Philosophical Studies Series

Volume 161

Philosophical Studies Series aims to provide a forum for the best current research in contemporary philosophy broadly conceived, its methodologies, and applications. Since Wilfrid Sellars and Keith Lehrer founded the series in 1974, the book series has welcomed a wide variety of different approaches, and every effort is made to maintain this pluralism, not for its own sake, but in order to represent the many fruitful and illuminating ways of addressing philosophical questions and investigating related applications and disciplines.

The book series is interested in classical topics of all branches of philosophy including, but not limited to:

- Ethics
- Epistemology
- Logic
- Metaphysics
- Philosophy of language
- Philosophy of logic
- Philosophy of mind
- Philosophy of religion
- Philosophy of science

Special attention is paid to studies that focus on:

- the interplay of empirical and philosophical viewpoints
- the implications and consequences of conceptual phenomena for research as well as for society
- philosophies of specific sciences, such as philosophy of biology, philosophy of chemistry, philosophy of computer science, philosophy of information, philosophy of neuroscience, philosophy of physics, or philosophy of technology; and
- contributions to the formal (logical, set-theoretical, mathematical, information-theoretical, decision-theoretical, etc.) methodology of sciences.

Likewise, the applications of conceptual and methodological investigations to applied sciences as well as social and technological phenomena are strongly encouraged.

Philosophical Studies Series welcomes historically informed research, but privileges philosophical theories and the discussion of contemporary issues rather than purely scholarly investigations into the history of ideas or authors. Besides monographs, *Philosophical Studies Series* publishes thematically unified anthologies, selected papers from relevant conferences, and edited volumes with a well-defined topical focus inside the aim and scope of the book series. The contributions in the volumes are expected to be focused and structurally organized in accordance with the central theme(s), and are tied together by an editorial introduction. Volumes are completed by extensive bibliographies.

The series discourages the submission of manuscripts that contain reprints of previous published material and/or manuscripts that are below 160 pages/88,000 words.

For inquiries and submission of proposals authors can contact the editor-in-chief Mariarosaria Taddeo via: massimo.durante@unito.it

Ugo Pagallo

A Theory of Legal Monsters: Repression, Resistance, Rebellion

Springer

Ugo Pagallo
Dipartimento di Giurisprudenza
Turin, Italy

ISSN 0921-8599 ISSN 2542-8349 (electronic)
Philosophical Studies Series
ISBN 978-3-032-10770-1 ISBN 978-3-032-10771-8 (eBook)
https://doi.org/10.1007/978-3-032-10771-8

This Springer imprint is published by the registered company Springer Nature Switzerland AG
The registered company address is: Gewerbestrasse 11, 6330 Cham, Switzerland

Gloria al Bravo Pueblo
Que el yugo lanzó
La ley respetando
La virtud y honor
(Venezuela's national anthem)

Preface

This book began to take shape in October 2024 on the southern coast of Sicily. Just a few hundred metres from the temples of Selinunte—the ancient Greek city of Σελινοῦς, or Selīnoûs—I wasn't far from some of the places that play an important role in the history of the ideas outlined in this book. Continuing east along the coast, one first encounters the Valley of the Temples in Agrigento and then, 70 km later, Gela. Once you reach the very tip of the island, travelling 60 km north along the coast, you'll arrive in Syracuse. It is within this triangle, nestled in the larger three-pointed shape of Sicily, or Trinacria, that I began to develop the themes of this book on despicable regimes and public resistance, clumsy laws and meta-jurisprudence, human tragedy and irony, the ugliest and noblest facets of the law. What all these topics have in common is a legal notion of 'monster', each with its own variables. Sicily was the most suitable place to frame the first type, the monstrous tyrant.

The image of tyrants as a monster can, in fact, be traced back to Aeschylus, the 'father of tragedy'. Aeschylus died in 'the wheat-bearing land of Gela', according to the inscription on his gravestone, in 456 or 455 BC. Aeschylus visited Sicily for the first time 20 years earlier, invited by Hiero, tyrant of Syracuse, the Corynthian colony that would rival—and even surpass in power—both Sparta and Athens less than a century later. The reason for Aeschylus' last journey to Sicily is unclear: ancient sources are often as inconclusive as the opinions of contemporary legal philosophers. Some, including Plutarch, attribute this journey to the poet's resentment towards his Athenian fellow citizens. The failure in a public competition, in which a Sophocles' tragedy was supposedly preferred to his own, led Aeschylus to take a break. For whatever reason, the people of Gela were more than happy to host Aeschylus in the last few years of his life. The city became a place of pilgrimage for writers soon after his death.

The awful depiction of the monstrous tyrant became extremely popular in Greek tragedy and was formalised by Plato in the following century. Plato finetuned his ideas on monsters and tyrants during three tumultuous journeys to Syracuse in 387, 367, and 361 BC under the imprint of two famous tyrants, namely, Dionysius, father and son. Any hope to implement Plato's political ideas of philosopher-kings in Sicily was in vain. However, the legal and political science of monsters that Plato outlines in *The Republic* would represent the model for centuries to come. The claim is valid regardless of opinions on Platonic philosopher-kings and even for those who are prone to follow the harsh anti-totalitarian remarks of Karl Popper. Three centuries after Plato's vicissitudes, among the many philosophers and jurists who followed suit in Roman times, Cicero took up these themes of monstrous tyrants and personalised them in the celebrated orations against the corrupt Sicilian governor Gaius Verres.

Verres' misdeeds against the city of Agrigento were indeed shameful. Although scholars still debate how reliable Cicero's criticisms of monstrosity are, his censures against Verres clear up what we are talking about when referring to a political monster: greed and disregard for the law and local culture, unlawful taxes, and fines to enrich oneself at the expense of the community, and gross thefts. Verres apparently stole a statue of Apollo during his first visit to Agrigento, and his very attempt to seize a massive statue of Hercules only failed because the statue was too large to move and snatch. When tourists visit en masse the Doric temples of old Greek Akragas today, they should reflect on how what they are admiring is, in fact, admirable notwithstanding all the damage caused by Verres in the last century BC.

My suggestion is, of course, wishful thinking. Tourists have far nobler things to consider than Cicero, Verres, and the latter's exile in Spain. Oppression, violence, and insatiability of rulers from times gone by, however, are only a warning of how the necessity to deal with the cruelty of monstrous tyrants persists. To substantiate the claim, this book's case study draws attention to that part of the world which—so goes the legend, because of the stilts that indigenous people used to build along Lake Maracaibo—was called 'Little Venice' since the early 1500s. After the wars of independence from the Spanish Empire, the region known as *Piccola Venezia* or *Veneziola* officially became Venezuela in 1830.

The case study is not a simple homage to the country in which I grew up, lived my youth, and visited regularly until the early 2010s. Instead, the dedication of this volume to the Venezuelan 'brave people' aims to stress the ways in which tyrannies can lead to a dire humanitarian crisis and economic collapse. In Chap. 10, I recall that more than half of the population's income was insufficient to meet basic nutritional needs at the peak of an escalating starvation in 2017. Four years later, in 2021, one Venezuelan out of five had already left the country. In 2024, the results of the presidential election were likely falsified. At the time of writing, while the tyrant is accomplishing its third 6-year term, the annual inflation rate is at 172%, the unemployment rate at 35,6%, the political prisoners around 2,000 and nearly 26 homicides are committed per 100,000 inhabitants annually. It adds to the tragedy that, according to current Venezuelan law, the national anthem must be played on all radio and television stations at least twice per day, giving a sinister aura to the 1800s anthem's verses on 'death to oppression' and 'the vile selfishness that had once prevailed'.

Cicero's remarks in the *Republic*, according to whom tyrants surpass the 'most savage monsters in infernal cruelty', therefore seem all but exaggerated. Plato even mentions cases of cannibalism in book VIII of his *Republic*, whether or not referring to the atrocities of Dionysius the elder: 'Whoever tastes of human flesh of the one man chopped up with the other sacrificial victims necessarily turns into a wolf. Haven't you heard the tale'? Roughly 2400 years later, the *Strait Times*, a journal close to the Chinese government, reported a variant of this story about another tyrant, North Korea's Kim Jong-un, who had ordered to throw his uncle, guilty of treason, to starving dogs. Reflecting on similar cases in his time, Cicero was the first renowned philosopher to appeal to the principles of natural law to support the legitimacy of tyrannicide against those who pretend absolute power in a free state. Nowadays, tyrants should not be executed, but rather, prosecuted according to the procedural safeguards of the law, for example, before the International Criminal Court in The Hague.

However, to put monstrous things in a proper context, we should widen the focus of the analysis. Two further types of monsters—which do not necessarily entail any capricious will of tyrannies—must be examined. The first type hinges on a more than 2500-year-long chapter of legal history that ideally ended with the Universal Declaration of Human Rights in 1948. In parallel with the rise of the Western tradition of monstrous tyrants, another Western legal tradition took shape regarding people with congenital disabilities. Offspring with no family resemblance to any member of the community represented another class of humans who were deemed monstrous. Philosophers and jurists, such as Cicero, did not find any paradox in dealing simultaneously with both types of monster, i.e. both tyrants and humans with 'certain natural defects'. Generations of Italian law students have been introduced to the nuances of the *monstrum vel prodigium* regulations in their first year courses of Roman law over the past decades. According to the Twelve Tables from 449 BC, 'notably deformed' children had to be suppressed 'immediately'. Aristotle would endorse a similar conclusion a century later in *Politics*. Crude as it can be, it was not a tyrant who had to decide whether to throw uncles to hungry dogs. Instead, it was the Roman *pater familias*, the head of a household, who had to determine what to do with a disabled child. The options included refusal of maintenance, suffocation, strangulation, exposition, i.e. putting the creature on the street at the whim of others (but only after having consulted five neighbours and obtained their consent); and, why not, sparing the kid's life. In graver cases, it was up to the Roman Senate to choose, on priests' advice, how to deal with such a monster.

Experts of Roman law have dissected clauses and status of the *monster vel prodigium* as much as legal philosophers and political scientists have examined the notion of tyranny and its evolution throughout the centuries. As far as I know, however, scholars have mostly overlooked how these two different types of monsters are connected and what implications follow in the legal domain.

The same holds for the second type of legal monster that, in addition to the *monstrum vel prodigium*, does not necessarily entail any tyrannical caprice. This further legal monster, admittedly, is less frightening than the legally dead people of both the civil and common law traditions. Attention is drawn to whimsical regulations that do not require any despicable institution, since decent institutions may also adopt monstrous acts. The formula of monster law—which used to be an oxymoron, according to some tenets of legal positivism—has become viral over the past years. Such a formula is increasingly at work in both courts' rulings and scholarly papers. Narrowing the scope of possible citations to the last few years, the opinion of the highest jurisdiction in Italy, i.e. the Court of Cassation's doctrine on monsters in rulings from the 2010s and 20s can be supplemented with the analyses of experts on the monstrous Singapore's 2021 foreign interference bill; the monstrous 2022 reform of an international trade agreement; Italy's monstrous 2024 right to image of cultural property; or the monstrous 2024 proposal of the European Commission on the so called 'Deforestation Law'. Since it is reasonable to suspect that the monstrosity of legal regulations is not exclusive to our times, the conjecture is that tenets of certain anachronistic forms of legal positivism have been dismissed to assess today's inconsistencies of regulators.

Still, it is harder to build than to tear down. The rule of experience applies to the misdeeds of politicians as much as the theoretical efforts of scholars. Despite the doctrine of Courts and dozens of papers focusing on the monstrosity of normative acts, there is a lack of robust work on the requirements of normative monstrosity and how to distinguish such monsters from the traditional monstrosity of tyrannical regimes. Although even sound institutions can occasionally embrace monster acts, a single act, edict, or piece of legislation may turn suitable regimes into a monster. What is the threshold?

To address these open issues on monstrous acts and institutions, it is not enough to examine the tyrants of the Platonic tradition, eventually supplementing them with the full repertoire of Cicero's monsters, such as corrupt governors, plotters, traitors, pirates or, for that matter, dear colleagues. The analysis must be complemented with the science of legislation and studies of meta-jurisprudence—which includes the examination of regulations such as those on people with congenital disabilities—to emphasise the two sides to the same monstrous coin. While, on the one hand, the monster metaphor is often employed to illustrate the repressive side of the law vis-à-vis the *monster vel prodigium* of the tradition; on the other hand, the image represents a symbol of criticism and even of open resistance and rebellion against the follies of the power on duty. We may wonder what the law is called to do in these cases and, moreover, what scholars should expect as a result.

Plutarch, Diogenes Laertius, and Diodorus Siculus all assert that Plato's first trip and his confrontation with Dionysius the elder did not end well, if it is true that the tyrant ordered to sell Plato as a slave. Scholars still debate how reliable such reports are, and yet, it is certain that a worse fate befell Cicero, who paid with his own life for criticising another tyrant, Mark Antony. The book dwells on further philosophers who had to face a similar dire fate: for example, another expert on legal monsters, such as Samuel Pufendorf, had to face political imprisonment. Despite such previous events, however, it seems safe to say that no algorithm decreeing strict correlations between monster expertise and tumultuous life exists. The intense work and peaceful death of two further experts of legal monsters, such as Lon Fuller and Herbert Hart, would confirm this conjecture in recent times.

Yet, the conjecture does not suggest any burst of optimism. Ours are indeed interesting times, according to the Chinese saying on what we should wish for our enemies. Several scholars and friends have been kind enough to read this book, pointing out errors and suggesting changes or additions. Notwithstanding such inputs, which include the gentle remarks of my Springer reviewers, the book may still contain ambiguities, imprecisions, or mistakes. Considering that only decent institutions are ready to concede their own monstrosities, I take full responsibility for what you are about to read on tyrants, despicable regimes, and monstrous laws. The heart aches not seeing again, among others, *mi querido pais* Venezuela.

September 2025
Turin, Italy

Ugo Pagallo

Contents

Abbreviations and Acronyms

AI	Artificial Intelligence
Art.	Article of a normative act
BC	Before Christ
C	Code of Justinian
CBS	Columbia Broadcasting System
CE	Common Era, or Anno Domini
CEO	Chief Executive Officer
CFR	Charter of Fundamental Rights in EU law
CIA	US Central Intelligence Agency
D	Digest of Justinian, or Corpus Iuris Civilis
EASA	European Aviation Security Agency
EC	European Commission
ECHR	European Convention on Human Rights
EEC	European Economic Community
ENAC	Italian Civil Aviation Authority
EP	European Parliament
EPP	European People's Party
ESO	European Source Online
EU	European Union
FLOPs	Floating Point Operations of computers
GDPR	General Data Protection Regulation of EU law
GM	Genetically Modified
GPT	Generative Pre-trained Transformer
HLEG	High Level Expert Group
ICC	International Criminal Court
ICT	Information Communication Technology
IEEE	Institute of Electrical and Electronics Engineers
IHL	International Humanitarian Law
LLMs	Large Language Models
MEP	Member of Parliament
MHC	Meaningful Human Control

MS	Member State of the European Union
Reg.	Regulation of EU law
UAS	Unmanned Aerial System
UAV	Unmanned Aerial Vehicle, or drone
UDHR	Universal Declaration of Human Rights
UK	United Kingdom
UN	United Nations
US	United States of America
WW II	Second World War (1939-1945)
ZI	Zero Intelligence agent or robot

Chapter 1
Introduction

Human culture has always been full of monsters, and our era is no exception. This book restricts the focus of the inquiry to the class of monsters related to the legal domain. All monsters pertaining to the fields of literature and aesthetics, philosophy and sociology, logic and economics, religion and mathematics, fall outside the scope of this book. Instead, the attention is drawn to both the normative side of the law and the monstrosity of political institutions. The focus is, so to speak, two-tiered: the primary legal sources of monstrosity — from the Roman Twelve Tables to some examples of today's legislation — and the opinion of jurists who discuss such primary legal sources. The book does not consider a potential third tier of discussion, i.e. the group of scholars who deem their colleagues' work monstrous. For example, in the words of Günther Teubner when discussing both Luhmann's concepts and Derrida's non-concepts, they shall be deemed as "autopoietic monsters in the world of deconstruction" (Teubner 2001).

Even with such constraints, there is still plenty of choice about what should be under scrutiny in this book. Jurists have been discussing monsters over the past 2500 years. The long list includes the founders of the natural law tradition, i.e. Plato and Aristotle; great Roman jurists and philosophers, from Cicero to Seneca; founding fathers of legal modernity, such as Thomas Hobbes and Samuel Pufendorf; precursors of today's public international law, like Christian Wolff and Emer de Vattel; or, advocates of contemporary schools of both natural law (Lon Fuller) and legal positivism (Herbert Hart). A confusing abundance can be the result. How will this book handle such a complexity?

The book adopts a twofold level of abstraction, namely, the stance through which this volume aims to identify observables and variables of the analysis of legal monsters. The first lens of this book is theoretical: the intent is to formalise a theory of legal monsters. To attain this end, attention is drawn to the requirements and functions of monstrosity, i.e. what a monster is supposed to be in the legal domain (its requirements), and what the formula on monsters is called to do (its functions). Such meanings and purposes are illustrated through the second lens of this book, which

U. Pagallo, *A Theory of Legal Monsters: Repression, Resistance, Rebellion*, Philosophical Studies Series 161, https://doi.org/10.1007/978-3-032-10771-8_1

is historiographical. Selection, examination, and assessment of legal texts follow a chronological order to complement the theoretical aim of this book. The reason does not hinge on a narrative expedient to put order into a panoply of legal sources. Instead, the chronological order of this history of ideas — which begins with the Greco-Roman culture, its legacy in the Middle Ages and down to Modernity — has a theoretical relevance. The stance aims to counter possible objections regarding the class of primary legal sources under scrutiny. Although most of such sources concern the Western legal tradition, the claim is that the results of the analysis do not only apply to Western countries and jurisdictions. Many examples of legal monstrosity in this book are indeed non-Western. Conditions of monstrosity may regard the U.S. or the European Union, but also China and Russia, North Korea and Venezuela.

The interplay between this book's theoretical and historiographical approach casts light on the crucial differences between our age's reflection and tradition. We shall never forget that monsters were deemed 'real' throughout most centuries of this history of ideas. Until recently, monsters were either associated with fantastic creatures or humans with congenital disabilities. It is noteworthy that still in the early 1700s, some philosophers, such as John Locke and Gottfried W. Leibniz, tried to convince their contemporaries that monsters, including human monsters, did not exist. We had to wait until Charles Darwin's investigations on the evolution of the species to gain empirical evidence and robust scientific conjectures on 'monstrosities' as a kind of congenital malformation in the mid-1800s. However, prejudices and superstition are challenging to eradicate, if they ever truly do. A few decades after Darwin's research, eugenics caused another terrible page of human history to be written. In the first decades of the 1900s, inhuman policies and criminal intentions materialised in the legal systems of the United States, Scandinavia, Canada and Germany, among others. Eugenics went beyond ideologies.

The end of one of the darkest pages of the Western legal tradition, such as the status of humans with birth defects treated as 'monsters' or 'prodigies' in ancient Roman law — the 'legally dead' people of civil law, common law, or canon law — can be traced back to the mid-1900s. The breakpoint is ideally represented by the Universal Declaration of Human Rights in 1948 and the foundation of medical teratology, a sub-field of medical genetics, some years later. Devoted to the examination of the abnormalities of physiological development in organisms, the Teratology Society was formally established in 1961. A new paradigm of scientific research and legal treatment of humans with congenital disabilities began to gradually assert itself through the 1970s and 80s. The formula 'legal monster' was progressively employed as a metaphor, rather than an image of what the formula intended to convey over the centuries. The transformation of old images into a metaphor went hand-in-hand with the demonstration that monsters do not exist. The monsters and prodigies of the legal tradition were indeed humans or, in the words of the Universal Declaration, "members of the human family".

Over the same span of years in which the new normative and epistemic paradigm started to gain track, however, scholars increasingly discussed the despicable regulation of the human monsters of positive law as an enlightening example of the repressive side of the legal phenomenon. This stance went viral with Michel Foucault's lectures on monsters and the abnormal at the College de France in 1974 and 1975 (Foucault ed. 2003). Such an understanding, which is still very popular today, must be complemented by all those interpretations of the law that present repression, coercion, and normalisation as the quintessence of the legal phenomenon. Still in the 1970s, Karl Marx's views on capitalist exploitation as "a live monster that is fruitful and multiplies" provided the archetype and scientific framework (Marx ed. 1887). The monsters and prodigies of strict positive law were just a symptom of a more structured, generalised, monstrous human condition that only the catharsis of communism could overcome. Although the status of the legally dead people of the tradition was formally abolished, legal monsters never died.

Foucault's transformation of the old human monster from the Middle Ages into the criminal monster of Modernity has become the monstrous terrorist and illegal immigrant of today's monstrous surveillance society: "The monster did it, not Victor Frankenstein" (Zuboff 2019, at 136). Variables of this stance on the eternal recurrence of the same concern capitalism's ideological, rather than structural, facets. Although monsters do not exist as living organisms in reality, either they persist as a legal category (Sharpe 2010); or, they may well reside in people's minds since monsters "inhabit an exterior that we cannot see, perhaps because we maintain a more fundamental relationship with it" (Lemos 2014). A further option is the creation of monsters not only in the legal domain, but also, by superimposing them upon our own sources of inspiration and imagination. Another Marxist thinker, the Italian philosopher Antonio Gramsci, has been a victim of this approach.

In *Past and Present*, a collection of writings and notes from the 1930s published in 1951 (Gramsci ed. 1977), Gramsci inspects the crisis of his times. He reckoned that the "masses" had detached themselves from traditional ideologies, no longer believing in what they had previously believed in, so the "ruling class" had lost consensus. Such a ruling class is no longer ruling but merely dominant, "the holder of pure coercive force". This is why, according to Gramsci, "the crisis consists precisely in the fact that the old is dying and the new cannot be born: the most varied morbid phenomena occur in this interregnum" (Gramsci 1977, at 311). To many, this assessment clarifies the troubles of our era, although with a symptomatic twist. Gramsci's "most varied morbid phenomena" have become, since Slavoj Zizek's free translation, "the time of monsters" (Zizek 2010). Dozens of scholars, journalists, and alleged opinion-makers have followed suit (Klein 2025). The internet propagates this legend of Gramsci's monsters, and only a few people take the time to check the authenticity of the source. This carelessness is not innocent but denotes a more general trend. Either monsters are invented where they do not exist or, following Foucault's method, monsters are removed from one's sources when inconvenient.

To substantiate this assumption in dealing with monsters and the law, it should be noted that the repression of the human monsters and prodigies of the tradition is only a part of this story. There is the proverbial other side to the coin. The historiographical approach of this book helps us to put the monster (and its legal theory) in a proper context. Since the philosophical inception of the formula in Plato's *Republic*, the 'monster' is not only the object of legal repression but rather the subject of this repression: the tyrant as the opposite of the philosopher-king in Plato's philosophy.

According to this further meaning of the formula, the monster represents a source of legal criticism. The image intends to transmit a sense of disapproval and, moreover, a call for resistance and even rebellion. Those who live by the monster, perish by the monster. This is the purpose that the formula has had — and according to which it has evolved — over the ages, from Cicero's *Republic* and Seneca's *Hercules Furens* to the Monarchomachs in the 1500s and down to all tyrants and theories of tyrannicide today. Every discourse on legal monsters without any reference to such sources of criticism and opposition would be like a history of Western philosophy deprived of the likes of Aristotle or Immanuel Kant.

This critical function of resistance that the use of the formula 'legal monster' has transmitted since its very beginning introduces a further class of requirements that monsters must have. Coercion is indeed a necessary but insufficient condition of the law's functioning. Should it not be the case, there would be no place for any sort of criticism and resistance in the name of monsters. In addition to the conditions that made humans look like monsters over more than 25 centuries — consequently treating them as legally dead people — a further class of requirements draws attention to the set of conditions that turn repression and even legal coercion illegitimate. Such conditions have arguably evolved through the centuries. The second meaning of the formula on monsters as a source of criticism, resistance and rebellion against forms of political repression, can be illustrated through different views and phases in the use of the formula. Contrary to every assumption of sheer legal relativism, such views and meanings in using the formula do not necessarily exclude each other but can be cumulative. Such political, rather than strict legal references to the formula on monsters concern four different facets of this history of ideas:

i. Plato's association of the tyrant with the image of monsters, which set the standard for the centuries to come. The Platonic archetype of the tyrant monster is not only a symbol of the Monarchomachs' theses of the late 1500s and a subject of the vibrant philosophical debate a century later and throughout the 1700s. It also forged our current notions of tyranny. In accordance with Aristotle's teachings, tyrants brutalise the institutions by making people slaves;
ii. The differentiation of monstrous institutions and monstrous normative acts in the late 1600s and through the 700s, which complements the archetype of the monstrous tyrant. Drawing on the teachings of the modern, rather than classical natural law school of Samuel Pufendorf, conditions of monstrosity regard the design of political institutions or specific pieces of legislation. This 'geometrical' monstrosity needs no face. As much as the tyrannies of the Greco-Roman tradition, this further meaning of monstrosity is well alive today;
iii. The eclipse of most references to the monstrosity of normative acts and institutions in the 1800s and until the mid-900s. Among the reasons, a major role in the eclipse of the formula was played by tenets of legal positivism as the principle of sovereignty and the theory of unconditional obedience, the supremacy of the legislative power and the declarative reading of the legal texts. The triumph of legal positivism materialised Thomas Hobbes' claims in the

Leviathan, according to which such a biblical monster should be conceived of as the 'ultimate monster' of politics and the law;
iv. The horrors of the Nazi regime and other totalitarian or post-colonial experiences that favoured the return of the use of the formula on monsters as a source of criticism, resistance and rebellion after the second world war (WW II). Such a use was initially supported by advocates of the natural law tradition. Today, it is admitted even by supporters of (certain variables of current) legal positivism.

Against this backdrop, the popularity of the metaphor can also be appreciated in today's digital societies. Some scholars stress the existence of institutional monsters, for example, with the threats of the surveillance society; others dwell on the drawbacks of some attempts to govern and regulate the challenges of digital technologies, for example, the monstrous regulation of cookies on the internet (Leenes and Kosta 2015). Further, the formula is often employed to emphasise the existential threats posed by technology. Joshua Bengio, among the 'godfathers' of Artificial Intelligence, sums up the menaces of technology as a "monster AI" (in Khorram 2024). The formula has gone hand-in-hand with viral narratives on the threats of super intelligences or general AI out of human control. Such scenarios supplement the traditional picture of monster laws or tyrant monsters. The meaningful control that humans must have over potentially monstrous technologies represents the other side to the coin of the control that institutions may attempt to exert over humans through the monstrous uses of technology, for example, the "syntax monster" of robotic courts (Ebrahimi Afrouzi 2024).

However, this popularity entails its own risks. The metaphor for monsters is often used for simple rhetorical purposes or employed with a certain theoretical leniency. The threat is that the more formulas on legal monsters are widespread today, the less clear the theoretical background against which such uses should be grasped. We may wonder how the monster should be conceived of against the tenets of the natural law tradition, or vis-à-vis the assumptions of legal positivism about the validity of the law and the legitimacy of political institutions (Pagallo 2024). Such uncertainties affect not only the meaning of the formula for monsters as subjects of legal criticism but also the idea of monsters as the target of legal repression. Scholars often resort to the metaphor to illustrate what the law intends to suppress because of its monstrosity. Since Cicero's times and up to the inception of international public law in the mid-1700s, jurists have grasped both meanings of the formula, i.e. both as the subject and as the object of legal regulation, as compatible. This twofold use of the formula is found in the common law tradition with Edward Coke in the early 1600s and William Blackstone in the mid-700s. They dub as monsters both people with birth defects and enemies of the institutions, such as traitors (Coke), and dishonest politicians (Blackstone). The same use is at work in continental Europe. In *The Law of Nations* from 1758, Emer de Vattel calls monsters both certain sovereigns and all pirates.

The monster can thus be a tyrant as much as every enemy of the institutions, be they pirates in the 1700s, criminals in the 1800s, terrorists in the 1900s, or immigrants in the 2000s. They complement the legal repertoire of human monsters, which started with the status of humans with congenital disabilities as the *monstrum vel prodigium* of Roman law. Politicians have often sparked this trend: for example, President George W. Bush's 'war on terror' in the early 2000s was not a simple rhetorical formula. On the contrary, it paved the way for abuses and tortures in Iraq as much as the 'legally dead' people of the U.S. Guantanamo facilities (Pagallo 2013). President Donald Trump has later led the "monstrification of immigrants" by calling them "migrant criminals", "gang members", "killers" and, of course, "illegal monsters" who "poison our country" (Eljaiek-Rodríguez 2024). It would seem that the Foucauldian thesis on the human monster who turns into a monster-criminal, who turns into a monster-terrorist, who turns into a monster-immigrant is hence confirmed. There is, however, a crucial difference regarding today's law. The monstrous treatment of pirates, criminals, terrorists and, nowadays, immigrants as a mere target of legal repression, should not only be deemed immoral but also unlawful (Johnson 2010; Lacy and van Houtum 2020). By portraying the current status of, for example, terrorists as monsters (Pinfari 2019), scholars must be attentive to this use of formulas that, although employed for simple rhetorical reasons, are dangerous, legally wrong, and politically misleading.

The increasing popularity of the formula and the abundance of legal monsters in today's debates, for better and worse, have thus recommended writing this book to elucidate the proper meaning of the metaphor against pure rhetorical uses, theoretical drawbacks, or controversial assumptions in the legal domain. The intent is to formalise functions and requirements of the legal formula, making it clear whether scholars refer to objects or subjects of the law, as much as what a monster would be under every observable and variable of the analysis with the different and even opposite functions of the metaphor. The assumption is that such a metaphor can still play a powerful role in denouncing cases of political oppression or against normative acts whose coercion is not simply bad or wrong, but monstrous. To preserve this critical role of the metaphor, it is essential to contrast all crying wolf trends in the use of the image. We have to flesh out what uses make sense, are coherent, and legitimate. To attain this end, the volume has been divided into ten chapters.

The next chapter provides a genealogy in accordance with the historiographical approach of this book. The attention is drawn to the Greco-Roman roots of the legal and political meanings of the formulas on monsters. The focus is on work by Plato and Aristotle, Cicero and Seneca, who still represent a reference point and continuous source of inspiration for every analysis on monsters. Key differences between Plato and Aristotle's practical reflection, as much as between Greek philosophy and Roman law, warn us against every simplification. Against Plato's equalisation of tyrants and monsters, for example, Aristotle suggests grasping such monsters as the beasts of the political community. In *Divination*, it is Cicero who claims that either "Nature herself", once resumed her sway, or surgery and medicine could restore "many persons who were born with certain natural defects" (Cicero ed. 1923, at 2, 96). This interplay of theoretics with natural philosophy, and politics with legal science, reminds us of the two sides to the same monstrous coin, that is, between the individual's physical body and the body politic, between monsters as the subject and as the object of the legal domain. It is necessary to understand, in particular, what Plato and Aristotle explained regarding the reasons why democracies occasionally turn into tyrannies. Despite today's confusion of tyrannies with some form of political absolutism, autocracy, despotic regime, dictatorship, or one-party ruler, what is at stake concerns the decisions of governments that break the law by seeking their profit against their own subjects.

The next three chapters of the book focus on the strict legal meaning of the formula, i.e. monsters as the object of repression handed down from the tradition of Roman law. Chapter 3 provides a concise history of the legal status of humans with congenital disabilities, starting with some tenets of the Roman *corpus iuris* down to civil and common law provisions. Chapter 4 illustrates the abolishment of such a status with the 1948 Universal Declaration and its philosophical grounds. They can be traced back to some teachings of Samuel Pufendorf, Jean-Jacques Rousseau, and Immanuel Kant with their own contradictions. Chapter 5 dwells on the opinion of those scholars who, following Foucault's lectures in Paris, still reckon that dismissing such old legal formulas on monsters would be deceptive. Even in this case, there is a form of irony in such analyses of the formula for they function as a way of criticism and resistance against the repressive side of the law. Today, every legal system or lawmaker still referring to any human being as a legal monster would be the only one who should be properly conceived of as a human monster.

The use of the metaphor for monsters as a form of criticism and resistance is the subject of the next three chapters of the book. Chapter 6 explores this use in accordance with the distinctions that Samuel Pufendorf drew between monstrous normative acts and the design of political institutions with their different requirements of monstrosity. Chapter 7 dwells on perhaps the most famous monsters of Modernity, i.e. Thomas Hobbes' Leviathan and Behemoth. Chapter 8 focuses on the debate between two advocates of the natural law tradition (Lon Fuller) and legal positivism (Herbert Hart), to ascertain different claims on the validity of the law vis-à-vis the acts of monstrous institutions. Despite the eclipse of the formula due to some tenets of legal positivism in the 1800s, the claim is that even advocates of legal positivism may concede today that either institutions or legislation can properly be grasped as legal monsters. The doctrine of the Italian Court of Cassation on monsters who defy the "logic of the system" supports this view.

On this basis, Chapter 9 provides a case study analysing the EU institutions and legislation. Since EU law has been a generous source of legal monsters for scholarly debates over the past years, the intent is threefold. First, the aim is to test the conditions of monstrosity for a certain legal and political organisation, such as the EU institutions, to determine whether the EU can be reasonably deemed as a legal monster vis-à-vis those thresholds, such as the protection of human rights at the international level and respect for constitutional safeguards at the national or regional level. Second, the purpose is to ascertain whether monstrous institutions represent a necessary condition of normative monstrosity or whether a decent institution may endorse monstrous acts. Third, the intent is to illustrate what a monstrous legislation may look like by distinguishing monstrous laws from wrong legislation through assessment criteria such as the congruency, consistency, coherence and intelligibility of every normative act.

Chapter 10 inspects the final function of the metaphor. After being employed as the image of legal repression (Chapters 3–5), or a source of legal criticism (Chapters 6–9), Chapter 10 examines the formula as a symbol of rebellion, namely, the open, organised, and armed resistance against rulers and governments. Drawing on the work and opposite claims of John Locke and Immanuel Kant, the analysis provides the background for current debates on the right to resist. The aim is to clarify the conditions of legal validity against the orders of monstrous normative acts as much as the legitimacy requirements concerning the persisting power of monstrous institutions. The analysis of what a monster is supposed to be and what a theory of legal monsters is called to do is further refined through the viewpoint of those who do not accept the rules of a certain legal order. Contrary to the political claims of most revolutionary men, for example, according to the tenets of Marxist revolutions, the attention is drawn to the legal side of the rebel's right to resist. Conversely, contrary to the formalisms of certain legal scholars, such as Kelsen's idea that the overall validity of the law ultimately hinges on its efficacy, the claim is that this Kelsenian assumption overlooks critical conditions for the existence of the law. We noted that coercion is a necessary but insufficient ingredient of the law's functioning.

The final chapter of this inquiry considers what we should expect in the future. Digital technologies and AI systems update traditional discussions on legal monsters, considering either the technology or its uses and applications as monstrous. The intent of Chapter 11 is to test the requirements of monstrosity regarding both the institutional and normative levels of abstraction, taking into account some exaggerations of today's debate on AI monsters, monstrous cookie laws, syntax monsters, or monstrous surveillance systems of private companies and sovereign states. Scholars often jump into the long-term threats of technology without dispensing any detail about how human societies may wake up one day dealing with superintelligences, sentient robots, or powerful AI systems out of control. Further types of monsters, such as Robert Nozick's "utility monster" and Imre Lakatos' "monster barring" and "monster adjustment", help us grasp the short- and mid-term challenges of the field. How the law will address such challenges is critical because those decisions will contribute to shaping the future. Considering cases of normative monstrosity that hinge on legislative incompetency, decent institutions may also adopt a monstrous normative act of technological regulation, and do so in candid good faith.

The overall intent of this book is both descriptive and prescriptive. It sorts out the manifold ways in which the metaphor of monsters is still used today to determine which uses are sound and appropriate. A theory of legal monsters must clarify essential conditions of the legal phenomenon, such as the validity of the rules laid down by tyrant monsters, as much as requirements of legal functioning, such as the norms of the law as guides to conduct, which can nonetheless provoke forms of criticism and opposition, resistance and open rebellion. A methodology on how to test the requirements of normative or institutional monstrosity aims to supplement the theoretical effort of this book. Assessing the conditions that make legal acts, statutes, practices, or institutions look monstrous may require particular expertise to grasp the specificities of every legal system with different traditions, customs, and cultures. And yet, such specificities find a twofold common ground. On the one hand, every institutional monstrosity rests on specific acts or practices: it would be difficult to demonstrate any institutional monstrosity or the evilness of a monstrous tyrant without adducing the monstrosity of this or that act or practice. On the other hand, such acts and practices can be grasped as monstrous in accordance with a restricted set of requirements, such as the congruency and consistency, coherence and intelligibility of normative acts that represent common principles of the law.

To proceed with the analysis, according to the two-tiered structure of this volume, the attention is drawn to the primary sources of the law, namely legislation and case law, statutory and customary law, and how scholars interpret them. Once we have accurately understood why some normative acts and political institutions can be properly deemed monstrous, the conditions for examining another class of requirements, i.e. what makes certain opinions of scholars look monstrous, will finally be met. However, this third-tiered level of analysis is left to further volumes of this inquiry. Criticism, resistance, and rebellion against all forms of political repression have theoretical priority in the following chapters of the book.

References

Cicero, M.T. 1923. *De Senectute, De Amicitia, De Divinatione*, trans. W.A. Falconer. Cambridge, MA: Harvard University Press.

Ebrahimi, Afrouzi A. 2024. John robots, thurgood martian, and the syntax monster: A new argument against AI judges. *Canadian Journal of Law & Jurisprudence* 37 (2): 1–28.

Eljaiek-Rodríguez, E. 2024. Blood: The monstrification of immigrants in U.S. politics, free voice, issue 40 (blood), August. Accessed on September 8, 2025 from https://shuddhashar.com/monsters-that-poison-the-blood-the-monstrification-of-immigrants-in-u-s-politics/.

Foucault, M. 2003. *Abnormal: Lectures at the College de France 1974–1975*. London: Verso.

Gramsci, A. 1977. In *Quaderni del carcere*, ed. A. Gerratana, vol. I. Turin: Einaudi.

Johnson, K. R. 2010. It's the economy, stupid: The hijacking of the debate over immigration reform by monsters, ghosts, and goblins (or the war on drugs, war on terror, narcoterrorists, etc.). *Chapman Law Review* 13 (3): 583–614.

Khorram Y. 2024. AI 'Godfather' Yoshua Bengio: We're 'creating monsters more powerful than us'. *Yahoo! Finance*, October 12. Accessed on September 8, 2025 from https://finance.yahoo.com/news/ai-godfather-yoshua-bengio-were-creating-monsters-more-powerful-than-us-120042014.html.

Klein, E. 2025. Now is the time of monsters. *The New York Times*, January 12.

Lacy, R. B., and H. van Houtum. 2020. Death as policy: The EU's criminalisation of solidarity with undocumented migrants. In *Expanding boundaries*, ed. J. P. Laine et al., 72–84. London: Routledge.

Leenes, R., and E. Kosta. 2015. Taming the cookie monster with Dutch law—A tale of regulatory failure. *Computer Law & Security Review* 31 (3): 317–335.

Lemos, F. 2014. Kant e o monstro. *Kriterion* 129:189–203.

Marx, K. 1887. *Capital: A critique of political economy, vol. I, book 1: The process of production of capital*. trans. S. Moore and E. Aveling. Moscow: Progress Publishers. Available at https://www.marxists.org/archive/marx/works/download/pdf/Capital-Volume-I.pdf.

Pagallo, U. 2013. Online security and the protection of civil rights: A legal overview. *Philosophy & Technology* 26:381–395.

Pagallo, U. 2024. Introduction to a theory of legal monsters: From Greco Roman teratology to the EU artificial intelligence act. *i-lex* 17 (1): 53–73.

Pinfari, M. 2019. *Terrorists as monsters: The unmanageable other from the French revolution to the Islamic state*. online ed. New York: Oxford Academic.
Sharpe, A. N. 2010. *Foucault's monsters and the challenges of law*. Abingdon: Routledge.
Teubner, G. 2001. Economics of gift-positivity of justice: The mutual paranoia of Jacques Derrida and Niklas Luhmann. *Theory, Culture and Society* 18:29–47.
Zizek, S. 2010. A permanent economic crisis. *New Left Review*, July/August, no. 64.
Zuboff, S. 2019. *The age of surveillance capitalism: The fight for a human future at the new frontier of power*. New York: Public Affairs.

Chapter 2
Genealogy

This chapter traces the contemporary conceptions of 'legal monsters' back to Greco-Roman antiquity. The attention is drawn to Plato's teratology in *The Republic*, Book IX, Aristotle's critique of these ideas, and the role of monsters in Roman culture. The aim is not only to highlight the differences between Plato's monsters and their naturalisation by Aristotle, or between natural law theories and Rome's 'body of law'. The intent is also to illustrate the genealogy of the dual meaning that the formula would convey in centuries to come, i.e. monsters as a source of criticism, resistance and rebellion, and as the object of legal repression. The analysis is complemented by an examination of the different criteria for monstrosity that arise from this distinction, namely, what a monster is supposed to be, either as a subject of the law or as a target of legal regulation.

2.1 Plato's Teratology

A history of ideas on legal monsters can accurately start with Plato's philosophy. Such an assumption does not imply that Plato's ideas emerged in isolation. Indeed, his work drew from popular stories of dreadful monsters that he, like all his contemporaries, grew up hearing. Some of these stories were related to the life of the political community and bring us back to Aeschylus, the 'father of tragedy' (Gentile 1930; Tarrant 1955). Together with later generations of Greek tragedians, from Euripides and Sophocles to Plato's own times, Aeschylus made this political use of the image familiar in Athenian culture. Athens' virtues clearly emerged through their opposition to tyrant monsters (Seaford 1998).

In Aeschylus' *Eumenides*, for example, the interplay of monsters, justice, and revolt unfolds through the trial of Orestes, guilty of murdering his mother Clytemnestra to avenge his father Agamemnon (Aeschylus ed. 2017). Whilst the Goddess Athena presides over the criminal trial, Apollo is Orestes' defence lawyer

U. Pagallo, *A Theory of Legal Monsters: Repression, Resistance, Rebellion*, Philosophical Studies Series 161, https://doi.org/10.1007/978-3-032-10771-8_2

against the Furies' prosecution. Upon entering the scene, Athena warns, "Yet to stand by and chide a monstrous form/Is all unjust from such words Right revolts". When it is time for Apollo to defend Orestes in the fourth episode of the tragedy, the divine attorney turns the charge of monstrosity in his favour. So goes the defence speech:

> Oh, monsters utterly loathed and detested by the gods! Zeus could undo fetters, there is a remedy for that, and many means of release. But when the dust has drawn up the blood of a man, once he is dead, there is no return to life. (Aeschylus ed. 2017, at 644)

A popular variant of this antithesis regards the image of tyrants as moral monsters vis-à-vis the merits of democratic Athens (Lanza 1977). The antithesis is displayed not only in Aeschylus' work but also in several other tragedies, such as Euripides' *Phoenissae* or Sophocles' *Oedipus Tyrannus*:

> Time the all-seeing has found you out against your will, and he judges the monstrous marriage in which parent and child have long been one. Alas, child of Laios, would that I had never seen you! (Sophocles ed. 1887, at 1212)

When distilling the meaning of the ideas transmitted by Aeschylus and the Tragedy in many of his dialogues, Plato is undeniably a son of his time. The author fully endorses and exploits the function of these images of tyrants as human monsters by adapting them to his own theoretical purposes.[1] What changes here pertains to the requirements of monstrosity, i.e. what a tyrant is supposed to be in contrast to its moral opposite. Book IX of Plato's *Republic* is specifically devoted to this task. He develops a 'science of monsters' or teratology — from the Greek words τέρας "monster" and λόγος "account" or "reason" — which helps illustrate his political ideas on the Philosopher-King. What better way to present this doctrine, *pace* the democratic ideas of Athens, than through an image accepted and admired for more than a century?

The central premise of Book IX in the dialogue between Socrates and Plato's brother, Glaucon, is that the soul of every man is made of three parts: Rational, spirited and appetitive. Drawing on the correspondence between man and state, according to which the state is a man written in capital letters, Socrates claims that three social classes correspond to the three parts of every man's soul. Such classes are the guardians (i.e. political rulers); the auxiliaries (soldiers); and the producers (workers

[1] Scholars often stress a paradox in Plato's *Republic* because Socrates and his interlocutors quote time and again several poets in the dialogue and yet, Socrates proposes the ban of poetry in Books II and III (*op. cit.*, at 398 a1 – b4). The paradox also regards Aeschylus. Although his tragedies should be silenced and dismissed from the polis (*op. cit.*, at 398 a), his work is mentioned at least seven times in the *Republic*, up to the point that tragedy may play an important role in a well-governed city (at 607c). Tragedy, so to speak, can be "redeemed" (Bakewell 2017, at 261). This rehabilitation of tragedy has been criticised by those who insist on the continuity of Plato's arguments and condemnation: see Naddaff (2002). Other scholars emphasise Aristotle's reconsideration of the genre in the *Poetics* "to defend it against Plato's strictures... The apparently fundamental opposition between the philosophers' responses to tragedy can be regarded as expressive of divergent presuppositions about the status of poetry as a whole in relation to other components of culture" (Halliwell 1984). We return to Aristotle's critique of Plato's subordination of politics to theoretical philosophy at the end of this section.

of the community). This distinction corresponds to that of Book II, in which Socrates clarifies the reasons why humans live in society. The reasons are explained through a form of phenomenology that traces the evolution of society from the expertise of producers and workers who satisfy basic human needs in the 'primitive society' to the emergence of two new social needs in the 'opulent society'. These needs regard the function of soldiers for defence and offence purposes, as well as the wisdom of the Philosopher-King.

Plato's idea of justice consists in the harmony of these functions or parts of the soul. An unjust state and an unjust man are those in which one part prevails over the other; moreover, the worst part has gained the upper hand over the other parts. It is against this idea of justice that Plato determines the conditions of monstrosity, which sets him apart from every democratic tradition. His distinction between justice and injustice in Book IX is, in fact, elucidated through a spectrum of different kinds of men and institutions. At one end of the spectrum, there is the royal state of the Philosopher-King; at the other, the tyrant. In between, Plato lists three different regimes with their rulers, i.e. timocratic, oligarch, and democrat. The aim is to make apparent the happiness of the royal state as opposed to the misery of every tyranny. Tyrants are slaves, poor, full of fear, and unhappy. They indulge without restraint in every kind of appetite that takes hold of them under the guidance of eros and lust. To counter the opinion of those who believe, like Thrasymachus, that injustice is "profitable to the completely unjust man who is reputed just", Socrates suggests addressing the whole issue through "a symbolic image of the soul". In his phrasing:

> "What sort of an image?" he said [Glaucon].
>
> "One of those natures that the ancient fables tell of," said I [Socrates], "as that of the Chimaera or Scylla or Cerberus, and the numerous other examples that are told of many forms grown together in one."
>
> "Yes, they do tell of them."
>
> "Mould, then, a single shape of a manifold and many-headed beast that has a ring of heads of tame and wild beasts and can change them and cause to spring forth from itself all such growths". (Plato ed. 2000, at 588d)

The correspondence between tyrants and monsters, such as the "Chimaera, Scylla or Cerberus", not only illustrates every tyrant's philosophical, political, and psychological state, but also emphasises how, according to Plato's *Republic*, human societies may surrender, from time to time, to such a tyrant. Every tyrannical man is the result of the progressive distancing from justice because, according to Plato, there exists, albeit sometimes dormant, a kind of appetite in every man which is tremendous, wild and contrary to the law. To clarify the corruption of customs and institutions, *The Republic*'s teratology depicts the distancing from the just man through another phenomenology, one which traces the transition from timocracies and oligarchies to the "democratic man, the man of the people". How, then, do democracies turn into tyrannies?

The first step in Socrates' phenomenology is to grasp how the oligarch turns himself into a democrat by leading a life which is neither mean nor lawless. The oligarch must bring up a young son who adheres to his own way of life. However, neither the father nor the rest of the household can control the young man without inadvertently fostering desires and appetites in his soul. Thus, democracy creates its own monsters.[2] In the phrasing of *The Republic*:

> He [the young democrat] is drawn toward utter lawlessness, which is called by his seducers complete freedom. His father and his other kin lend support to these compromise appetites while the others lend theirs to the opposite group. And when these dread magi and king-makers come to realize that they have no hope of controlling the youth in any other way, they contrive to engender in his soul a ruling passion to be the protector of his idle and prodigal appetites, a monstrous winged drone. Or do you think the spirit of desire in such men is aught else? (*op. cit.*, at 372e – 373a)[3]

Plato was a harsh critic of democracy, which explains the equally harsh criticism he received from some advocates of democracy.[4] Contrary to the previous generation of tragedians, in fact, the conflict for Plato does not concern the monstrosity of tyranny as opposed to the virtues of democracy, but rather, the opposition lies between tyrants and Philosopher-Kings. The antithesis is political, psychological and theoretical, and remarkably, it can even be measured. Plato's teratology, in other words, does not offer a simple qualitative inquiry but a proper quantitative science. According to some scholars, especially those from the Tübingen school, Plato would be hinting at his esoteric doctrines and the ideal numbers of One and the Dyad (Reale 1997). Although controversial, this part of Plato's doctrine is particularly interesting for understanding the history of political ideas about monstrous tyrants because it sheds light on a second kind of criticism we must consider in addition to Plato's ideas and preferences on kingdoms, tyrannies and democracies. The focus should be on the overall theoretical basis of Plato's political theory.

Going back to the arithmetic of *The Republic*'s Book IX, tyrants are indeed presented as three steps away from oligarchs — today, in network theory's jargon, we may refer to a degree of separation — because democrats, the "man of the people", stand between tyrants and oligarchs. The same degree of separation holds for the ideal distinction between just kings and oligarchs: the tyrant's distance from true pleasure should thus be thought of as "three times three". Yet, according to Plato's calculus, it would be insufficient to flesh out such difference as a mere "plane number" because

---

[2] Plato's opinion may apply to modern democracies (Talmon 1919). Many dictators have come to power through democratic elections in the 1900s, for example, from Adolph Hitler to Hugo Chávez in Venezuela. We return to the monsters of democracy below in Chapter 4, dealing with Jean Jacques Rousseau's own monsters.

[3] I'm quoting here the translation by P. Shorey, Cambridge, MA, Harvard University Press,1969, online at accessed on September 8, 2025 from https://www.perseus.tufts.edu/hopper/text?doc=Perseus%3Atext%3A1999.01.0168%3Abook%3D5%3Asection%3D471e.

[4] Among such critics of Plato's doctrines, it is worth mentioning Karl Popper depicting Plato as a monster (Popper ed. 1962), and how critics of Popper's readings, for example Paul Levinson, refer to Popper as the real monster: "there is no text which Popper can cite in support of such a change; it arises solely from his picture of Plato as a third head upon the double-headed monster whom he has created, called 'the Old Oligarch and Gritias'; it is guilt by association, the very ultimate example of the witch-hunt technique" (in Popper ed. 1962, at 324). As stressed in the introduction, however, this third tier of the analysis on scholars deeming their colleagues' work monstrous falls outside the scope of this book.

we should both "square" and "cube" it. Correspondingly, the life of the Philosopher-King is conceived as being 729 times more pleasurable than the tyrant's, whose life is accordingly more miserable by the same amount. All in all, $9 \times 9 \times 9 = 729$!

> [Socrates]: 'Numerically, then, the tyrant is three times three removed from true pleasure.'
>
> [Glaucon]: 'So it seems.'
>
> 'And as for the total length of this distance,' I said [Socrates], 'it looks as if the image of the tyrant's pleasure is a plane number.'
>
> 'Just so.'
>
> 'And by squaring and cubing it becomes clear how far removed the tyrant is.'
>
> 'Clear enough,' he said [Glaucon], 'to anyone who can do the arithmetic.'
>
> 'Conversely, if you are talking about how far removed the king is from the tyrant, in terms of true pleasure, you will find, when you complete the multiplication, that his life is nine-and twenty- and seven hundred-fold more pleasurable, and that a tyrant is more wretched by the same amount. (Plato, *op. cit.*, at 586 d-3)

Experts have comprehensibly struggled with the interpretation of this part of Plato's arguments on the monstrous tyrant. It remains unclear, for example, why Plato counts the oligarch twice and, moreover, why he was not content with 9 as the tyrant's distance from true pleasure, but felt compelled to square and cube that number.[5] As a disciple attending Plato's lectures at the Academy, Aristotle likely heard some of those doctrines. However, later on, as a colleague, he sharply criticised Plato's oral teachings in his own work. Books XIII and XIV of *Metaphysics* are devoted to refuting Plato's numerology. The same holds for the *Nicomachean Ethics*, in which Aristotle neatly distinguishes practical sciences from theoretics. Contrary to the theoretical sciences, which comprise physics, metaphysics, and mathematics, the subject of the practical sciences is "the philosophy of human nature" (Aristotle ed. 2000, 1181 b). This branch of philosophy concerns reflection on that part of the world that is doable, feasible, and practicable for human beings. Although Aristotle follows several of Plato's ideas on natural justice and tyranny as the worst of all political regimes, he argues that Plato failed to note the distinction between metaphysics and politics, mathematics and practical sciences and, further, between natural virtue and virtue in the strict sense.

---

[5] Further Platonic dialogues help at times clarify *The Republic*'s numerology, for instance, Plato's *Philebus*: see Pagallo (2005). Even in this case, however, it seems fair to concede that Plato's ideal numbers remain scientifically infertile. Plato's "nuptial number" in Book VIII, at 546 b-c, clarifies this claim: "For the birth of a divine being there is a period embraced by a perfect number, while for a human being it is the first number in which increase to the power of roots combined with squares — taking on three dimensions and four defining limits — of the numbers which create likeness and unlikeness, and which wax and wane, makes all things conversable and rational with one another. Of these numbers the ones that form the basis of the musical fourth, when coupled with five and three times increased, produce two harmonies. The first harmony is a square, the product of equals, so many times 100. The second harmony is of equal length one way, but a rectangle. One side is the square of the rational diagonal of a five-by-five square, minus one, times 100, or the square of the irrational diagonal of a five-by-five square, minus two, times 100. The other side is three cubed times 100. Taken as a whole, this geometrical number is master of this domain — of better and worse births" (Plato 2000, at 255–256). For the more curious readers, it is worth mentioning that the spectrum of interpretations concerning this Platonic calculus ranges from 216 to 12,960,000.

Aristotle's differentiation between theoretics and political philosophy is relevant for a theory of legal monsters because, *pace* Plato's wisdom of his Philosopher-King, only *phronesis* allows us to ascertain what is right in general terms and what is right in a given context. Socrates — the quintessence of a political thinker — erred in claiming that all virtues are forms of practical wisdom. Pericles, rather than Socrates, should be considered the model of the true politician. As stressed in Book VI of the *Nicomachean Ethics* (1141 b 2):

> From what we have said, then, it is clear that wisdom is scientific knowledge, combined with intellect, of what is by nature most honourable. This is why people say that Anaxagoras, Thales, and people like them are wise, but not practically wise, when they are seen to be ignorant of what is in their own interest; and that their knowledge is extraordinary, wonderful, abstruse, godlike, but useless, because it is not human goods they are looking for. (Aristotle ed. 2000, at 109–110)

Aristotle's ideas diverge from Plato's political philosophy, and yet, this does not mean that every reflection on monsters would be meaningless. If it is true that Aristotle does not refer any longer to monsters in his political theory, we should be attentive to how Plato's teachings reappear in *Politics* and the *Nichomachean Ethics*. Otherwise, the outcome would resemble that of the first generations of comparative law scholars who, in examining Chinese culture, failed to find any strict legal principles because they were simply looking for them in the wrong places (Ruskola 2013). What changes vis-à-vis Plato's philosophy is the field of research in which we can properly analyse Aristotle's perspective on monsters.

As stressed in the following section, Aristotle's distinction between theoretics and praxis, mathematics and ethics, metaphysics and the law, entails a new scientific approach to the monsters of the tradition. We should not look for any reference to monsters in the realm of politics, as the investigation on monsters concerns physics and natural philosophy (Asma 2009, at 45). The 'naturalisation of the monster', so to speak, requires a new kind of anthropology in Aristotle's reflection. What kind of monster emerges as a result? How did Aristotle reinterpret the monstrous tyrants of Plato's teratology in the *Republic*? What is the connection between Aristotle's theoretical sciences and practical philosophy, between physiology and the law, biology and ethics?

2.2 The Critical Colleague

Aristotle's critique of Plato's subordination of politics to theoretical philosophy yields two main results relevant to a theory of legal monsters. On the one hand, his critique precludes every application of quantitative methods to the world of human things, an approach that would later characterise much of modern legal and political thought.[6] On the other hand, there is no room for monsters in Aristotle's *Politics*

[6] We return to this below in Chapters 6 and 7, dealing with geometry as a source of inspiration for the ideas of Hobbes and Pufendorf, Leibniz and Rousseau, among others.

and *Nichomachean Ethics*. In the first book of *Politics* (1253 a), Aristotle illustrates the famous thesis — a hallmark of the natural law tradition — arguing that humans are inherently a political species, or *zoon politikón*. Justice is conceived of as the bond of men in the political community so that both the law and the determination of what is just represent the principle of order within this society. By following Plato's teachings, Aristotle distinguishes two kinds of justice: natural and conventional.[7] However, the political dimension of human nature is grasped according to a new distinction: instead of Plato's opposition of humans to monsters, Aristotle opposes humans to brute animals.

Aristotle's new differentiation should be grasped in two dimensions: upward and downward. Upward, in the sense that only the beings who do not have needs or are self-sufficient do not participate in the human community: these beings are gods. Downward, in the sense that individuals who are unable to live in society should not be considered proper humans but rather beasts. Although humans are a 'political species', Aristotle freely admitted that all humans seek wealth, prioritise themselves and are governed by their own habits. Men are, at times, the worst of all earthly beasts. In the phrasing of the *Nicomachean Ethics* (VII.7, 1150 a 1):

> Brutishness is not as bad as vice, though it is more to be feared, because it consists not in the corruption of the superior element, as in human beings, but in its absence. (Aristotle ed. 2000, at 130)

The 'naturalisation of the monster' means, *pace* Plato, that tyrants are neither monsters nor necessarily beasts. Tyrants are 'able to live in society' and, in some cases, they rule over it. Entire parts of Aristotle's *Politics* and *Nichomachean Ethics* are devoted to the anatomy of tyrannies. For instance, Book XI of *Politics* examines the arts, marks, and practices used by tyrants to grasp why they get power and how tyrannies are preserved. In the *Nicomachean Ethics*, Aristotle even suggests strategies for tyrants to sustain their power, i.e. by presenting themselves as a steward, or king, before their people. Such tricks of power emphasise how much tyrannies and tyrants are despicable. Aristotle follows Plato's arguments on the kind of appetites that lie behind tyrannies — tremendous, wild and contrary to the law — although in connection with the new image of a 'human beast' who is slavish in tastes and acts under passion and revenge.

In Book X of the *Nichomachean Ethics*, Aristotle examines this form of institutional enslavement through the lens of Plato's dichotomy between tyranny and monarchy. Both forms of political community can be understood as a one-man rule system, and yet, tyrants look to their own advantage, kings to that of their subjects. In Book V of *Politics*, tyranny is presented as embodying the worst aspects of both oligarchy and democracy (1311 a). Tyranny is the most deplorable among all forms of political community because tyrants brutalise the institutions. To clarify the assumption, an entire section of the *Nicomachean Ethics*, i.e. VIII.12, focuses on the

[7] See Aristotle, *Nicomachean Ethics*, at 1134 b: "As regards what is politically just, one part is natural, the other legal. What is natural is what has the same force everywhere and does not depend on people's thinking. What is legal is what originally makes no difference whether it takes one form or another, but does matter when people have adopted it" (Aristotle ed. 2000, at 93).

correspondence among different kinds of constitutions and various forms of familial relationships, i.e. between justice and friendship. Aristotle meticulously analyses the multiple social classes existing in society — from peasants and handcrafters, merchants and retailers, employees and soldiers, to judges and advisors, managers and the wealthy — to illustrate why different forms of political and economic organisation govern human societies. Monarchies are traced back to the relationship between fathers and sons; aristocracies and republics are linked to the relationship between husbands and wives; oligarchies hinge on the dominion of husband and wife over everything else; and Aristotle likens democracies to a state of anarchy between brothers. Therefore, it is against this framework that we can appreciate the lesson learned from seven generations of Athenians, from Aeschylus to Aristotle via Plato: what makes tyrannies the worst of all political institutions is that tyranny enslaves its people. In *Politics* (1267 a), drawing on the history of Athens, Aristotle reminds us of the honour bestowed to those who kill a tyrant, "but not to one who kills a thief".[8]

The Aristotelian substitution of monsters with beasts in the political domain does not mean that the philosopher lacked curiosity for other kinds of monsters in further fields of scientific investigation: humans are featherless bipeds, after all. The naturalisation of the monster in the political arena is integrated with the analysis of several kinds of monsters in physics and physiology. In *Generation of Animals*, for example, Aristotle carefully examines the case of humans with birth defects, anomalies, or physical deformations, calling them 'monsters'. Although it is still debated whether Aristotle comprehends as a human monster both children who do not resemble humans and offspring with no family resemblance to any of its members, Aristotle's spirit of scientific investigation would be associated centuries later with the analysis of the abnormalities of physiological development in organisms and genetics. In the phrasing of *Generation of Animals* (IV, 769 b):

> Still it is not easy, by stating a single mode of cause, to explain the causes of everything, (1) why male and female are formed, (2) why female offspring often resembles the father and male offspring the mother, and again (3) the resemblance borne to ancestors, and further (4) what is the cause why sometimes the offspring is a human being yet bears no resemblance to any ancestor, sometimes it has reached such a point that in the end it no longer has the appearance of a human being at all, but that of an animal only — it belongs to the class of monstrosities, as they are called. (Aristotle ed. 1943, at 417)

[8] Athenians used to celebrate Harmodius and Aristogeiton, the "tyrant-slayers" of Hipparchus, brother of the tyrant Hippias. Harmodius and Aristogeiton paid with their own life for the tyrannicide, being executed in 514 BC. According to Andocides in *On the Mysteries*, Athens instituted the following oath a few decades later: "I shall kill, by both word and deed, by vote and by my own hand, if I can, anyone who subverts the democracy at Athens, and anyone who holds any office after the democracy has been subverted" (Andocides ed. 1998, at 126). Tyrannicide was increasingly common and popular also in Aristotle's times: "it bears noting that Academy students did commit assassinations at about the time [Plato's] *Statesman* was written. Python of Aenus killed the king of Thrace, one Cotys, in 360 BC, with help from another follower of Plato; both escaped from Thrace and made it safely back to Athens, where they were honored as heroes. Then in 353 a third Academy member, Chion, slew the ruthless tyrant of Heraclea (on the Black Sea), Clearchus" (Romm 2025, at 242).

Truth, however, is the child of time. *Generation of Animals* focused on the formal and material nature of the being, wondering whether the former still has control over the latter (*op. cit.*, IV, 770 b). Doubts are moreover cast on the final cause of such being, that is, its ultimate purpose or what is discussed as a possible "failure in the purposive effort" in Book II of *Physics* (199 b). In the *Generation of Animals*, Aristotle notes that monsters show how Mother Nature may be "strawed from the generic type" (*op. cit.*, 767 b), though monsters entail a sort of deformity which is, luckily, rare (772 b). To be fair, in ancient times such views were challenged by different schools of thought. Despite Aristotle's authority, Stoicism and followers of Zeno on the one hand, and supporters of the Epicurean theory of knowledge on the other, aimed to defuse popular beliefs on the individual and irregular phenomena of monsters (Del Lucchese 2019, at 180). Yet, roughly 2200 years of history were necessary to attain a clearer picture of the category of monstrosities under scrutiny in Aristotle's work.

Beyond issues in scientific research and natural philosophy, another challenge arising from the Aristotelian distinction between theoretical and practical sciences, physics and politics, physiology and the law, monsters and beasts, concerns their own interplay. Some interpreters have suggested that Aristotle's distinction between theoretics and praxis may lead to a paradox: Aristotle supports the idea that theoretics is nobler than praxis — its virtues pertain to eternity, after all — yet, the supremacy of theory does not entail that *sophia* and its theoretical virtues prevail over *phronesis*, or the normative dimension of human life (Gadamer 1983). While examining the structure, functions, and even *telos* of this peculiar animal, Aristotle's remarks on human monsters are strictly connected to a physical and metaphysical level of abstraction that nevertheless opens the question of how the political community should deal with physical bodies that stray from the generic type. Although, from a theoretical viewpoint and dealing with the genealogy of today's debates on legal monsters, this interplay between science and politics could be dismissed as anachronistic, it is not.[9] It is Aristotle himself who, in *Politics* (1335 b), asserts that "concerning exposure and rearing of offspring when they are born, let there be a law that no deformed child should be raised" (Aristotle ed. 2013, at 218).

From a historiographical perspective, however, the role of the law in such cases has often led to misapprehensions. Considering the history of ancient Roman law vis-à-vis the natural law tradition of Plato and Aristotle, for example, the German philosopher G.W.F. Hegel stressed in his *Philosophy of History* that a crucial difference between Greeks and Romans would revolve around the idea of positive law and the separation between law and morals. Although Roman law endorsed an approach similar to Aristotle's normative suggestion on "deformed children", such a convergence would be misleading. In the phrasing of Hegel's *Philosophy of History*:

> In contrast with the beautiful, harmonious poetry and well-balanced freedom of Spirit among the Greeks — here, among the Romans the prose of life makes its appearance — the self-consciousness of finiteness — the abstraction of the Understanding and a rigorous principle

[9] The analysis of this interplay and then the overt conflict between science and politics is postponed to Chapter 4, when dealing with the theses of Charles Darwin in *On the Origin of Species* and the foundation of genetics with Gregor Mendel's experiments with pea plants.

> of personality … To the constrained, non-spiritual, and unfeeling intelligence of the Roman world we owe the origin and the development of positive law. (Hegel ed. 2001, at 307)

It seems fair to admit that such a harsh alternative between Greek philosophy and Roman law may be overstated. Nonetheless, we may concede to Hegel that the principles and influence of Roman law — that is, Roman private law, rather than Roman public law; *ius privatum* rather than *ius publicum* (Mousourakis 2012; Russell 2016) — have been unique throughout the centuries. Some of these principles were later incorporated into further legal systems and considered as a part of natural law or, with Kant's example on the legal notion of deposit, as the form in which the moral law immediately manifests itself (Kant ed. 1997, at 25).[10] Unfortunately, the same holds for the ancient Roman law concept of 'monster'. Aristotle's brief remark in *Politics* ended with an intricate network of legal notions and formal mechanisms that disciplined the status of the human monsters under scrutiny in *Generation of Animals*. Jurists developed a strict understanding of the formula on monsters and prodigies because they had to clarify the aim or material scope of the legislation that would have established the standard across Western legal systems for centuries.

The following section dwells on these Roman conceptions of monsters and how they adopted the Greek tradition of political theory, natural law, and natural philosophy. Although Hegel's claims on what distinguishes the two cultures is clearly exaggerated, he has a point in stressing the relevance of the Roman 'body of law' or *corpus iuris* for centuries to come. As noted in the introduction, the focus is on the origin and development of one of the darkest pages in the history of Western law.

2.3 Roman Monsters

Roman jurists were great experts on monsters. In Aristotelian terms, we may say that their focus was more on the 'monsters' as discussed in *Generation of Animals*, than the 'monsters' understood according to the meaning of Greek tragedians or in Plato's philosophy. With time, sophisticated legal principles and a complex case law developed from the governance and regulation of humans with birth defects, regardless of the formal, material or final cause of the abnormal human being under scrutiny within the 'body of law'. Such deformity is repeatedly illustrated in the *Digest* of Justinian (Watson ed. 1997), where legal monsters concern:

> "Whenever something contrary to nature is born, perhaps in the three hands or feet, or in some other part of the body, which is contrary to nature" or "when something prodigious appears, which the Greeks call phantasmata" (Dig. 50.16.38).[11]

Roman lawyers did not develop any general definition of what kind of 'person' a monster might be, nor did they determine the overall status of the parents and

[10] It comes as no surprise that Hegel would typically reject Kant's arguments as empty formalism: see, for example, Hegel ed. (1999: 125–126). Kant's ideas on monsters never significantly dealt with their inhuman legal status: see Chapter 4 below.

[11] All translations of the *Digest* in this section and in Chapter 3 below are mine.

third parties involved in the governance and regulation of deformed people, such as offspring lacking any family resemblance to members of a Roman village. Instead, the definition of the *monstrum vel prodigium* — the 'monster or prodigy' of the Digest — shall be grasped in accordance with a network of rights and obligations concerning legal actions and parties to a lawsuit. The aim was to determine practical things such as patrimonial conditions and inheritance relationships; or, duties and obligations that parents may have in cases such as the burial of their monstrous offspring. Although the birth of a human monster could entail legal consequences, such a being did not enjoy any 'legal subjectivity' of its own. Since the foundation of Roman law and later, pursuant to the Twelve Tables from 449 BC, deformity was deemed a discriminating element between monsters and humans. In the wording of the first paragraph of Table IV on paternal power, "a notably deformed child shall be killed immediately".[12]

In addition to principles and regulations of Roman law, however, the Platonic meaning of the monstrous tyrant persisted in Roman culture as much as the Aristotelian image of the human beast.[13] Such political formulas were often used interchangeably and further evolved with various nuances. Perhaps no one clarifies the convergence of old and new meanings of the formula more effectively than Cicero, the great lawyer, philosopher, and statesman. In *The Republic* (2, 26), Cicero refers to the tyrant as the ruler who "deviates into unjust rule ... surpassing, although in the human form, the most monstrous wild beasts in cruelty" (Cicero ed. 1829, at 100). Further, a recurring trope of Cicero's work is to refer to political foes and adversaries as beasts or inhuman monsters. For example, in 70 BC, during the corruption and extortion trial of Gaius Verres, governor of Sicily, Cicero delivers one of the most famous series of speeches in his rise to the consulship: *The Verrine Orations* (Cicero ed. 1928a). According to Cicero's eloquence, Verres is an "importunum animal", a "portentum", even more dangerous than Scylla or Charybdis — a second Cyclops. In a nutshell, a "novum monstrum".[14] The same holds a decade later when Cicero was

[12] The first regulations of monsters are traditionally traced back to the first Roman king, Romulus. According to our main source, Dionysius of Halicarnassus in *Roman Antiquities* (II, 15), "in the first place, he [Romulus] obliged the inhabitants to bring up all their male children and the first-born of the females, and forbade them to destroy any children under three years of age unless they were maimed or monstrous from their very birth. These he did not forbid their parents to expose, provided they first showed them to their five nearest neighbours and these also approved. Against those who disobeyed this law he fixed various penalties, including the confiscation of half their property" (Dionysius ed. 1937, at 356). We return to the nuances of Roman law below in the first section of Chapter 3.

[13] A well-established tradition of Roman playwriters and comedians contributed to making popular the image of the human beast. For example, around 200 BC, in the *Asinaria*, Plautus coins the formula of the 'human wolf' which would ignite the political and philosophical reflection in the 1500s (Erasmus and Montaigne), and in the 1600s (Francis Bacon and Thomas Hobbes): "*Lupus est homo homini, non homo, quom qualis sit non novit*", namely, "man is no man, but wolf, to strangers" (*op. cit.*, Act II, 495). As stressed in the introduction, a similar idea is at work in Plato's *Republic*, according to which "anyone who tastes [human innards] will inevitably turn into a wolf" (Plato ed. 2000, at 279). Still, we must render unto Plautus the things that are Plautus. We return to his image in Chapters 6 and 7.

[14] See Cicero (1928a, at § 2.1.42, 2.1.40, 2.5.146, and 2.5.145, respectively).

embroiled in the Catilinarian affair: the conspiracy leader becomes a misbegotten monster, "*monstrum illud atque prodigium*" (in May 1996). Therefore, the formula is meant to include not only tyrants but also corrupts, conspirators and enemies of the institutions. Such a political use of the formula is still at work in the first century CE with Seneca's *Hercules Furens* and his fight against monsters by the killing of tyrants (Seneca ed. 1917).[15]

Legal and political notions of monstrosity in Roman culture have to be complemented with the meaning of the formula in the realm of natural philosophy. Superstitions and popular beliefs in the existence of monsters went hand in hand with dissenting opinions and attempts at scientific research. As noted in the previous section, among those who contested, in various ways, the existence of monsters, were the Stoics and Epicureans, as referenced, for example, by Diogenes Laertius and the Christian reception of Stoicism with Tertullian, Minucius Felix, or Pelagius (Del Lucchese 2019, at 170–222). Among scientific investigators, a prominent role must be recognised to Pliny the Elder (Beagon 1992). Pliny devoted his life to examining the nature of things in the fields of zoology and botany, ethnography and anthropology, physiology and pharmacology, and more. Child of his time, Pliny's multi-volume *Natural History* is full of monsters. In particular, Book VII of the *Natural History* — focused on the origins and diversity of humans — dwells on bestial monsters such as griffins and hippocentaurs, cannibals, one-eyed Cyclopes, backward-footed Antipodes, swift one-legged Sciapods, and a dog-headed Cynocephali. Such monstrous beings are occasionally presented as "monstrous races".

Despite what, in retrospect, appears to be a fantastic description of the natural world, Pliny's *Natural History*, drawing on Herodotus and other authorities, set the standard for later encyclopaedias and scholarly work encompassing all fields of scientific research. Pliny paved the way for the spirit of Italian humanism, which persisted into the Renaissance and its naturalistic concepts (Murphy 2004). Before the multifaceted variety and diversity of the world, Pliny was indeed interested in the causal and physical explanation of monstrous phenomena, such as the hereditary transmission of genetic characters, even sincerely admitting the limits of human understanding: "one should not forget that the modern meaning of scientific enquiry recognisable in Aristotle or Pliny's did not pre-exist" (Del Lucchese 2019, at 200).

The threefold backdrop of legal, political, and philosophical meanings of what a monster is supposed to be, or what it represents in Roman culture, warns us against

[15] There is not only room for tragedy in Seneca's reflection on monsters. See his satire on the Roman emperor Claudius in *Apocolocyntosis (divi) Claudii*, namely, the *Pumpkinification of (the Divine) Claudius*, in which Hercules reacts to the "first glimpse he got" of the Emperor, just arrived among the gods after his death, being "really much taken aback, although not all the monsters in the world could frighten him; when he saw this new kind of object, with its extraordinary gait, and the voice of no terrestrial beast, but such as you might hear in the leviathans of the deep, hoarse and inarticulate, he thought his thirteenth labour had come upon him. When he looked closer, the thing seemed to be a kind of man" (Seneca ed. 2009, at 16–17). Another monstrous emperor, however, i. e. Nero ordered Seneca to kill himself, which Seneca did in 65 CE. We return to Nero, the monstrous tyrant par excellence in the 1500s, below in note 2 of Chapter 4.

every simplification. The attention should be drawn to how such meanings interplay through two observables of the analysis with their variables:

i) The interplay between legal science and natural philosophy as regards thresholds of monstrosity: although legislation on the *monstrum vel prodigium* of Roman law would persist over the centuries, the demarcation between humans and monsters, legal persons and legally dead people, should not be taken for granted and would evolve under Roman law.[16] In *Divination*, for example, Cicero claims that "many persons who were born with certain natural defects have been restored completely by Nature herself, after she had resumed her sway, or by surgery or by medicine" (Cicero ed. 1923, at 2, 96);
ii) The interplay between the two meanings of the formula on monsters in the political and legal domain, that is, the political use of monsters as symbols of criticism, resistance and rebellion, such as the monstrous tyrants of Plato, Cicero, and Seneca; and monsters as targets of repression, that is, in addition to the *monstrum vel prodigium*, Cicero's enemies of the institutions. Cicero paid with his own life for the consequences of such a tension between the two meanings of the formula.[17]

Against this framework, it is therefore necessary to prevent every one-size-fits-all view, whether theoretical or historiographical. We noted in the previous section Hegel's attempt to provide one of such views with the Roman notion of positive law and its separation from morals. Cicero's work, however, is once again instructive in grasping this intricacy of the different meanings of formulas on monsters that readings such as Hegel's view on natural law and positive law, private law and public law, overlook. On the one hand, according to the Roman jurist, there was no contradiction between the different legal and political meanings of the formulas on human monsters. Yet, on the other hand, their opposite function — either referred to as the object of legal regulations or source of criticism and even rebellion and tyrannicide — could hardly be consistent with any form of proto-positivism. How else should we interpret what Cicero claims in *On Duties* (III, 4), i.e. that the killing of the tyrant is the most noble of all deeds worthy of renown? (Cicero ed. 1887, at 180).

To be fair, risks of simplification have been popular even after Hegel's historiographical and philosophical reconstructions. The crucial differences arising from

[16] On the evolution of the 'body of law' and its regulation of human monsters, especially considering the case of the hermaphrodites, see below the first section of Chap. 3. As regards the minority opinion of ancient times that human monsters, properly speaking, would not exist, this opinion played a role of reference in centuries to come. See below in Chap. 4.

[17] Cicero reckoned that the killing of Julius Caesar, the tyrant, was justified (*On Duties* III, 4); however, he later dared to criticise Mark Antony, who rose to power after Julius Caesar's death. Presented by Cicero as a new tyrant, Mark Antony finally ordered to assassinate the philosopher: Cicero was killed in Formia on 7 December 43 BC (see Hall 2009). To grasp the spirit of those times and the popularity of the formula on monsters, it is worth mentioning that Crassus and Pompey, who managed Caesar's election as consul in 59 BC, were all portrayed by a bold satirist of those times, i.e. Marcus Terentius Varro, as the "three-headed monster". See Stothard (2022).

the multiple uses of the formulas concerning monsters — particularly the differentiation between subjects and objects of legal regulation, natural law and positive law, private law and public law, down to potential conflicts between scientific research and political institutions — have been overlooked in scholarly work over the past decades. The next section claims that most hermeneutical shortcomings hinge on a distorted vision of the requirements and functions of the law. A theory of legal monsters should be attentive to the historiographical nuances under scrutiny in this section. Next, the focus is on how far this claim goes, drawing on Cicero's ideas on the legal and political uses of the formula on monsters.

2.4 A Complex Legacy

Hegel's dichotomy between natural and positive law represents a crucial topic of this book. Different schools and variants of both traditions will be under scrutiny in the next chapters of the volume, suggesting once again the need to prevent risks of simplification. Although commonly recognised among the founders of the classical natural law tradition, in the previous sections of this chapter, we noted crucial differences between Plato and Aristotle. Aristotle strongly criticised Plato's theoretical foundation of the practical sciences and sometimes even poked fun at his intent to apply mathematical methods to morals and politics. However, both philosophers agreed that alongside and above positive law, justice — as the bond of the political community — does not depend on conventions or people's mutable thinking. By contrast, legal positivism can be deemed as a theory that does not admit the existence of any natural law besides positive law or maintains that no law other than positive law exists for practical purposes.[18]

Drawing on this standard demarcation, *pace* Hegel, it seems fair to concede what most scholars do, i.e. that a pillar of the Digest in the arguments of Gaius, Paul, or Ulpian, together with the tenets of Cicero's legal philosophy, firmly rest in the natural law tradition.[19] However, what is even more important to stress — in addition to different variants of this natural law tradition since ancient times — has to do with the critical issues that follow due to the co-existence of positive law and natural law. By considering in particular Cicero's ideas, this perspective casts light on three critical issues:

i) The interplay between theory and praxis;
ii) The connection between law and morals;
iii) The repressive side of the law.

Cicero's remarks in *The Republic*, *On the Laws*, and *On Duties* make it clear that the Roman jurist considered positive law in relation to a hierarchy of superior laws,

---

[18] The attention is drawn to the variables of legal positivism below in Chapter 8.

[19] The assumption does not intend to underestimate, for example, "a larger philosophical conflict in the ancient world between Aristotle and the Stoics" reflected in the Digest: see Kroger (2017), and Weinreb (1987).

which he dubbed *vera lex, suprema lex, communis lex naturae, naturae jus, naturae lex, naturalis lex, jus naturale, universum jus* or *sempiterna lex*. Whether these ideas shall be interpreted in light of the Stoic natural law school or the Greek school of natural rights remains an open issue (Strauss 1953, at 127). Yet, it is certain that Cicero was neither sceptical nor Epicurean. As he claims in *On the Laws* (Cicero ed. 1928b), humans are born for justice and formed by nature to share justice and impart it to everybody (*op. cit.*, 1.33); we belong to the same species (1.29); and our possession of reason is what distinguishes us from other creatures (1.30). Moreover, it is reason that provides a sense of mutual fellowship and union between human beings (1.28). On this basis, Cicero provides the celebrated definition of the law as right reason, *recta ratio* (1.23), which grounds the legitimacy of what is commanded or forbidden in the legal domain (1.33; 1.42). The fact that Cicero freely admitted the opposition of the real world to the ideal world of *recta ratio* is not a good motive to claim that such *recta ratio* does not exist, or has no function. Indeed, the opposition of theory and praxis does not entail any separation of morals and the law but, rather, just mediation and proper dialectics.[20]

As a result, the broader political — rather than strictly legal — meaning of the formula on 'monsters', which Cicero develops in *The Verrine Orations*, the Catilinarian conspiracy and many other essays, speeches and letters, should be understood in connection with this interplay between law and morals, positive law and natural law, rather than just the byproduct of their separation. The targets of Cicero's criticism and sarcasm were not only the enemies of the institutions but also colleagues and rivals. Ironically, this meaning of the formula is also evident in Hegel's preliminary remarks in *Philosophy of History*, though his historiographical claims on the separation of law from morals obscure this connection. So goes Hegel's argument:

> Among us, the so-called 'higher criticism,' which reigns supreme in the domain of philology, has also taken possession of our historical literature. This 'higher criticism' has been the pretext for introducing all the anti-historical monstrosities that a vain imagination could suggest. (Hegel ed. 2001, at 21)

The Hegelian (and Ciceronian) use of the formula persists today: some colleagues are indeed monstrous and, their work, a monstrosity. However, the nuances of Cicero's references to a legal monster vanish as soon as they are disconnected from their corresponding moral assessment. Cicero, admittedly, is partly responsible for this kind of semantic impoverishment when his references to monsters insist on the repressive side of the law against corrupt governors (Verres), conspirators (Catiline 'the monster'), or a brutish bunch of people. The interchangeability of monsters with the Aristotelian beasts of *Politics* and the *Nicomachean Ethics* makes this repressive function of the law crystal clear, for example, when dealing with a squad of pirates.

[20] Experts in Hegel's thought may object that the German philosopher discussed the interplay between law and morals just in terms of mediation and dialectics in his philosophy of right (Brooks 2012). The claim of this section is however historiographical, that is, related to how Hegel interpreted the nuances of Roman law. Leaving aside Hegel's ideas of legal philosophy, we return to this mediation and dialectics in Chapter 8, dealing with the opposite theses of a legal positivist (Herbert Hart), and an advocate of the natural law tradition (Lon Fuller).

In the phrasing of *On Duties* (3.29.107), "a pirate is not included in the list of belligerents, but is the common enemy of all [*communis hostis omnium*]" (Cicero ed. 1887, at 236).[21] This is the class of enemies who deserve no mercy.

The natural foundation of the law and its *recta ratio* work both ways, i.e. they can oppose or justify harsh legal coercion in the name of justice. This assumption is critical, especially considering, in retrospect, the detailed Roman legislation and case law about slaves or children with birth defects. Most Romans did not object that both slaves and monsters were legitimate objects of repression. Even Aristotle conceded that certain humans are things; others, monsters with no right to live. This repressive face of the law is apparent in the formula of Roman law on their *monstrum vel prodigium*, which encapsulates the twofold aim to check or inhibit human actions or desires, and to hold down and control humans unfairly or evilly. Leaving aside the technical considerations on how *ius*, *lex* or *consuetudo* were conceived of in legal detail — we return to their differentiation in the following chapters of this book — it is noteworthy that Roman law survived an impressive turmoil of traditions and cultures, economies and moral values, as if it were impervious to any change of opinions also, but not only, concerning the regulation of humans with congenital disabilities.

This success of Roman law would confirm the impression that, regardless of the idea of justice we may embrace, the formalisms of the law function as a mechanism of social repression.[22] As stressed in the introduction of this book, Foucault made this repressive function of the law popular through his research on legal monsters in the Middle Ages and down to the 1600s and 700s (Foucault ed. 2003). On this basis, some scholars have proposed unlikely interpretations linking Cicero's ideas to Foucauldian monstrosities (Troshynski and Weiner 2016). Although the hard side of the law clearly exists — and has materialised through the governance and regulation of monsters and prodigies since ancient Roman law until the Universal Declaration of Human Rights in 1948 — this is only a part of the story of the meaning and uses of the formula 'legal monster'.

The chapter has emphasised the complex legacy handed down by the Greco-Roman tradition. Not only some scholars and, admittedly, a few philosophical schools have claimed that monsters do not exist or should be treated more humanly. Also, in accordance with Cicero's ideas on monsters, such monsters regard both objects and subjects of the law, both physical and political bodies, both birth defects and the

---

[21] A.P. Peabody translates the Latin 'pirata' as robber, claiming that the word assumes in this context the same meaning of 'praedo', i.e. a robber by land. I maintained the original meaning, especially considering the relevance of Cicero's ideas for the modern debate about pirates as monsters in the 1700s. See below Chapter 5. On the other hand, I kept Peabody's translation of belligerents, although some English editions make the concept more similar to modern ideas, such as those of 'lawful combatants'.

[22] This idea fits like hand into glove with Hegel's readings of Roman law and the separation of law from morals: "The Romans then completed this important separation, and discovered a principle of right, which is external — i.e. one not dependent on disposition and sentiment. While they have thus bestowed upon us a valuable gift, in point of form, we can use and enjoy it without becoming victims to that sterile Understanding — without regarding it as the ne plus ultra of Wisdom and Reason" (Hegel ed. 2001, at 307).

tragedy of tyrants. These two sides to the same coin should not be understood in light of any strict separation of law and morals, *pace* Hegel, but rather, with the different legal, political, and philosophical meanings that the formula has had since antiquity. This view is all the more necessary since the next chapter focuses on the first side of the coin. In fact, in Chapter 3, principles and rules of the law will strictly refer to the abnormalities of physiological development in human organisms that have been under the radar of scholars from a scientific viewpoint since Aristotle's *Generation of Animals* and, later, Pliny the Elder's *Natural History*. By focusing on the repressive side of the law against offspring with no resemblance to any of the members of the community, we should keep in mind the complexities of a topic that has misguided the likes of Hegel, or Foucault.

References

Aeschylus. 2017. *Eumenides*, trans. E.D.A. Morshead. Melbourne: Scribble. Accessed on September 8, 2025 fromhttp://classics.mit.edu/Aeschylus/eumendides.html.

Andocides. 1998. *Antiphon & Andocides*, trans. M. Gagarin and D.M. MacDowell. Austin: University of Texas Press.

Aristotle. 1943. *Generation of animals*, trans. A.L. Peck. Cambridge, MA: Harvard University Press.

Aristotle. 2000. *The nichomachean ethics*, trans. R. Crisp. Cambridge: Cambridge University Press.

Aristotle. 2013. *Politics*, trans. C. Lord. Chicago and London: Chicago University Press.

Asma, S. T. 2009. *On monsters: An unnatural history of our worst fears*. Oxford: Oxford University Press.

Bakewell, G. W. 2017. The voice of Aeschylus in Plato's republic. In *Voice and voices in antiquity: Orality and literacy in the ancient world*, ed. N. Slater, vol. 2, 260–276. Leiden: Brill.

Beagon, P. 1992. *Roman nature: The thought of Pliny the elder*. Oxford: Clarendon Press.

Brooks, T. 2012. *Hegel's political philosophy*. Edinburgh: Edinburgh University Press.

Cicero, M.T. 1829. *The republic*, trans. G. W. Featherstonhaugh. New York: Carvill.

Cicero, M.T. 1887. *De officiis*, trans. A.P. Peabody. Boston: Little, Brown & Co.

Cicero, M.T. 1923. *De Senectute, De Amicitia, De Divinatione*, trans. W.A. Falconer. Cambridge, MA: Harvard University Press.

Cicero, M.T. 1928a. *The Verrine Orations*, trans. L.H.G. Greenwood. Cambridge, MA: Harvard University Press.

Cicero, M.T. 1928b. *On the laws*, trans. C.W. Keynes. Cambridge, MA: Harvard University Press.

Del Lucchese, F. 2019. *Monstrosity and philosophy: radical otherness in Greek and Latin culture*. Edinburgh: Edinburgh University Press.

Dionysius of Halicarnassus. 1937. *Roman antiquities, vol. I: Books 1–2*, trans. E. Cary. Cambridge, MA: Harvard University Press.

Foucault, M. 2003. *Abnormal: Lectures at the College de France 1974–1975*. London: Verso.

Gadamer, H. G. 1983. *Dialogue and dialectic: Eight hermeneutical studies on Plato*. New Haven, CT: Yale University Press.

Gentile, M. 1930. Platone autore di drammi filosofici. *Rivista di Filosofia Neo-Scolastica* 22:427–435.

Hall, J. 2009. Serving the times: Cicero and Caesar the dictator. In *Writing politics in imperial Rome*, ed. W. J. Dominik, J. Garthwaite, and P. A. Roche, 89–110. Leiden, The Netherlands: Brill.

Halliwell, S. 1984. Plato and Aristotle on the denial of tragedy. *Proceedings of the Cambridge Philological Society* 30:49–71.
Hegel, G.W.F. 1999. On the scientific ways of treating natural law, on its place in practical philosophy, and its relation to the positive sciences of right. In Political writings, ed. L. Dickey and H.B. Nisbet, trans.H. B. Nisbet. 102–180. Cambridge: Cambridge University Press.
Hegel, G.W.F. 2001. *The philosophy of history*, trans. J. Sibree. Kitchener: Batoche Books.
Kant, I. 1997. *Critique of practical reason*, trans. M. Gregor. Cambridge: Cambridge University Press.
Kroger, J. R. 2017. The philosophical foundations of Roman law: Aristotle, the stoics, and Roman theories of natural law. In *Cicero and modern law*, ed. R. O. Brooks, 229–268. London: Routledge.
Lanza, D. 1977. *Il tiranno e il suo pubblico*. Turin: Einaudi.
May, J. M. 1996. Cicero and the beasts. *Syllecta Classica* 7:143–153.
Mousourakis, G. 2012. *Fundamentals of Roman private law*. Heidelberg: Springer.
Murphy, T. 2004. *Pliny the elder's natural history: The empire in the encyclopaedia*. Oxford: Oxford University Press.
Naddaff, R. 2002. *Exiling the poets: The production of censorship in Plato's republic*. Chicago and London: University of Chicago Press.
Pagallo, U. 2005. Plato's Daoism and the Tübingen school. *Journal of Chinese Philosophy* 32 (4): 597–613.
Plato 2000. *The Republic*, trans. T. Griffith. Cambridge: Cambridge University Press.
Popper, K. R. 1962. *The open society and its enemies*. London: Routledge and Kegan.
Reale, G. 1997. *Toward a new interpretation of Plato*. Washington, DC: Catholic University of America Press.
Romm, J. 2025. *Plato and the tyrant*. New York: Norton.
Ruskola, T. 2013. *Legal orientalism: China, the United States, and modern law*. Cambridge, MA: Harvard University Press.
Russell, A. 2016. *The politics of public space in republican Rome*. Cambridge: Cambridge University Press.
Seaford, R. 1998. Tragic Money. *The Journal of Hellenic Studies* 118:119–139.
Seneca, L.A. 1917. *Tragedies*, trans. F.J. Miller. Cambridge, MA: Harvard University Press.
Seneca, L.A. 2009. *Apocolocyntosis*, trans. by W.H.D. Rouse. Auckland: The Floating Press.
Sophocles 1887. *Oedipus tyrannus*, trans. R. Jebb. Cambridge: Cambridge University Press.
Stothard, P. 2022. *Crassus: The first tycoon*. New Haven: Yale University Press.
Strauss, L. 1953. *Natural right and history*. Chicago: University of Chicago Press.
Talmon, J. 1919. *The origins of totalitarian democracy*. London: Mercury Books.
Tarrant, D. 1955. Plato as dramatist. *The Journal of Hellenic Studies* 75:82–89.
Troshynski, E. I., and J. D. Weiner. 2016. Freak show: Modern constructions of Ciceronian monstra and Foucauldian monstrosity. *Law, Culture and the Humanities* 12 (3): 741–765.
Watson, A., ed. 1997. *The digest of Justinian*. Philadelphia: University of Pennsylvania Press.
Weinreb, L. L. 1987. *Natural law and justice*. Cambridge, MA: Harvard University Press.

Chapter 3
Sources of Repression

This chapter provides a concise history of human monsters, i.e. people with birth defects, anomalies and deformations as the target of repressive regulation. The twofold aim of the law covers both sides of this repression: to hold down and control persons, and to check or inhibit their actions or desires—in the case of generations of human monsters, quite unfairly and evilly. The focus is on ancient Roman law and centuries of civil law and common law tradition, from the Middle Ages to Modernity. The legal repression under scrutiny in this chapter illustrates one of the darkest pages in the history of Western thought and societies.

3.1 Civil Law

Generations of experts in Roman law have dissected the clauses on legal monsters and prodigies. Over the centuries, jurists have elaborated on the fundamental discrimination between monsters and humans established with the Twelve Tables and based on an obvious deformation: "a notably deformed child shall be killed immediately".[1] Jurists occasionally had to address extraordinary phenomena and even social and political pressure: we shall not overlook that life at the time was permeated by magic and full of monsters. For example, Livy, the great Roman historian, reported the birth of a hermaphrodite and a boy with an elephant's head in 209 BC, dubbing

[1] See above chapter 2, section 3, where we noted that the first regulations of monsters, or prodigies, are traditionally traced back to Romulus, the first Roman king. According to Raymond Bloch, the notion of prodigy is however of Etruscan origin and shapes the Roman culture at the times of the Etruscan kings, starting with Tarquin the Elder (Bloch 1963). Annie Allély distinguishes five kinds of monsters, namely, androgynes, deformed children, precocious children, monsters half-man half-beast, and multiple births (Allély 2003). Her conclusion is that "the fear of the hermaphrodite disappeared in the imperial era… although this was a marginal phenomenon, involving the wealthy classes, since Seneca notes that weak and monstrous children were always eliminated" (*op. cit.*, at 156). We return to this differentiation in the next note of this chapter.

U. Pagallo, *A Theory of Legal Monsters: Repression, Resistance, Rebellion*, Philosophical Studies Series 161, https://doi.org/10.1007/978-3-032-10771-8_3

them "prodigies" (A*b urbe condita*, XXVII 11). That same year, other monsters were reported. These reports prompted the Roman Senate to convey Haruspices from Etruria to interpret the birth of a hermaphrodite in Sincussa and then, in 207, a 4-year-old kid with monstrous forms in Frosinone. The response of the law was unequivocal: "The creature was locked alive into a cage and in full sea the whole lot was set overboard". A customary rite followed: the choral expiation of the monster. According to some scholars, "in striking contrast to this impassioned description of the fate of these monstra… stands the apathetic approach to the phenomenon of the monsters in the Corpus Iuris Civilis" (Schrage 1995, at 469).

Roman jurists had indeed no pathos for their *monstrum vel prodigium*. They primarily focused on the birth of an individual as a potential bearer of rights and properties. There were three conditions for legal birth:

(i) Separation from the human mother;
(ii) Of a living being;
(iii) With a human form.

Jurists discussed all three circumstances, i.e. whether a separation from the mother had occurred, what conditions should be considered indicative of life, and what should be conceived of as human form as opposed to any abnormality or deformation. Most discussions on Roman 'legal monsters' must thus be grasped against this framework. The antithesis of humans and monsters determined whether a living being separated from the mother was born or 'legally dead'. Variables of this threshold are consequences of the axiom that, in legal terms, human monsters had never rights of their own. However, the birth of deformed children or monsters half-man half-beast could have legal consequences, such as benefiting their parents, or affecting third parties' claims. For example, in Justinian law, a title of merit, such as a right to *ius liberorum*, was recognised to the monster's parents when the woman was the mother of more than one child. Also, in this case, the human monster or prodigy remained a simple object of regulation.[2]

[2] The legal regulation of hermaphrodites represents a special case among the monsters of Roman law (Crifò 1999; Franchini 2016). Whereas, until the end of the Roman republic, hermaphrodites were often considered the most alarming prodigies, their status changed considerably in the imperial period. In fact, contrary to the cruel treatment of hermaphrodites reported by Livy's *Ab urbe condita*, the legal issue of jurists in the *Digest* revolved around the preponderant sexual features of such human being. This is for example the opinion of Ulpian, drawing on the teachings of Sabinus: "The question is: to whom do we compare a hermaphrodite? And I think that the sex that predominates in him should be considered more" (D. 1.5.10). Furthermore, so goes Ulpian, "the hermaphrodite, if his virile qualities prevail in him, will clearly be able to establish a posthumous heir" (D. 28.2.6.2). Paul follows suit: "Whether a hermaphrodite can be used in a will depends on the quality of the predominant sex" (D. 22.5.15.1). Scholars often interpret this radical social and legal change with "a forgetfulness of Roman tradition and an interest in Greek rationality" (Evêque 2020, at 139). In the phrasing of Horace's *Epistles* (II, 1, 156), "Graecia capta ferum victorem cepit", i.e. Greece took its Roman captor captive. A more colorful picture of this cultural change is in the *Attic Nights* of Gellius (IX, 4, 15): "I myself in Africa saw Lucius Cossutius, a citizen of Thysdrus, who had been changed into a man on his wedding day and was still living when I wrote this". Then, quoting Pliny the Elder's *Natural History* (VII, 34), "there are persons who from birth are bisexual, whom we call 'hermaphrodites'; they were formerly termed androgyny and regarded as prodigies, but

The Digest is full of such legal monsters (Watson ed. 1997). Paul employs the formula for three purposes: to differentiate monsters and hermaphrodites, to establish that monsters are not free and, nevertheless, to acknowledge that their birth can have legal effects.[3] In Paul's wording:

> They are not free, them who are procreated contrary to the form of the human race: as if a woman were encumbered with something monstrous or prodigious. But birth, which has expanded the functions of human members, seems to be an effect to some extent and therefore will be counted among children. (D. 1.5.14)

Ulpian, drawing on the authority of Labeo, refines the definition of Paul:

> Labeo defines 'portent' everything that is born and made contrary to the nature of each thing. But there are two kinds of portent: one, whenever something is born contrary to nature, perhaps with three hands or feet or some other part of the body, which is contrary to nature: the other, when something seems prodigious, which the Greeks call them phantoms. (D. 50.16.38)

In accordance with the provisions of the *Lex Papia et Poppaea*, Ulpian uses the formula even for rhetorical purposes to support the opinion that a monster's birth should not prejudice the parents:

> Let someone ask if a woman has given birth to something portentous or monstrous or weak, or something new in appearance or in crying, not of a human figure, but of another, more of an animal than a man, whether, because she is pregnant, should it benefit her? And it is more likely that these things should also benefit the parents: for there is no reason to blame them for having complied with the statutes as best they could, nor should that which came fatally entail harm on the mother. (D. 50.16.135)

In other contexts, the understanding is that a monster's birth is relevant for the purposes of inheritance law and the rights of succession. Consider Justinian's ruling addressed to Julianus, Praetorian Prefect, on "a dispute among the ancients" (C. 6.29.3). The case concerned a posthumous child and whether her birth could break a testament. To interpret the parent's will, some jurists reckoned that a posthumous child who was indeed brought into the world but died without emitting a sound, would not break the will; on the contrary, others, such as the Sabinians, "thought that if the child was born alive, the testament would be void, despite it uttered no sound, which would also apply had it been mute". Justinian follows this latter opinion, ordering that whenever a child was born "completely alive" the testament is void, "provided only that it arrived in this world as a human being and not as a monster or prodigy" (C. 6.29.3).

---

now are instruments of pleasure" (Gellius ed. 1927, at 170). As stressed in the previous chapter, the translations of the Latin texts in this section, unless otherwise indicated, are mine: "D" stands for the Digest; "C" refers to the Code of Justinian.

[3] In addition to the differentiation between hermaphrodites and proper monsters (see the previous note of this chapter), the attention must be drawn to the fundamental distinction of Roman law between two kinds of persons. According to the *Institutes* of Gaius (1, 9), considering the different conditions of men, "the greatest division in the law of persons is this, that all men are either free or slaves" (D. 1, 5, 3). Paul's claim that monsters or prodigies are not free does not mean, however, that such beings were slaves. See the next note of this chapter.

There is no empathy, or pathos, in Roman legal texts: monsters simply are not human, or rather, *ad nullum declinans monstrum vel prodigium*, they indeed "decline to nothing" (C. 6.39.3.1). Therefore, going back to the previous question on whether a human being was born, the answer is that a free human being was never born if it is a monster; and if it is a monster, then, only the parents' rights and eventually the claims of third parties shall be considered for legal purposes. The solution goes hand-in-hand with the ethos of that era and the moral grounds on which the political community rests. In the previous chapter, we noted that Aristotle, like the Romans, deemed it natural that certain human beings were things and, therefore, slaves; on the other hand, other beings — such as the human monsters under scrutiny in Aristotle's *De generatione animalium* or in Livy's *Ab urbe condita* — should not be considered as humans, either legally alive or free. The proverbial exceptions mostly concerned the regulation of hermaphrodites in the imperial period and the monster's parents: we noted a right to *ius liberorum* for the mother of a monster if she had more than one child. These provisions suggest evolving social expectations, perhaps as a form of solidarity towards the monster's parents facing such a tragedy: from the rite of choral expiation for the monster to new social rights under Justinian's empire in the mid-500s (Maas 2005). However, crude as it can be, once a prodigy was born, or a child turned into a monster, the law did not consider them legally free, or humans, because they were less than things, or slaves.[4] Human monsters were rare enough but still dangerous.

Roman culture would wonder about what kind of empathy we may ever have for those sorts of beings lacking any human resemblance. Human superstition in a world of magic, such as the monsters of Livy, would cement this lack of Roman pathos throughout the centuries. The transmitter of this moral apathy was no other than the law with its cases and formalities. Yet, this lack of pathos is not unique to Roman culture. It is possible to find similar notions on the status of 'legal monsters' even in cultures not directly influenced by Roman law, such as the English common law. Generations of scholars have dissected the role of Roman law in this legal tradition, in particular, considering the summa of Henry de Bracton's *On The Laws and Customs of England 1240–1260*, written in Latin (Bracton ed. 1968).[5] A substantial convergence with the legal treatment of monsters in Roman law seems apparent, and still, the formula on monsters assumed its own English character with Bracton's case

[4] Although Roman slaves were conceived of as things, some slaves enjoyed a significant autonomy. The elite of the slaves, as in the case of the emperor's slaves, were estate managers, bankers and merchants, holding important jobs as public servants, or entering into binding contracts, managing and making use of property for their masters' family business. Consequently, Romans distinguished multiple types of activities and status of the slaves *as dispensatores, ordinarii*, etc., for each of which specific lawsuits or *actiones* were established: in addition to the Institorian action, the *actio exercitoria, actio tributaria*, and so forth (Pagallo 2013: 103–104). Slaves could do business through a separate unit, such as the peculium, which remained however the property of the head of the household: see Watson (1997).

[5] The translations of Bracton's Latin texts in the next section are mine, unless otherwise noted. We return to Bracton's constitutional ideas below in the fourth section of Chapter 6, where the Medieval dualisms of *jurisdictio* and *gubernaculum, dominium politicum et regale*, are examined in connection with the bane of the modern natural law tradition.

law and, then, with the monsters of Edward Coke in *The Institutes of the Law of England 1628–1644* (Coke ed. 1817); and, of William Blackstone's *Commentaries on the Laws of England* from the mid-1700s (Blackstone ed. 1871).

The aim of the next section is to illustrate how a new 'legal monster' was born in the common law tradition.

3.2 Common Law

Among the founders of the common law tradition, Henry de Bracton and Thomas Coke laid down the constitutional basis of the rule of law in England, drawing on the Medieval ideas of *jurisdictio* and *gubernaculum, dominium politicum et regale.* The aim was to prevent the monsters of tyranny and the enslavement of the subjects in the kingdom by distinguishing between the individuals' rights, their liberty, and the rulers' power. This overall intent included the regulation of another kind of monster, i.e. people with birth defects, anomalies, or deformations. The summa of medieval and modern common law, from Bracton to Coke, from the mid-1200s to the early 1600s, reminds us of this twofold meaning handed down from the tradition: on the one hand, the political monsters of the Greek tragedy and Plato's philosophy and, on the other, the monsters of Aristotle's physiology and the prodigies of ancient Roman law. Blackstone's *Commentary on the Laws of England* is no exception. Humans with birth defects, or anomalies, were the common target of principles and regulations that converged with the basics of Roman law under scrutiny in the previous section of this chapter. Bracton's *On The Laws and Customs of England* set the precedent for Coke's *Institutes* and Blackstone's *Commentary.*

In the second volume of *On The Laws and Customs of England* (Bracton 1968), Bracton's opinion on human monsters is presented exactly where expected according to the classifications of Roman law, i.e. dealing with "persons, things, and actions" (*op. cit.*, 2, 31). As much as occurs in Roman law, the aim was to classify humans and specify who shall be deemed free and freeborn, in a nutshell, who can be conceived of as a child. Contrary to Roman law, however, Bracton classified mankind into three genres: "male, female, and hermaphrodite". His prudent opinion is that "those born of unlawful intercourse, as out of adultery, are not reckoned among children, nor those procreated perversely, against the way of humankind, as where a woman brings forth a monster or a prodigy". Yet, the legal outcome that follows such a circumstance is so harsh — namely, the legal death of the human monster as occurred throughout centuries of ancient Roman law — that Bracton suggests a restrictive interpretation of the category. Accordingly, "an offspring who has a larger number of members, as one who has six fingers, or if he has but four, [or only one,] will be included among children" (*op. cit.*, 2, 31, 26–28).

Against this general framework, we can dwell on the case law under exam in the volumes of Bracton's work.[6] For example, a case regards a pregnant woman vis-à-vis the administration of justice and, in particular, the causes of legitimate delay concerning the writes of a sheriff that "cause her to come before the justices at Westminster". The issue entails a doctrinal conflict that must be solved:

> Some say, though others are of a contrary opinion, that the woman cannot exceed the gestation period by a single day, even where the issue dies *in utero* or turns into a monster, the risk falling on the mother, but may anticipate the time of birth and deliver prematurely. If such a monster or prodigy is born, it will not be reckoned as a child nor taken into account with respect to succession. Nevertheless, if an infant is born with more or fewer than the usual number of limbs – as six fingers on one hand, or no more than four – yet otherwise appears to be fully human, he or she (they) shall be considered as a child for the purpose of succession. (*op. cit.*, 2, 203–204)

Further cases regard "disseised" people, particularly whether tenants have had a child and whether "it was born a monster and not a child" (vol. 3, 151). Another case concerns a wife's claim to be put into possession *ventris nomine*, making it crucial to determine whether the "heir apparent" or "him who is in the womb" develops into a monster or dies in the womb (vol. 4, 198). Also, warranties can be suspended for several reasons, such as the uncertainty of the warrantor or the heirs in the case under scrutiny, for example, "if a woman is pregnant and it cannot be established whether the child will be born alive or dead or, when it is born, whether it will be a human being or will turn into a monster" (vol. 4, 227). Another issue has to do with a child, particularly whether "it is a monster and if it cries by uttering a roar" (4, 361). Once again, the problem revolves around whether such a child is to be considered a monster, although in accordance with the restrictive interpretation that "I do not call a child a monster, even when nature has given it too few or too many members: too few, as where fingers are lacking; too many, as where there are too many fingers or joints... And note that this exception lies both in a possessory action ... [or] in a proprietary, by writ on entry or a writ of right" (*ibid*).

In *The Institutes of the Law of England*, Coke follows suit. The assumption is that "monsters are begotten on account of the corruption of some principle". Monsters are legally dead, *civiliter mortui*, and therefore, "cannot purchase much less retain anything" or "be heir or inherit any land". In the *Mary Portington's* case, Coke recalls "the honourable Funeral of fond and new-found Perpetuities, a monstrous Brood, carved out of meer Invention, and never known to the ancient Sages of the Law" (in Gest 1909, at 526). Coke clarifies that "yet I say honourable, for that these Vermin have crept into many honourable Families". Coke had no problem attending the solemn funeral and accompanying the monster to the "grave of oblivion", although not mourning it. As much as occurs in Roman law, the priority is that of providing certainty regarding the status of individuals and their property, "for

[6] Drawing on this case law, which includes some five hundred decisions, scholars have emphasised Bracton's Englishness in the treatment of human monsters. See Kelley (1990, at 167), who adopts Maitland's overall interpretation of Bracton's doctrine (Maitland 1963). However, the importance of Roman law should not be underestimated, at least, as regards monsters lacking any human resemblance.

that the Commonwealth rejoyced, that fettered Freeholds and Inheritances were set at liberty, and many and manifold Inconveniences to the Head and all the Members of the Commonwealth thereby avoided". In the conclusion of Chapter XXIV of *The Institutes*' first volume, this approach ends up with a perverse sort of sexist paradox, because "a hermaphrodite, if the male sex be predominant, shall have an appeal of death as heir, but if the female sex does exceed the other, no appeal does lie for her as heir".[7]

In the Preface to Part V of the *Reports* (Coke ed. 1826), however, Coke warns the "good Reader" that the kind of monster he is dealing with does not only concern abnormal people who do not look like humans. Both the strict legal and political meanings of the formula are at work in Coke's argumentations. In addition to the *monstrum vel prodigium* of the tradition, Coke claims that error, together with its "inseparable twin" ignorance, multiplies infinitely, thus producing "such monstrous & strange Chimaeras". After all, the main intent of the English institutions, according to Coke, is to prevent any comeback of monsters, whether they be the tyrants of Greek tragedy or Plato's philosophy, or the enemies of the institutions, such as corrupt politicians, conspirators, or traitors, as described in Cicero's eloquence.[8] The trial of Sir Walter Raleigh, accused of committing treason against the Crown by attempting to establish Arabella Stuart as queen of England in 1603, provides the proper framework. Coke was, in fact, the prosecutor in such a case, in which, in his own words, "no speedier expedition hath been used in these proceedings, considering the monstrousness and continual horror of this so desperate a case" (in Johnson 1845, at 173). The exchange between prosecution and defence went down in history:

> "Oh do I, Sir?" exclaimed Coke. "I will prove you the notoriousest traitor that ever came to the bar, after you have taken away the King, you would alter religion, as you, Sir Walter Raleigh, have followed them of the bye, in imitation, for I will charge you with the words".
> "Your words," retorted Raleigh, "cannot condemn me, my innocency is my defence; prove one of these things wherewith you have charged me, and I will confess the whole indictment, and that I am the most horrible traitor that ever lived, worthy to be crucified with a thousand torments".
> "Nay," replied the attorney-general; "I will prove all: thou art a monster; thou hast an English face and a Spanish heart". (in Johnson 1845, at 158)[9]

[7] Scholars have stressed that the early common law tradition did not conceptualise sex as purely binary, although not hinging on medical opinions: see Fishbayn (2007), and Sudai (2022). On the contrary, we noted in the previous section of this chapter that the Roman conceptualisation of sex was strictly binary. What dramatically changed in Roman times was the legal reaction to cases of androgyny, intersex, or hermaphrodism. Regarding the legal subtleties of the *Mary Portington*'s case, see Boyer (1997).

[8] Coke's vision of the English institutions is under scrutiny below in Chapter 7, dealing with the opposite ideas of Thomas Hobbes, "the monster of Malmesbury".

[9] For the curious readers, it is worth adding that Coke won his case: Raleigh was found guilty in 1603. However, Raleigh was not executed, but rather imprisoned in the Tower of London. After many years, Raleigh was released to lead an expedition to South America in search of El Dorado. The mission was a catastrophe: El Dorado was, of course, never found; the English expedition clashed with Spanish forces; and Raleigh's son died in the fight. Furthermore, upon his return home, Raleigh was arrested again and executed in 1618 for violating the terms of his pardon and the peace treaty with Spain. See Wallace (2015). Coke's monster j'accuse is also in *op. cit.*, at 205.

This twofold meaning of monster, both strictly legal and political, is similarly at work in Blackstone's *Commentaries on the Laws of England* with further refinements. Regarding how to deal with abnormal humans, Blackstone draws on the tradition and the authority of Bracton, including in the class of "public nuisances" not only those making great noises in the streets at night with trumpets or similar, but also with suffering mischievous animals and by "exhibiting monsters". Likewise, when a sentence of death is pronounced — and "it is now clear beyond all dispute that the criminal is no longer fit to live upon the earth" — such a criminal must be "exterminated as a monster and a bane to human society". All in all, human monsters, "which hath not the shape of mankind", cannot be heirs, for they do not have "inheritable blood". Although Blackstone admits the Justinian idea that the monster's parents could reap some advantage, for example, the *jus trium liberorum*, because a monster's birth represents "the misfortune, rather than the fault, of that parent" (Blackstone ed. 1871, at 246), the legal effects of such a birth depend on a familiar threshold (C. 6.29.3). That is, whether the monster "bears the resemblance of brute creation" or, despite its deformities, it has "human shape". In Blackstone's words, "this is a very ancient rule in the law of England; and its reason is too obvious and too shocking to bear a minute discussion" (Blackstone ed. 1871, at 246–247).

The political meaning of the formula, however, did not vanish from the *Commentaries*. Since the very beginning, Blackstone sets his level of abstraction by stressing, as much as Coke did before him, that "in times of ignorance and superstition that monster in true policy may for a while subsist, of a body of men residing in the bowels of a state and yet independent of its laws". Such monstrosity does not only regard any attempt to put at risk the "original contract of government" or "the united will of the community" (Blackstone ed. 1871, at 372–373). Also, specific statutes and acts of legislators can be monstrous. This differentiation between monstrous institutions and monstrous normative acts was very popular in the mid-1700s.[10] In *Of the Absolute Rights of Individuals*, Blackstone makes the example of rules *ad personam*, i.e. normative acts in which the goal is to protect a particular interest through the adoption of some general rule, or with the further example of a retrospective legislation with a similar purpose. Such normative acts are simply monsters (Blackstone ed. 1979, at 127).[11]

It is worth mentioning that both meanings of the formula on monsters handed down by Bracton, Coke and Blackstone still persist today in British debates regarding either the physical body of the individuals or the body politic, either abnormal human objects of legal regulation or monsters conceived of as the result of evil intentions or ignorance of the law. On the one hand, among the last cases in which the legal authority on human monsters had to be judicially debated in the UK, *Re A (Children)*

[10] We return to this popular differentiation, which can be traced back to the teachings of the natural law tradition, in Chapter 6.

[11] Interestingly, Blackstone's jurisprudence has also been discussed in connection with a further type of monster, i.e. debates on the uncontrolled lawsuits phenomenon of the American tort law system devouring corporation as "monsters" (Hazleton 1995). Although Blackstone never uses the term tort in his writings, his jurisprudence in the *Commentaries* would anticipate current US debates over tort reform: see Rustad and Koenig (2002).

from 2000 concerned the medical separation of conjoined twins (Sharpe 2007). On the other hand, both sides made a series of monster accusations during the Brexit row. On 1 April 2019, for example, Professor John Finnis argued that only one option remained with Brexit—in the phrasing of *The Telegraph*'s title, "prorogue Parliament and allow us out of the EU with no-deal". The day after, on his website *Public Law for Everyone*, Cambridge's colleague Mark Elliott criticised suggestions such as suspending Parliament or ignoring legislation. The kind of criticism aimed at a natural law advocate such as Professor Finnis speaks volumes. In the colleague's words, "in truth, it is those suggestions, as distinct from Parliament's entirely legitimate decision to undertake indicative votes, that represent the real 'constitutional monstrosity'."[12]

3.3 From Middle Ages to Modernity

In his Lectures on the "abnormal" at the College de France in 1974–1975, Foucault brings to life the image of the abstract monster depicted by the rules of the law through the strict formalisms of its jurists (Foucault 2003). His lecture on 22 January 1975, in particular, draws attention to "a story of two Siamese twin brothers" (*op. cit.*, at 65); the killing of a hermaphrodite in 1599 (*ib.*, 67); and the Lyon case from 1765, which "transposes the old category of the monster from the domain of somatic and natural disorder to the domain of pure and simple criminality" (Foucault 2003, at 74). Foucault sums these cases up with a periodisation:

(i) The human monster of ancient Roman law;
(ii) That of the Renaissance; and,
(iii) The legal monster of the 1600s and 700s.

The Roman monster had the features of a being who was half human and half animal; this image would persist until the Middle Ages.[13] Then, according to the French philosopher, the monster became "the double individual" of the Renaissance. Finally,

[12] Since the introduction of this book, I stressed that this kind of debate of scholars presenting the opinion of their fellow colleagues as monstrous falls outside the scope of the analysis. It is fair, however, to grant Finnis the right to reply: "I agree with Mark Elliott in finding my April 1 argument about prorogation and assent astonishing and monstrous, once the argument's important premises have been omitted, as he has omitted them". The reply is in the UK Constitutional Law Association website (8 April 2019) accessed on September 8, 2025 from at https://ukconstitutionallaw.org/2019/04/08/john-finnis-royal-assent-a-reply-to-mark-elliott/.

[13] See Foucault (2003, at 63 and 66). We noted, however, that the monster half-man half-beast was only one of five different types of monster in Roman times: dramatic social and legal changes in the treatment of hermaphrodites represent a special case. In addition, scholars have often proposed more nuanced readings also concerning the treatment of people with congenital disabilities in the Middle Ages. For example, according to John Block Friedman, "we can conclude that monstrum came to be defined indirectly as something that could have both a soul and a legal status, and therefore partake of humanity from the social and theological points of view" (Friedman 1981, at 183). Along the same lines, Lisa Verner stresses that "not all infants with significant deformities or impairments did die quickly… and thus must have received assistance from caretakers for much if not all of their lives [so that] for the Middle Ages, I believe, we can substitute 'monstrosity' for

it was the turn of the hermaphrodite, who gave rise to "so many problems in the seventeenth and eighteenth centuries" (*op. cit.*, at 324). In particular, Foucault dwells on the case of Antide Collas. Doctors concluded that such a being really had both sexes, but only because of the relations of that monster with Satan: "the hermaphrodite confessed to having had relations with Satan and was burnt alive in Dole in 1599" (*op. cit.*, at 67). Similar cases of hermaphrodites in 209 BC, as reported by Livy — see the first section of this chapter — suggest that the destiny of all these monsters was often brutal. Foucault properly emphasises this ugly side of the law in which Antide's sole fault was being a hermaphrodite.

However, such an anomaly or deformation entails a legal disorder problem because of its 'natural exception'. In Foucault's wording (*op. cit.*, at 324):

> A monster is not only... an exception to the form of the species but also... introduces disorder into the legal system (whether it is a question of marriage laws, canons of baptism, or laws of inheritance).

This legal disorder can be understood in connection with the hard cases of the law, i.e. cases of disagreement among jurists that may regard the meaning of the terms framing the legal question, the ways such terms are related to each other in legal reasoning, or the interpretation of the principles that are at stake in the case. Foucault's analysis is full of such hard cases. For example, regarding a Siamese twin monster, "the problem was whether one or both of them should be executed. If one were executed, then the other would die; but if the innocent brother was allowed to live, then the other also had to be allowed to live" (*op. cit.*, at 65). Work by the Italian priest Cangiamila, who published his "holy embryology" in Palermo in 1745, translated into French in 1762 — who "seems to me to be of absolutely fundamental importance for understanding the question" — provides further hard cases related to the baptism of monsters with a rational soul. The difficulties are a 'source of disorder' for canon law because we may wonder whether two Siamese twin brothers deserve one or two baptisms. Likewise, "if a monster has two bodies which, despite being joined, each possess its own limbs", we may ask whether two separate baptisms are necessary. In such a case, we may say, *ergo ego vos baptiso.*

On the other hand, Foucault's legal disorder is more radical than a strictly legal affair: monsters affect the ethos of the community and its pathos. The problem concerns the moral grounds on which every political community and the law rest in Aristotelian terms. It is noteworthy, however, that Foucault interrupts his history of legal monsters with the transformation of the somatic being and beasts of the Middle Ages "[in]to the domain of pure and simple criminality" in the late 1700s. Foucault could examine the reasons why — and the ways in which — the legal monsters of positive law went legally extinct two centuries later. Instead, starting from the fourth lesson on 29 January 1975 and until the end of the course in Paris, the focus dwelled

---

'disability'" (Verner 2014, at 44 and 56). A similar viewpoint in Newman-Stille (2010). We return to Foucault's historiographical difficulties below in Chapter 5.

on forming new Western monsters, leaving aside the repression and final extinction of the old Western monster of positive law.[14] So goes the reasoning:

> What prevented the formation of this category of monstrous criminality? What was it that prevented aggravated criminality from being seen as a kind of monstrosity? How was it that the extremity of crime and the aberration of nature were not linked together? Why was it that we had to wait until the end of the eighteenth and the beginning of the nineteenth centuries for the appearance of this heinous figure of the criminal monster in whom the most extreme breach of the law joins up with the aberration of nature? And it is not the aberration of nature that in itself is a breach of the law, but the breach of the law that refers — as if to its origin, cause, excuse, or framework, it matters little — to something that is the aberration of nature itself. (Foucault 2003, at 75)

It is not a motive for self-congratulation contrasting Foucault's narrative with the end of the formula on the legally dead, i.e. the abolishment of the monsters of Roman law and common law in modern times. However, the history of how and why the legal monsters of Roman and common law were dismissed is instructive because it casts light not only on the role that moral opinions and social customs play in the functioning and constitution of every body politic, i.e. Aristotle's *politeia* and *nomoi*.[15] Furthermore, this perspective draws the attention to the core of Foucault's own investigation: how should we interpret the repressive function of the law, which has been under scrutiny throughout this chapter with the regulation of the legal monsters in Roman law, the common law tradition, and from the Middle Ages to the late 1700s?

According to this book's historiographical and theoretical stance, the question needs clarification. Foucault's analysis on the transformation of the traditional legal monster into a modern criminal monster must be supplemented with the further transformation of the traditional monster into a legal rights bearer. This conversion can ideally be traced back to the Universal Declaration of Human Rights in 1948. And yet, this double transformation demands a preliminary elucidation about the subject

---

[14] In addition to the monsters found in Brunswick (in 1625); Bologna (1625); Salamanca (1655); Geneve (1658); and Hungary (1686), Foucault could dwell on the monsters of the 1800s, among which the monsters of Luton (1855); Montpellier (1860); Betschler (1861); and Schoenborn Carol (1863), described in Taruffi (1886, at 73 and 153 ff.). As stressed below in Chapter 5, the medieval monster and the modern monster lived indeed together as much as the Australopithecus, Paranthropus and Homo erectus did two million years ago (Leakey and Walker 1976; Herries et al. 2020). Foucault's criminal monster, in other words, never replaced, but complemented the analysis and legal treatment of humans with birth defects in the 1800s.

[15] The role that ethos and social customs play in Aristotle's legal theory is twofold. Most of the time, scholars focus on the "true lawmaker" who should take care of virtue, "for he wishes to make his fellow citizens good and obedient to the laws" (Aristotle ed. 2000, at 1102 a). According to the *Nichomachean Ethics*, the aim of the legislator is thus to form "habits" in citizens (*op. cit.*, 1103 b). However, we should be also attentive to how the opinions and habits of citizens affect the resilience of the institutions. As Aristotle stresses in *Politics*, the legislator must "take care to preserve it because, whatever the form of the constitution, it is not difficult for it to last a day or two or three" (Aristotle ed.1944, 1319 b). Arguably, one of the main reasons for the thousand-year history of oppression of human monsters in legal history has depended on the lack of pathos on the part of the fellow citizens. We return to this public attitude below in the next section of this chapter and in Chapter 4.

of this chapter, i.e. the 'sources of repression'. We noted in Chapter 2 that the issue is as old as Plato's *Republic,* in which the repressive side of the law is related to the different ideas on justice under scrutiny in the first book of the dialogue. In addition to the candid opinions of Cephalus and Polemarchus, Socrates' ideas on justice aim to oppose in particular the claim of Thrasymachus, "that the just is nothing else than the advantage of the stronger" (Plato ed. 2000, at 338 c).

All in all, Thrasymachus' position does not seem too distant from Foucault's own ideas, although scholars have stressed that such an idea of justice can also be understood as obedience to the laws of one's state, a position which is not dissimilar to some tenets of legal positivism (Hourani 1962; Hadgopoulos 1973). Dealing with the tenets of the natural law tradition, as discussed in Chapter 2, the sources of legal repression may however stem from the very idea of justice as the bond of humans in the political community against its own monsters. Therefore, clarifying the terms of this classic debate of legal philosophy appears crucial before going on with any history of ideas about monsters and their double transformation, i.e. both the transformation of the *monstrum vel prodigium* of this chapter into a rights bearer of our times (Chapter 4), and Foucault's conversion of this human monster into a monstrous criminal occurred in "the end of the eighteenth and the beginning of the nineteenth centuries" (Chapter 5).

A theory of legal monsters without historical support would be empty, and however, a historical reconstruction deprived of any theory would simply be blind. How should we grasp the sources of repression?

3.4 Modern Times

The legal repression discussed in the previous sections of this chapter represents some of the darkest pages of Western history. It is not a source of legal self-congratulation to stress the moral and epistemic differences between the treatment of human monsters in ancient times and today's law. That is, from the Haruspices of Etruria called to interpret the birth of the hermaphrodite in Sincussa in 209 BC, to current analysis in genetics and legal forensics as regards the abnormalities of physiological development in organisms. However, the difference between today and then raises a fundamental issue: how to understand the repression of legal monsters over more than two millennia. Two different meanings and approaches must be considered. They regard either the assumption of repression as the essence of the legal phenomenon, or the thesis that coercion is a requirement or function of the law.

Regarding repression as the essence of the legal phenomenon, we dwelt on the opinion of Thrasymachus in Plato's *Republic*: the law is a means of power, a tool of repression, according to what a stronger man, the ruler, deems useful or good. The definition applies regardless of any difference among multiple forms of states and governments, such as Plato's distance of 729 between kings and monstrous tyrants.[16] So goes the dialogue:

> Thrasymachus: 'All right,' he said. 'You must be aware that some cities are tyrannies, some are democracies, and others aristocracies?'
>
> Socrates: 'Of course'.
>
> 'And what is in control in each city is the ruling power?'
>
> 'Yes.' 'Every ruling power makes laws for its own good. A democracy makes democratic laws, a tyranny tyrannical laws, and so on. In making these laws, they make it clear that what is good for them, the rulers, is what is just for their subjects. If anyone disobeys, they punish them for breaking the law and acting unjustly. That's what I mean, my friend, when I say that in all cities the same thing is just, namely what is good for the ruling authority. This, I take it, is where the power lies, and the result is, for anyone who looks at it in the right way, that the same thing is just everywhere - what is good for the stronger'. (Plato ed. 2000, at 338e–339 a)

In opposition to Thrasymachus' ideas, the thesis of natural law (from Plato to Cicero), and the common law tradition (from Bracton to Coke and Blackstone) is that coercion is a requirement of the legal phenomenon rather than its essence. Plato, Aristotle and Cicero, along with Coke and Blackstone, would find it hard to buy into Thrasymachus' argument that every kind of constitution and political community is what rulers or the stronger deem useful.[17] On the contrary, we can argue about monsters when referring to a tyrant, a corrupt, a traitor, or even a whole institution — as Plato and Cicero, Coke and Blackstone did — because the principles of natural law or the tenets of English constitutionalism would justify this distinction against every repression by political monsters. The issue, as a result of this latter perspective, revolves around what kind of constitution and normative acts can be deemed monstrous and

---

[16] Plato's numerical distinction of philosophers-kings from tyrants can be considered as an attempt to formalise what later would be dubbed as a form of legitimate power: see the first section of Chapter 2. In its basic form, power refers to a relation between people, according to which "A can get B to do something that B would not otherwise do" (Dahl 1957). In the legal domain, as stressed in the text, such power is further qualified as coercive power to stress that legal provisions hinge on the threat of physical or pecuniary sanctions. In the phrasing of Leslie Green's *The Authority of the State*, "coercion threats provide secondary, reinforcing motivation when the political order fails in its primary normative technique of authoritative guidance" (Green 1988, at 75). Such coercion threats are further qualified as repression when the aim is to hold down and control persons, or to check and inhibit their actions or desires. Going back to the discussion in the first book of *The Republic*, legal power is thus legitimate when coercion and repression are justified either in the name of justice (Plato), or according to its radical critique (Thrasymachus). See also below note 17 of this chapter.

[17] The objection also applies to the interpretation of Thrasymachus' theses as a proto legal positivist, which entails the duty of obedience to the laws of one's state. A solution is just to force the Platonic text and interpret Thrasymachus' theses in a Marxist sense, so that, in the phrasing of the *German Ideology*, "the ideas of the ruling class are in every epoch the ruling ideas, i.e. the class which is the ruling material force of society, is at the same time its ruling intellectual force" (Marx and Engels ed. 1976). It follows that all institutions and law are destined to be monstrous until the catharsis of communism (Marx ed. 1887). This hermeneutical option of a Marxist Thrasymachus, so to speak, is endorsed in Nicholson (1974) and Vavouras (2021). Long (2009) deems it superficial. We return to the troubles with every catharsis in Chapter 5.

repressive, and not the other way around, that is, why all constitutions and legislations potentially have a uniform monstrous repressive shape.

Both views on 'legal repression' acknowledge that power and the use of force are critical features of the law: they concern the enforceability of legal provisions. This threat is what makes the law, law: a system of toothless provisions would be legally irrelevant, a simple theoretical exercise, or a cause of concern for governments in exile. In the 1900s, the quintessence of the modern legal formalist, such as Hans Kelsen, freely admitted this point with the efficacy of the law as a necessary condition for the validity of the legal norms (Kelsen 1945). Although distinguishing the primary and the secondary rules of the law, statutory and customary law, Hart concedes this point to Kelsen (Hart 1994).[18] Later, Dworkin would find this point indisputable despite his harsh critiques of both Hart and Kelsen (Dworkin 1986). What the law is supposed to do through the means of coercion remains, nonetheless, controversial. From the viewpoint of Thrasymachus and his followers, down to Foucault's analysis on old human abnormalities and new social monsters, repression is the other side of the coin to power and efficacy as conditions of the legal phenomenon. From the classical natural and common law perspectives, down to the tenets of constitutionalism in modern times, power and coercion are a necessary but insufficient ingredient for understanding the law's functioning. Either justice, Hart's "rule of recognition", or the role that principles play in the legal system according to Dworkin's view, would allow us to discern whether we are dealing with decent institutions and sound legislation, or vice versa, monstrous regimes and repressive acts. For example, in Dworkin's words:

> The most abstract and fundamental point of legal practice is to guide and constrain the power of government in the following way. Law insists that force not be used or withheld, no matter how useful that would be to ends in view, no matter how beneficial or noble these ends, except as licensed or required by individual rights and responsibilities flowing from past political decisions about when collective force is justified (Dworkin 1986, at 93).

It is against this philosophical debate that the sources of repression under scrutiny in this chapter shall be assessed. Followers of the natural law tradition stemming from Plato, Aristotle and Cicero, or the common law tradition from Coke and Blackstone, or the modern legal theory of Hart and Dworkin, can grasp the death of the legal formula on the *monstrum vel prodigium* as an example of how legal coercion is selective, and the law can be ameliorated. Supporters of the repressive nature of the law, such as some interpreters of Thrasymachus or Foucault, can object that the end of the legal formulas on old monsters, as a matter of physical deformity and control

---

[18] The primary rules of the law, in accordance with Kelsen's ideas, aim to directly govern individual and collective behaviour on the basis of the threat of physical or pecuniary sanctions: "if A, then B ought to follow". The secondary rules of the law concern the procedural rules of adjudication, the rules of change, and of recognition (Hart 1994). In particular, the rules of change allow the creation, modification, and suppression of the primary rules of the system, whereas the "rule of recognition" provides the criteria for determining the validity of the law. We return to Hart's concept of validity below in Chapter 8, dealing with the debate between Hart and Fuller on the separation of law from morals and why, according to Hart, a clear distinction between law and morality may encourage, rather than discourage, every resistance to tyranny.

over the bodies of individuals, does not contradict the idea that the law is a repressive force of power, from both an institutional and organisational view. What matters is the transformation of such a target: the monster who turns into a modern criminal. This stance — still popular among Foucauldian followers[19] — perfectly aligns with Thrasymachus' assumption that every ruling power determines what is just for its subjects: if a tyranny makes tyrannical laws, and a democracy democratic laws, then a human rights international regime can well endorse universal declarations.

Both sides of today's debate can concede, however, that the sources of repression under scrutiny in this chapter were not only selective but also evil. Human rights advocates of people with congenital disabilities can reverse the meaning of Blackstone's argument in defence of monsters: "its reason is too obvious and too shocking to bear a minute discussion" (Blackstone ed.1871, at 247). This is also Foucault's view on the despicable treatment of hermaphrodites, twin Siamese brothers, or other abnormal humans who were, for over two millennia, killed without mercy. As far as I know, today, nobody claims that the law has done well to repress such monsters.

Still, the aim of this section is not to discern decent institutions from monsters or sound legislation from repressive acts.[20] Instead, the goal is to clarify the repressive side of the law to determine a methodological framework for analysis. As regards the notion of legal repression, the attention was drawn so far to four readings of this notion:

(i) Repression understood as the essence of the legal phenomenon in accordance with Thrasymachean approaches to the law with their variables;
(ii) Repression understood in connection with the hard tools of the law that hinge on the threat of sanctions. Hart's distinctions between primary and secondary rules of the law, statutory and customary law, emphasise that coercion is a necessary but insufficient condition to determine what the law is supposed to be, or is meant to do;
(iii) Repression further understood in accordance with Dworkin's arguments on the ways in which political decisions may provide a necessary condition for the use of public coercion. A community licenses coercion because responsibilities and rights flow from "past decisions of a right sort";

[19] The group of Foucauldian scholars is under scrutiny in Chapter 5: see, among many, Rai (2004); Sharpe (2010); Nuzzo (2013). Such opinions on legal functions and requirements can be grasped as variables of the Thrasymachean claim that power, coercion, and repression represent the very essence of the legal phenomenon.

[20] This twofold distinction is the subject of Chapter 6 below in connection with the modern natural law tradition and tenets of contractualism. This approach aims to make political institutions legitimate through the justification of coercive legal power. This approach, namely, contractualism, is still at work in, for example, Rawls (2005). Contrary to the geometrical claims of the modern natural law tradition, however, Rawls argues that reasonableness, not truth, provides the "final criterion of correctness" (*op. cit.*, at 126). According to Dworkin, "whatever we may think of his suggestion, it has no direct connection to our present problem of legitimacy in the circumstances of ordinary politics where Rawls's principles of justice are very far from dominion… because it does not tie political obligation sufficiently tightly to the particular community to which those who have the obligation belong; it does not show why Britons have any special duty to support the institutions of Britain" (Dworkin 1986, at 192–193).

(iv) Repression understood in historiographical terms, that is, in connection with the specific target of a particular legal order at a certain historical moment.

Drawing on this basis, we can go back to the analysis of monsters and Foucault's "abnormal", and proceed in our history of ideas with method. Whatever the legal theory scholars intend to embrace — i.e. the Thrasymachean, Hartian, and Dworkinian readings (i), (ii), and (iii) above — they shall confront themselves with the analysis of some transformations in the target of such a repression. That is, according to the fourth observable of the analysis, the reasons why the legally dead people of the tradition became legal rights bearers in modern times as well as the transformation of beasts and prodigies from the Middle Ages into a new generation of monsters in the late 1700s, i.e. that on which Foucault focused in his Paris lectures. A theory of legal monsters should be attentive to both sides of this transformation. From a theoretical view, such a twofold transformation casts light on the requirements and functioning of the law with a series of oppositions between the natural law tradition and legal positivism concerning the validity of the law and how to assess normative acts and institutions. From a historiographical viewpoint, the attention must be drawn to the moral, political and epistemic differences between the treatment of human monsters up until recent times and their status in today's law. This status clarifies what was under exam in Foucault's lectures, i.e. the advent of new social monsters since the late 1700s. Further post-Foucauldian discussions on the monstrous treatment of either terrorists or illegal immigrants shall be understood against this general legal framework as well.

To clarify this framework, the next chapter examines a sort of Copernican revolution that complements the history of the legal treatment of humans with birth defects, which was under scrutiny in this chapter. A theory of legal monsters must be up to one of the most radical transformations of our times, i.e. the change of status concerning the monsters of the tradition from pure objects to subjects of the political community. The reasons for this profound transformation regard as many factors as philosophical arguments on why monsters, strictly speaking, do not exist; empirical evidence and scientific conjectures on what birth defects or physical malformation would be; human rights advocacy of why the legal status of the *monster vel prodigium* should be abolished; down to changes in social attitudes and the public opinion concerning the lack of pathos towards 'monsters' that characterised human societies over the ages.

Foucault and a generation of glossators have simply overlooked this transformation of a specific class of human beings from old objects of repression to new subjects of the law: good news is scarcely a best seller.

However, the death of old formulas about legally dead people is a matter of fact, i.e. alethic information about the states of reality. Epistemic reasons and moral arguments paved the way for the acceptance of scientific methods in politics, society, and the legal arena. How should we interpret this overall phenomenon?

References

Allély, A. 2003. Les enfants malformés et considérés comme prodigia à Rome et en Italie sous la République. *Revue des études anciennes* 105 (1): 127–156.

Aristotle. 1944. *Politics*, trans. H. Rackham. Cambridge, MA: Harvard University Press; London: Heinemann.

Blackstone, W. 1871. *Commentaries on the laws of England: In four books*. Chicago: Callaghan and Cockcroft.

Blackstone, W. 1979. Commentaries on the laws of England. In *Of the rights of things*, vol. 2. Chicago: University of Chicago Press.

Bloch, R. 1963. *Les prodiges dans l'antiquité classique: Grèce*. Étrurie et Rome, Paris: PUF.

Boyer, A. D. 1997. Understanding, authority, and will: Sir Edward Coke and the Elizabethan origins of judicial review. *Boston College Law Review* 39 (1): 43–94.

Bracton, H. 1968. *On the laws and customs of England 1240–1260*, trans. S. E. Thorne, vols. 1–4. Cambridge, MA: Harvard University Press.

Coke, E. 1817. *The institutes of the law of England 1628–1644*. Vol. 4 vols. London: W. Clarke.

Coke, E. 1826. *The reports of Sir Edward Coke*, ed. J. H. Thomas and J. H. Fraser, 13 parts in 6 vols. London: J. Butterworth and Son.

Crifò, G. 1999. *Prodigium e diritto: il caso dell'ermafrodita*. Naples: Jovene.

Dahl, R. A. 1957. The concept of power. *Behavioral Science* 2 (3): 201–215.

Dworkin, R. 1986. *Law's empire*. Cambridge, MA: Harvard University Press.

Evêque, R. 2020. The legal treatment of hermaphroditism in ancient Rome. From persecution to integration, gender based approaches to the law and Juris Dictio in Europe, hal open science. Accessed on September 8, 2025 from https://hal.science/hal-03891789/document.

Fishbayn, L. 2007. Not quite one gender or the other: Marriage law and the containment of gender trouble in the United Kingdom. *American University Journal of Gender Social Policy and the Law* 15 (3): 413–441.

Foucault, M. 2003. *Abnormal: Lectures at the College de France 1974–1975*. London: Verso.

Franchini, L. 2016. Lo status dell'ermafrodita ed il problema della determinazione del sesso prevalente, Teoria e storia del diritto privato. *Rivista Internazionale on line* 9:1–35.

Friedman, J. B. 1981. *The monstrous races in medieval art and thought*. Cambridge, MA.: Harvard University Press.

Gellius. 1927. *Attic nights*. Volume I: Books 1–5, trans. J. C. Rolfe. Cambridge, MA: Harvard University Press.

Gest, J. M. 1909. The writings of Sir Edward Coke. *The Yale Law Journal* 18 (7): 504–532.

Green, L. 1988. *The authority of the State*. Oxford: Oxford University Press.

Hadgopoulos, D. J. 1973. Thrasymachus and legalism. *Phronesis* 18 (3): 204–208.

Hart, H. L. A. 1994 [1961]. *The concept of law*, 2nd ed. Oxford: Clarendon.

Hazleton, R. 1995. The tort monster that ate Dow Corning. *The Wall Street Journal*, May 17, at A21.

Herries, A. I., et al. 2020. Contemporaneity of *Australopithecus, Paranthropus*, and early *Homo erectus* in South Africa. *Science* 368 (6486): eaaw7293.

Hourani, G. F. 1962. Thrasymachus' definition of justice in Plato's 'Republic'. *Phronesis* 7 (2): 110–120.

Johnson, C. W. 1845. *The life of Sir Edward Coke: Lord chief justice of England in the reign of James I with Memoirs of His Contemporaries*. London: H. Colburn.

Kelley, D. R. 1990. *The human measure: Social thought in the western legal tradition*. Cambridge, MA: Harvard University Press.

Kelsen, H. 1945. *General theory of the law and the State*, trans. A. Wedberg. Cambridge, MA: Harvard University Press.

Leakey, R. E., and A. C. Walker. 1976. *Australopithecus, Homo erectus* and the single species hypothesis. *Nature* 261 (5561): 572–574.

Long, R. T. 2009. Thrasymachus and the relational conception of authority. In *An anthology of philosophical studies, 3*, ed. P. Hanna, 27–36. Athens: Atiner.
Maas, M., ed. 2005. *The Cambridge companion to the age of Justinian*. Cambridge: Cambridge University Press.
Maitland, F. W.. 1963 [1908]. *The constitutional history of England*. Cambridge: Cambridge University Press.
Marx, K. 1887. *Capital: A critique of political economy, vol. I, Book 1: The process of production of capital*, trans. S. Moore and E. Aveling. Moscow: Progress Publishers. Accessed on September 8, 2025 from https://www.marxists.org/archive/marx/works/download/pdf/Capital-Volume-I.pdf.
Marx, K. and F. Engels. 1976 [1846]. *The German ideology*. Moscow: Progress Publishers.
Newman-Stille, D. 2010. Morality and monstrous disability in topographia hibernica. In *The treatment of disabled persons in Medieval Europe*, ed. W. J. Turner and T. V. Pearman, 231–257. Lewiston, N.Y.: Edwin Mellen Press.
Nicholson, P. P. 1974. Unravelling Thrasymachus' arguments in "The Republic". *Phronesis* 19 (3): 210–232.
Nuzzo, L. 2013. Foucault and the enigma of the monster. *International Journal for the Semiotics of Law-Revue internationale de Sémiotique juridique* 26:55–72.
Pagallo, U. 2013. *The laws of robots: Crimes, contracts, and torts*. Dordrecht: Springer.
Plato. 2000. *The Republic*, trans. T. Griffith. Cambridge: Cambridge University Press.
Rai, A. S. 2004. Of monsters: Biopower, terrorism and excess in genealogies of monstrosity. *Cultural Studies* 18 (4): 538–570.
Rawls, J.. 2005 [1993]. *Political liberalism*. New York: Columbia University Press.
Rustad, M. L., and T. H. Koenig. 2002. Taming the tort monster: The American civil justice system as battleground of social theory. *Brooklyn Law Review* 68 (1): 1–122.
Sharpe, A. 2007. Structured like a monster: Understanding human difference through a legal category. *Law and Critique* 18 (2): 207–228.
Sharpe, A. 2010. *Foucault's monsters and the challenge of law*. London: Routledge-Cavendish.
Schrage, E. J. H. 1995. Capable of containing a reasonable soul. In *Colatio Iuris Romani*, ed. R. Feenstra, A. S. Hartkamp, J. E. Spruit, P. J. Sijpesteijn, and L. C. Winkel, vol. 2, 469–488. Amsterdam: J. C. Gieben.
Sudai, N. 2022. Sex ambiguity in early modern common law (1629–1787). *Law and Social Inquiry* 47 (2): 478–513.
Vavouras, E. 2021. Natural right and historicism: from Thucydides to Marx. *Cogito-Multidisciplinary Research Journal* 1:7–20.
Verner, L. 2014. Medieval monsters, in theory and practice. *Medicina nei Secoli [Journal of History of Medicine and Medical Humanities]* 26 (1): 43–68.
Taruffi, C. 1886. *Storia della teratologia*. Vol. 4. Bologna: Regia Topografica.
Wallace, W. M. 2015. *Sir Walter Raleigh*. Princeton, NJ: Princeton University Press.
Watson, A., ed. 1997. *The digest of Justinian*. Philadelphia: University of Pennsylvania Press.

Chapter 4
A Legal Death

The end of formulas on legally dead people, such as the monsters of Roman law and common law, can be ideally traced back to the 1948 Universal Declaration of Human Rights. This chapter illustrates the philosophical, moral, political, epistemic, social and scientific reasons that led to the Declaration with the principle of dignity and the universal dimension of this legal framework. The aim is to sum up this transformation of the *monstrum vel prodigium* of the tradition — from object of legal repression to subject of legal rights — drawing on two main arguments, i.e. either monsters do not exist in the real world or they should not exist in the legal domain. The chapter warns, however, against threats of strict legal formalism that could lead scholars to overlook the open problems of the field.

4.1 Good News

The status of legally dead people with birth defects, abnormities, or deformations ideally ended with the 1948 Universal Declaration of Human Rights (UDHR).[1] The UDHR Preamble enshrines the principle "of the inherent dignity and of the equal and inalienable rights of all members of the human family" as "the foundation of freedom, justice and peace in the world". The Universal Declaration paved the way for what soon was called the International Bill of Rights, which includes the International

[1] The adverb 'ideally' in the text intends to stress not only the noble principles of the Declaration, but also, two different kinds of problems. The first issue regards the fact that those rights, in accordance with tenets of international public law, are not legally binding: the Declaration and the enforceability mechanisms of the European Convention on Human Rights (1950) with the adjudicatory powers of the corresponding Court in Strasbourg makes this difference between UDHR and ECHR clear. The second issue concerns the time-consuming assimilation and implementation of every new paradigm: once the letter of the Preamble was understood as including, among "all members of the human family", individuals with congenital disabilities, their concrete protection took hold only in the 1970s and 80s.

U. Pagallo, *A Theory of Legal Monsters: Repression, Resistance, Rebellion*, Philosophical Studies Series 161, https://doi.org/10.1007/978-3-032-10771-8_4

Covenant on Civil and Political Rights from March 1966 (entered into force in March 1976); and the Covenant on Economic, Social, and Cultural Rights from December 1966 (entered into force in January 1976).

The international Bill of Rights is complemented by further specialised declarations and principles of protection for the safeguarding of people's rights, for example, the achievement of human dignity in healthcare regarding people with birth defects, mental illness, and disabilities. The UN General Assembly adopted two non-binding Declarations on the rights of people affected by mental illness, i.e. who, in 1971, were dubbed 'mentally retarded' people; and later, in 1975, the protection of people with disabilities. Scholars have examined this work in progress over the past seven decades "through the insight, hard work and dedication of a select group of people and organisations", especially the World Health Organization, in such new fields, such as cytogenetics, immunogenetics, population genetics and molecular genetics, among others (Christianson 2013).

A complex set of moral, political, epistemological and even theological ideas led to the acceptance of scientific methods in the legal arena. Work in clinical genetics did not come out of the blue. On the contrary, science and technology gained acceptance in judicial debates and politics — dealing with the legally dead people of positive law — only at the end of a very long process that started in the mid-1500s (and, even earlier, for the 'savages' of the new world in the Americas). Images and allegories of monsters are not only related to terrible creatures (Freedman 2024), human anomalies (Ghadessi 2018), or the tyrants of Greek tragedy and Plato's philosophy, as in Erasmus' *The Education of a Christian Prince.*[2] Also, monsters were increasingly associated with the miserable, weak, wretched condition of our Western civilisation.[3] Michel de Montaigne's *Essays* from 1580 clarify this 'socialisation' of the monster with the example of "A Monster Child" in chapter 30 of Book II. Montaigne does not reference the *mostrum vel prodigium* of positive law as a threat or object of repulsion regarding a certain body, gender, or race. Instead, the deformed sort of animal inherited from antiquity and the Middle Ages is presented as the consequence of human vanity, the narcissism of Europe and its culture, and all the knowledge systems that create further monsters by themselves (Long 2016). In Montaigne's own words:

---

[2] See Erasmus (ed. 2003, at 27): "This is the picture of a tyrant, unless something even more hateful can be depicted. Claudius and Caligula were this sort of monster". The monstrous tyrant par excellence in the 1500s, however, was probably Nero. Ariosto, Sir Thomas Elyot, or John Foxe, all refer to Nero as a monster: see Gwyn (1991). We return to this political use of the image with the analysis of the *Vindiciae contra tyrannos* from 1579 below in Chapters 6 and 10.

[3] As the example of Montaigne's *Essays* clarifies in the text, this use of the image on monsters is often related to the old teachings of the Stoic and Epicurean schools mentioned in Chapter 2. See, among many, Bouwsma (1975), and Joy (1992). Remarkably, Montaigne delighted in "pricking the bubble of human vanity" and its pride, despite being a child of his time and thus adhering to the old geocentric cosmography: "the geocentric cosmography served rather for human's humiliation than his exaltation... Copernicanism was opposed partly on the ground that it assigned too dignified and lofty a position to his dwelling-place" (Lovejoy 2001, at 102). Lovejoy's history of the idea of a "great chain of being" remains a methodological and historiographical reference point for the analysis of the *querelle des monstres*, examined in the next section of this chapter.

> What we call monsters are not so for God who sees the infinite number of forms which he has included in the immensity of his creation: it is to be believed that the figure which astonishes us relates to, and derives from, some other figure of the same genus unknown to Man. God is all-wise; nothing comes from him which is not good, general and regular: but we cannot see the disposition and relationship. (Montaigne ed. 2003, at 738)

The idea that monsters do not really exist but, rather, are the byproduct of our customs and culture became the subject of a vibrant philosophical debate in the 1600s and 700s. The legally dead humans with birth defects handed down from the tradition of Roman law and crystallised by positive law in the Middle Ages down to Modernity, posed new questions on human knowledge and nature, epistemology and ontology, mathematics and metaphysics, and occasionally even medicine. There are two ways in which we can appreciate this overall debate. From a legal standpoint, we should distinguish the thesis that monsters do not exist from the argument that monsters should not exist. Hans Kelsen made this difference a point of honour in the 1900s with the rigid demarcation between being and having to be, *sein und sollen*, causal explanation of physical phenomena versus legal normativity (Kelsen 1950). Although this differentiation is followed in the subsequent parts of the analysis, it must be embraced with a methodological warning.

In the legal domain, the physical constraints of the natural world do, in fact, impact the normative claims of the law, a principle succinctly summarised by Roman lawyers with the axiom *ad impossibilia nemo tenetur* (nobody is bound to the impossible). This condition entails a methodological order — from the elucidation of facts to the interpretation of acts — which is still relevant in the practice of courts: *da mihi factum, dabo tibi ius*, "tell me the circumstances of the case, and I will give you the legal response". This means that the interpretation of human behaviour and its normative impact on other humans must consider such behaviour as a natural fact and, hence, as Kelsen admits, "according to a law of nature to be determined by other facts as an effect by its causes" (Kelsen 1950, at 7). The constraints of physics can thus entail legal consequences: for example, according to Art. 49(2) of the Italian penal code on "impossible crimes", it is established that individuals are not punishable "when, due to the unsuitability of the action or the non-existence of its object, the harmful or dangerous event is impossible".

Such legal provisions, on the other hand, remind us of the normative limits of physical constraints. It is up to lawmakers to determine how to regulate the intentions of the individual who intended to commit an impossible crime. Furthermore, it can be tricky to determine whether an "event is impossible". A popular example of impossible crime among Italian lawyers illustrates this point: the aim to kill someone through acts of magic. Although it is reasonable to expect that contemporary Italian courts would set such a sorcerer free, it is equally fair to concede that the sorcerer would have faced a much harsher trial in earlier centuries. Leaving aside the exaggerations of all followers of Friedrich Nietzsche, according to whom no facts exist, only interpretations — we return to this radical form of perspectivism in Chapter 5—I am ready to admit that the human understanding of the physical universe has evolved alongside its legal machinery. After all, as noted earlier in Chapter 3, the bane of civil and common lawyers throughout history was determining whether a being, once born, had to be considered human or a monster. This was the preliminary factual issue to be determined before defining the legal consequences of such a birth.

Drawing on this differentiation of facts and acts, physics and politics or, in epistemic terms, 'information about reality' and 'information for reality',[4] the assumption of the following sections of this chapter is that the argument that monsters do not exist paved the way for new discussions about the rights of a *mostrum vel prodigium.* To corroborate the assumption, the analysis adopts the methodology of a trial, discussing first the 'facts of the case' (section 4.2) and then their relevance for its legal outcomes (section 4.3). The overall intent is to flesh out the set of reasons that eventually led to the abolishment of the legal status of human monsters in the second half of the twentieth century (section 4.3).

Therefore, the next section examines the first part of this historical account concerning the trial of legally dead individuals before the court of reason. Among the advocates of this case, we find Locke, Leibniz, Diderot, and the Enlightenment. Darwin serves, so to speak, as the scientific consultant. By examining the facts of the case, jurists had to ascertain whether the monsters under scrutiny over the centuries, from Roman law to their times, really existed. Indeed, if monsters do not exist, then, the subsequent step consists in discussing whether or not humans with congenital disabilities shall be granted their own rights. *Sum cuique tribuere.*

4.2 Monsters Do Not Exist

Gottfried W. Leibniz and Charles Darwin are the leading figures of our case. The current idea that legal monsters do not exist and that, therefore, we should begin seriously considering their rights is rooted in their work on metaphysics and natural sciences (Leibniz in the early 1700s) and evolution (Darwin in the mid-1800s).

Leibniz's reference point is John Locke. Leibniz wrote the *New Essays on Human Understanding* as a chapter-by-chapter critique of Locke's *An Essay Concerning Human Understanding* from 1689 (Locke ed. 1997). In Aristotelian terms, Locke's approach to monsters is formal rather than substantialist. He mocks current debates on the nature of man: his ironic example recalls the hard legal cases on baptisms, later discussed by Foucault in his lectures on the abnormal.[5] This pertains, for Locke, to whether or not infants should be baptised, depending on their 'form', as in the Abbé Malotru case regarding the odd shape of the kid (*Essays*, III, vi, 26). Locke's response is non-substantialist: if the kid can speak, he is no monster, and therefore has rights (III, xi, 16). The word 'monster' denotes a nominal rather than a real essence; there is no way to determine what monsters really are. Instead of a "natural

[4] Information about reality refers to semantic information which instructs us about the states of reality, and which is alethically qualifiable. Information for reality concerns the set of rules or instructions that determine the way of being or behaving of other entities. See Floridi (2013).

[5] See above the third section of Chapter 3 on Foucault's example of Siamese twin brothers.

kind", monsters refer to the way in which humans represent their world (III, iii, 15–19). This is why, since the "frequent production of monsters, in all the species of Animals, and of Changelings" does exist, Locke proposes to tackle such anomalies through an atomistic or corpuscular explanation of these phenomena. Rather than substantial forms or similar, the attention should be drawn to the stance that allows for the explanation of every anomaly in the course of nature, such as the features of motion, shape, and position of the minute particles of matter (Wolfe 2005).

Leibniz's critique of Locke is radical. There is a way to determine, pace Locke, whether monsters really exist. The claim rests on the metaphysical assumption that *nihil est sine ratione*, that is, nothing is without reason in the best of all possible worlds. In Part III of *Theodicy* (1710), dealing with "the justice of God and the freedom of man in the origin of evil", Leibniz explains the reasons for this assertion (Leibniz ed. 1995). The argument goes as follows:

> One must believe that even sufferings and monstrosities are part of order; and it is well to bear in mind not only that it was better to admit these defects and these monstrosities than to violate general laws, as Father Malebranche sometimes argues, but also that these very monstrosities are in the rules, and are in conformity with general acts of will, though we be not capable of discerning this conformity. (*op. cit.*, § 241)

Later in his work, Leibniz clarifies the opinion with a mathematical similarity: "It is just as sometimes there are appearances of irregularity in mathematics which issue finally in a great order when one has finally got to the bottom of them" (§ 277). Leibniz was proud of his results in mathematics, which he applied to his work as much as he could. In the *Discourse on Metaphysics*, for example, Leibniz refers to geometry to support his theses on order, complexity, and randomness in the universe (Chaitin 2006). Drawing on the case of someone who haphazardly draws points on a page, Leibniz demonstrates that it is always possible to generate the equation regardless of the intricacy of a continuous line (*Discourse*, at § 6). Likewise, in the legal domain, despite Aristotle's warnings against extending mathematical methods to practical sciences,[6] Leibniz's ambition was to turn legal arguments into computing through probability calculus, combinatorial analysis, and binary arithmetic. The project was already underway in his doctoral thesis and *de Arte Combinatoria* from 1666 (Leibniz was 20 years old). The overall aim was to show that disputation among jurists, or legal philosophers, was a matter of calculation. Leibniz even started building machines that hinged on probabilities and digital calculus to tackle legal disputes!

The same approach is held in the *Theodicy* in the case of monsters and monstrosities. According to the metaphysical tenets of Leibniz's philosophy, the argument is

---

[6] See the end of the first section in Chapter 2. It is worth mentioning that Leibniz was developing these (neo-Pythagorean) ideas with Erhard Weigel, also mentor of Samuel Pufendorf, as I mention below in the second section of Chapter 6. Leibniz follows the logical-mathematical side of Weigel's teachings as well as the opinion that the ancient philosophy, and Aristotle in particular, have shown the path to truth. Unlike Hobbes or Descartes, the problem, in Leibniz's opinion, does not consist in opposing classical wisdom to modern philosophy, but rather, in integrating it with a new logical-mathematics, new even for Hobbes and Descartes. See Pagallo (2016, at 8); and, Bringsjord et al. (2023). We return to Leibniz's legal philosophy in Chapter 6, dealing with the different ideas of Pufendorf on sovereignty and justice, voluntarism and the German Holy Roman Empire.

that whatever the complexity of the form of such monsters, they follow rules and, moreover, conform to God. The existence of monsters, in other words, does not simply depend on popular credulity, or the subjective view of our species — "the workmanship of the understanding" in the phrasing of Locke.[7] Instead, we shall take into account the confusion of philosophers vis-à-vis the complex fabric of our world, between the will of God and human freedom:

> Those who have confused this determination with necessity have fabricated monsters in order to fight them. To avoid a reasonable thing which they had disguised under a hideous shape, they have fallen into great absurdities. (Leibniz 1995, at § 362)

Leibniz's theses had a certain impact among his contemporaries and the enlightened, for example, Diderot (Wartofsky 1952). Diderot adheres to an opinion quite common in his times: "There can be no monsters, prodigies, marvels or miracles in Nature. What we call monsters are merely combinations with which our eyes are not familiar" (d'Holbach ed. 1990, at I, 93). Diderot supports such theses beyond strictly anatomical questions of the *querelle des monstres*, following the ideas of both Leibniz and Locke. On the one hand, according to Diderot, monsters are fiction because they are human 'names of substances' which rest on acritical beliefs regarding the regularity of Mother Nature, i.e. Locke's way in *D'Alembert's dream* (Diderot et. 2001, at V, 637). On the other hand, drawing on the infinite number of possible organic developments, Diderot draws on Leibniz's arguments to embrace a principle of plenitude: "the chain of being is not interrupted by the variety of forms", so that "there is nothing imperfect in nature, not even monsters" (in Wolfe 2005, at 200). However, this conclusion begets a crucial question: if humans are not monsters, how should we represent their abnormities and deformations?

Natural philosophers made significant conjectures in the early 1800s, more than a century after Leibniz's intuitions on "entelechies", software engineering, and evolution. Étienne Geoffroy Saint Hilaire stressed the role of environmental agents as a cause for birth defects and arrested development (Saint Hilaire 1822); his son and successor, Isidore Geoffroy Saint Hilaire, further showed that congenital malformations are more common than what naturalists used to think at that time. Rather than legal repression, from slaughter to humiliation, the approach should be scientific, and evidence suggested that all monsters or prodigies of the tradition should not be distinguished and separated from their own species: those monsters were indeed humans (Mann 1998).

In *On the Origin of Species*, drawing on the ideas of Étienne Geoffroy Saint Hilaire, it was Darwin who made apparent what was at stake in the case of people with birth defects.[8] The conjecture is a congenital malformation, i.e. "monstrosities" which

[7] See Locke (1997, at III.iii.14). In addition to the monsters related to the limits of human understanding, however, Locke also uses the monster formula for further polemical purposes. In *A Letter Concerning Toleration*, the monster becomes symbol of political intolerance: "it seems monstrous for men to be so blind as not to perceive the necessity and advantage of it [toleration] in so clear a light" (Locke ed. 1993, at 393). On the connection between the intolerant monster and the monster in the Abbé Malotru case, i.e. the Abbot of St. Martin, see Shanks (2014).

[8] Scholars have traced Darwin's "many references to monsters and anatomical deformities" back to the late 1830s, i.e. "in Darwin's early transmutation notebooks" (Richards 1994, at 407). From

"cannot be separated by any clear line from mere variations" although "injurious or not useful to the species" (Darwin ed. 1964, at 8). Almost two decades later, in *The Descent of Man* from 1871, the conclusion is that "monstrosities, which graduate into slight variations, are likewise so similar in man and the lower animals … the same terms can be used for both, as has been shown by Saint Hilaire" (Darwin ed. 1901, at 20). In the phrasing of *On the Origin of Species*:

> It is commonly assumed, perhaps from monstrosities often affecting the embryo at a very early period, that slight variations necessarily appear at an equally early period. But we have little evidence on this head — indeed the evidence rather points the other way… The question is not, at what period of life any variation has been caused, but at what period it is fully displayed. The cause may have acted, and I believe generally has acted, even before the embryo is formed; and the variation may be due to the male and female sexual elements having been affected by the conditions to which either parent, or their ancestors, have been exposed. (Darwin ed. 1964, at 443)

Darwin's findings can hardly be exaggerated in the trial of human monsters before the court of reason. Among others, Darwin paved the way for the understanding of humans with birth defects, i.e. the *monstrum vel prodigium* of the tradition, in accordance with the new field of scientific investigation: genetics.[9] We may say that the assumptions of Leibniz's metaphysics and natural philosophy, down to the claims of the Enlightenment on materialism and monsters, were vindicated.

However, the intent of this section is not to provide a triumphal ride of progress before the court of reason. The collection of sound empirical evidence showing that the *mostrum vel prodigium* does not exist covers only half of this story. In 1883, Darwin's cousin, Francis Galton, published his first work in "eugenics", a program developed over the decades and supported by lawmakers and public institutions (Galton 1904). The infamous treatment of people with abnormalities in physiological development in the late 1800s and down to the first decades of the 1900s is another criminal page of Western legal history. Empirical evidence against the *monstrum vel prodigium* was not enough to grant rights to a 'new human'. Kelsen would remind us of the difference between is and ought to be. We noted the normative part of this

---

a sociological viewpoint, the claim is that "Darwin's domestication of the monster was one critical element in his long-drawn-out negotiation of the highly political problem of packaging and presenting a theory associated with atheism and revolution in such a way as to make it scientifically and socially respectable" (*op. cit.*, at 410). We should not overlook that the 1800s were, in fact, still full of monsters and fantastic creatures (Halberstam 1995). However, from a scientific view, it is noteworthy that, after 1859, Darwin's theory became the reference point for every sound research on the topic, such as, for example, Hugo de Vries' mutation theory (Mangham 2023).

[9] The field of genetics is universally traced back to Gregor Mendel's work and his experiments with pea plants in the 1850s — Darwin lacked a clear understanding of the mechanism of inheritance. Although Mendel likely knew much about Darwin, Darwin knew nothing of Mendel (Fairbanks 2020; Berry and Browne 2022). Today's paradigm of evolutionary biology can be understood, according to the formula of Julian Huxley, as the "modern synthesis" of their ideas, i.e. Darwin's theory of evolution and Mendel's ideas on heredity.

argument with Locke's *Essays* (III, xi, 16): children who can speak are not monsters but humans, and therefore, they have rights.[10]

The following section provides the context for this philosophical debate on the transformation of monsters — from pure object of repression and dominion, to the status of human rights bearers. Drawing on the evidence that monsters do not exist (Saint Hilaire and Darwin), the focus is next on the normative arguments on why monsters should not legally exist, for all human beings have rights.

4.3 Monsters Should Not Exist

The transformation of the monstrous legally dead people of the tradition into rights bearers starts with the Universal Declaration of Human Rights, which, in turn, hinges on certain teachings of modern natural law schools.[11] Almost all philosophers of the 1600s and 700s belong to this legal and political tradition.[12] Every great mind – – from Hobbes to Locke, or, in continental Europe, from Pufendorf and Spinoza to Rousseau and Kant—provided its own version of basic concepts of legal and political reflection, such as the state of nature, natural rights, social contract, or civil society, i.e. the State. What is crucially at stake with this natural law tradition concerns the balance that must be struck between the individuals' rights and the powers of the institutions. Considering the legal condition of the *monstrum vel prodigium* endorsed by positive law until the 1900s, we may wonder about the status of humans with congenital disabilities within this natural law context.

By focusing on key features of the 1948 Declaration, such as the notion of human dignity and the universal dimension of human rights, the natural law sources of the Declaration draw attention to two main issues:

(i) Whether humans with congenital disabilities can be a part of the social covenant;
(ii) What rights, if any, would such humans have.

To tackle these issues, the ideas of Pufendorf, Rousseau, and Kant are particularly fruitful because those ideas on dignity and universality help us grasp the philosophical grounds of the Declaration as well as the challenges of the whole enterprise. Pufendorf is often presented as a forerunner of the principle of human dignity enshrined in the Preamble of the UDHR. In *Elementorum jurisprudentiæ universalis*, and later, *De*

[10] Locke's argumentation in the *Essays* must in fact be supplemented with his formalisation of the social contract in the *Two Treatises of Government* (Locke ed. 1823). We return to Locke's normative ideas in Chapters 6 and 10.

[11] There is not a one-size-fits-all way to distinguish classical and modern natural law traditions due to their multiple and even opposite opinions. However, dealing with the UDHR, we may follow John Finnis' thesis (we met Finnis above in the previous chapter, concerning accusations of monstrosity in the Brexit row). According to Finnis, whereas the classical (or traditional) natural law schools worked with "the idea of natural right", the modern natural law approach elaborated the "concept of natural or human rights": see Finnis (2004).

[12] Leibniz is perhaps the most outstanding exception until Hegel.

iure naturae et gentium from 1672 — books extremely popular but controversial in his times — Pufendorf refers to dignity as the moral ground on which the 'institutional design' of the political community hinges.[13] Human moral standing has to do with the sociable dimension of human nature, which, according to Pufendorf, rests on reciprocity, i.e. the way in which a person would address another person directly (Darwall 2012). As Pufendorf says in *The Whole Duty of Man*, "the last and most efficacious Argument to curb the Arrogance of insulting Men, is usually, *I am not a Dog but a Man as well as yourself*" (Pufendorf ed. 2003, at 67). But how should we treat human beings who are unable to speak or make their own case?

Notably, Pufendorf's remarks on human moral standing also apply to the treatment of a "child born with some bodily defect" (*op. cit.*, at 201). The "great Aristotle" is openly criticised for his harsh recommendations in *Politics* (VII, xvi)—see above in Chapter 2—to stress that "it is a certainty that in various times and various places there were laws that were unjust". However, Pufendorf's normative approach, resting on the "sociable" nature of human beings who "reciprocate", can only be stretched to a certain point. Dignity does not hinge on any inherent value of human beings making them equal. Instead, Pufendorf's reflection is related to the notion of self-esteem with regard to the glory of God who has raised human beings above all other creatures, that is, humans having a higher moral standing than other animals. The assumption is comparative rather than absolute. From this strict viewpoint, Pufendorf's idea of dignity was not yet 'universal' (Haara and Saastamoinen 2022; Hunter 2023).[14]

Rousseau arguably provides this dimension. His reflection on the nature of man and the current human condition revolves around a popular trope of his times, i.e. the monstrosity of customs, culture, and institutions. Rousseau depicts this state of affairs as monstruous in several works, such as *On the Origin of Inequality Among Men* and *Emile, or Concerning Education.* In the preliminary general remarks of *Emile*, for example, he claims that "man overturns everything, disfigures everything; he loves deformity, monsters; he desires that nothing should be as nature made it, not even man himself" (Rousseau ed. 1889). The assumption has both a psychological

[13] The meaning and content of such a design is elucidated below in Chapter 6.

[14] As stressed in the previous note, we return to Pufendorf's political and legal ideas, in particular, his views on monsters in Chapter 6. However, it is worth mentioning another use of the monster formula in his work. We noted that Pufendorf's philosophical doctrine was highly controversial. For example, two of his colleagues at the University of Lund, i.e. the jurist Nikolaus Beckmann and the theologian Josua Schwartz, accused Pufendorf of theological errors and even heresy. Pufendorf had to defend himself in several works, later collected in *Eris Scandica*, which was published in 1686. Leaving aside the reasons for the bitter debate on voluntarism, empiricism, and divine vis-à-vis human justice, the stakes of the controversy were so high to explain the impetus of Pufendorf's remarks. His fellow colleagues were not only ignorant, envious, and in bad faith, but also, "filthy charlatans, scapegallows, slanderers, worms born from bung, liars, idiots, sycophants, asses" and, of course, "a two-bodied monster composed of Josua Schwartz as author of the *Index Novitatum*, and of Nikolaus Beckmann, as his voice". See Palladini (2023, at 266–267). This kind of debate on monstrous colleagues is set aside in this book according to the methodological remarks provided in the introduction of the volume. Instead, the attention should be drawn to what it is like to be a victim of such claims. See below note 16 of this chapter as regards the monstrosity of Jean Jacques Rousseau.

and institutional implication. On the one hand, nobody wants to be "a half-developed being… a man left to himself among others from his birth would be the most deformed among them all" (*op. cit.*, 12). On the other hand, Rousseau insists on the institutional side of this treatment, such as the practices of those countries in which "the bodies of children" are cruelly deformed by putting them into a press. In his phrasing:

> Can we conceive of any creature's being truly happy out side of what belongs to its own peculiar nature? … The man unacquainted with suffering would not know the tender feelings of humanity or the sweetness of compassion; he would not be a social being; he would be a monster among his kind. (Rousseau 1889, at 48)

From a legal and political standpoint, *The Social Contract* instructs on what should be done against this monstrous condition. According to the tenets of modern natural law, the solution concerns the contract, in this case, between the "man", *homme*, and the "citizen", the *citoyenne*. Rousseau admits that this individual contract does not exist, but rather, it is the level of abstraction according to which we can grasp what must be done against the monstrosity of current customs and institutions.[15] Such formulations on man, citizen, and their contract may include not only *Emile*'s deformed children, but also, the legal monsters of positive law. In Chapter 3, we noted the scandal of the Lyon case in 1765, i.e. three years after the publication of *The Social Contract*. Rousseau could just wonder about how such human monsters, hermaphrodites, and deformed people should interplay with the able-bodied civil society.

However, we will never know what kind of rights this *homme* — namely, humans with birth defects — could have, according to Rousseau. Either this problem is up to the decisions of the General Will in Assembly, as described in Book II of *The Social Contract*, or Rousseau simply had other kinds of issues in mind, but certainly not the status of the *monstrum vel prodigium*. Years later, in 1782, Rousseau confesses in *The Reveries of the Solitary Walker*, that "I who believed myself honored, cherished, as I deserved to be; I saw myself suddenly misrepresented as a dreadful monster the likes of which has never existed" (Rousseau ed. 1992, at 112).[16] Other types of priorities put the *monstrum vel prodigium* in the background, even for the men of the

[15] See Chapter 6 of Book I on the definition of social contract: "I suppose men to have reached the point at which the obstacles in the way of their preservation in the state of nature show their power of resistance to be greater than the resources at the disposal of each individual for his maintenance in that state. That primitive condition can then subsist no longer; and the human race would perish unless it changed its manner of existence" (Rousseau ed. 2003, at 8).

[16] A likely source of this monstrous misrepresentation is David Hume, who offered to find a refuge for Rousseau in London, which they actually reached in January 1766. Things turned soon ugly, however. According to a letter of Rousseau, "Yes, Mr. Hume, you have me, I know it. All the prejudices are in your favour… It costs you nothing to let me appear as a monster, in the way you have already begun, and I already heal the barbaric rejoicings of my enemies" (in Noyes 1890, at 423). Accusations of monstrosity, in any case, did not only concern personal relationships: the image of a monstrous Rousseau became popular just a year after his arrival in London. It speaks volumes the print published in London 1767 and made by Charles Grignion depicting "Justice and Liberty hanged, while Voltaire rides monster Humanity and Jean-Jacques Rousseau takes his measure". See the print at the British Museum images: https://www.bmimages.com/preview.asp?image=00084941001, accessed on 8 September 2025.

Declaration of the Rights of Man and of the Citizen, set by the National Constituent Assembly in 1789. The formulas and principles of the Declaration hinge, in fact, on Rousseau's ideas: "men are born and remain free and equal in rights" (Art. 1); and the "law is the expression of the general will" (Art. 6). The legal status of the *monstrum vel prodigium* of positive law could thus be transformed into a human rights bearer in the name of brotherhood. And yet, on the other hand, it seems fair to concede that the revolution men had to face other priorities and kinds of monsters: "the first monster is the king", Louis XVI (Foucault 2003, at 94).[17]

The third philosopher under consideration in this section is Kant. His monsters sum up the contradictions of the modern natural law tradition on the status and dignity of the *monstrum vel prodigium* in moral theory (Pufendorf), and the rights of this legal prodigy or citizen monster (Rousseau). In a series of legal and political essays of the 1780s and 90s, Kant illustrates the moral foundation on which every political community lies, that is, the categorical duty to treat persons "as an end" and never merely "as a means" (Kant ed. 2013, at 73). There is an inherent value or dignity in persons because of their "autonomy" as "rational agents" (*op. cit.*, at 24). Kant's wording is, however, open to multiple and even opposite interpretations as to whether personal dignity is related to any 'absolute inner value' that humans possess. This question is critical because it entails determining whether and to what extent the *monstrum vel prodigium* could be considered a moral person with specific legal rights of its own. Although scholars may speculate on what Kant might have thought, he simply had other theoretical priorities concerning monsters. They do not pertain to the connection between natural and positive law, between private and public law, but rather, to the limits of human reasoning and understanding.

The pre-critic Kant is full of monsters. They illustrate that which challenges reason: the "sublime".[18] In literature and philosophy, Shelley's Frankenstein is arguably at the top of the list of this particular Kantian monster.[19] The discussion about the limits of reason that generate monsters — as well as monsters as a fruitful term for assessing the human faculty of judgement, not only in the field of aesthetics — is nonetheless unrelated to Kant's legal and political arguments in the writings from the 1770s and 80s. The same holds for his three Critics, especially *The Critique*

[17] From a theoretical viewpoint, it is not by chance that generations of scholars have presented Rousseau as a frontrunner of Marx's revolution: see, among many, Colletti (1972) and Levine (1993). The overall idea is that current institutions and the law are monstrous and only the General Will or the Revolution can free humanity from this monstrous condition.

[18] The sublime works both ways in scholarly papers, i.e. either from morality to art (Crowther 1989), or from art to freedom (Clewis 2009).

[19] There is plenty of bibliographical choice in this regard: see, for example, Freeman (1987). However, according to certain scholars, it is Rousseau who "overshadows all other philosophical influences upon Shelley, except perhaps for the influence of her parents" (Bök 1992, at 415, drawing on David Marshall's *Frankenstein, or Rousseau's monster*). Along the same lines, see Richardson (1991). Still, we can leave the reader to question the main philosophical source of Shelley's monster due to the irrelevance of this kind of debate for the purposes of our investigation.

of Judgment from 1790.[20] Scholars have dissected the Kantian treatment of monsters throughout his work, arguing that since Kant's critical writings leave no room for monsters, this could be interpreted as the "failure of aesthetics" (Angelucci 2022). Regardless, it is clear that this kind of monster has no relevance in the legal field, especially considering positive law in Kant's times. The elimination of the image from the field of critical philosophy does not entail any abolishment of the 'legal deaths' of the tradition because, whether pre-critic or critic, Kant overlooked the question, i.e. what the status of people with congenital disabilities should be in accordance with the principles of individual liberty, equality, and independence.

In the previous section, we noted that only a few decades after Kant's work, Geoffroy Saint Hilaire and Charles Darwin finally put humans on the right track to abolish the legally dead people of positive law. However, to prevent any self-complacency, we also noted the horror of eugenics that soon followed in the late 1800s. As Francis Galton declared in the early 1900s, the aim was to develop "the science that deals with all influences that improve the inborn qualities of a race; also those that develop them to the utmost advantage" (Galton 1904, at 1). This monstrous scope of the field, i.e. "to cause the useful classes in the community to contribute more than their proportion to the next generation" (*op. cit.*, at 3), was endorsed by legislation in the 1910s and 20s, progressively adapted to the different national practices in the United States, Scandinavia, Canada, and Germany, among others. Dramatically, eugenics simply went beyond ideology (Kevles 1999).

This new horrific chapter in the history of Western legal monsters was vivid in the minds of the drafters of the 1948 Universal Declaration. It is against this framework of eugenics and the holocaust that the Declaration intended to refer to all members of the human family. The formula was progressively interpreted to include humans with congenital disabilities. In the mid-1900s, scholars such as David W. Smith and James Wilson laid down the basis for a new field, medical teratology, which aims to study the abnormalities of physiological development in organisms, today's bread and butter of a sub-field of medical genetics (Finnell 1999; Polifka and Friedman 2002). The Teratology Society was formally established in 1961 (Shepard et al. 2000). In an ideal handover, legal regulations became gradually ancillary to medical-scientific research on what was once regarded as a prodigy, or monster (Brent 1967). Over the past six decades, for example, generations of Italian law students have learned to appreciate this epochal transformation in 'legal medicine' courses, which include forensics. These courses cover further declarations that regard the rights of people with congenital disabilities, such as the Convention for the Protection of Human Rights and Dignity of the Human Being with regard to the Application of Biology and Medicine, i.e. the European Bioethics Convention, or Oviedo Convention from 1997.

[20] In the analytic of the sublime, as a part of the critique of the aesthetical judgement, Kant claims, "nature contains nothing monstrous... An object is monstrous if, by its size, it destroys the purpose which constitutes the concept of it" (Kant ed. 1951, at 91).

Just 3 years later, a case of medical separation of conjoined twins was discussed before English courts: *Re A (Children)* from 2000.[21] According to the tenets of the rule of law, parties to the case still had to discuss doctrines of common law and case law to determine what must be done in cases of medical separation of twins. The Court formally dismissed all prudent opinions transmitted throughout centuries, whether from Paul and Ulpian to Justinian, or from Bracton to Coke and Blackstone: "It would seem that in English law the concept of the monster is now, if it was not already, legally dead" (Sharpe 2007, at 208). The same holds true for the multiple variants of civil law tradition in continental Europe. Legal paradigms do not change overnight. The judicial disavowal of the monsters of the tradition in *Re A (Children)* ideally concludes this chronicle of a legal death.

4.4 Against Formalisms

The eradication of legal formulas on repression — against the *monstrum vel prodigium* of the tradition — occurred after more than 2500 years of Western history concerning formally dead people. Today, we shall say that the only monster would be a lawmaker still targeting humans as simple objects of repression. The gist of the 1948 Declaration is that all members of the human family cannot be deprived of their rights, be they a criminal, a terrorist, a combatant enemy, an immigrant, or people with congenital disabilities. There is no room for legal monsters an as object of repression because humans must always be considered subjects with rights of their own.[22] The use of the formula is either legally incorrect (i.e. monster as an object), or refers to other meanings of the formula (i.e. monster as a subject) that do not strictly pertain, however, to the discussion of today's positive law. Instead, what is at stake with current debates on monsters concerns, in the best possible light, the fields of politics and rhetorics, or sociology, literature, and aesthetics, that add little to the thresholds of legal evaluation in such cases, such as the conjoined twins of *Re (A) Children.*

This conclusion does not entail that we should be contented; on the contrary, we must be vigilant. Scholars are concerned with the enforcement of legal rights and how the provisions of today's international and national legal frameworks can be improved. The contrast between law in the books (principles of human and fundamental rights) and law in the making (the praxis of sovereign states) reminds us

---

[21] The case was already mentioned in the third section of Chapter 3.

[22] Such rights can be conceived of as either 'absolute' or 'relative'. Absolute rights refer to the protection of rights that do not admit any balancing, for example, ban on torture. Relative rights vice versa admit such balancing according to the proportionality principle. Absolute and relative rights are enforceable once they are enshrined in national constitutions and regional or international agreements. As stressed in the subsequent chapters, on the one hand, the new status of the *monstrum vel prodigium* of the tradition as rights bearer refers to the class of absolute rights; on the other hand, such a status must be understood as binding at both national and international levels. See Pagallo (2013).

of persisting problems in the field: it is all about the classical contrast inherited from both ancient and modern traditions of natural law. The opposition can be that between natural and positive law, as noted by Cicero, or similarly, the opposition can be illustrated by Kant's remark, "this may be true in theory, but it does not apply in practice" (Kant ed. 1974). Even critics of the Universal Declaration who stress limits of this framework, either regarding the design of the international Bill of Rights or its problematic enforcement, would admit, however, that discrepancies between ideals and praxis do not affect the soundness of the principles: in our case, monsters shall not exist in the legal domain. No serious scholar would claim nowadays that a certain class of individuals can legitimately be the legal target of pure control and repression.[23]

What certain scholars claim, however, is different. Although the old formula over the legally dead people of the tradition is formally extinct, it is contended that monsters persist as a category of the law: it is something with a continuing legal life (Sharpe 2010). We should not find easy shelter in simple legal formalisms about the value of the Universal Declaration and the enforceability of its norms and principles. Either monsters persist in the praxis, that is, we still deal with humans who are treated as the legally dead of the tradition; or the praxis provokes new monsters. The monsters of our age can thus be understood not only as a pathological but also physiological phenomenon. The first interpretation is the reading endorsed in this chapter with the 'legal death' of the *mostrum vel prodigium.* Every inhuman or degrading treatment must be deemed as morally and, moreover, legally intolerable under today's international legal framework, i.e. Art. 5 UDHR,[24] or at the regional level, e.g., Art. 3 ECHR,[25] or under constitutional law in most national legal orders.[26]

On the other hand, this inhuman or degrading treatment is considered physiological by all those scholars who think that such treatment is consistent with the repressive nature of the law, its functions, and categories.[27] We noted the birth of new types of monsters related to certain interpretations of Rousseau's citizen monster, or Kant's Frankenstein. As occurs with the monsters of Aristotle's political philosophy or efforts of the first generation of comparative law scholars studying Chinese law,

---

[23] The same conclusion holds for those scholars who draw the attention to "the monstrosity of human rights" to stress "the long history of efforts to actualize equality, to realize, that is, the promise of the right to representation for everyone". See Cadava (2006).

[24] Art. 5 UDHR states, "no one shall be subjected to torture or to cruel, inhuman or degrading treatment or punishment".

[25] Art. 3 of the European Convention on Human Rights (ECHR) is a copy and paste of Art. 5 UDHR: "no one shall be subjected to torture or to inhuman or degrading treatment or punishment in all circumstances". We return to the European Court of Human Rights' interpretation of this absolute right below in the third section of Chapter 5.

[26] The potential conflict between positive law and moral principles is under scrutiny in Chapter 8. The further conflict of national law with principles of international law in Chapter 10.

[27] The careful readers will note that we are back to the alternative stressed in the last section of Chapter 3. Contrary to the idea that coercion is legally selective and, moreover, a necessary although insufficient condition of the law, some scholars claim that the nature of the law is essentially repressive. This is the thesis under scrutiny in the next chapter of this book.

we would not find or appreciate the monsters of today's law because we are looking for them in the wrong places. For example, as regards Kant:

> The Monster withdraws from this new topography of Reason. However, the elimination of this figure from the field of critical philosophy seems to confine it to a slightly more threatening place: it begins to inhabit an exterior that we cannot see, perhaps because we maintain a more fundamental relationship with it. (Lemos 2014)

Whether addressing the shortcomings of formal law or confronting the horrors of the praxis, it thus seems that the monster transmigrates, akin to the ancient cults of metempsychosis in which the human soul travels into other bodies. Legal monsters never die. Many experts, philosophers, and scholars have endorsed this assumption over the past decades. Against the ideas of Locke and Leibniz, or the empirical evidence of Darwin and today's medical genetics, the chronicle of the legal death under scrutiny in this chapter should be grasped as a novel Arabian phoenix, a new legal chronicle of life after death. In fact, even if such a legal death has concerned the status of people with birth defects, current law would demonstrate that we have not solved our problems at all. On the contrary, monsters do not only represent one of the darkest pages of ancient and modern history, but they would also denote that the very essence of the law, its repressive nature, remains the same despite the appearances.

Michel Foucault made this view on monsters extremely popular half a century ago. According to this perspective, it makes sense to dwell on the monsters of the law — even after the formal extinction of any *monstrum vel prodigium* in positive law — because it is not by chance that the repression of people with congenital disabilities is as old as the Western legal tradition. The dismissal of old formulas on monsters would be deceptive, for they persist in disguise. The legal monster trial before the court of reason must thus be integrated with an additional investigation. Welcome to the masters of suspicion.

References

Angelucci, D. 2022. From the sublime to the monstrous. two interpretations of Kant. *Con-textos Kantianos: International Journal of Philosophy* 15:287–296.

Berry, A., and J. Browne. 2022. Mendel and Darwin. *Proceedings of the National Academy of Sciences* 119 (30): e2122144119.

Bök, C. 1992. The monstrosity of representation: Frankenstein and Rousseau. *ESC: English Studies in Canada* 18 (4): 415–432.

Bouwsma, W. J. 1975. The two faces of humanism: stoicism and augustinianism in renaissance thought. In *Itinerarium italicum: The profile of the Italian renaissance in the mirror of its European transformations*, ed. H. A. Oberman, 3–60. Leiden: Brill.

Brent, R. L. 1967. Medicolegal aspects of teratology. *The Journal of Paediatrics* 71 (2): 288–298.

Bringsjord, S., N. S. Govindarajulu, and J. Oswald. 2023. Universal cognitive intelligence, from cognitive consciousness, and Lambda (Λ). In *Computational approaches to conscious artificial intelligence, vol. 5 of machine consciousness*, ed. A. Chella, 127–168. Singapore: World Scientific Publishing.

Cadava, E. 2006. The monstrosity of human rights. *PMLA* 121 (5): 1558–1565.

Chaitin, G. 2006. *Meta-math! The quest for Omega*. New York: Knopf Doubleday.

Christianson, A. L. 2013. Attaining human dignity for people with birth defects: A historical perspective. *South African Medical Journal* 103 (12:1): 1014–1019.

Clewis, R. R. 2009. *The Kantian sublime and the revelation of freedom.* Cambridge: Cambridge University Press.

Colletti, L. 1972. *From Rousseau to Lenin.* New York: NYU Press.

Crowther, P. 1989. *The Kantian sublime: from morality to art.* Oxford: Clarendon Press.

Darwall, S. L. 2012. Pufendorf on morality, sociability, and moral powers. *Journal of the History of Philosophy* 50 (2): 213–238.

Darwin, C. 1964 [1859]. *On the origin of species, facsimile of the first edition.* Cambridge: Harvard University Press.

Darwin, C. 1901. *The descent of man.* new ed. London: John Murray.

d'Holbach, P-H. T. 1990 [1781]. *Système de la nature*, ed. J. Boulad-Ayoub. Paris: Fayard.

Diderot, D. 2001. *Rameau's nephew, and other works*, trans. J. Barzun and R. H. Bowen. Indianapolis/Cambridge: Hackett.

Erasmus 2003 [1516]. *The education of a Christian prince*, trans. L. Jardine. Cambridge: Cambridge University Press.

Fairbanks, D. J. 2020. Mendel and Darwin: Untangling a persistent enigma. *Heredity* 124:263–273.

Finnell, R. H. 1999. Teratology: General considerations and principles. *Journal of Allergy and Clinical Immunology* 103 (2): S337–S342.

Finnis, J. 2004. Natural law: The classical tradition. In *The Oxford handbook of jurisprudence and philosophy of law*, ed. J. L. Coleman and S. J. Shapiro, 1–61. Oxford: Oxford University Press.

Floridi, L. 2013. *Ethics of information.* Oxford: Oxford University Press.

Foucault, M. 2003. *Abnormal: Lectures at the college de France 1974–1975.* London: Verso.

Freedman, L. 2024. The revival of classical monsters in the Italian renaissance. In *The Oxford handbook of monsters in classical myth*, ed. D. Felton, 470–492. Oxford: Oxford University Press.

Freeman, B. 1987. Frankenstein with Kant: A theory of monstrosity, or the monstrosity of theory. *SubStance* 16 (1): 21–31.

Galton, F. 1904. Eugenics: Its definition, scope and aims. *American Journal of Sociology* 10 (1): 1–25.

Ghadessi, T. 2018. *Portraits of human monsters in the renaissance: Dwarves, hirsutes, and castrati as idealized anatomical anomalies.* Kalamazoo, MI: Medieval Institute Publications.

Gwyn, W. B. 1991. Cruel Nero: The concept of the tyrant and the image of Nero in western political thought. *History of Political Thought* 12 (3): 421–455.

Haara, H., and K. Saastamoinen. 2022. Esteem and sociality in Pufendorf's natural law theory. *British Journal for the History of Philosophy* 32 (2): 265–283.

Halberstam, J. 1995. *Skin shows: Gothic horror and the technology of monsters.* Durham and London: Duke University Press.

Hunter, I. 2023. Introduction: Life, work and historical context. In *The Cambridge companion to Pufendorf*, ed. K. Haakonssen and I. Hunter, 1–32. Cambridge: Cambridge University Press.

Joy, L. S. 1992. Epicureanism in renaissance moral and natural philosophy. *Journal of the History of Ideas* 53 (4): 573–583.

Kant, I. 1951 [1790]. *Critique of judgement*, trans. J. H. Bernard. New York: Hafner.

Kant, I. 1974 [1793]. *On the old saw: That may be right in theory but it won't work in practice*, trans. E. B. Ashton. Philadelphia: University of Pennsylvania Press.

Kant, I. 2013 [1785]. *The moral law. groundwork of the metaphysic of morals*, trans. H. J. Paton. London/New York: Routledge.

Kelsen, H. 1950. Causality and imputation. *Ethics* 61 (1): 1–11.

Kevles, D. J. 1999. Eugenics and human rights. *BMJ* 319 (7207): 435–438.

Leibniz, G.W. 1995 [1710]. *Theodicy: Essays on the goodness of God, the freedom of man and the origin of evil*, trans. E. M. Huggard. La Salle, IL.: Open Court.

Lemos, F. 2014. Kant e o monstro. *Kriterion* 129:189–203.

Levine, A. 1993. *The general will: Rousseau, Marx, communism.* Cambridge: Cambridge University Press.
Locke, J. 1823 [1689]. *Two treatises of government*. London: Tegg & Co.
Locke, J. 1993 [1690]. A letter concerning toleration. In *Political writings*, ed. D. Wootton, 390–436. Indianapolis: Hackett Publishing.
Locke, J. 1997 [1689]. *An essay concerning human understanding*. London: Penguin.
Long, K. 2016. Montaigne on monsters and monstrosity. In *The Oxford handbook of Montaigne*, ed. Philippe Desan, 715–731. Oxford: Oxford University Press.
Lovejoy, A. 2001 [1936]. *The great chain of being: A study of the history of an idea.* Cambridge, MA: Harvard University Press.
Mangham, A. 2023. *We are all monsters: How deviant organisms came to define us.* Cambridge, MA: MIT Press.
Mann, J. 1998. Dignity and health: The UDHR's revolutionary first article. *Health and Human Rights* 3 (2): 30–38.
Montaigne. M. 2003 *The complete essays*, trans. M. A. Screech, London: Penguin.
Noyes, W. 1890. The insanity of Jean Jacques Rousseau. *The American Journal of Psychology* 3 (3): 406–429.
Pagallo, U. 2013. Online security and the protection of civil rights: A legal overview. *Philosophy & Technology* 26:381–395.
Pagallo, U. 2016. *Leibniz*. Milan: Kluwer.
Palladini, F. 2023. Polemics and controversies: Regarding the eris scandica. In *The Cambridge companion to Pufendorf*, ed. K. Haakonssen and I. Hunter, 263–294. Cambridge: Cambridge University Press.
Polifka, J. E., and J. M. Friedman. 2002. Medical genetics: 1. Clinical teratology in the age of genomics. *Canadian Medical Association Journal* 167 (3): 265–273.
Pufendorf, S. 2003. *The whole duty of man, according to the law of nature*, ed. I. Hunter and D. Saunders, trans. A. Tooke. Indianapolis: Liberty Fund Press.
Richards, E. 1994. A political anatomy of monsters, hopeful and otherwise: Teratogeny, transcendentalism, and evolutionary theorizing. *Isis* 85 (3): 377–411.
Richardson, A. 1991. From Emile to Frankenstein: The education of monsters. *European Romantic Review* 1 (2): 147–162.
Rousseau, J. J. 1889 [1762]. *Emile, or concerning education*, trans. E. Worthington. Boston: Heath & Co.
Rousseau, J. J. 1992 [1782]. *The reveries of the solitary walker*, trans. C. E. Butterworth. Indianapolis/Cambridge: Hackett.
Rousseau, J. J. 2003 [1765]. *On the social contract*, trans. G. D. H. Cole. New York: Dover.
Saint-Hilaire, E. G. 1822. *Philosophie anatomique des monstruosité humaines.* Paris: Rignaux.
Shanks, T. 2014. Toleration and democratic membership: John Locke and Michel de Montaigne on monsters. *Political Theory* 43 (4): 451–472.
Sharpe, A. 2007. Structured like a monster: Understanding human difference through a legal category. *Law and Critique* 18 (2): 207–228.
Sharpe, A. N. 2010. *Foucault's monsters and the challenges of law.* Abingdon: Routledge.
Shepard, T. H., M. Barr Jr., R. L. Brent, A. Hendrickx, D. Kochhar, G. Oakley, and W. J. Scott Jr. 2000. A history of the teratology society. *Teratology* 62 (5): 301–316.
Wartofsky, M. W. 1952. Diderot and the development of materialist monism. *Diderot Studies* 2:279–329.
Wolfe, C. T. 2005. The materialist denial of monsters. In *Monsters and philosophy*, ed. C. T. Wolfe, 187–204. London: College Publications.

Chapter 5
Masters of Suspicion

In the 1960s, Paul Ricoeur identified three masters of suspicion: Nietzsche, Marx, and Freud. This chapter adds a fourth philosopher to the list, Michel Foucault, with his analysis of legal monsters. The aim is twofold. On the one hand, it is fair to agree with Foucault that the treatment of the *monstrum vel prodigium* of positive law is a shame of Western legal systems as a mere object of repression and suppression. However, on the other hand, almost 2500 years of Western thought on tyrants and tyrannicides show, *pace* Foucault, that the formula on monsters has further meanings. Monsters do not only concern objects, but also subjects of the law; not only physical bodies, but also the body politic; not only targets of oppression, but also sources of criticism, resistance, and rebellion. A theory of legal monsters must be reflective. It is only on this basis that, from time to time, scholars can deem monstrous what the law aims to set up and enforce through means of coercion and normalisation.

5.1 A Band of Four

Paul Ricoeur's analysis on the 'masters of suspicion' revolves around an opposition which is critical for a theory of legal monsters. Work by Nietzsche, Marx, and Freud can be understood according to the alternative between interpreting the meaning of the texts — as in classical and modern hermeneutics, which can be traced back to the Aristotelian teachings — and the radical critique of any notion of human understanding (Ricoeur 2013). It goes without saying that generations of scholars have interpreted this interpretation. In the opinion of an authority of the field, such as Hans Georg Gadamer (Gadamer 1984), what is at stake would concern "the relationship between traditional hermeneutics, its philosophical situation, and this radical form of interpretation, which is almost at the opposite end of the spectrum of interpretation". Concerning this latter end of the spectrum, the masters of suspicion's claim is that traditional distinctions between facts and the law — i.e. in Kelsenian terms,

U. Pagallo, *A Theory of Legal Monsters: Repression, Resistance, Rebellion*, Philosophical Studies Series 161, https://doi.org/10.1007/978-3-032-10771-8_5

between 'is' and 'ought to be', description and prescription — are deceptive. It is just like the old Italian proverb, according to which "apply the law to the enemies, but interpret it for your friends".[1]

How the hermeneutics of suspicion works in practice can be illustrated with some tenets of this inquiry on the legal death of the *monstrum vel prodigium*. Dealing with the human monster trial before the court of reason, under scrutiny in Chapter 4, the attention was drawn to different kinds of semantic information, i.e. meaning over data related to reality.[2] Three observables of the analysis followed as a result:

(i) Information 'as' reality: the focus is on the scientific investigation of the causes that explain abnormalities of physiological development in human organisms, i.e. a sub-field of medical genetics;
(ii) Information 'for' reality: the attention is drawn to the tenets of modern natural law and principles of the human rights tradition as a series of legal instructions for the behaviour of individuals and institutions;
(iii) Information 'about' reality: the claim of Chapter 4 concerned an alethic proposition about the states of the world, such as the dismissal of old formulas on legal monsters in the second half of the 1900s.

The hermeneutics of suspicion conflates these different orders of meaning into a single macro area, that of interpretation, regardless of whether we are dwelling on scientific research in genetics, legal principles on human rights, or the epistemic frameworks that define the representation of our world. Even the conclusion of Chapter 4 — on how formulas on the *monstrum vel prodigium* were legally abolished — can be grasped either as a self-complacent and deceitful interpretation (Freud); or, as a fruit of false self-consciousness (Marx), which misses the proverbial elephant in the room, i.e. the eternal recurrence of the same (Nietzsche). In Ricoeur's wording:

> Hermeneutics seems to me to be animated by this double motivation: willingness to suspect, willingness to listen; vow of rigor, vow of obedience. In our time we have not finished doing away with idols and we have barely begun to listen to symbols. It may be that this situation, in its apparent distress, is instructive: it may be that extreme iconoclasm belongs to the restoration of meaning. (Ricoeur 1970, at 20)

[1] Against the masters of suspicion, this volume rests on the legal differentiation between plain cases and hard cases. Drawing on Herbert Hart's distinction (Hart ed. 1994), the hard cases of the law entail a general disagreement among scholars that may revolve around the meaning of the terms framing the legal question; or how such terms are related to each other in legal reasoning; or the principles that are at stake in the case. The plain cases of the law, on the other hand, hinge on a generally shared opinion on the terms of their application, thus appearing straightforward and even open to automation: such cases abound in everyday life and are familiar to readers of this book every time they buy a book, shop at a mall or on the internet, enjoy a dinner at the restaurant, etc. The differentiation between plain and hard cases is not only theoretical, but has also practical relevance. In addition to purchases, shopping, and other contracts of both readers and masters of suspicion, the distinction concerns several legal provisions and regulations on, for example, cases of vexatious litigation under Art. 96 of the Italian civil procedural code. We return to this differentiation of plain and hard cases in Chapters 7, 9 and 10 of this book.

[2] See above note 4 of Chapter 4.

To restore any meaning, in particular, against the argument that legal monsters never die but rather evolve or transmute into new kinds, it is fruitful to examine the method of these 'extreme iconoclasts'. A specific feature of this method is to substantiate the token by transforming it into a type, e.g. from the *monstrum vel prodigium* of the Roman tradition to the categories of monstrosity and the abnormal. The method is at work in Foucault's lectures at the College de France (Foucault ed. 2003). Drawing on the second edition of George Canguilhem's book *On the Normal and the Pathological*, which helped clarify Foucault's ideas on 'the abnormal', the assumption is that the law is "an element on the basis of which a certain exercise of power is founded and legitimized" (Foucault 2003, at 50). Whether legal norms represent a "polemical concept" (Canguilhem ed. 1991, at 239), or a "political concept" (Foucault 2003, at 50), what matters is the process of "technical normalisation" that is implemented through the norms of the law. Such a perspective aims to cast light on the long history of the *monstrum vel prodigium* based on, however, a normative bias and a mental reserve. The normative bias has to do with the law merely understood as a set of norms, or rules, "to impose a requirement on an existence, a given whose variety, disparity, with regard to the requirement, present themselves as a hostile, even more than an unknown, indeterminant" (Canguilhem 1991, at 238). Foucault follows suit, leaving aside every difference between *consuetudo*, *lex*, or *ius*.[3] On the other hand, regarding the mental reserve of the Paris lectures, the legal death of formulas and norms on the *monstrum vel prodigium* becomes irrelevant for Foucault because what is important does not concern the transformation of the 'legally dead' subjects of positive law into bearers of human rights. Instead, what is significant is the transformation of the Medieval monster into the modern criminal monster, i.e. from the Rouen case in 1601 to the Lyon case in 1765 (Foucault 2003, at 74). The trick of the Master of suspicion consists in the analysis of the old monster of civil and canon law as a member of the family, i.e. the token superseded by the type. What happened to the human monster of the tradition is irrelevant because what matters is the series of transformations regarding the repressive side of the law, namely, the traditional monster who turns into a modern criminal monster who then turns into the abnormal (Foucault 2003, at 110).

[3] The tripartition is illustrated since the first book of the Digest. Drawing on the definition of law (*ius*) as what is good and fair (D. 1.1.1), Modestinus distinguishes three sources of the law based on consensus, necessity, and customs (1.3.40). The interplay of statutes (*lex*) and customs (*consuetudo*) is clarified in D. 1.3.32.1 (Julianus) and D. 1.3.33 and 34 (Ulpian). These distinctions are still preserved in European civil law systems. Among many legal philosophers, Friedrich Hayek made the differentiation of legal acts and facts his strong theoretical point according to the further distinction of political constructivism and unintentional orders, i.e. *taxis* and *cosmos*: see below the first section of Chapter 6. To be fair, such differentiation is not overlooked by Foucault's master: "Even while recognizing that the law, private as well as public, has no source other than a political one, we can admit that the opportunity to legislate is given to the legislative power by a multiplicity of customs which must be institutionalized by that power into a virtual juridical whole. Even in the absence of the concept of juridical order, dear to Kelsen, the relativity of juridical norms can be justified" (Canguilhem 1991, at 249). It remains of course an open question whether and to what extent the legislative power is able to domesticate the customs of the legal order. This set of issues is simply ignored by Foucault.

In the beginning of his cosmogony *Timaeus* (at 17 a 1-3), Plato has Socrates ask, “One, two, three — but where, my dear Timaeus, is the fourth of those guests of yesterday who were to entertain me today?” (Plato ed. 1977, at 9). Following Ricoeur’s triad, it seems fair to suggest that the fourth, in our case, is Foucault.

Foucault has significantly influenced generations of scholars over the past 50 years. By following the method and historiographical sources of the lectures at the College de France, it is remarkable that such scholars often disregard all the legal and political sources — which are numerous, since Chapters 6 and 7 of this book are devoted to their analysis — that do not align with their views. For example, the transformation of the *monstrum vel prodigium* into the modern criminal monster is more than questionable, given the evidence under scrutiny in Chapter 4. We may say that the medieval monster and the modern monster lived together as much as the Australopithecus, Paranthropus and Homo erectus did two million years ago. The Foucauldian trick of his followers consists in supporting the methodology of the Master regardless of deficiencies in historical evidence and conceptual frameworks. Even in the aftermath of the legal death of formulas on monsters and prodigies, according to the principles and declarations under scrutiny in Chapter 4, it is contended that the law creates and represents bodies and human desires as something “unnatural” so that “at least some constructions or representations of human difference, both legal and non-legal, are informed by the monster category” (Sharpe 2007).[4]

The abnormal appears as something with a persisting legal life, i.e. the object of legal repression and normalisation, which transcends the historical features of the *mostrum vel prodigium*. Against every kind of legal formalism, so goes the argument, we should be attentive to the continuum of the monster who turns criminal who turns abnormal — extending, ultimately, to the monstrous terrorists and immigrants of today’s legal systems — despite the principles and regulations of current positive law. Relevant information about reality, as an alethic proposition about the states of the world, either is ignored, dissolved into interpretation, or is irrelevant in case of blatant contradiction.

The previous chapter of this book illustrated the death of legal formulas on monsters, drawing on empirical evidence (e.g., Darwin); philosophical arguments (e.g., Leibniz); and political activism (e.g., the human rights tradition). Foucault and his followers recommend an additional investigation. Their narrative on legal monsters has drawn the attention of sociologists, criminologists, philosophers, and experts of aesthetics, discussing formulas that jurists and lawyers consider simply dead. The first step in this additional investigation — concerning the legal monster trial before the court of reason — has to do with Foucault’s categories of “monster”, “monstrosity”, and “abnormal”. Since today’s positive law experts think these formulas are dead, what are they missing?

[4] The monster category is an extremely popular topic among scholars: see Cohen (1996); or Weinstock (2020). Some of this research is strictly related to some masters of suspicion, such as Freud: see e.g., Schneider (1999); or, Nietzsche (O’Hara 2003). Others are devoted to aesthetics: see Tedeschini (2021). As stressed in the text, however, this research has little relevance either for the body politic or the law (*corpus iuris civilis*).

5.2 The Abnormal

Foucault's legal monster is the first incarnation of the abnormal. On 15 January 1975, the lecture focused on the status of the *mostrum vel prodigium* from the Middle Ages to the late 1700s from a legal standpoint. Foucault could have dwelt on other cases, for example, on idiots and disabled, lunatics and lepers, and yet, there is something unique to the status of the *mostrum vel prodigium*. The monster — from the Roman Digest to the sources of common and civil law — is a non-human considered 'legally dead'. This status makes monsters different from other beings such as slaves, for example, who were 'legally alive'. The Roman slaves' elite was, after all, a bunch of estate managers, bankers and merchants, holding important jobs as public servants, entering into binding contracts, managing and making use of property for their masters' family business.[5] The regulation of both kinds of object is thus totally different, despite common issues on the status of such beings, such as whether slaves and monsters could ever enjoy patrimonial conditions.

Foucault captures the uniqueness of the legal monster in accordance with "a juridico-natural complex" in which "the monster appears and functions precisely at the point where nature and law are joined" (Foucault 2003, at 65). This interpretation of the monster — which revolves around the physical dimension of bodies — entails a twin breach or transgression, namely, a breach of nature and a breach of law, which "comes up against, overturns, or disturbs civil, canon, or religious law" (*op. cit.*, at 63). The monster, in fact, "combines the impossible and the forbidden" (at 56); it "is the casuistry that is introduced into law by the confusion of nature" (at 64). The legal sources would confirm this hermeneutical approach. In Foucault's words:

> For medieval thought, and definitely for seventeenth- and eighteenth-century thought, the breach of natural law is not enough to constitute monstrosity. Monstrosity requires a transgression of the natural limit, of the law-table, to fall under, or at any rate challenge, an interdiction of civil and religious or divine law. There is monstrosity only when the confusion comes up against, overturns, or disturbs civil, canon, or religious law. The difference between disability and monstrosity is revealed at the meeting point, the point of friction, between a breach of the natural law-table and a breach of the law instituted by God or by society, at the point where these two breaches of law come together. (Foucault 2003, at 63-64)

However, the sources of the legal and political thought of the 1600s and 700s suggest a more complex normative framework. In addition to efforts of jurists and philosophers to provide a more lenient reading of requirements and effects of monstrosity according to positive law,[6] in Chapter 4, we noted a vibrant debate from Locke

---

[5] Among the sources of the Digest, see for example Book XL, titles 1, 7, 8, and 9.

[6] The analysis has so far illustrated many such efforts both in ancient times (e.g., Cicero), and the Middle Ages (e.g., note 13 of Chapter 3). At the end of the 1500s, the threshold remains that of Roman law, and can be illustrated with Ubaldo Baldo's *Commentari in Digestum vetus* (published in Venice 1599), according to which, "since form gives being to a thing, he who does not have the form of a man is not a man, nor consequently is he free"; and yet, "in our law, anyone who is completely devoid of a limb, but has the form of a rational animal, although he is defective, is still considered a man, breaks the will and must be nourished like all demi-humans" (in Taruffi 1886, at

to Leibniz, whose main thesis was that human monsters did not exist. Instead of monsters and prodigies of positive law, a common trope of this era presents the law and current institutions as the real monsters.[7] This popular image, which can be traced back to the Greco-Roman antiquity, represents the other side to the coin of monsters and monstrosity. For example, in 1667, in *De statu imperii Germanici* or *The present state of Germany*, Samuel Pufendorf, examining the political structure or constitution of the German Holy Roman Empire, found it so arbitrary and irregular to consider it a "monster".[8] Moreover, complementing the very idea of the body politic as an institutional monster, another popular trope of that era was to similarly present the anomaly and abhorrence of single normative acts as a monster. For example, in 1736, the Royal Order of 10 July, regulating the appointment of Deans to the University of Valencia, is keen to inform us that "quorum utrumque monstruum arti, & naturæ contrarium esse, dubium non extitit" — that is to say, "there was no doubt that both of these monsters were contrary to art and nature".[9] Three years later, in 1739, it is time for a German scholar to once again protest against the monstrosity of certain acts: the title of a work by Gottlieb Samuel Treuer is eloquent, "*Monstrvm Arbitrarii Iuris Territorialis A Legibus Imperii E Germania Profligatum*", namely, "a monster of arbitrary territorial law unleashed by the laws of the empire from Germany".[10]

The political meaning of the formula 'legal monster' supplements our understanding of the functions of the image. Foucault's lectures overlook this part of the story — namely, how the transformation of the *mostrum vel prodigium* of the tradition

65, the translation is mine). The same approach is at work in Alessandro Tartagni's *Commentaria (Digesti)* (published in Venice 1576); and Andrea Alciati's *Opera* (published in Basel 1582). In particular, Tartagni agrees with Baldo that "the statutes that punish homicide include the murder of a sick or monstrous man" (in Taruffi 1886, at 65). A century later, we noted Pufendorf's remarks in *The Whole Duty of Man*, according to whom Aristotle's advice on children "with some bodily defect" is deemed "bad" and the corresponding regulations, "unjust laws" (quoted in the third section of Chapter 4). Likewise, Locke's opinion in the *Essays* is that a kid who can speak is no monster, and therefore, that kid has rights: see above the second section of Chapter 4.

[7] References in the text to the sources of civil law are only a part of this more complex history. As stressed in Chapter 3, the claim of this section also concerns the common law tradition. We noted that in the early 1600s Edward Coke had no problems to refer to both monsters as enemies and traitors of the institutions (the Sir Walter Raleigh trial), and as the deformed beings of the tradition (from the Digest to Bracton). The same holds a century later for the ideas of William Blackstone, whose views on humans with congenital disabilities and thresholds of monstrosity are not too dissimilar from the Roman law views of Baldo Ubaldo, Alessandro Tartagni, and Andrea Alciati in the late 1500s (see previous note).

[8] See Pufendorf (ed. 2007, at IV, § 9). We return to Pufendorf's ideas below in Chapter 6.

[9] The document is collected in *Real Provisión de su Magestad y Señores y de su Consejo Supremo de Castilla* (Universidad Literaria de la Ciudad de Valencia, Dolz Publisher, Valencia 1737). The Royal Order is online at https://crowd.loc.gov/campaigns/herencia-centuries-of-spanish-legal-documents/laws-statutes-governance-administration/2018751508/2018751508-60/ (the quote is at p. 116, section 92).

[10] See G. S. Treuer, *Monstrvm Arbitrarii Iuris Territorialis A Legibvs Imperii E Germania Profligatum*, Schroeter, 1739, available at https://books.google.it/books?id=PXUHvwEACAAJ; and, on Internet Archive, at https://archive.org/details/bub_gb_Z5rQ0LN7rqwC/page/n19/mode/2up?q=thomasius

into a human rights bearer during the second half of the 1900s shall be understood as a result of this interplay between the two functions of the formula: monsters as a target of repression and monsters as a source of criticism, resistance, and rebellion. Foucault prefers to focus on another transformation: the *monstrum vel prodigium* into the modern criminal monster in the late 1700s and 800s. The reason for this level of abstraction is twofold, i.e. Foucault's intent to shed light on the repressive side of the law through its "techniques of normalisation", and to stress "a fundamental kinship between the criminal and the tyrant, between the lawbreaker and the despotic monarch" (Foucault 2003, at 93). Leaving aside centuries of natural law reflection on monstrous tyrants and the distinction between tyrants and despots, as well as the reasons why, since Greco-Roman times, the killing of a tyrant was differentiated from the murdering of a thief, Foucault presents such monsters as epiphenomena of a new economic regime of punitive power. So goes his argument in the 29 January 1975 lecture:

> The first juridical monster to emerge in the new regime of the economy of punitive power, the first monster to appear, to be identified and defined, is not the murderer, the transgressor, or the person who breaks the laws of nature, but the person who breaks the fundamental social pact. The first monster is the king. The king, I believe, is the general model from which, through successive historical shifts and transformations, the countless little monsters who people nineteenth-century psychiatry and legal psychiatry are historically derived. In any case, it seems to me that the fall of Louis XVI and the problematization of the figure of the king mark a decisive point in this history of human monsters. (Foucault 2003, at 94-95)

In this sort of mirror image, the parallel between criminals and monstrous kings is complemented by the parallel between the monstrous king and the revolutionary people who "break the social pact by revolt" (*op. cit.*, at 98). The despotic sovereign and the people in revolt, that is, the monster from above and the monster from below, the "incestuous monster" and the "cannibalistic monster" of the 1800s, are presented as the two sides to the coin of "the new economy of punitive power" that is "at the very heart of the juridico-medical theme of the monster" (*op. cit.*, at 101). The trick of suspicion consists of shifting the focus of the analysis from the tension between the political and legal meanings of the formula on monsters, between the body politic and the individuals' physical bodies, between subjects and targets of legal repression, between public and private law, to the means of legal normalisation brought forth by criminal psychiatry and medical power, i.e. "a transition from the monster to the abnormal" (at 110). By drawing attention to the type superseding the token, Foucault's dialectics of abnormality and normalisation can leave aside every tension between natural and positive law, public and private law, sovereignty powers and the right to resist, as the two sides to the same monstrous coin. Instead, the intent is to review the domain of sexuality, the technologies of eugenics and psychoanalysis (at 132), or the medicalised family (at 254), where "the functioning of the theme of incest should be situated in the century-old practice of the crusade against masturbation" (at 268).

Foucault's eternal recurrence of the same, i.e. the monster who turns into a criminal who turns into the abnormal — in the transition from "a juridico-natural complex" to "the juridico-medical theme" — omits the conditions that make such legal repression and normalisation legitimate or monstrous. In the lecture from 12 February 1975, although Foucault briefly mentions "Hobbes, Locke, or later French theorists" who distinguish "between good and bad political regimes", he dismisses "these juridico-political theories" first, in the name of history and then, of "psychiatry, and psychology in general" (*op. cit.*, at 152-153). Any argumentation about the body politic and the 'real monster' of both the natural law and common law traditions in continental Europe and England becomes irrelevant because what matters has to do with the "techniques of normalisation" and the "new regime of the economy of punitive power" which turn the legal repression into a sort of Aristotelian second nature.[11] So much so that such repression of the law should not only be considered normal but also trivial. It is significant that Foucault's modern criminal monster ultimately became a freak show in courtrooms and crime newspapers, i.e. an outcome of that normalisation through the norms of the law. All Italian fellows from my generation recall the Monster of Florence, the Italian media formula for a serial killer active within the city of Florence between 1968 and 1985. The medieval monster who turns into the modern criminal who turns into the abnormal who then turns into a media freak show may all be viewed as historical forms or illustrations of Foucault's dialectics of punishment and normalisation. Although the brute repressive face of the law does not vanish with the normalisation process, which is brought forth by the norms of the law, Foucault's 'abnormal' aims to embrace both.

However, the problems with this dialectics of monstrous repression and normalisation through a new economy of punitive power — which internalises the morphological abnormity of traditional monsters — are both conceptual and historiographical. Regarding legal concepts, conflicts between natural law and positive law, public law and private law, habeas corpus and the body politic, and subjects and objects of regulation are either ignored or omitted in Foucault's lectures. Concerning the two meanings, legal and political, of the formula on monsters, it is hard to buy into Foucault's thesis that natural law and positive law went hand-in-hand in the repression of the polyform monster (*op. cit.*, at 65); that "the moral monster… appears on the threshold of the nineteenth century" (at 90); that theories of tyrannicide can be

[11] On Foucault's transition from "a juridico-natural concept" to "the juridico-medical theme", i.e. from the morphological monstrosity of traditional prodigies to the normalisation of people's interiority or psyche, see the *Nichomachean Ethics*: "Those who have become unrestrained through habit are more easily cured than those who are unrestrained by nature, since habit is easier to change than nature; for even habit is hard to change, precisely because it is a sort of nature" (Aristotle 2000, at 1152a). In modern times, Rousseau adopts this Aristotelian idea in accordance with the distinction between the *homme de la nature* and the monstrous *homme de l'homme*, so that, in the phrasing of the *Emile*, "habit adds a new want to those of nature, and this must be prevented. The only habit a child should be allowed to form is to contract no habits whatever" (Rousseau ed. 1889, at 24). In his work on postmodernism, Stephen Hicks has brilliantly described the parable that leads from Rousseau's ideas on human nature to Foucault's social criticism: "Postmodern debates thus display a paradoxical nature. Across the board, we hear, on the one hand, abstract themes on relativism and egalitarianism. Those themes come in both epistemological and ethical forms… Coexisting with those relativistic and egalitarian themes, we hear, on the other hand, deep chords of cynicism" (Hicks 2004, at 20).

understood as a simple criminal affair (at 94); that "all human monsters are descendants of Louis XVI" (at 95); or, that the only right to be considered is either the right to punish, or "the right to cook" (at 103).

On the other hand, as regards the limits of Foucault's historiography, we noted that the 'real monsters' of both the natural law and common law tradition in continental Europe and England throughout the modern ages were often normative acts and institutions, rather than humans with congenital disabilities. Those who live by the monster, die by the monster. After Plato, Cicero or Seneca, the list of sources on political monsters or monstrous normative acts — from the early 1500s to the late 1700s — includes the reflection of Erasmus, Ludovico Ariosto, Sir Thomas Elyot, the Monarchomachs, Edward Coke, Jean Racine, Samuel Pufendorf, Emer de Vattel, Montesquieu, and William Blackstone, among many others.[12] The further omission of the transformation of the old monster of positive law into a human rights bearer exacerbates such limits of Foucault's storytelling on monsters. The trick of suspicion consists of removing all this information or interpreting it as a sort of false consciousness in Marx's slang.[13] Why should we prioritise the rights of people with congenital malformations in a world which is still full of slavery, sex trafficking, or the death penalty for gay people?

To test this latter trick, we can update the debate on the abnormal with a more recent case study. The analysis of the 'legally dead' people of the tradition takes the form of today's terrorist. Many examples of extra-judicial rendition over the past decades — which are increasing with the use of drones, AI systems, and myriad lethal autonomous weapons (Pagallo 2011) — would illustrate the status of terrorists as monsters, for example, with the 'legally dead' people of the U.S. Guantanamo facilities (Steyn 2004; Gregory 2006). Several scholars have dissected the details of tortures and abuses, rapes and killings, following this new incarnation of the abnormal. To some, the cruel and tragic photos of Manadel al-Jamadi (see next section) confirm this logic of suspicion, according to which terrorist monsters perpetuate the method of the Master. It is all about the *monstrum vel prodigium* who turns into a criminal who then turns into a terrorist: all treated as non-humans and legally dead — the eternal recurrence of the same.

---

[12] The list of jurists, poets, philosophers, and politicians, has of course theoretical relevance. As stressed below in Chapter 6, a further layer of complexity is added to the traditional equalisation of tyrants with monsters through the differentiation between classical and modern natural law schools, and the further distinctions between monstrous normative acts and institutions, between tyrants and despots.

[13] The notion of false consciousness is discussed in Marx and Engels (ed. 1976). The reference text was in the early 1900s, G. Lukács (ed. 1972). On Marx's notion of false consciousness see today Eyerman (1981) and Pines (1993). Regarding Foucault's analysis on monsters, every discourse on legal rights, including the right to resist, would be a byproduct of such false consciousness because the focus on individual and collective rights with the corresponding limits of sovereignty, coercion, or the economy of punitive power would make disappear the hard face of the law. According to the analysis of Günther Teubner, "Foucault's problem, however, is his obsessive fixation on the phenomenon of power, which leads him into a senseless inflation of the concept of power" (Teubner 2019, at 22). The last section of this chapter illustrates the reasons why this "obsessive fixation" does not fit the legal phenomenon.

5.3 The Terrorist

The formula for 'terrorist monsters' has a long history. It can be traced back to Greco-Roman antiquity with the very distinction between friend and foe. In *The Republic,* Plato metaphorically illustrates the Philosopher-King, who distinguishes friend from foe, as a dog (375 a); in *Politics,* Aristotle harshly opposes Greeks and Barbarians (1252 b); and, in *On Duties,* Cicero distinguishes between lawful enemies and pirates as "the common enemy of all" (3.29.107).[14] Foes are depicted as monsters, human beasts, or both: in *The Republic*, Plato's dog opposes the tyrant monster; in *Politics,* Aristotle's Greeks oppose the bestiality of Barbarians and those who are not a part of any city; and in *On Duties,* Cicero opposes the Roman institutions to monsters and beasts as enemies of such institutions.

This tradition was still very much alive in the early 1600s,[15] so much so that Cicero's formula on pirates as 'enemies of all' triumphed under the label of a new 'legal monster' in the mid-1700s. The parallelism is formalised in the most important treaties of that era across fields such as the "laws of the people", the "laws of nations", or what today is known as public international law. This is the claim of the German philosopher Christian Wolff in the *Jus Gentium Methodo Scientifica Pertractum*, or *The Law of Nations According to the Scientific Method* (Wolff ed. 1934). According to Wolff, nothing could be "too harsh… against those who plainly show that they are enemies of the whole human race". By seeking war as an end in itself, thus threatening the security of all nations, such "robbers whose malice extends to the farthest limit" should be properly understood as *humani generis monstrae*, "monsters of the human race". Hence, Wolff's conclusion:

> The right to punish them [i.e., the monsters of the human race, the robbers, the pirates] belongs to all nations, and by this right they can remove from their midst those fierce monsters of the human species. (*op. cit.*, § 6.627)

Such ideas were endorsed a few years later, in 1758, by Emer de Vattel in *The Law of Nations*, which soon became a renowned treatise of international law (Vattel ed. 2008). Focus of Books II and III of this work is on the relations among sovereign states. In § 56 of Book II — "Of a Nation considered in its Relations to others" — Vattel draws on Wolff's arguments with a crucial difference: the monster does not only refer to pirates and robbers, but also "to those monsters who, under the title of sovereigns, render themselves the scourges and horror of the human race". These public monsters are also presented as "savage beasts". Whether pirates or sovereigns, Vattel's conclusion still draws on Wolff's authority: "every brave man may justly exterminate [the monsters] from the face of the earth" (*op. cit.*, § 56). This very idea of a legal monster is also under the lens of Book III, "Of War":

---

[14] We dwelt on Cicero's pirates above in the last section of Chapter 2.

[15] In Chapter 3 and in Sect. 2 of this chapter we noted that, in the Sir Raleigh trial, Edward Coke's j'accuse against the pirate is that Raleigh is a "monster". Of course, Raleigh is a monster not because he is a pirate, but because he is a traitor.

> Nations that are always ready to take up arms on any prospect of advantage, are lawless robbers: but those who seem to delight in the ravages of war, who spread it on all sides, without reasons or pretexts, and even without any other motive than their own ferocity, are monsters, unworthy the name of men. They should be considered as enemies to the human race. (Vattel ed. 2008, at III, § 34)

In this context, to restrict the focus of the analysis to the idea of 'pirate monsters' as an object of suppression, we can set aside Vattel's ideas on 'sovereign monsters' as a target of repression and extermination.[16] This idea of 'pirate monsters' as 'enemies to humankind' has indeed become popular in the current age of terrorism (Land 2008). The atrocities of terrorist attacks may, in fact, turn them into a non-human status as much as the legally dead monsters of the tradition. The risk materialised with U.S. President George W. Bush's declaration of war in the aftermath of the 2001 Twin Towers attacks. In 2003, during the early stages of the Second Gulf War and the 'war on terror', members of the U.S. Army and the CIA physically abused and tortured some 'monsters' in the Abu Ghraib prison in Iraq. The practice included the killing of Manadel al-Jamadi with the desecration of his body. In April 2004, CBS News drew public attention to this series of human rights violations and war crimes with the publication of photographs. The scandal was vibrant. However, the debate which followed was also, at times, confusing and misrepresentative. The more scholars debate the scandal of this legal monster — the terrorist — the more we should be attentive to the different meanings of the formula, in particular, the legal and political meanings of monster in this context.

From a strictly legal viewpoint, positive law admits no legal monster, whether criminal, abnormal, combatant enemy, or terrorist. All humans have basic rights that shall be respected at the international level (i.e. human rights); and the national level (their fundamental or constitutional rights). This assumption does not mean that institutions, scholars, national security experts, anti-terrorism authorities, or secret services ignore the challenges of enforcing principles and rules of law. However, most scholars and experts of international humanitarian law warn against the use of such a dangerous and misleading formula — such as presenting terrorists as monsters — for a twofold reason (Luban 2018; de Wilde 2018). On the one hand, the formula is incorrect because it suggests thinking about terrorists as a legitimate target of legal repression, i.e. an object rather than the subject of certain rights of positive law. On the other hand, the formula is dangerous because it can legitimise practices of oppression. For example, Bush's 'war on terror' was not a simple rhetorical formula but paved the way for abuses and tortures (Pagallo 2013).

The political meaning of the formula 'terrorist monster', therefore, concerns the material practice of public actors or sovereigns at the national and international levels. Issues with the enforcement of the international Bill of Rights and multiple cases of extra-judicial rendition may remind us of Foucault's thesis on the monster who turns into a criminal who may ultimately turn into a terrorist, as the last sequel of

[16] We return to this part of the analysis on public monsters in Chapter 10. Dealing in this chapter with the abnormal, the attention is drawn to the alleged monstrosity of those private actors, such as the pirates as the "enemies of humanity". See Piirimäe (2019).

the 'legally dead' in Western law. There is, however, a crucial difference.[17] Whereas, strictly speaking, the human rights framework and the Bill of Rights leave no room for the legally dead persons of tradition, politically speaking, it may make sense to refer to the treatment of terrorists as monsters either to stress the problems with the enforcement of the law or to emphasise the monstrosity of institutions in their war on terror. In both cases, attention is no longer drawn to instances of lawful repression or normalisation, but rather to illegal acts under international and regional conventions, for example, in accordance with the European Court of Human Rights' doctrine on Art. 3 of the 1950 Convention, or 'ECHR'.[18]

[17] The remarks of the text also apply to illegal immigrants as monsters. We noted in the introduction of this book that the U.S. President Donald Trump has led the "monstrification of immigrants" who "poison our country" (Eljaiek-Rodríguez 2024). Such narrative and corresponding practices have been widely debated over the past years: see Johnson (2010); Román and Olivas (2013); Kaplan (2022); among many. Such practices and rhetoric find their counterpart in their critique as monstrous acts, not only in the U.S. (e.g. Graff 2014), but also, in the EU (Lacy and van Houtum 2020); and the UK (Tyerman and Van Isacker 2024); among others. See also the next note of this chapter.

[18] As stressed above in note 25 of Chapter 4, Art. 3 of the European Convention on Human Rights (ECHR) refers to the prohibition of torture, inhuman or degrading treatment or punishment. Such prohibition includes not only the treatment of criminal and terrorists, but also, immigrants: see Moya and Milios (2021). The Court of Strasbourg has traditionally considered such rights as 'absolute'. In *VM and others v. Belgium* from 2015, for example, the Court found that Belgium had violated Art. 3 by exposing some asylum seekers to conditions of extreme poverty for four weeks. A year later, in *Paposhvili v. Belgium*, the Grand Chamber unanimously held that there would have been a violation of Art. 3 if the applicant had been removed to Georgia without the Belgian authorities having assessed the risks of the removal. Yet, some scholars stress a "problematic interpretation" of Art. 3 by the Court when it comes to migrants (Dembour 2015; Spalding 2022). Diplomatic assurances, 'healthcare removals', and returns to situations of general violence would compromise the immigrants' human right against any inhuman treatment, so much so that, paradoxically, the standard of protection would be lower than the standard afforded to individuals convicted of criminal offences, i.e. what Amanda Spalding dubs the immigrants' under-criminalisation. This criticism is nonetheless subject to criticism because the absoluteness of the right under Art. 3 must be considered under the circumstances of each case and moreover, the fact that the notion of absoluteness is "better understood within the wider context of the Convention as a whole" (Addo and Grief 1998). It is on this basis that we shall assess, for example, the alleged healthcare removal in *N. v. The United Kingdom* from 2008: "Article 3 does not place an obligation on the Contracting State to alleviate such disparities [of medical science and treatment] through the provision of free and unlimited health care to all aliens without a right to stay within its jurisdiction. A finding to the contrary would place too great a burden on the Contracting States" (§ 44 of the ruling). The same holds for some more recent rulings of the Court from the early 2020s, upholding Spain's so-called 'pushback practices'. Such decisions would stress "the basic tension between the prohibition of *refoulement* and the absence of a right to asylum" (Thym 2020). Drawing on this brief review of case law, the conclusion is threefold. First, such a case law falls well below the threshold of monstrosity discussed in the text. Second, the absolute nature of the rights enshrined in Art. 3 does not preclude the existence of hard cases to which scholars are attentive. Third, the principles of existing law that make the monstrous treatment of human beings illegal may be violated by further national legislation or practices, and hence, courts' rulings upholding them. Among such cases, consider Uganda's law from May 2023 establishing the capital punishment for certain gay behaviour: see Ehirim (2025) and Butler (2025). This circumstance does not contradict the approach of this volume, but rather, confirms it. Should no monstrous laws or institutions exist, there would be no need to resort to the political use of the formula on monsters as a source of legal criticism, resistance, and rebellion.

In the series of permutations of the abnormal, the crucial difference that every follower of the Master of suspicion shall consider is that Foucault's chain of the abnormal is all about people legally declared (or presumed as) dead or repressed in both positive and natural law. Today, it is clear that the monstrous oppression or normalisation of people with congenital disabilities, criminals, terrorists, immigrants, lesbian or homosexuals, is not only immoral but also unlawful in accordance with principles and provisions of international law. This conclusion does not entail that we can ignore many jurisdictions that still endorse monstrous normative acts and practices. The following chapters of this book are devoted to analysing the conditions that make legal coercion illegitimate. The political and legal meanings of the formula on monsters in the tradition of Western law do not suggest any self-complacent historical reconstruction. The formula on monsters functions as a source of criticism, resistance, and rebellion precisely because the interplay between the individuals' bodies and the body politic, between objects and subjects of legal regulation, represents a double-edged sword. This is a lesson learned from almost 2500 years of Western thought on monstrous tyrants. A theory of legal monsters must be reflective.

5.4 Redemption Song

We have reached the end of the trial on legal monsters before the court of reason. Considering the first meaning of the formula on monsters as the object or target of legal repression, Chapter 4 examined three different kinds of semantic information on why monsters do not exist (Sect. 4.2); why monsters shall not exist (Sect. 4.3); and the alethic statement according to which old formulas of the legal tradition were abolished in the second half of the twentieth century (Sect. 4.4). Against this backdrop, this chapter has carried out an additional investigation concerning the claims of Foucault and followers, considering both Foucault's analysis of the abnormal (Sect. 5.2), and debates on terrorists and illegal immigrants (Sect. 5.3). The additional investigation has provided four different means of proof regarding the shortcomings of Foucault's analysis and that of his followers vis-à-vis the development of strict legal formulas of positive law on monsters. They regard:

(i) The interplay between objects and subjects of the law;
(ii) The interplay between physical bodies, people's minds, and the body politic;
(iii) The tension between natural law and positive law, and, furthermore, between today's human rights framework and its enforcement;
(iv) The tension between legal oppression and civic liberties.

As regards the interplay between objects and subjects of the law, both of which the image of the monster intends to convey, we noted that Foucault and followers consider the 'legal monster' only as an object of repression and normalisation: the subject of the law is only the legal oppressor, the normaliser. The history of the *mostrum vel prodigium*, or today's terrorist monster, shows a more complex picture. The old prodigies and monsters of Foucault (and the tradition) have turned into human rights bearers, whilst the repression of pirates, criminals and terrorists that Cicero, Wolff, Vattel, or George W. Bush would deem appropriate, is nowadays illegal. There is no room for any kind of legally dead people or abnormal in current law. Should it be the case, such a law must be deemed a monstrosity. Masters of suspicion and their followers have neither interest nor expertise in dissecting the legal reasons for this normative monstrosity.

The second point regards the interplay of two different bodies. Monsters cover both the individuals' bodies (*monstrum vel prodigium*), and the body politic of legal philosophy. This second political meaning of the formula can be traced back to Plato's political monster (the tyrant), and Cicero's institutional monsters (e.g., the corrupted governor of Sicily). In the second section of this chapter, we noted how this meaning is taken up with certain variants in both the common law tradition (from Coke to Blackstone), and the modern natural law schools (from Pufendorf to Vattel). In addition to institutional monsters, specific normative acts can also be deemed monstrous. This political use of the formula either complements or goes hand-in-hand with the strict legal meaning of the formula regarding positive law, whether Roman law, common law, continental Europe's civil law, or canon law.[19] In either case, the interplay of the body politic with the natural body of the individuals, which follows as a result of the use of the formula, is essential because it casts light on the constitution and law of those societies as well as the moral grounds on which the body politic lies. The very fact that, most of the time, the legal and political reference to monsters in the 1600s and 700s shall be understood as a form of rebellion, rather than oppression — of legal criticism, rather than normalisation — simply falls outside the radar of Foucault and followers.

The third point concerns the tension between natural and positive law, between today's human rights framework and its enforcement. Foucault ignored this tension by changing the meaning of the formula on monsters according to the circumstances. We noted that the starting point of Foucault's analysis is the convergence of the repressive powers of canon and civil law, as well as natural and positive law. Since the 1600s and down to the 1800s, however, a fierce philosophical and scientific debate has discussed this very convergence either as a matter of fact (monsters do not exist), or in

[19] Among the scholars who used the image of monsters both as an object and subject of the law, we noted Coke and Blackstone (in Chapter 3), Pufendorf (Chapter 4), and Vattel (third section of this Chapter). This double use of the image can be traced back to Cicero. As stressed in the text, the interplay between the body politic and the physical bodies of the individuals is apparent or, in the phrasing of Blackstone, "too obvious and too shocking to bear a minute discussion" (quoted in the second section of Chapter 3). Whereas, in the case of Pufendorf, the moral pillars and natural rights of the political community prohibit every treatment of humans with congenital disabilities as the legally dead people of the tradition, Blackstone deems this status compatible with the tenets of the common law. However, the political use of the formula can be disconnected from any reference to the *monstrum vel prodigium* of positive law in certain cases, such as Samuel Pufendorf's remarks on the German empire (above in the second section of this chapter). Such uses differ from Plato's identification of the monster with the tyrant because either they refer to the impersonal monstrosity of the institutions, or the monstrosity of certain normative acts. The interplay of the body politic with the physical body of the individuals, *pace* Foucault and followers, becomes evident in these cases with the political use of the formula against forms of repression or oppression.

normative terms (monsters should not exist). All tensions which Foucault overlooked — whether between facts and norms or positive law and certain versions of natural law — would be overcome and realigned in a new convergence only after the Second World War and the Universal Declaration, which Foucault likewise overlooked.[20] As a result, the more Foucault and his followers insist with their analysis of the repressive side of the law, the more legal coercion, which undoubtedly exists, has to be grasped in accordance with the political meaning of the use of the formula on monsters. This other side of the coin does not suggest any self-complacency by drawing on the glorious tradition of natural law or the tenets of English constitutionalism. On the contrary, from Plato to Cicero, and in modern times, from Coke to Blackstone, or in continental Europe, from Pufendorf to Vattel, these traditions refer to monsters to stress some of the most difficult and even tragic moments of their lives: Plato's tyrants, Cicero's enemies of the institution, Coke's traitors, Pufendorf's disgraceful state of Germany, and so on.

The final point concerns the tension between coercion and civic liberties that the formula on monsters transmits since ancient times and throughout modernity. A generation of scholars, following Foucault's method, has dissected the transmutation of the monster who turns into a criminal who turns into an abnormal who may turn into a terrorist or illegal immigrant, leaving aside any discourse on civil liberties, rights and freedoms as a result of false consciousness, according to the Marxian slang. However, the function that the formula 'legal monsters' has had throughout the centuries also entails an act of resistance, or opposition to certain men, laws, and institutions. In 1667, Pufendorf sums up *The Present State of Germany* as a monstrous

[20] Consider the ban on torture as a painful example of this realignment of natural law and positive law since torture was deemed morally and legally acceptable until early modern societies (Einolf 2007). On the one hand, Art. 5 UDHR prohibits torture and cruel, inhuman, or degrading treatment or punishment: this absolute right has been enshrined in the ad hoc Convention that the UN General Assembly adopted in 1984. 173 countries have so far ratified it. We noted that regional conventions, such as the ECHR, complement these international law provisions: see above note 18 of this chapter. Yet, on the other hand, torture is a plague that still afflicts the world. In 2013, Juan Méndez, the UN special rapporteur on torture and special advisor to the prosecutor of the International Criminal Court, declared that "one hundred countries use torture" (the interview is in *Refugee Transitions*, 2013, 28, pp. 51-53). See also his report to the General Assembly in Méndez (2015). A decade later, the picture has become even more discouraging. The UN website on the international day in support of victims of torture quotes the opinion of another UN special rapporteur, Alice Jill Edwards, according to whom, "there is an increase in the use of torture worldwide. It's partly correlated to the fact that... we have more wars going on in this world since 1945. The International Committee of the Red Cross says there are 100 armed conflicts currently going on. And regrettably, with armed conflict comes an uptick in the use of torture and other forms of inhuman treatment". See the new report to the General Assembly in Edwards (2025), which draws attention to the practice of hostage-taking. In addition to the recommendations of the UN Special Rapporteurs on how to address this bleak scenario, we should not overlook the ways in which the monster problem has realigned in today's law. Cases of monstrosity are not based on moral principles or despicable orders applied in the name of law, but rather, national practices and legislative acts that blatantly violate the principles and provisions of international law. We might ask whether such national practices and legislative acts should be considered 'valid law', and what legal thresholds of monstrosity follow as a result of this new realignment of positive law and natural law. These are the topics covered in Chapters 8 and 9.

condition; in 1689, Locke discusses an act of resistance against monsters (turned into beasts) in the second of the *Two Treatises of Government*; in 1736, a Spanish Royal Order stigmatises the monstrous regulation for the appointment of Deans in Valencia; in 1739, Gottlieb Samuel Treuer denounces a monstrous territorial law of the German empire; in 1748, Montesquieu warns against the violence of monstrous governments that run counter to a nation's way of thinking; in 1753, William Blackstone depicts every attempt to put at risk the "original contract of government" and "the united will of the community" as a monstrous practice.[21] In Foucault's terms, all such claims — and many others, under scrutiny in the following parts of this book — oppose some kind of 'normalisation'. The monster represents the face of oppression that reminds us of the conditions making political obligation and legal coercion legitimate. It is hard to buy into Foucault's view that "principles of civility and procedural justice simply serve as masks for hypocrisy and oppression born of asymmetrical power relations" (Hicks 2004, at 20).

New forms of monsters pop up as a result of this framework. By examining the interplay and even tension between monsters as the target of normalisation and repression, and monsters as a source of criticism, we can dismiss the Master of suspicion's method and focus on that very legal and political debate of the 1600s and 700s that Foucault and followers neglected. To grasp the meaning of formulas such as 'institutional monster' or 'normative monster', which today remain particularly popular, it is necessary to dwell on their political meaning vis-à-vis the teachings of the modern natural law school, as occurs with the monsters of Hobbes and Pufendorf. This historiographical level of abstraction has a conceptual and methodological advantage.

Regarding the conceptual gains, the political, rather than strict legal use of formulas on monsters helps cast further light on the coercive means of the law, its repressive side. In the last section of Chapter 3 we noted the limits of this side, meaning that coercion is a necessary but insufficient condition of hard law and, moreover, that repression is one of the manifold functions of the legal phenomenon which must be specified in connection with certain targets. The subsequent step of the analysis concerns the conditions making such coercion legitimate or, conversely, monstrous. It is either incorrect, misleading, or deceitful, to simply present the law as a sort of normalising procedure. The next chapters of this book will address the substantiation of this assumption.

From a methodological point of view, this exercise of legal theory on the repressive side of norms and institutions suggests that a theory of legal monsters must be reflective. The image of the monster can be considered as a double-edged sword between the individuals' natural bodies and the body politic, between the objects of normalisation and the sources of legal criticism or, in legal theory, between positive and natural law, between public and private law, between international and national law. To appreciate this double-edged sword, attention should be drawn to the conditions that, in ascendent order, make criticism, resistance, and rebellion meaningful and legitimate against monstrous normative acts, brutalising institutions, or tyrants. This

[21] All those authors' reflection on monsters are discussed below in Chapter 6.

is the meaning of the formula on monsters that, after the abolishment of the status of the *monster vel prodigium*, is, strictly speaking, the only legally alive formula today.

The next chapter scrutinises this other side to the coin of Foucault's arguments on legal monsters and the normalisation efforts of the law, drawing on the teachings and limits of the modern natural law tradition from the 1600s and 700s. As done in the previous parts of this volume, arguments of legal theory are clarified through the sources of positive law, law in the making, and references to political philosophy. The aim is to cast further light on the repressive side of the legal phenomenon, complementing a history of ideas on monsters with the work of those scholars who took up and developed the political use of the image in Plato and Cicero. This image of monsters can be summed up with new forms of 'natural resistance'. Contrary to legally dead formulas on the *monstrum vel prodigium* with their criminal or terrorist variables, it is this resistance that has a proper strict legal meaning today.

References

Addo, M. K., and N. Grief. 1998. Does article 3 of the European convention on human rights enshrine absolute rights? *European Journal of International Law* 9 (3): 510–524.
Aristotle. 2000. *The Nichomachean ethics*, trans. R. Crisp. Cambridge: Cambridge University Press.
Butler, J. 2025. *Who's afraid of gender?* London: Penguin.
Canguilhem, G. 1991. *The normal and the pathological* [1966]. New York: Zone Books.
Cohen, J. J. 1996. *Monster theory: reading culture*. Minneapolis: University of Minnesota Press.
De Wilde, M. 2018. Enemy of all humanity: The dehumanizing effects of a dangerous concept. *Netherlands Journal of Legal Philosophy* 47 (2): 158–175.
Dembour, M.-B. 2015. *When humans become migrants*. Oxford: Oxford University Press.
Edwards, A. J. 2025. Report of the special rapporteur on torture and other cruel, inhuman or degrading treatment or punishment. U.N. Doc. A/HRC/58/55 (8 September 2025). https://docs.un.org/en/A/HRC/58/55.
Ehirim, U. G. 2025. Public morality and constitutionalism in restricting LGBTQ+ rights: A legal analysis of Nigeria, Ghana, and Uganda. *International Journal of Constitutional and Administrative Law* 1 (1): 42–68.
Einolf, C. J. 2007. The fall and rise of torture: A comparative and historical analysis. *Sociological Theory* 25 (2): 101–121.
Eljaiek-Rodríguez, E. 2024. Blood: The monstrification of immigrants in U.S. politics. *Free Voice*, Issue 40 (Blood), (8 September 2025). Available at/from https://shuddhashar.com/monsters-that-poison-the-blood-the-monstrification-of-immigrants-in-u-s-politics/.
Eyerman, R. 1981. False consciousness and ideology in marxist theory. *Acta Sociologica* 24 (1-2): 43–56.
Foucault, M. 2003. *Abnormal: Lectures at the college de France 1974-1975*. London: Verso.
Gadamer, H. G. 1984. The hermeneutics of suspicion. *Man and World* 17:313–323.
Graff, G. M. 2014. The green monster. *Politico*, (8 September 2025). Available at/from https://www.politico.com/magazine/story/2014/10/border-patrol-the-green-monster-112220/.
Gregory, D. 2006. The black flag: Guantánamo Bay and the space of exception. *Geografiska Annaler: Series B, Human Geography* 88 (4): 405–427.
Hart, H. L. A. 1994. *The concept of law* [1961]. Oxford: Oxford University Press.
Hicks, S. R. C. 2004. *Explaining postmodernism: Skepticism and socialism from Rousseau to Foucault*. Tempe and New Berlin/Milwaukee: Scholargy Publishing.

Johnson, K. R. 2010. It's the economy, stupid: The hijacking of the debate over immigration reform by monsters, ghosts, and goblins (or the war on drugs, war on terror, narcoterrorists, etc.). *Chapman Law Review* 13 (3): 583–614.

Kaplan, J. 2022. Undocumented zombies: US-Mexican immigration, The Walking Dead, and the effort/shape of monsters. In *Monsters in performance*, ed. M. Chemers and A. Santana, 213–227. London: Routledge.

Lacy, R. B., and H. van Houtum. 2020. Death as policy: The EU's criminalisation of solidarity with undocumented migrants. In *Expanding boundaries*, ed. J. P. Laine et al., 72–84. London: Routledge.

Land, I., ed. 2008. *Enemies of humanity: The nineteenth-century war on terrorism.* New York: Palgrave Macmillan.

Luban, D. 2018. The enemy of all humanity. *Netherlands Journal of Legal Philosophy* 47 (2): 112–137.

Lukács, G. 1972. *History and class consciousness: Studies in Marxist dialectics* [1927]. Cambridge, MA: MIT Press.

Marx, K. and F. Engels. 1976. *The German ideology* [1846]. Moscow: Progress Publishers.

Méndez, J. E. 2015. Report of the special rapporteur on torture and other cruel, inhuman or degrading treatment or punishment. U.N. Doc. A/HRC/28/68, (8 September 2025). Available at/from https://www.refworld.org/pdfid/550824454.pdf.

Moya, D., and G. Milios, eds. 2021. *Aliens before the European court of human rights: Ensuring minimum standards of human rights protection.* Leiden: Brill.

O'Hara, D. T. 2003. Neither gods nor monsters: An untimely critique of the "post/human" imagination. *Boundary 2* 30 (3): 107–122.

Pagallo, U. 2011. Robots of just war: A legal perspective. *Philosophy & Technology* 24:307–323.

Pagallo, U. 2013. Online security and the protection of civil rights: A legal overview. *Philosophy & Technology* 26:381–395.

Piirimäe, P. 2019. Men, monsters and the history of mankind in Vattel's law of nations. In *Early modern natural law*, ed. S. Zurbuchen, 159–185. Leiden: Brill.

Pines, C. L. 1993. *Ideology and false consciousness: Marx and his historical progenitors.* Baltimore: SUNY Press.

Plato. 1977. *Plato's cosmology. The Timeus of Plato*, trans. F. M. Cornford. Indianapolis/Cambridge: Hackett.

Pufendorf S. 2007. *The present state of Germany* [1667], trans. E. Bohun. Indianapolis: Liberty Fund.

Ricoeur, P. 1970. *Freud and philosophy: An essay on interpretation.* New Haven and London: Yale University Press.

Ricoeur, P. 2013. *Le conflit des interprétations. Essais d'herméneutique.* Paris: Média Diffusion.

Román, E., and M. A. Olivas. 2013. *Those damned immigrants: America's hysteria over undocumented immigration.* Vol. 1. New York: NYU Press.

Rousseau, J. J. 1889. *Emile, or Concerning Education* [1762], trans. E. Worthington. Boston: Heath & Co.

Schneider, S. 1999. Monsters as (uncanny) metaphors: Freud, Lakoff, and the representation of monstrosity in cinematic horror. *Other Voices* 1 (3): 167–191.

Sharpe, A. 2007. Structured like a monster: Understanding human difference through a legal category. *Law and Critique* 18 (2): 207–228.

Spalding, A. 2022. *The treatment of immigrants in the European Court of Human Rights.* Oxford: Hart.

Steyn, J. 2004. Guantanamo Bay: The legal black hole. *International & Comparative Law Quarterly* 53 (1): 1–15.

Taruffi, C. 1886. *Storia della teratologia.* Vol. 4. Bologna: Regia Topografica.

Tedeschini, M. 2021. Il mostro è un paradosso. *Studi di estetica, XLIX, IV* 2:240–259.

Teubner, G. 2019. *Critical theory and legal autopoiesis: The case for societal constitutionalism.* Manchester: Manchester University Press.

Thym, D. 2020. The end of human rights dynamism? Judgments of the ECtHR on ‘hot returns’ and humanitarian visas as a focal point of contemporary European asylum law and policy. *International Journal of Refugee Law, 32*(4) 569–596.

Tyerman, T., and T. Van Isacker. 2024. ‘Here there be monsters’: Confronting the (post) coloniality of Britain’s borders. *Review of International Studies* 1–21.

Vattel, E. de. 2008. *The law of nations, or, principles of the law of nature* [1758], ed. B. Kapossy and R. Whatmore. Indianapolis: Liberty Fund.

Weinstock, J. A., ed. 2020. *The monster theory reader*. Minneapolis: University of Minnesota Press.

Wolff, Ch., 1934. *The law of nations according to the scientific method* [1749], trans. J.H. Drake. Oxford: Clarendon Press.

Chapter 6
Natural Resistance

This chapter examines two further meanings of the formula 'legal monster': 'institutional monsters' and 'monstrous normative acts', with their variables. These new formulas can be traced back to the modern natural law schools of the 1600s and 700s, complementing ancient ideas on tyrants, traitors, or enemies traditionally presented as monsters. According to some modern natural law scholars, laws and institutions are monstrous when they contradict their own conditions or requirements following the claims of a geometric reason. These ideas developed and spread with the further claim that even decent institutions can adopt monstrous acts. However, multiple variants of the natural law tradition make it tricky to determine whether an institution should be properly understood as monstrous and, moreover, what legal effects would follow such an institutional monstrosity. This is the bane of the modern natural law tradition.

6.1 Modern Natural Law

The function of resistance transmitted by the image of Greco-Roman monsters was still popular in the 1600s. To corroborate this popularity, consider the famous Huguenot essay *Vindiciae contra tyrannos*, published in Basel under the pseudonym of "Stephen Junius Brutus" in 1579 (Brutus ed. 1924). The essay's main problem concerns whether the King's commands are binding when contradicting the law of God. The classic reference to a monster illustrates — and justifies at the same time — all claims of resistance against unjust acts. In the phrasing of the pamphlet:

U. Pagallo, *A Theory of Legal Monsters: Repression, Resistance, Rebellion*, Philosophical Studies Series 161, https://doi.org/10.1007/978-3-032-10771-8_6

> Briefly, if man becomes a wolf to man, who hinders that man (according to the proverb), may not be instead of God to the needy? And therefore the ancients have ranked Hercules amongst the gods, because he punished and tamed Procrustes, Busiris, and other tyrants, the plagues of mankind, and monsters of the earth. (Brutus 1924, at 104)[1]

More than a century later, this early modern tradition is still alive in England as well. In 1689, in the second of the *Two Treatises of Government* (Locke ed. 1823), Locke supports people's power to resist their king (*op. cit.*, § 232), and to provide for "their safety anew" (§ 226). "Great mistakes in the ruling part, many wrong and inconvenient laws, and all the slips of human frailty" suggest why revolutions happen, and people have the right to make them (§ 225). Locke exposes the shortcomings of most popular critiques to people's right to resist, suggesting that such critiques are worse than the political crisis in which the right is exercised. Locke's argument in constitutional law anticipates Wolff and Vattel's views on the treatment of pirates under international law (see Chapter 5). In Locke's phrasing:

> But if they who say it lays a foundation for rebellion mean that it may occasion civil wars or intestine broils… they may as well say, upon the same ground that honest men may not oppose robbers or pirates because this may occasion disorder or bloodshed. (Locke 1823, at § 228)

However, there is a clear difference between the right to resist in the *Vindiciae* and the one in the *Two Treatises*. The natural law right to people's rebellion in the Huguenot pamphlet is anchored to a specific legal and political tradition which rests on ancient authority: this is Edward Coke's style in the early 1600s when presenting — to some, reinventing — the tenets of the common law in England.[2] Although Locke may even support these views, the basis of his arguments does not hinge on traditional authority or strict legal sources when addressing the practical problems of politics and the government.[3] As Locke affirms in § 226 of the second treatise, the opposition against the monsters of the tradition does not regard "persons, but authority", and this authority is legitimate to the extent that it protects the natural rights of individuals, in particular, their right to property in accordance with the dictates of nature and reason.

Scholars have dissected — and have been deeply divided by the interpretation of — the differences between ancient and modern natural law theories.[4] Discussions

[1] The page regards the online version at https://www.yorku.ca/comninel/courses/3020pdf/vindiciae.pdf. The "proverb" of the *Vindiciae* refers to Plautus' *Asinaria*, which is mentioned above in Chapter 2 (see note 13). We return to his proverb below in the next chapter, dealing with the extraordinary popularity of the adage in the 1500s and 600s.

[2] We return to Coke's style and constitutional ideas in the last section of this chapter and in Chapter 7.

[3] Locke's approach poses other kinds of problems or even open contradictions between his political and epistemological reflection. It remains to be seen, for example, how human reason with its limits and artificial moral concepts can grasp a natural law which is not created by men, but rather, transcends human reason. See von Leyden (1981). On Locke's paradox on the legitimacy of the English political order, see Dunn (1982).

[4] The distinction between classical and modern natural law theories was under scrutiny in Chapter 4, where I stress that no one-size-fits-all interpretation exists to sum up their complex differences, which includes differences among advocates of the same tradition: see note 11 of Chapter 4. Accordingly,

have concerned, also but not only, interpretations of Locke's work.[5] For example, in 1816, Benjamin Constant opposed the Liberty of the Ancients to that of the Moderns, claiming that ancient freedoms "consisted of the active and constant participation in the collective power" and, thus, in the direct exercise of some sovereign power. In contrast, modern liberty would be regarded as a state in which "individual rights and commerce are respected" (Constant ed. 2016). Another liberal thinker, Friedrich von Hayek, claimed the opposite in 1982. In *Law, Legislation, and Liberty*, Hayek opposes the classical natural law forces of the 'cosmos' to the modern natural law constructivism of 'taxis'. Whereas ancient natural law was deeply anchored in the customs and ethos of the political community with rules that "spontaneously" or "unintentionally" emerge from social interaction, modern natural law and social contracts — which must be traced back to the tenets of René Descartes' philosophy – – are the forerunners of legal and political social planning: "This intellectual tradition can be shown to be false both in its factual and in its normative conclusions, because the existing institutions are not all the product of design" (Hayek ed. 2021, at 19).

Dealing with a theory of legal monsters, the concept of design is particularly fruitful even without buying into Hayek's thesis (or Constant's, for that matter). Hayek's view on 'constructivist design' clarifies crucial differences between ancient and modern times as well as persisting differences among advocates of modern natural law theory, all of which help clarify the meaning of resistance in the use of the formula on legal monsters. It is the design of the modern natural law tradition with its monsters, from Hobbes to Pufendorf, that explains most differences with the political use of the formula handed down from the tradition, i.e. the monster as a symbol of resistance, which is still used in the late 1500s in the *Vindiciae contra tyrannos*.[6]

Design concerns the ways in which humans shape not only objects, processes, or environments, but also legal and political ideas (Pagallo 2015a). Institutional design has been the bread and butter of generations of scholars over the past 30 years, dealing with the regulation of technology and the 'science of design' (Simon 1996). Pace Hayek, the aim of political design does not necessarily result in despicable forms of constructivism, such as the Soviet Union's economic planning. Indeed, design can aim to tackle the prevarication of human political planning, for example, as occurs

---

the analysis of this section draws on Hayek's distinction between cosmos and taxis with some caution. Although political constructivism, institutional design, and geometry clarify pillars of the modern natural law school — that can be reasonably opposed to the tenets of the classical natural law school — critical differences persist between Hobbes and Pufendorf, Rousseau and Kant, among others. All in all, Hayek even claims that "Locke's contention that in a free society all law must be 'promulgated' or 'announced' beforehand would seem to be a product of the constructivist idea of all law as being deliberately made" (Hayek ed. 2021, at 149).

[5] Scholars usually agree that Locke breaks with the classical natural law tradition, although they disagree on how to interpret his modern natural law views. See for example Laslett's review of Macpherson (1962) in Laslett (1964). An overall view of scholarly disagreements in Euchner (2017).

[6] The main difference is that Hobbes and Pufendorf refer to legal, political and institutional monsters whilst rejecting every kind of right to resistance. By contrast, as argued in § 212 of the second treatise, Locke defends the right to resist because every government's break-up does not entail the civil society's dissolution. We return to Locke's right to resist below in Chapter 10.

with Locke's "many wrong and inconvenient laws". The multiple 'social covenants' of the modern natural law tradition show that design not only has multiple aims, but it is also a regulatory system of its own — for better or worse. This normativity has become even more trivial in the age of artificial intelligence. Back in the late 1990s, Lawrence Lessig used to summarise such normative effects of technological design with a catchphrase that soon turned viral, 'code is law' (Lessig 1999).

Hayek's historiographical problems with the equalisation of the modern natural law tradition with political constructivism remind us that every design has its own style and personal touch. Hayek simply overlooked crucial differences among the great minds of the 1600s and 700s. It is remarkable that, from Hobbes and Pufendorf to Spinoza and Rousseau — along with many other philosophers, the so-called 'minors' of this tradition, such as Christian Wolff — were all openly inspired by the methods and working ways of geometry. However, this common source of inspiration, which went hand-in-hand with fundamental contributions in mathematics, such as Leibniz's infinitesimal calculus, often led to opposite conclusions in the moral, legal, and political domains. Therefore, although the medium may be the message, those formulas, such as 'state of nature' and 'social contract', can convey multiple theses as different as the manifold schools of the modern natural law tradition. The spectrum of hermeneutical possibilities spans from human rights to absolutism.

To prevent generalisations, attention should be drawn to how the formula on 'legal monsters' has been employed differently in modern times. This stance helps clarify three critical points:

i) The difference between classical and modern natural law schools, i.e. the starting point of this section;
ii) Further differences among philosophers of the modern natural law tradition, i.e. the claim of this section;
iii) Some continuities between the modern natural law tradition and our times, i.e. the assumption of this chapter.

The level of abstraction on the legal monsters of the modern natural law tradition can fruitfully start with the illustration of a specific style of monster, i.e. Pufendorf's. We first met his ideas in Chapter 4 when dealing with the philosophical sources of the 1948 Universal Declaration. Pufendorf's monster not only differs from those of Plato and Cicero, or Coke and the *Vindiciae*, but also from Hobbes' biblical monsters Leviathan and Behemoth. Pufendorf's meaning of the formula 'legal monster' anticipates some of today's uses in accordance with certain tenets of institutional design. His ideas persist notwithstanding open debates of legal theory between natural law advocates and supporters of legal positivism. To appreciate this influence, it is worth mentioning that scholars often debate who should be considered the 'father of modern natural law'. Until the late 1800s, Hugo Grotius was often presented as such a father (Bobbio 1993). Although scholars have changed their minds and today consider Hobbes as "one of the fathers of modern philosophy and political theory" (Martinich 1999) — which includes modern natural law theories and contractualism — it seems fair to say that Pufendorf should be similarly deemed a founding father of the modern natural law tradition, and not only a grandfather of the Universal Declaration of Human Rights.[7]

The following section aims to support this claim as regards, also but not only, Pufendorf's ideas about monsters.

6.2 Monstrous Institutions

Pufendorf's mathematical approach to morals, politics, and the law can be traced back to his early academic years under the direction of Erhard Weigel, professor in Jena since 1653. Weigel published works on "philosophical mathematics", such as *Analysis Aristotelica ex Euclide restituta* (1658); *Idea mathesis universale cum speciminibus inventionum mathematicarum* (1669); and the *Ethica Euclidea* in 1674. Pufendorf's first works present arguments on moral demonstrations and legal axioms clearly developed under Weigel's mathematical influence. The same holds for another great scholar (maybe the greatest) of that era, i.e. Leibniz. In 1663, a 17 year old Leibniz visited Weigel in Jena. In that very year, Leibniz published his own first research in 'legal mathematics', obtaining the title of magister in philosophy at the University of Leipzig. In his thesis, *Specimen quaestionum philosophicarum ex iure collectarum*, Leibniz quotes Pufendorf's first major work, *Elements of Universal Jurisprudence* from 1660. The common aim is to attain demonstrative certitude in legal affairs and moral matters, thus supplementing methods and syllogisms of Aristotelian logic (Pagallo 2016). This is the German context in which, from Pufendorf to the non-contractualist Leibniz, they inherited and confronted the ideas of Descartes and Hobbes.

In particular, Pufendorf integrated the geometrical approach to morals and politics with the study of history and empirical evidence, which provided a realistic view of the contemporary events of his own troubled life. In his masterpiece of 1672, *Of the Law of Nature and Nations*, Pufendorf aimed to attain the "certainty of moral science" as the ground on which the constitution and legislation of commonwealths should lie. In his phrasing:

> But, besides this Reason, which the Goodness of God will not permit us to doubt of; there is still another drawn from the Nature of the Thing itself and which alone would be of Force enough to convince any reasonable Person, of the Possibility of reducing the Science of Morality to a System, as well connected, as those of Geometry, for example, or Mechanicks; and founded on as certain Principles. (Pufendorf ed. 1729, chapter II)[8]

---

[7] Some scholars have gone even further claiming that "if Smith can be called the father of modern economics... Pufendorf can be called the grandfather": see Saether (2017). We can skip this further claim in this context.

[8] Pufendorf's argument "besides this reason" echoes Grotius' claim in his 1625 *On the Law of War and Peace*, according to which, "even when God were assumed not to exist", the principles of natural law would stand: *etsi deus non daretur*. Pufendorf quotes time and again Grotius in *Of the Law of Nature and Nations*.

On this basis, Pufendorf defines the 'state of nature' as a geometry of human passions, just as Hobbes had done before him. Contrary to the English philosopher, however, Pufendorf insists on the functioning of cooperative institutions — the cosmos side of the law, such as language and contracts, family and property — although admitting that these forces are not robust enough to establish a peaceful body politic. From a methodological point of view, to establish a "civil society" or commonwealth through a social covenant, Pufendorf formalises principles and definitions of law and politics, drawing on axioms. There are several absolute requirements that humans have for other humans. The first natural law represents the condition of every social life: "do not injure another"; however, in case of damage, there must be reparation. Pufendorf develops definitions and observations hinging on this natural law basis. His style consists of a complex normative network of concepts and principles on rights and duties, prohibitions and obligations, designed for computing the legal system as much as Leibniz was trying to do in those very years. The all-encompassing focus of the modern natural law theorist comprehends moral duties and moral entities, the nature of promises and pacts, content and conditions of promises, agents concerned with contracting obligations for other men, property and dominion, wills and testaments, usucapion and prescription, up to the production of the 'civil sovereignty' with different forms of commonwealth, sovereign properties and duties, and the rights of war. It is no exaggeration that Pufendorf set the standard of moral assessment and legal expertise for generations of scholars in positive law and legal theory in civil — as opposed to common — law (Seidler 2021).

Against this theoretical framework, we can further appreciate Pufendorf's assessment of *The Present State of Germany* introduced in Chapter 5. The political structure, or constitution, of the German Holy Roman Empire was so arbitrary and irregular that Pufendorf called it a monster.[9] So goes Pufendorf's argument:

> There is now nothing left for us to say, but that Germany is an Irregular Body, and like some misshapen Monster, if, at least, it be measured by the common Rules of Politicks and Civil Prudence, and that nothing similar to it, in my opinion, exists anywhere else on the whole globe. (Pufendorf ed. 2007, at IV, § 9)

Pufendorf's "misshapen Monster" is particularly relevant to this history of ideas on legal monsters because it established a new meaning for the formula.[10] The old

---

[9] Pufendorf's theses gave rise to a broad and lively debate. Among his many critics, it is worth mentioning Leibniz's comments in *De jure suprematus ac legationis* from 1671. In addition to general ideas on sovereignty and justice, the reasons for the disagreement mostly revolved around duties of esteem in diplomatic relations. See Piro (2011), and Blank (2021). Several decades later, in 1756, Voltaire would comment, with his distinctive wit, that the German Holy Roman Empire was "neither holy nor Roman nor an empire". See Voltaire (ed. 2012, at I, 683). The Empire would finally end on 6 August 1806.

[10] Scholars have stressed that "monstrum" had a rather ordinary descriptive meaning in Pufendorf's times, i.e. "simply equivalent to irregular" (Seidler 2007, at xviii). Pufendorf previously used the word in *De rebus gestis Philippi Amyntae filio* from 1664 (at § 3), and later in *Addenda* to *De republica irregulari* –a part of the *Dissertationes academicae selectiores* – in 1675. However, the empire's apologists deemed Pufendorf's "misshapen Monster" as deeply offensive since, traditionally, the formula was employed to blame tyrannic institutions. Pufendorf deleted the scandalous

political image of tyrants and enemies of the body politic as monsters is supplemented with an institutional meaning that revolves around the balance between the powers of the sovereign state. The standard is set by geometrical clarity and the elegance and beauty of mathematics. Contrary to Plato's tyrants, Cicero's corrupt governors, or Coke's traitors, this new monster needs no face because it corresponds to the irregularities of geometrical lines, i.e. the design of the body politic that can generate or ease the arbitrariness of politics. As a result, Pufendorf's monster is concerned with the role of authority and not that of any specific human.[11] The two political meanings of the formula — that of classical natural law and of Pufendorf's modern natural law — are thus cumulative: they can reinforce each other but may also regard two different kinds of problems. On the one hand, Cicero's corrupts or Coke's traitors do not entail any kind of institutional monstrosity, but instead can be appreciated just against the tenets of a sound institution. On the other hand, by deeming a commonwealth monstrous, the problem of tyrants and arbitrary rulers is anticipated because the focus is on that which can trigger them, such as an uncertain or chaotic distribution of competences among the state bodies; an improper balance between such powers of the state; or, a fragile system of safeguards for the protection of individual rights. Alas, human history is full of such examples.

However, although they interplay, the monsters of the classical and modern natural law traditions should be distinguished and examined separately. Their differentiation is critical — especially in the civil law context of continental Europe — considering that some of Pufendorf's ideas set the standards for moral evaluation and legal assessment over the following decades. Since the early 1700s, references to legal monsters in legal and philosophical essays, or political pamphlets, should be divided into two groups, i.e. the group of those concerned with the classical natural law tradition and the group hinging on Pufendorf's authority. Therefore, going back to some of the examples presented in Chapter 5, the 1736 Royal Order regulating the appointment of Deans to the University of Valencia refers to "monsters contrary to art and nature" in accordance with some teachings of Aristotle and Thomas Aquinas: the focus is

term from the second edition. Still, the new meaning of the formula was meant to stay. In the 1700s, Pufendorf's *The Present State of Germany* was considered "as one of the best short guides to the nature and politics of the empire" (Whaley 2022). According to Zedler's *Universal-Lexicon* (Leipzig and Halle, 1745, vol. XXI), monstrum meant not only "that which is or is born against nature", but also, "that which hides or changes the true origin of its birth by assuming a foreign shape" (in Seidler 2007, at xviii).

[11] This faceless monster, so to speak, is also at work in other legal contexts and even for opposite reasons. The differentiation, for example, is crucial in Locke's argument in support of a right to resist in the *Two Treatises*: resistance and opposition are "not to persons, but authority, which is founded only in the constitutions and laws of the government" (*op. cit.*, II, § 226). The same differentiation holds for William Blackstone's criticism against unscrupulous politicians half a century after Locke's remarks. We return to Blackstone's institutional monsters in the next section of this chapter. Such differences between Pufendorf and Locke, between civil law and common law, remind us of the manifold schools of the modern natural law tradition and how the spectrum of hermeneutical possibilities spans from the protection of natural rights to the defence of sovereign powers against any right to resist. Pufendorf's ideas on the right to resist are illustrated below in notes 23 and 24 of this chapter.

on the binding force of customs and the institutional wisdom handed down by the tradition.[12] Vice versa, the 1739 Treuer's volume on "a German monster of arbitrary territorial law" refers to Pufendorf's meaning of legal and political design through the mediation of Christian Thomasius: the attention is drawn to the rationality and logic of the whole institutional construct.[13] The same differentiation holds more than two centuries later. In the late 1990s, some scholars still presented irregularities and arbitrariness of political institutions — such as, for example, the European Union — as a monstrous entity (see Chapter 9). This is, arguably, the meaning that Pufendorf made popular with his work and authority since the late 1600s. Scholars may refer to an institutional monster, such as the European Union, without any necessary connection with the tragedy of Plato's monsters, or that of Sir Walter Raleigh's trial, because what is at stake does not concern any binding custom or traditional wisdom but rather the geometrical soundness of the whole institutional enterprise.

To be sure, the classical political meaning of the formula on monsters that, from time to time, sums up the tragedy of the human condition persists. This use of the formula may overlap with the Pufendorf-like institutional meaning of a legal monster. The same holds true for Montesquieu's new meaning of the formula in the mid-1700s. In the *Spirit of the Laws* (III, 9), referring to Persia, the claim is that "one cannot speak of these monstrous governments without shuddering" (Montesquieu ed. 1989, at 28). The crucial difference with the classical natural law tradition is that monstrous institutions no longer refer to tyrannies, although considered as a synonym of "the violence of the government", which establishes "things that run counter to a nation's way of thinking" (*op. cit.*, XIX, 3, at 309). Instead, what is monstrous becomes synonymous with despotism. "Despotism was transformed into a general category which included tyranny, oligarchy and ochlocracy" (Turchetti 2008, at 172).[14]

These different meanings of monstrosity coalesced in the later condemnation of totalitarian institutions and dictatorships. For example, Lon Fuller, arguably among the most important advocates of natural law theory in the late 1950s, referred to the abhorrence of the Nazi regime as monstrous (Fuller 1958). In *Positivism and Fidelity*, Fuller deems a Nazi 1934 statute a "legislative monstrosity" (*op. cit.*, at 654); a secret act enacting the wholesale killings in concentration camps the greatest "legal monstrosity" (at 651); and the improvement of planning authorities

[12] See above note 9 of Chapter 5.

[13] See above note 10 of Chapter 5. Treuer was in fact a student of Thomasius (von Friedeburg 2003). Some scholars have depicted Thomasius as "the uncritical admirer of Pufendorf" (Chroust 1979, at 79). For a more balanced opinion, see however Riley (2009). Leaving aside Thomasius' intellectual debts to Pufendorf, Treuer's *Monstrvm Arbitrarii Iuris Territorialis* can be understood as an example of monstrous institutional design that, nevertheless, distinguishes between the assessment of the whole body politic and the evaluation of specific normative acts. We return to this differentiation in the next section of this chapter.

[14] Montesquieu's new views have been often criticised and even deemed monstrous. For example, "the assumption that human nature is everywhere the same, the only variable being the physical environment... is the source of Montesquieu's monstrous and historically barren error in attributing all human differences to geographic environment" (Stromberg 1951, at 301). Although such criticism is clearly exaggerated, we can dismiss it in this volume. This criticism belongs to the class of scholarly opinions that deem others' philosophical ideas on monstrosity as monstrous.

lowering the market value of the land on which a house was built "an unmortgageable monstrosity" (at 665). The monstrosity of certain normative acts in the Nazi era could indeed be understood against a political regime which was overall monstrous. However, the different meanings of monster must be differentiated because, drawing on Pufendorf's teachings, an institution can be deemed monstrous regardless of fear and terror, tragedies and scandals, wars and spies. Contrary to the old tyrants of the tradition and Montesquieu's despots, the threshold of institutional monstrosity may entail a Pufendorf-like meaning of reason in the design of political organisations: the question is more about coherence and congruence in such a design than blatant violations of human rights and fundamental legal principles.[15] Correspondingly, the difference between Pufendorf's monster of institutional anomalies and irregularities, and the political monsters of both the classical natural law tradition and modern claims on despotism begs the question of how to grasp their interplay.

As regards Pufendorf's legal philosophy, it seems fair to concede that it deeply anchors the institutional design into human nature: we noted this approach in Chapter 4, regarding Pufendorf's notion of dignity as a forerunner of the human rights tradition. Still, we do not have to buy into Pufendorf's assumptions on natural law theory to admit that a certain body politic is monstrous regardless of moral arguments. For example, by distinguishing requisites and functions of the law — that is, between what the law is supposed to be and what the law is meant to do — Herbert Hart suggested that discussions of legal theory should focus on the means chosen for effective legislation, which appears only as moral as the enterprise they make possible (Hart 1965). By drawing attention to how a body politic can either contradict its necessary conditions of existence, or its proper ways of functioning, four monsters follow as a result of this distinction:

i) The political meaning of the formula handed down from the classical natural law tradition with the equalisation of tyrants and monsters;
ii) The modern meaning of the formula which can be traced back to Montesquieu with the equalisation of despots and monsters;
iii) The institutional meaning of legal monster established with Pufendorf's modern natural law theory;
iv) The functional meaning of the institutional monster under scrutiny in more recent debates of legal philosophy.

This differentiation is critical for a theory of legal monsters because it casts light on the further assessment of single normative acts. In the classical natural law tradition, as well as in modern representations of despotic regimes, the aim to distinguish monsters from decent institutions entails that monstrous practices or normative acts go hand-in-hand with the existence of monstrous institutions. By contrast, the institutional and functional meanings of the formula may entail that also decent institutions can adopt monstrous acts. Since the 1700s, this further differentiation has not only

[15] See for example Allott (2003). We return to this differentiation between congruous institutional design and the protection of human rights below in Chapter 9. As suggested in this section, the distinction can also be grasped according to Hart's differentiation between law and morals, between requirements and functions of the law. This differentiation is under scrutiny below in Chapter 8.

spread among followers of the modern natural law tradition but also in some variants of the classical school. We noted this use of the formula with the distinction between monstrous institutions and monstrous acts with the appointment of Deans in Valencia. Therefore, whether dealing with some tenets of classical natural law, modern natural law, or variants of legal positivism today, the legal assessment of acts, rather than whole institutions, demands a different class of requirements on monstrosity. Such conditions are not only related to the distinction between decent institutions and monstrous laws, but also, to the further analysis of what turns 'bad laws' into monsters: a new level of abstraction.

The aim of the next section is to examine what a monstrous legislation may look like.

6.3 Monstrous Normative Acts

Formulas on monsters as a source of legal criticism, opposition, and resistance must be used selectively. The target of such criticism, opposition and resistance cannot only be the body politic as such, admittedly a rarer case. Instead, the target can be this or that normative act of a commonwealth, i.e. a sovereign state. In the 1700s, drawing on the (classical and modern) natural law tradition, the claim used to be that acts of lawmakers, or edicts of the authority, were monstrous when they contradicted their nature or essence. This use of the formula is at work in both civil and common law traditions. For example, in *The Absolute Rights of Individuals* from 1753 (Blackstone ed. 1893), William Blackstone discusses the monstrosity of the law that depends on the lawyers' violation of the "oath of office" and "a comprehensive view of their duty to the constitution and laws". Blackstone depicts this state of affairs as "a most monstrous practice… such laws [that] are very frequently urged by men having causes pending, who dare not boldly ask that a law should be made for their particular case, but who do not hesitate to impose upon the legislature, by plausible arguments, the adoption of some general rule, which by a retrospective construction will have the same operation" (Blackstone ed. 1893, at 127).

What turns laws and practices into monsters is thus a vice, or contradiction, that does not necessarily entail the monstrosity of the whole institution. The levels of analysis on monstrous institutions and monstrous laws or practices can — and should accurately — be distinguished. The monster law is neither necessarily associated with a tyrant, nor the necessary consequence of a monstrous body politic. The monstrosity of an edict or a practice can, in fact, be determined regardless of any assessment of the whole jurisdiction or legal system. The assessment is specific, potentially more effective and, all in all, less controversial. Only decent institutions may admit that they not only adopted bad laws but even proper monsters. This is how the formula is still used today, i.e. when scholars dubbed as monstrous either Singapore's 2021 foreign interference bill[16]; the 2022 reform of an international trade agreement[17]; or Italy's 2024 right to image of cultural property.[18]

There have been a few attempts to formalise the principles and conditions according to which certain acts are monstrous (Pagallo 2024). For example, in *The Morality of Law*, Fuller aims to establish the conditions that turn legal rules into genuine laws, namely, what Fuller calls the "internal morality of law" (Fuller 1964). He illustrates his ideas with the image of a fictional king, Rex, to show that every attempt to govern a society would be impossible when departing from eight minimal conditions of law. This perspective can be reversed in this context to flesh out eight cases in which the law looks not simply bad, but rather monstrous. The conjecture is supported by what was stressed above in the previous section concerning the meaning of monster as the image of abhorrent institutions, i.e. Fuller's "legislative monstrosity" of the Nazi era (Fuller 1958, at 654), vis-à-vis the greatest "legal monstrosity" of secret acts (*op. cit.*, at 651).

Drawing on Fuller's minimum conditions, the eight new legal monsters are:

(i) A normative act which is particular, i.e. *ad personam* or laid down on an individual basis, rather than for general purposes;
(ii) A normative act which is secret, rather than public;
(iii) A normative act which is retroactive, rather than prospective;
(iv) A normative act which is unintelligible, rather than decently clear;
(v) A normative act which is incongruous or inconsistent, rather than non-contradictory;
(vi) A normative act which is subject to over-frequent revision, rather than resistant to changing circumstances;
(vii) A normative act which defies human nature, rather than being feasible to obey; and,
(viii) A normative act which is randomly dispensed, rather than coherently administered, as regards the obvious meaning of the law.

There are myriad possible examples to illustrate all classes of these legal monsters. Consider the first of Fuller's minimal conditions of the law vis-à-vis such legislation of the Italian Parliament as Act no. 140 from 2003; Act no. 46 from 2006; and Act no. 124 from 2008; all under Silvio Berlusconi's governments (Pagallo 2015b, at 39–40). Those acts aimed to protect the particular interests of the political leader under the guise of a general legislative act. The Italian Constitutional Court declared such acts void with rulings no. 13 from 2004; no. 26 from 2007; and no. 262 from 2009. (These cases raise the further issue of whether court rulings, in addition to acts of lawmakers, can be monstrous. It seems evident that regardless of different legal traditions and jurisdictions, for example, between civil law and common law,

[16] See at https://rsf.org/en/singapore-s-foreign-interference-bill-legal-monstrosity-totalitarian-leanings

[17] For the "investment law's monstrous reform" see Neufeld (2022).

[18] See at https://www.finestresullarte.info/en/opinions/a-legal-monster-roams-italy-the-right-to-the-image-of-cultural-property

case law and courts' doctrines can be monstrous as much as acts of parliaments can occasionally be.)

This strict meaning of 'legal monster' — referred to this or that normative act or court ruling — is very popular today (Pagallo 2024). However, this popularity of the formula entails its own risks because those who use it may do so fleetingly. The monstrosity of certain normative acts may depend on assumptions of natural law schools, either classical or modern; or, vice versa, on some teachings of legal positivism (Raz 1979). For example, in his review of Fuller's book *The Morality of Law*, Hart asked in what sense Fuller's conditions of genuine law could ever be called a "morality" since they seemed more like means for effective legislation (Hart 1965). This diatribe has practical relevance (Romano 2013). Remarkably, Italian Courts, from the Court of Cassation to some administrative and civil or criminal tribunals, have intended to clarify their own use of the metaphor on monsters since the threat is that the very use of the formula can trigger further issues of legal certainty. Therefore, in a ruling from 2009, the highest jurisdiction in the country, i.e. the Italian Court of Cassation, intended to put order in the use of the image by defining a legal monster as every act that presents "uncomprehensible legal solutions that defy the logic of the system".[19]

However, what the "logic of the system" is, remains controversial. Scholars and courts may converge in the opinion that a certain normative act is monstrous, and yet, it can be tricky to determine the requirements of such a monstrosity and, moreover, whether a monstrous normative act belongs to a decent or monstrous commonwealth or 'civil society'. The problem has arguably opposed the classical and modern schools of natural law as much as the advocates of modern legal positivism against the tenets of such natural law schools. Corollaries of legal positivism, such as the dogma of positive law and legislative normativism as the unique or main sources of the system, precluded every discussion about the monstrosity of normative acts and institutions for centuries.[20] In addition, we noted in the first section of this chapter that, *pace* Hayek, even the aim to attain a geometrical demonstration of the moral and legal principles that shall govern the 'civil society' did not prevent advocates of the modern natural law tradition from reaching opposite conclusions.

These uncertainties affect the overall "logic of the system", either considering different notions of monster at the institutional level, or how they may interplay with the reasons that make certain normative acts look monstrous in a particular jurisdiction. As a result, attention must be drawn to this 'legal logic' as a meta-requirement of what may make the law and its normative acts look monstrous. The

[19] The ruling of Cassazione penale (Italy) is from Section I, 3 March 2009, no. 17854. Further rulings on monsters include the united sections of Cassazione civile, 21 June 2010, no. 14890; Cassazione penale section II, 5 December 2012, no. 853; Cassazione civile section III, 4 April 2019, no. 9324; Cassazione civile section VI, 8 May 2020, no. 8658; and Cassazione penale section VI, 21 February 2024, no. 20677. Among the rulings of Italy's administrative tribunals, see T.A.R. Friuli-Venezia Giulia section I- Trieste, 28 October 2013, n. 530. Regarding ordinary jurisdictions, see Tribunale section III in Como from 27 March 2018.

[20] We return to the tenets of legal positivism which precluded any discussion on monsters in Chapter 8.

next section aims to show why and how this 'logic' is the bane of modern natural law schools.

6.4 The Bane

Both ancient constitutionalism and the modern natural law tradition revolve around a series of critical dualisms as their own logic. In ancient constitutionalism, dualisms were summed up with formulas such as the 'king's two bodies' — i.e. the body natural and the body politic of the king — or according to the interplay between *lex regia* and *lex digna*, or between *gubernaculum* and *jurisdictio*, that is, grasping the body politic as a *dominium politicum et regale*. The medieval history of these formulas has often been understood in connection with the birth of the modern notion of sovereignty in the 1500s.[21] However, such dualisms also refer to the opposition to every form of royal absolutism. For example, in the mid-1200s, Henry de Bracton was concerned with dualisms to determine whether the King should be deemed above or under the law, instead of father or son of justice. Although Bracton admits that there is no way to legally enforce the limits of the King's powers under current law, in *On the Laws of England*, he repeatedly insists that the King is under God and the law (Kantorowicz ed. 2016).

Edward Coke followed suit in the early 1600s. In the *Reports*, mentioning Bracton, Coke opposes the 'natural reason' of the King to the 'artificial reason' of the law. In a series of judicial cases, Chief Justice Coke defines the limits of the royal prerogative in accordance with the principles of the common law. In the *Bonham case*, Coke declares that every act which contradicts the common law is void; in the *Peacham's case*, Coke inspects what we may say were the constitutional grounds of the Royal methods to raise money from his subjects; in the *Case of Commendams*, the dispute regarded the claims of King James to delay trials on the royal prerogative (Drinker Bowen 1985). In the *Reports*, Coke mentions the famous speech he made before the King and all the chief authorities of the Kingdom on 10 November 1607. The speech sums up Coke's dualistic view on English institutions and the stark opposition to every Royal absolutism. So goes Coke's report on the reaction of James:

> The King was greatly offended, and said that he was then under the law, and that it was treason to say such a thing… to which I [Coke] said that Bracton said that the King ought not to be under men, but under God and the law. (in Lee Malcolm 1999, at 18)

[21] An illustrious contemporary of Bracton, Frederick II, i.e. the Holy Roman Emperor, argued that it would be legitimate to reverse the relationship between the king and the law, so that the king, and not the law, should establish who has the right to decide a controversial case. The interpretation of the legal norm concerning the sovereignty of the prince could have brought, in other words, within the scope of the king's prerogatives: see Pagallo (1995, at 240). Also, see McIlwain (ed. 2008), Kantorowicz (ed. 2016), Calasso (1957), and Skinner (1978). Dealing with the political meaning of the image on monsters, the analysis of this section draws the attention to the opposite conclusion: the interplay of *lex regia* and *lex digna*, between *imperium* and people's *potestas*, entails limits to the ruler's powers.

Coke's resistance and opposition to King James is still anchored in historical evidence (the Magna Charta), and the power of legal authority (Bracton). Coke's artificial reason has nothing to do with the geometrical reason of the modern natural law tradition, lest we indulge in more recent hermeneutical narratives on the invention of traditions.[22] In fact, for Coke, resistance and opposition do not rest on moral demonstrations about justice and legal principles, but rather, on case law and authoritative sources: "I said that Bracton said". Instead, in the modern natural law tradition, dualisms and resistance mostly concern how human nature and natural rights may interplay with the political design of civil society. How to combine them in a win-win game is the problem of modern natural law with all its variants. It is not by chance that this is still a Rousseau's problem in the *Social Contract.* On 26 July 1767, Rousseau explains to Mirabeau this problem in a purely geometrical way. In Rousseau's phrasing:

> Here, according to my ideas, is the great problem of politics, which I compare to that of squaring the circle in geometry, and of longitudes in astronomy: To find a form of government that might place the laws above man. (Rousseau ed. 1997, at 269)

Dualisms affect the modern notion of social contract, and it is noteworthy that even Pufendorf's social covenant is itself dual with an intervening decree of sovereignty (Pufendorf ed. 1729). On the one hand, the social agreement is between members of a multitude — the future's citizens — starting prosaically with the assent of family-fathers and patriarchs: they all agree to bond together for mutual security. On the other hand, the second agreement sets up a specific form of civil society, either monarchy, aristocracy, or democracy, so that every future subject agrees to bring itself under this political authority. Pufendorf recognised the emergent powers and qualities of the sovereign: the whole is greater than the part. However, even in this case, Pufendorf establishes a series of conditions and limits to the golden rule, according to which it is the sovereign's right to govern, and it is the subject's duty to obey.[23] Rephrasing the concept with the legislative technique of many lawmakers today, such as the European Parliament and the Council in Brussels, a golden rule is often complemented with a more or less detailed list of exceptions, or derogations. In the case of the modern natural law tradition, it remains to be seen how the limits to the exercise of sovereign powers could ever work and prevail, for example, through the extreme remedy of a right to resist.[24]

---

[22] We return to Coke's controversial constitutional ideas below in Chapter 7.

[23] Such limits and conditions to the subjects' duty to obey may be found in the third chapter of book VII, in *Of the Law of Nature and Nations* (Pufendorf 1729), "on promises and covenants". The claim is that "promises of things impossible are void" (section II); and moreover, focus is on "whether our utmost endeavour is sufficient" (section IV); or, "whether a man be obliged to bear such afflictions as are above man's courage and strength" (V). See Saastamoinen (2006). However, there is no such a thing as a right to resist in Pufendorf. See below the next note of this chapter.

[24] Scholars have often stressed that Pufendorf follows a Hobbesian suit by rejecting every subject's right to resist: see Behme (2002) and Dobelmann (2020). Interestingly, however, in the ninth chapter of book VIII, in *Of the Law of Nature and Nations* (Pufendorf 1729), it is granted the freedom to leave one's own country, although such a freedom to emigrate does not entail any right to enter into

The aim of this book, however, is not to dissect the dualities and contradictions of modern natural law schools, from Pufendorf to Rousseau. Instead, the intent is to inspect such dualities in connection with probably the most important monsters of modernity, that is, Hobbes' Leviathan and Behemoth. Hobbes addressed the series of moral, legal, and constitutional dualities mentioned in this section, that is, the dualities of ancient and modern constitutionalism that Coke endorsed in his times (the Behemoth), by giving the shape of a biblical monster to the sovereign (the Leviathan). Framing Hobbes' work retrospectively, Karl Marx and Friedrich Engels depicted the English philosopher in *The Holy Family* as a sort of Baconian materialist, although restyled through geometry. In the wording of the *Critique of Critical Criticism*:

> In its further evolution, materialism becomes one-sided. Hobbes is the man who systematizes Baconian materialism. Knowledge based upon the senses loses its poetic blossom, it passes into the abstract experience of the geometrician. Physical motion is sacrificed to mechanical or mathematical motion; geometry is proclaimed as the queen of sciences. Materialism takes to misanthropy. If it is to overcome its opponent, misanthropic, fleshless spiritualism, and that on the latter's own ground, materialism has to chastise its own flesh and turn ascetic. (Marx and Engels ed. 1956, at VI,3,d)

In Chapter 5, we noted that, according to Ricoeur, we should consider Marx, together with Nietzsche and Freud, a 'master of suspicion'. Ricoeur's methodological warnings extend to Marx and Engels' interpretation of Hobbes vis-à-vis the teachings of Francis Bacon and the tenets of French materialism.[25] Hobbes' political geometry, detached from the value of experience may, in fact, resemble some approaches of modern natural law theory on moral demonstrations and legal corollaries. After all, it is just Hobbes who affirms in Chapter 20 of the *Leviathan* that "the skill of making, and maintaining Commonwealth, consisteth in certain Rules, as doth Arithmetique and Geometry; not (as Tennis-play) on Practice onely" (Hobbes ed. 2004, at 157). However, a passionate, hot-tempered style persists in Hobbes' argumentation and makes it vibrant even in the post-Marxist, post-materialist times of our digital era. It speaks volumes that Hobbes sums up the gist of his geometrical work against every dualism of ancient and modern constitutionalism, including the tenets of a right to resist, just with the images of those Biblical monsters, such as the Leviathan and the Behemoth.

Those monstrous images, of course, did not emerge in isolation. This chapter has stressed that monsters still played a role in the moral demonstrations and legal principles of the modern natural law tradition. In addition to the image of monsters as tyrants, traitors, and other enemies of the institutions, the focus was on the geometrical design of the civil society as an antidote against monstrous institutions and blatant

another country: see Chetail (2016), and above note 18 of chapter 5 as regards the "basic tension" of today's immigration law. As stressed in the text, the analysis of limits and contradictions in Pufendorf's natural law theory falls outside the scope of this book.

[25] Chapter VI (3, d) of the *Holy Family*, from which the quote on the geometrical Hobbes is taken, is in fact presented as a "critical battle against French materialism". We dwelt on these 'materialistic' ideas, in particular, concerning their views on monsters above in the second section of Chapter 4. Regarding the teachings of Francis Bacon, on the other hand, see below note 15 of Chapter 7 on 'the naturalisation of monsters'.

contradictions of certain normative acts. Unresolved dualisms of legal and political thought had to deal with both kinds of monsters, i.e. those conveyed by the political meaning of the image handed down from the tradition and the institutional meaning of the formula as a source of criticism against arbitrary commonwealths (Hill 1997). However, the rigour of geometrical methods applied to the normative realm did not prevent multiple and even opposite solutions among modern natural law scholars on how to tackle old and new monsters. This is the bane that Hobbes intends to tackle. It remains to be seen why the geometrical terms of Hobbes' own argumentation took the shape of a monster, such as the Leviathan, and how this monster could fix the dualities that modern political geometries could not reconcile, i.e. another monster such as the Behemoth. All in all, scholars must take any reading of the geometrical Hobbes with caution.

References

Allott, P. 2003. Epilogue: Europe and the dream of reason. In *European constitutionalism beyond the state*, ed. J. H. H. Weiler and M. Wind, 202–225. Cambridge: Cambridge University Press.

Behme, T. 2002. Pufendorf's doctrine of sovereignty and its natural law foundations. In *Natural law and civil sovereignty*, ed. I. Hunter and D. Saunders, 43–58. London: Palgrave Macmillan.

Blackstone, W. 1893. Commentaries on the laws of England. In *On the rights of persons*, ed. G. Sharswood, vol. 1. Philadelphia: Lippincott.

Blank, A. 2021. Pufendorf and Leibniz on duties of esteem in diplomatic relations. *Journal of International Political Theory* 18 (2): 186–204.

Bobbio, N. 1993. *Thomas Hobbes and the natural law tradition.* Chicago: University of Chicago Press.

Brutus, S. J. 1924 [1579]. *Vindiciae contra tyrannos. A defense of liberty against tyrants*, trans. Ch. H. McIlwain. London: Bell & Sons.

Calasso, F. 1957. I glossatori e la teoria della sovranità. In *Studio di diritto comune pubblico.* Milan: Giuffrè.

Chetail, V. 2016. Sovereignty and migration in the doctrine of the law of nations: An intellectual history of hospitality from Vitoria to Vattel. *European Journal of International Law* 27 (4): 901–922.

Chroust, A. H. 1979. Some critical remarks about Samuel Pufendorf and his contributions to jurisprudence. *American Journal of Jurisprudence* 24 (1): 72–85.

Constant, B. 2016. The Liberty of the Ancients Compared with that of the Moderns. In *Democracy: A Reader*, ed. R. Blaug and J. Schwarzmantel, 108–110. New York Chichester, West Sussex: Columbia University Press.

Dobelmann, J. 2020. The right to resist in the approach of Samuel Pufendorf's de iure naturae et gentium and de officio hominis et civis. *Archiv für Rechts und Sozialphilosophie* 106 (4): 487–508.

Drinker Bowen, C. 1985 [1956]. *The lion and the throne. The life and times of Sir Edward Coke.* Boston: Little, Brown & Company.

Dunn, J. 1982. *The political thought of John Locke: An historical account of the argument of the 'two treatises of government'.* Cambridge: Cambridge University Press.

Euchner, W. 2017. *John Locke zur Einführung.* Hamburg: Junius Verlag.

Fuller, L. L. 1958. Positivism and fidelity to law: A reply to professor Hart. *Harvard Law Review* 71 (4): 630–672.

Fuller, L. L. 1964. *The morality of law.* revised ed. New Haven, CT: Yale University Press.

Hart, H. L. A. 1965. Book review: Lon Fuller, the morality of law. *Harvard Law Review* 78:1281–1296.

Hayek, F. A. 2021 [1982]. *Law, legislation and liberty: A new statement of the liberal principles of justice and political economy*, ed. J. Shearmur. Chicago: Chicago University Press.

Hill, Ch. 1997. The many-headed monster. In *Intellectual origins of the English revolution–revisited*, ed. Ch. Hill, 327–337. Oxford: Oxford University Press.

Hobbes, Th. 2004 [1651]. *Leviathan*. New York: Barnes & Noble.

Kantorowicz, E. 2016 [1957]. *The king's two bodies: A study in medieval political theology*. Princeton: Princeton University Press.

Laslett, P. 1964. Market society and political theory. *The Historical Journal* 7 (1): 150–154.

Lee Malcolm, J., ed. 1999. *The struggle for sovereignty: Seventeenth-century English political tracts*. Vol. 1. Indianapolis: Liberty Fund.

Lessig, L. 1999. *Code and other laws of cyberspace*. New York: Basic Books.

Locke, J. 1823 [1689]. *Two treatises of government*. London: Tegg & Co.

Macpherson, C. B. 1962. *The political theory of possessive individualism: Hobbes to Locke*. Oxford: Clarendon Press.

Marx, K. and F. Engels 1956 [1844]. *The holy family, or critique of critical criticism*, trans. R. Dixon. Moscow: Foreign Languages Publishing House.

Martinich, A. P. 1999. *Hobbes: A biography*. Cambridge: Cambridge University Press.

McIlwain, Ch. H. 2008 [1940]. *Constitutionalism: Ancient and modern*. Indianapolis: Liberty Fund.

Montesquieu 1989 [1748]. *The spirit of the laws*, trans. A. M. Cohler, B. C. Miller and H. S. Stone. Cambridge: Cambridge University Press.

Neufeld, R. 2022. Investment law's monstrous reform. In *The Oxford handbook of International Trade Law*, ed. D. Bethlehem et al., 2nd ed. Oxford: Oxford University Press.

Pagallo, U. 1995. *Homo homini deus*. Padua: Cedam.

Pagallo, U. 2015a. Good onlife governance: On law, spontaneous orders, and design. In *The onlife manifesto: Being human in a hyperconnected era*, ed. L. Floridi, 161–177. Cham: Springer.

Pagallo, U. 2015b. *Il diritto nell'età dell'informazione*. Turin: Giappichelli.

Pagallo, U. 2016. *Leibniz*. Milan: Kluwer.

Pagallo, U. 2024. Introduction to a theory of legal monsters: From Greco Roman teratology to the EU Artificial Intelligence Act. *i-lex* 17 (1): 53–73.

Piro, F. 2011. Rationality of the irregular. *Political Communities and Constitutional Devices in Leibniz, Studia Leibnitiana* 43 (1): 36–53.

Pufendorf, S. 1729 [1672]. *Of the law of nature and nations*, Carew ed. London: Walthoe et al. publishers.

Pufendorf, S. 2007 [1667]. *The present state of Germany*, trans. E. Bohun. Indianapolis: Liberty Fund.

Raz, J. 1979. *The authority of law*. Oxford: Oxford University Press.

Riley, P. 2009. The legal theory of Pufendorf. In *A treatise of legal philosophy and general jurisprudence*, ed. E. Pattaro et al., 421–431. Dordrecht: Springer.

Romano, B. 2013. Giudizio giuridico e giudizio estetico. In *Da Kant verso Schiller*. Turin: Giappichelli.

Rousseau, J. J. 1997 *Rousseau's social contract and other later political writings*, ed. and trans. V. Gourevitch. Cambridge: Cambridge University Press.

Saastamoinen, K. 2006. Liberty and natural rights in Pufendorf's natural law theory. In *Transformations in medieval and early-modern rights discourse*, ed. V. Mäkinen and P. Korkman, 225–265. Dordrecht: Springer.

Saether, A. 2017. *Natural law and the origin of political economy: Samuel Pufendorf and the history of economics*. London/New York: Routledge.

Seidler, M. 2007. Introduction. In *The present state of Germany*, ed. S. Pufendorf, ix–xxviii. Indianapolis: Liberty Fund.

Seidler, M. 2021. Pufendorf's moral and political philosophy. In *The Stanford Encyclopaedia of philosophy*, ed. E. N. Zalta. available at https://plato.stanford.edu/entrieS/pufendorf-moral/.

Simon, H. A. 1996 [1969]. *The sciences of the artificial.* Cambridge, MA: MIT Press.
Skinner, Q. 1978. The foundations of modern political thought. In *The age of reformation*, vol. 2. Cambridge: Cambridge University Press.
Stromberg, R. N. 1951. History in the eighteenth century. *Journal of the History of Ideas* 12 (2): 295–304.
Turchetti, M. 2008. 'Despotism' and 'Tyranny'. unmasking a tenacious confusion. *European Journal of Political Philosophy* 7 (2): 159–182.
Voltaire 2012 [1756]. *An essay on universal history, the manners, and spirit of nations*, trans. Th. Nugent. London, Nurse: Ulan Press.
von Friedeburg, R. 2003. Natural jurisprudence, argument from history and constitutional struggle in the early enlightenment: The case of Gottlieb Samuel Treuer's polemic against absolutism in 1719. In *Early Modern Natural Law Theories*, ed. T. J. Hochstrasser and P. Schröder, 141–167. Dordrecht: Springer.
von Leyden, W. 1981. *Hobbes and Locke: The politics of freedom and obligation.* New York: Palgrave.
Whaley, J. 2022. Politics and the constitution of the empire. In *The Cambridge companion to Pufendorf*, ed. L. Haakonssen and I. Hunter, 33–59. Cambridge: Cambridge University Press.

Chapter 7
The Monster of Malmesbury

This chapter examines the monsters of Hobbes' reflection, namely, the tenets of his legal and political philosophy (the Leviathan) and the causes of the English civil war (the Behemoth). The analysis illustrates the complexity and manifold understandings of this work: it is the magic of Hobbes' monsters to be open to such many readings and even opposite interpretations. To corroborate the claim, attention is drawn to the interplay between natural and positive law and between morals and Hobbes' definition of sovereignty. Despite hermeneutical disputes that persist to this day, Hobbes remarkably set the standard for the use of the formula on 'legal monsters' in the centuries to come. A long eclipse of the formula would follow in accordance with his theoretical claims.

7.1 The Naturalisation of Monsters

Hobbes shares a common destiny with Rousseau, for both were considered monsters during their lifetimes.[1] As regards Hobbes, the reasons are clear. The philosopher of Malmesbury became the monster of Malmesbury because of Hobbes' extremely controversial and even subversive ideas on the body politic, civil society, or the commonwealth.[2] In 1658, in his review of Hobbes' the *Leviathan*, Bishop John Bramhall summed up this popular opinion by dubbing Hobbes' ideas a "Rebel's Catechism". Although Hobbes used to present himself as an ardent defender of royal rights and an advocate of the absolute character of authority – the sovereign – Bramhall had little difficulty exposing Hobbes' true intentions. Instead of a King's divine right, according to the standard doctrine of that era, the rights of Hobbes' sovereign were grounded in the individuals' natural rights and their 'true liberty'.

[1] We dwelt on Rousseau's monsters and own monstrosity in the third section of Chapter 4.

[2] The epithet 'monster of Malmesbury' was probably coined in "a typically sympathetic sermon from 1679" (Parkin 2007, at 335).

U. Pagallo, *A Theory of Legal Monsters: Repression, Resistance, Rebellion*, Philosophical Studies Series 161, https://doi.org/10.1007/978-3-032-10771-8_7

The sovereign's right was ultimately defined by human power, or *potentia* (Bramhall ed. 1844).[3]

To further put Hobbes' rebel ideas into perspective, the comparison with Robert Filmer is instructive: Filmer was born the same year as Hobbes, i.e. in 1588, the year of the Spanish attempt to invade England with the "Invincible Army". Sons of the same era, Hobbes and Filmer represent the two ends of a spectrum of natural law theories. Filmer epitomises the orthodoxy with his ideas on paternal power and the divine right of the King, against which Hobbes embodies a radical departure from the tradition. It is not by chance that decades later, in 1689, when Locke published the *Two Treatises of Government*, he ignored Hobbes and devoted the entire first treatise to a harsh criticism of Filmer's ideas.[4] It is against this backdrop of English political philosophy and the spread of modern natural law theories that we can properly start appreciating Hobbes' Leviathan. Although Filmer's ideas have fallen into oblivion, his opinions allow us to understand both Locke's severe criticisms and the monstrosity of Hobbes' ideas in the eyes of his contemporaries.[5]

Filmer likely began to write the *Patriarcha, or The Natural Power of Kings,* between 1628 and 1632 (Tuck 1986). The book was probably completed before the outburst of the Civil War in 1642 and yet, it was published only decades later, after the Restoration in 1680. In his work, Filmer criticises the assumptions of modern natural law theory, especially the theses of Hugo Grotius, to stress that the ultimate power to establish a government does not rest on the people and their abstract natural rights, but rather, on the natural and divine right of the King, supported by the authority of the Holy Scriptures. This theory was extremely popular during the years of the Civil War, expressing the need for continuity in the life of the country.[6] The same success held after the Civil War: the King's power is natural, not artificial; absolute, not limited;

---

[3] In Bramhall's opinion, the problem does not only regard the interplay between power and the law. Also, the issue is methodological because, *pace* Hobbes, state policy "is not all like Arithmetic and Geometry, which are altogether abstracted from matter, but much more like Tennis play… There is no room for liberty in Arithmetic and Geometry". See also Bowle (1969, at 120). In addition to the criticisms of his compatriots, mentioned in later notes of this chapter, criticisms levelled at Hobbes also came from his contemporaries in continental Europe, including Leibniz. Like Bramhall, Leibniz emphasises Hobbes' contradictory ideas on power and political authority, linking such ideas to the English philosopher's materialism and a mechanistic understanding of nature. See Cairns (1946) and Friedrich (1966). This kind of debate continues today, for example, with the interpretation of Hobbes as supporter of a *de facto* theory of obligation (Skinner 1974). We return to this debate in the third section of this chapter.

[4] According to Peter Laslett in his *Introduction* to the *Patriarcha* (Laslett 1949), "in this period (1681/8) of seven years the thought of Sir Robert Filmer turned the *ipsissima verba* of the established order… By 1688, therefore, the cult of Filmer had become an organic part of the cult of monarchical legitimacy" (*op. cit.*, at 34). For the development of Locke's ideas in these turbulent times of English history see Ashcraft (1986).

[5] Contemporary critics to Hobbes, admittedly, include "forerunners of the Whig tradition", such as Philip Hunton and George Lawson, whose *Examination of the political part of Mr. Hobbs his Leviathan* is from 1657. An overall view in Bowle (1969).

[6] According to John Neville Figgis (1922), "the singularly orderly character of English constitutional development… would not have been obtained but for the influence of this doctrine" (*op. cit.*, at 146). In the opinion of Laslett, Filmer's ability was "to combine the subtleties of the doctrine of

paternal, not strictly political. This paternalism is in full display in Chapter VII of the *Patriarcha*, in which Filmer insists on the "agreement" of royal and paternal power: "As the Father over one family, so the King, as Father over many families, extends his care to preserve, feed, clothe, instruct and defend the whole commonwealth" (Filmer 1680, at 13).

By contrast, the ultimate source of legitimate power, in Hobbes' opinion, has to do with a social contract. Since the introduction of the *Leviathan*, Hobbes explains that the biblical monster stands for any commonwealth, state, or Roman civitas, the crucial difference with the classical natural law tradition being that such a body politic is an "artificial man" (Hobbes ed. 2004, at xxxvii). Hobbes substantially develops the theses discussed a few years earlier in *De Cive* (Hobbes ed. 2003). The parties to the social contract are the individuals or, more specifically, each individual who unilaterally gives up his claims at the 'state of nature'. Although scholars still discuss the role of Hobbes' sovereign – who is not a party to such a contract – what is striking about the Hobbesian state of nature, that is, the political anthropology on which both the social contract and the commonwealth lie, is the potential conflict among individuals in this state. To illustrate the potential state of war in *De Cive*, Hobbes uses the 'human wolf' formula that the Roman playwright Plautus coined around 200 BC.[7]

The fact that Hobbes employs the adage may have caused a scandal among the bigots of the time, including supporters of the idea that the King was the father of his subjects, the shepherd of the (lost) sheep.[8] By the mid-1600s, however, the image of the man as a wolf to other man was commonplace. Erasmus of Rotterdam made the adage popular with the many editions of his *Essays* in the early 1500s, probably coupling for the first time the formula of the 'human wolf', *homo homini lupus*, with its opposite *homo homini deus* (Pagallo 1995, at 339). In the late 1500s, the double formula is at work in Montaigne's *Essays* to stress the blessing and curse of every marriage[9]; whereas the image of the human-wolf is still equalised with the political monsters of the tradition, for example, in the *Vindiciae contra Tyrannos*.[10]

---

sovereignty with the crude assumptions of conventionalism patriarchalism, and he might have been less effective had he been less naïve" (Laslett 1949, at 31).

[7] See above note 13 of Chapter 2.

[8] For example, Reverend John Eachard, in *Mr. Hobbes' state of nature considered in a dialogue*, claims that the assumption "man as arrant wolfe" is contrary to experience: see Bowle (1969, at 193).

[9] Indeed, in the phrasing of Montaigne, marriage is "une convention à laquelle se raporte bien à point ce qu'on dict, homo homini ou Deus ou lupus" (Montaigne ed. 1965, at 852). In the opinion of Hiram Haydn, this "double concept is a Renaissance motif" (Haydn 1950, at 406). Haydn also stresses the popularity of the adages in England, for example, in John Owen's *Epigrammata* from 1612, and years earlier, i.e. in 1592, in an unpublished essay by John Dee: "Certain Considerations, and conferring together, of these three sentences, (anciently accounted as Oracles) Nosce te ipsum: Homo Homini Deus: Homo Homini Lupus" (in Haydn 1950, at 406).

[10] See above note 1 of Chapter 6. Admittedly, the image of the human-wolf was not only used according to the political aims of the Monarchomachs. Also, the formula was employed or criticised in connection with the discovery of the 'new world' and the colonisation of the 'barbarians' by Christians. What was at stake, in particular, concerned whether the "Indios" had the right – even

No surprise then if, in 1642, in the dedication of *On the Citizen*, Hobbes uses the twofold adage to sum up his own doctrine:

> There are two maxims which are surely both true: Man is a God to Man, and Man is a wolf to Man. The former is true of the relations of citizens with each other, the latter of relations between commonwealths. (Hobbes 2003, at 3–4)

What is less evident in Hobbes' use of this well-known dual adage is the relationship between the wolf-man of his anthropology and the image later employed in the *Leviathan*, i.e. the identification of the sovereign with a monster. To understand such an interplay between Hobbes' anthropology and the monsters of the political reflection, we have to trace this connection back to Aristotle's 'naturalisation of the monster'. In *Generation of Animals*, as noted in Chapter 2, Aristotle examines humans with congenital disabilities, classifying them as 'monsters' within the domain of physics and natural science. Vice versa, in the field of politics and practical science, Aristotle dismisses the old monsters of the tradition, from the Tragedians to Plato, replacing them with a beast. This transformation of Plato's political monsters into the beasts of political thought became widespread in Roman antiquity and gained further popularity in the late Middle Ages and the Renaissance. In the early 1300s, for example, monsters and dreadful beasts crowd Dante Alighieri's *Inferno,* and still, it is noteworthy that Dante's political and legal reflection concerns humans who may well turn into wild animals rather than monsters.[11]

Two centuries later, in the early 1500s, Machiavelli completed the naturalisation of the monster. Machiavelli's work is full of animals to depict a doctrine of human power in which beasts, rather than monsters, are protagonists in line with Aristotle's *Politics.* What changes in Machiavelli's *Prince* is, however, radical. The Prince must not control the worse part through the better part of every man, as still occurs in Alighieri following the teachings of the Master of those who know. Instead, it is all about making the Prince a mix of man and beast. The aim is to depict how politics really works, rather than what the body politic should ideally be, i.e. the subject matter of the *Florentine Histories* (published posthumously in 1532).[12] In the wording of *The Prince*'s Chapter 18, on whether a prince should remain true to his word:

> It should be understood that there are two types of fighting: one with laws and the other with force. The first is most suitable for men, the second is most suitable for beasts, but it

though they were "infidels" – to claim the legitimate ownership of their lands and possessions. See De Vitoria (ed. 1967, at 80–81). We will note below in the next section of this chapter that Hobbes extends the formula *homo homini lupus* to certain Indian tribes in North America.

[11] The beast can, of course, bring along a monstrous trait. As Dante writes at the end of *De Monarchia*: "O human race, in how many storms and misfortunes, in how many shipwrecks must you be tormented, since, having become a many-headed beast, you are toiled in conflicting disparities, unhealthy in both intellect and in affection". The English translation is mine, drawing on the critical edition of the Latin text in Alighieri (2021).

[12] Scholars often stress a fundamental parallelism between *Principe* and *Discorsi.* In both cases, what is at stake is the Machiavellian teaching of 'virtue' either to the prince or to the whole political community. See Skinner (1981). Yet, for better or worse, this led Machiavelli to conceive the liberty of the political community as a form of self-government which soon clashed against the hard facts of his own city's history. See Chabod (1964, at 91).

> often happens that the first is not enough, which requires resorting to the second. Therefore, it is necessary for a prince to know how to act both as a man and a beast. (Machiavelli ed. 2014)[13]

From the mid-1500s and throughout the 1600s, the centrality of power in human affairs earned Machiavelli the English nickname 'old Nick', meaning the devil in person – but not a monster.[14] Hobbes was well aware of this tradition of political realism. He was introduced to 'Old Nick' during his years at Chatsworth House in the 1620s as a secretary of Sir Francis Bacon, the former Lord Chancellor. Bacon would even declare that that young secretary from Malmesbury was the only one who could understand what he, Bacon, used to say in those sad years (Aubrey 1898, at 331), i.e. after Bacon's political failure following the first constitutional impeachment in modern history. The Chief Prosecutor against the King's Chancellor was none other than Sir Edward Coke. After the trial – in which Coke was strangely kind to Bacon, despite the 17 indictments against the Lord Chancellor (Drinker Bowen 1985, at 385) – Bacon transmitted to that young scholar, Hobbes, his ideas on sovereignty, legal monism and, of course, *homo homini deus* and *homo homini lupus* (Pagallo 1998).

Hobbes absorbs the naturalisation of the monster in his talks with Bacon and adapts it to his new views on science, politics, and legal geometry.[15] Hobbes' wolf illustrates what is typical of his social contract, namely, the fact that individuals,

[13] The English translation is mine, drawing on the critical edition of Giorgio Inglese (Machiavelli ed. 2014).

[14] Scholars have inspected far and wide the adventures of Old Nick in England. See Weissberger (1927), Scott (1984), and Arienzo and Petrina (2013). The (allegedly) diabolical nature of *The Prince*'s teachings does not mean that later authors, in other contexts, have not considered Machiavelli a monster. Among the most famous examples is the 1740 introduction to *Anti-Machiavel*: "I venture to undertake the defense of humanity against this monster, whose aim is to destroy it; I venture to confront sophism and crime with reason and justice; and I have dared to present my reflections on Machiavelli's The Prince" (Frederick the Great ed. 2024, at 13). Without wishing to make any official defense, it is worth noting that, in turn, the great Italian writer Vittorio Alfieri referred to the Florentine secretary as the "divine Machiavelli" in *The Prince and the Letters* (Alfieri ed. 2023, at 24). I entrust the reader with the task of tackling Machiavelli's enigma, warning however that those who, like Thomas Babington Macaulay, have attempted to solve it (Macaulay ed. 1967, at 237), run the risk that, "instead of one enigma, we have two finally resolved into one, but at the cost of denying Machiavelli any individuality or originality" (Villari 1891, at 233).

[15] We noted above in the last section of Chapter 6, Marx and Engel's interpretation of Hobbes as a simple Baconian systematist. Kuno Fischer made this reading popular in his 1856 monograph *Franz Baco von Verulam. Die Realphilosophie und ihr Zeitalter*. The thesis is reiterated in the tenth volume of Fischer's *Geschichte der neuem Philosophie* in *Francis Bacon und seine Schule. Entwicklungsgechichte der Erfahrungsphilosophie*: "The task is obvious: the moral sciences should obey natural science, the moral world should be explained by natural laws, founded on the natural state of man, and derived from it… This task is grasped and solved by Thomas Hobbes, Bacon's immediate successor and student" (Fischer 1904, at 354, the German translation is mine). The opinion that Hobbes was a simple follower of Bacon is however criticised, first, by Friedrich Albert Lange in *Geschichte des Materialismus und Kritik seiner Bedeutung in der Gegenwart* from 1866, and then by Henry Sidgwick in *Outlines of the History of Ethics for English Readers* in 1886. Ten years later, in his monograph *Thomas Hobbes: Leben und Lehre*, Ferdinand Tönnies would have put an end to the question of Hobbes' mere baconism (Tönnies ed. 1989).

rather than representatives of families or cities, are the parties to such a contract. However, what is unique to Hobbes' view is that the response to this condition of humans, potentially the beasts of every war, needs no further wolves or a mix of man and beast like in Machiavelli. Hobbes' response entails the creation of a monster. This has been the message of the *Leviathan*'s cover book since the first edition in 1651. The monster is the 'artificial man' of modern natural law standing against every kind of 'artificial reason' then popular with Coke's ideas on the common law and the constitutional distinctions between the realm of the subjects' rights and the king's prerogatives – between a king below the law and the king as the source of the whole legal system (see above Chapter 6).

Years later, in 1668, Hobbes summed up the analysis of the causes that triggered the English Civil War from 1640 to 1660 with the image of another biblical monster, the Behemoth. The pains and sufferings of the civil war among dreadful wolf-like men could have been well depicted as a monster itself. Hobbes died at 91 a decade later, in 1679, ten years before the Glorious Revolution; the Behemoth would have been published only posthumously, two years later, in 1681. In the *Leviathan*, the analysis is "not of this or that Commonwealth in particular, but of a Commonwealth" (part 2, XXVI); in the *Behemoth*, the focus is on the dualisms of ancient and modern constitutionalism under scrutiny in the previous chapter of this book. Such dualisms between common law and royal prerogatives played a critical role in one of the most tragic decades of English history. The *Leviathan* is the response to this state of nature, *homo homini lupus*, which includes the potential war between sovereign states in what is known today as the international arena.

Following the traditional legal distinction and order of exposition between the facts of a trial and the corresponding doctrine, the following section focuses on the facts of the Civil War in England. The aim is to inspect the set of reasons why Hobbes summarised the causes that led to two decades of civil war and human tragedy as a biblical monster, the Behemoth.

7.2 The Behemoth

Scholars have dissected the possible causes and drivers of the English Civil War, such as the weakening of aristocracy and the emergence of a new power of the gentry; the spread of Puritan ideas; and the lack of both a permanent army and decent bureaucracy in the hands of the King. All of this went together with the increasing confrontation between King and Courts in the 1610s, and later, King and Parliament from the 1620s onwards. From a legal viewpoint, as noted in Chapter 6, such a confrontation revolved around the absolute – divine and natural – right of the King on the one hand and, on the other, the 'legal dualism' of the English institutions, according to Sir Edward Coke. The clash between King and Courts, between James and Coke, culminated in the defeat of Chief Justice Coke in the *Commendams' case* (1616); and yet, a few years later, the antagonism resumed as a conflict between King and Parliament with its first opposition leader, once again, Coke. The reasons at stake with the institutional confrontation concern critical problems of taxation and judicature, legislation and administration. However, Coke's ideal – that Magna Charta is such a fellow that it will have no sovereign – "soon perished" (Maitland 1963, at 301). By the 1630s, the Courts' reputation was in decline and, in the 1640s, their role even became irrelevant (Kenyon 1966, at 105). The dispute increasingly concerned who had to be considered the English sovereign, that is, either the King or the King-in-Parliament.

In Part I of the *Behemoth*, written as a dialogue between an eyewitness of those events and a legal student, Hobbes endorses the royal cause (Hobbes ed. 1889). The student asks the master why King Charles I had to face a rebellion. The eyewitness (Hobbes) draws the attention to three factors of the conflict: (i) religion, for example, the role of such sects as the Papists, Independents or Presbyterians; (ii) politics, i.e. the Parliament's opposition to the King's requests for funds or percentage of customs revenue; and, (iii) academy, i.e. universities. In Part II, Hobbes provides a concise history of this 'institutional factor' in the breakthrough of the Civil War. The Parliament's opposition to the King's requests was overall unhinged because, traditionally, the Parliament's institutional role was that of a council, not of control over the King's decisions (Hobbes 1889, at 77).

Generations of scholars have discussed Hobbes' legal version of the English Civil War vis-à-vis the robustness (or weakness) of Coke's strict legal arguments. Some scholars concede that both defenders of the royal prerogative and the opponents had their good reasons. For example, in the analysis of Charles Howard McIlwain, the royalists relied on specific legal precedents, while the opponents, on the general principles of the ancient constitution: "one side relied on the letter, the other on the spirit, of English monarchical institutions; and in the courts the letter naturally prevailed. But their arguments never met each other" (McIlwain ed. 2008, at 75–76). Whether or not Hobbes endorsed the wrong side of the Civil War falls outside the scope of this book. Instead, the attention should be drawn to the outcome of this legal quarrel on jurisdiction and control over the King's power. Dealing with a theory of legal monsters, what is relevant concerns the reasons why, according to Hobbes, a civil war among wolf-like men should be understood in accordance with the shapes of a biblical monster.

The *Behemoth* describes the salient moments of the Civil War. Part II focuses on the Parliament's control over the militia and its *Humble Petition* in 1642; Part III deals with both the rise of Oliver Cromwell with the Parliamentary army in 1644 and the execution of King Charles in 1649; Part IV dwells on Cromwell's power as Lord Protector until his death in 1658. These parts of the *Behemoth* – from Charles' imprisonment to his son's journey to Scotland – do not only concern the subtleties of ancient and modern constitutionalism, but they also express solidarity with the victims of the rebellion.[16] After all, in Hobbes's opinion, rebellions are either "an unwise or failed experiment" or "a complete blunder arising from ignorance" (in

[16] For this reason, claims such as those of Bernard Willms, are limited: "Behemoth is first of all a picture of a confusion of political language or confusion of the political discourse – in some way a new tower of Bable" (Willms 1992, at 307).

Williams 2003, at 34). In addition to the reasons that make rebellions look monstrous, Hobbes insists on what it is like to be a victim of these cases of monstrosity. Years earlier, in the *Leviathan*, Hobbes admitted three cases in which a 'state of nature' materialises. Contrary to other advocates of the modern natural law tradition,[17] the state of nature is not a philosophical conjecture or hypothetical; rather, the potential beast turns real with the savage people of the Americas, in the relations among sovereign states, and every civil war.[18] This is Hobbes' argument in Chapter 13, Part I, of the *Leviathan*:

> For the savage people in many places of America, except the government of small families, the concord whereof dependeth on natural lust, have no government at all, and live at this day in that brutish manner, as I said before. Howsoever, it may be perceived what manner of life there would be, where there were no common power to fear, by the manner of life which men that have formerly lived under a peaceful government use to degenerate into a civil war (Hobbes 2004, at 92).

Hobbes' political anthropology in the *Leviathan* drew on the tragic experience of the Civil War, as reported later in the *Behemoth.* Regardless of his partisan positions – nobody is a prophet in their own land – Hobbes' 'state of nature' reminds us of the potential conflict of the man who turns himself into a wolf, and moreover, of how the warfare of wolf-like men creates monstrosity, such as the Civil War detailed in the *Behemoth.* From the viewpoint of legal theory and moral philosophy, this interplay of wolves and monsters is not simply rhetorical or ornamental. It is critical. Hobbes argues that it is not enough to follow Machiavelli and turn the Prince, or the sovereign, into half a man and half a beast to tackle every wolf-like man's rebellion. Instead, it is apparent that only a monster, such as the Leviathan, can defeat another monster, such as the Behemoth.[19]

---

[17] This is, for example, Rousseau's approach: see above the third section of Chapter 4. According to some scholars, the same applies to Locke's state of nature conceived of as subject of theological reflection, rather than anthropology. See, for example, Dunn (1982). However, it seems fair to concede that Locke's claim in the second treatise is that the state of nature is not a mere hypothesis. Although, in § 101, he concedes, "that it is not at all to be wondered that history gives us but a very little account of men that lived together in the state of Nature", he later adds that "I have given several examples out of history of people, free and in the state of Nature, that, being met together, incorporated and began a commonwealth" (*op. cit.*, § 103).

[18] Hobbes, as many of his contemporaries, was impressed by the news referring to cannibalism among tribes in today's East Cost. Reporting the cruelties inflicted by a population of Canadian Indians, the Iroquois, on their Algonquin enemies in 1642, a Jesuit father, a certain Vimont, commented that "bref, ils les font roustir et bouillir et puis les mangent avec tine délicieuse rage. Homo homini lupus; l'homme devient un loup anvers un homme quand il se laisse gouverner aux Démons" (in Landucci 1972, at 126).

[19] The necessity of the monster becomes particularly evident in those parts of *Leviathan* where the issue concerns "Those Things that Weaken or Tend to the Dissolution of a Commonwealth", according to the title of chapter XXIX, i.e. the distinction and potential opposition between temporal and spiritual power, secular and religious authority. "When therefore these two Powers [the Civill and the Ghostly Authority] oppose one another, the Common-wealth cannot but be in great danger of Civill warre, and Dissolution" (Hobbes ed. 2004, at 254). In particular, Part IV of the Leviathan deals with "the Kingdom of Darkness", i.e. the spiritual darkness that hinges on the "misinterpretation of scripture" (chapter XLIV), and the darkness that comes from "vain philosophy" (chapter XLVI).

The following section examines the requirements and functions of Hobbes' monster, namely, what the Leviathan is supposed to be (requirements), and what the Leviathan is meant to do (functions). As one of the fathers of modern legal and political thought, Hobbes' monster's shadow grew ever larger in the centuries to come.

7.3 The Leviathan

Hobbes worked meticulously on the frontispiece of Leviathan around 1650, during his exile in Paris, in close collaboration with the engraver and perspective theorist, the Huguenot Abraham Bosse (Bredekamp 2020, at 32). The frontispiece shows a monster – the sovereign – as a crowned giant rising above the landscape. The Leviathan wields a sword with the left hand and a crosier with the right, symbols of earthly and ecclesiastical authority. On the lower left, the sovereign's earthly power is illustrated with a castle, a coronet, a cannon, a trophy made up of muskets, sticks, flags and a battlefield with a drum; on the lower right, the ecclesiastical power is depicted with a church, a bishop's mitre, and a dispute before a court. The detail is in the sovereign's body and his arms, which are protected by a chainmail and made of the bodies of hundreds of people. Most of them look at the sovereign. Others, however, look at each other and talk among themselves. Far from being a reproduction of anonymous male figures, there are also women, children, families with a liveliness and personality of their own, "according to Bosse's way of representing the costumes and daily life of the inhabitants of the houses in the Flemish and Dutch manner" (Casanovas 2017, at 78). We can only imagine what the faces of all such individuals look like and what these people might say. The monster that contains them is the only one whose face stares back at us. This unity represents the first message of the book's frontispiece. In the phrasing of the *Leviathan*'s Chapter XVI, Part 1:

> A multitude of men are made one person when they are by one man, or one person, represented; so that it be done with the consent of every one of that multitude in particular. For it is the unity of the representer, not the unity of the represented, that maketh the person one. And it is the representer that beareth the person, and but one person: and unity cannot otherwise be understood in multitude. (Hobbes 2004, at 121)

How we should interpret the 'artificial' person and, hence, how people look at the monster and what they might say remains controversial. For example, scholars have proposed to interpret the interplay between the one and the multitude in the *Leviathan* either in accordance with an 'agency theory' (Hampton 1986) or an 'alienation

---

Here, it is obvious that Hobbes' Monster does not only have to tackle human-beasts, but also, a "confederation of deceivers" who subtly evoke "the rulers of the darkness of this world", "the kingdom of Satan", "the principality of Beelzebub over demons", and "the prince of the power of the air". We noted that, according to Hobbes, religion, together with politics and academia, is one of the three driving factors of the English Civil War. What better way to deal with ignorance and false religious doctrines on Satan and demons, Beelzebub and the "children of darkness", than with another biblical monster?

theory' (Gauthier 2022). In fact, according to Chapter XVII of Part 2, the social contract is a unilateral act of every individual at the state of nature, giving up "my right of governing myself to this man". However, it is the bane of scholars how to grasp this "consent" and, hence, "the generation of that great LEVIATHAN, or rather, to speak more reverently, of that mortal god to which we owe, under the immortal God, our peace and defence". Although Hobbes aims to contain any wolf-like man through the unity of a political monster, according to the tenets of the 'alienation theory', the 'agency theory' has a point when considering some borderline cases in Hobbes' reasoning, such as the capital punishment paradox, or the assessment of the sovereign's powers. Hobbes' "true liberties of subjects" can sometimes be at odds with any claim of absolute sovereignty: the Rebel's catechism, in the jargon of Bishop Bramhall.

Consider the sovereign's failure to provide adequate protection to subjects in cases where the monster's power should be competent to keep wolf-like men under control within its borders (civil war) or outside (wars among sovereigns). In the jargon of civil lawyers, such cases may affect the 'cause of the contract', namely, its declared aim or purpose, making the pact inapplicable or void. In Chapter XXI, part 2, for example, Hobbes claims that it is up to the subjects to assess the extent of the monster's protection and, hence, whether the obligation to obey has to be considered appropriate. In his phrasing:

> When therefore our refusal to obey frustrates the end for which the sovereignty was ordained, then there is no liberty to refuse; otherwise, there is. (Hobbes 2004, at 164)

Hobbes' difficulties with the limits of political obligation are real.[20] However, they do not suggest that his contribution to legal philosophy can be overestimated. On the contrary, Hobbes' principle of sovereignty – the formal face of the artificial man, the monster – would set the standard for centuries, notwithstanding some uncertainties or even contradictions between what it is and what it ought to be.[21] This is a crucial point for a theory of legal monsters. Against every kind of dualism handed down from ancient or modern constitutionalism, which includes Coke's version of the common law in England, Hobbes provides the tenets of every legal monist doctrine as a corollary of sovereignty in Chapter XXVI, part 2, on 'civil laws'. Whether monarchy, democracy, or aristocracy, as Hobbes stresses in Chapter XIX, such tenets of legal monism can be summarised in accordance with five main points:

(i) Civil laws establish what is right and what is wrong in civil society in connection with that which is contrary or not to the rule;
(ii) The legislator is only the sovereign who is above the civil laws;

[20] Chapter 14, part I of the *Leviathan* seems to support this view: "a covenant not to defend myself from force by force, is always void" (Hobbes 2004, at 102). On the other hand, a corollary of sovereignty is the right to impose the death penalty (*op. cit.*, at 239). Hobbes' difficulties are examined in Heyd (1991) and Schrock (1991), among others.

[21] Hampton insists on this class of contradictions as the "failure of Hobbes" for supporting the social contract with the subjects' moral duty to respect the pact: see Chapter VII of Hampton (1986). Her claim that scholars mostly overlook this problem is however debatable since many have stressed a sort of Hobbes' 'natural fallacy'. See for example Scarpelli (1981, at 50).

(iii) Every custom – the cosmos side of the law – is not binding as such, that is, because of "the length of time that maketh the authority", but rather, the sources of the law shall always be traced back to the "will of the sovereign", in this case, customs "signified by his silence";
(iv) The same holds for the rulings of courts: they are not binding because of the content of the ruling, but rather, because they hinge on the formal authority of the court interpreting the will of the sovereign;
(v) The sovereign has the last word on the meaning and interpretation of all civil laws. There is no room for dualism because the legal sources must be defined formally. Hobbes ironically mentions Coke's doctrine about an 'artificial reason', to stress that it is not, in Coke's words, a "long study, observation, and experience" that can determine right from wrong before courts, considering that "it is possible long study may increase and confirm erroneous sentences" (Hobbes 2004, at 206).

Generations of scholars, from Howard Warrender to Quentin Skinner, have warned against every reading of Hobbes' texts as a simple forerunner of legal positivism.[22] Each of the five corollaries of Hobbes' principle of sovereignty in the *Leviathan* does not entail any separation of natural law and positive law, nor the irrelevance of natural law in the making of the civil laws in society. This interplay is not only evident in Hobbes' incongruities regarding power and the cause that extinguishes political obligations, as in the natural law tradition. Also, we may take Hobbes at face value when he declares in Chapter XXVI of *Leviathan* that "natural law and civil law contain each other" (Hobbes 2004, at 204). What is at stake for Hobbes does not concern any binary between natural law and positive law, as would later occur with most teachings of legal positivism, because the Leviathan intends to incorporate both. Scholars may wonder how much natural law and positive law, rights and obligations of the sovereign's subjects "are of equal extent". However, what is at stake in this context, that is, dealing with a theory of legal monsters, is different, i.e. why Hobbes could consider his own personal solution as the 'ultimate monster' of politics and the law.

At the very beginning of the *Leviathan*'s chapter on 'civil laws', Hobbes illustrates his own design:

> But that is not it I intend to speak of here; my design being not to show what is law here and there, but what is law; as Plato, Aristotle, Cicero, and diverse others have done, without taking upon them the profession of the study of the law. (Hobbes 2004, at 202)

---

[22] This common output brought forth by different interpretation of Hobbes' legal theory did not prevent Warrender and Skinner to criticise each other: see Warrender (1979) and Skinner (1988). By denying that Hobbes was a forerunner of legal positivism, however, it does not follow that crucial aspects of this tradition cannot be traced back to his work: see Murphy (1995), Coyle (2003), and Bix (2005). In the wording of Norberto Bobbio, "I wish us to avoid mistaking it [i.e. Hobbes's system] for contemporary positivism because of the closeness of his system to the theory of legal positivism" (Bobbio 1993, at 167). From a historiographical view, "we have to remember that when in the middle of the seventeenth century Hobbes put forward a theory of sovereignty which was substantially that of Bentham and of Austin, this was a new thing, and it shocked mankind" (Maitland 1963, at 101).

The co-extensivity of natural law and positive law in Hobbes' *Leviathan* represents the condition for understanding his sovereign as the 'ultimate monster' of politics and the law. On the one hand, this is because, against the ancient natural law schools, there is no sense in any old *j'accuse* of a monster against the institutions: calling Hobbes' Leviathan a monster would be a tautology (and Hobbes was a nominalist in philosophy). On the other hand, in accordance with the teachings of a certain legal positivism today, every reference to monsters in positive law would be either illegitimate or meaningless – for it is only the Leviathan, or sovereign, who can determine whether and to what extent another legal monster can exist; for example, the monsters of the common law tradition which was valid law in Hobbes' times.[23] This conclusion is supported by the relatively clear claims of Chapter XXVI, part 2, on 'civil laws', according to which not only the sovereign monster is above the civil laws, but he also has the last word on the meaning and interpretation of such civil laws (Hobbes 2004, at 212).

Hobbes' twofold aim of sovereignty – the ultimate monster of morals and the law – set the standard for centuries. As a matter of fact, the most relevant part of Hobbes' influence would concern the debate on legal monsters related to the second facet of Hobbes' Leviathan (legal theory) rather than the first one (moral philosophy). In Chapters 5 and 6, we noted that, by the early and mid-1700s, most discussions on legal monsters concerned either the classical natural law tradition or the modern natural law authority of Pufendorf's monsters regarding institutional design.[24] This is not to say that Hobbes' 'ultimate monster' played no role in the moral and legal assessment of both normative acts and commonwealths. Indeed, Hobbes' ideas on sovereignty and its legal corollaries would gain track in the 1800s with claims on the separation of morals from the law, and of ethics from legal sovereignty. The crucial convergence of some ideas as different as English utilitarianism, French positivism, or German formalism would all strengthen the assumption that, at the end of the day, the Leviathan is the ultimate monster because it is up to the sovereign to determine whether and to what extent another monster can legally exist within its borders.

Remarkably, a sign of Hobbes' own success is the silence of certain philosophical debates and systematisations of legal theory about monsters. To address this silence, the focus should be on what the *Leviathan* suggests about the binding nature of normative acts "signified by silence" for "silence is sometimes an argument of consent" (Hobbes 2004, at 204). This silence echoes in today's everyday work of administrative law experts who deal with self-certifications that become valid after a certain period – for example, in Italy, two months after the silence of the public authority. Although it can be tricky to ascertain the relevant lack of monsters in arguments of legal theory, a theory of legal monsters should be attentive to flesh out such significant "silences" as well.

[23] This conclusion does not extend, of course, to the relation among sovereign states. The co-existence of monsters in the international arena is Hobbes' legacy that modern international law has intended to govern. See Armitage (2006). We return to this scenario in Chapter 10.

[24] As regards the English political debate, Locke's authority was crucial throughout the 1700s, although fading away in the early 1800s under the influence of utilitarian ideas. See Stephen (1876, at I, 5).

7.4 The Cape Horn of Legal Science

The separation of moral arguments from legal reasoning is at the core of the triumph of multiple schools of legal positivism in England and continental Europe in the 1800s and through the mid-1900s. The separation of law and morals is a pillar of Bentham and Austin's teachings through the lens of utilitarianism and command theory in legal philosophy.[25] Likewise, the separation is an axiom of legal positivism in France over the 1800s strengthened by Auguste Comte's scientific project.[26] Further, the separation is even a point of honour in Kelsen's pure doctrine of the law. This latter assumption is relevant for a theory of legal monsters because the separation of law and morals can also be understood epistemologically through the differentiation of science and value judgements. According to Kelsen, legal arguments can be as much a subject of science as physics or chemistry.[27] No moral consideration is necessary to discern right from wrong in the legal domain because the law differentiates itself from morals by hinging on a proper technique: If A, then B ought to follow (Kelsen 1950). Such a normative proposition is as formal as the corollaries of Hobbes' principle of sovereignty.[28] It is remarkable that Kelsen, like the great minds of the 1600s and 700s, openly admitted geometry as his theoretical model or source of inspiration.

> To declare purely formal concepts of the law worthless for being empty formulae would be tantamount to dismissing the concepts of geometry for merely capturing corporeal forms and saying nothing about corporeal content... With reference to its formal character, jurisprudence can be characterized – without of course suggesting a likeness in every respect – as a geometry of all manifestations of the law (Kelsen 1911, at 93).[29]

---

[25] It is worth mentioning Bentham's *Anarchical Fallacies*, according to which "right, the substantive right, is the child of law: from real laws come real rights; but from imaginary laws, from laws of nature, fancied and invented by poets, rhetoricians, and dealers in moral and intellectual poisons, come imaginary rights, a bastard brood of monsters, 'gorgons and chimaræ dire'" (Bentham ed. 1843, at 523).

[26] The lack of interest for monsters may arguably depend also on scientific reasons. In fact, according to Comte's "examination of exceptional organizations, or cases of monstrosity", his opinion was that "these organic anomalies were the last to pass over from the gaze of a barren curiosity to the investigation of science; but we are now learning to refer them to the laws of the regular organism, and to subject them to pathological procedures" (Comte ed. 1858, at 313). However, drawing on this basis, Comte still indulges in the use of the metaphor. For example, the "colonial slavery of our day" appears as a "social monstrosity" (*op. cit.*, at 586); whereas such ideas that "impute pathological monstrosity to whole classes" should be considered as "simply absurd" (at 487).

[27] There is, of course, a crucial difference between natural and legal sciences, i.e. how the connection between any 'A' and 'B' should be grasped for Kelsen: as stressed in the text, the causal interpretation of nature should be carefully distinguished from the technique of legal imputation.

[28] As occurs with discussions on Hobbes' interplay between natural and positive law (see the previous section of this chapter), also the foundation of Kelsen's legal formalism is controversial or problematic. See for example Paulson (2000). We return to the problems of Kelsen's formalism in Chapter 10.

[29] The English translation of Kelsen in Paulson (2008, at 38).

The aim of this section is not to address the evergreen problem of legal theory on morals and the law, whether considering Hobbes' distinction between civil laws and natural law, or Kelsen's separation between legal science and natural law, or current debates of multiple positivistic schools (both inclusive and exclusive) vis-à-vis tenets of natural law theory. In the early 1900s, Benedetto Croce used to sum up such efforts of philosophers to distinguish law from morals with the image of the "Cape Horn" of legal science because jurists would end up in a "conceptual storm" and "wreckage" by trying to circumnavigate the issue (Croce 1907). Dealing with a theory of legal monsters, what is interesting to stress is that every reference to monsters, according to Hobbes' auspices in the *Leviathan,* became increasingly irrelevant in the legal debate from the 1800s and down to the mid-1900s. There are three different reasons for this kind of silence:

(i) The assumption that every natural law claim on political monsters, as occurs in the tradition of Plato and Cicero, would be irrelevant in legal reasoning;
(ii) The argument that further monsters, such as Pufendorf's monsters of legal design, would be similarly irrelevant because they hinge, once again, on the self-defeating tenets of natural law theory with its value judgements;
(iii) The irrelevance of monsters in legal theory and positive law because the metaphor is either meaningless or devolved to a formal decision of lawmakers concerning, for example, the status of the *monstrum vel prodigium* of positive law in the 1800s and until the mid-1900s.

The monumental *System of Modern Roman Law* by Friedrich August von Savigny is particularly instructive.[30] The *System* in some ways facilitated the triumph of legal positivism in Germany by the late-1800s (Kelly 2007, at 324). Savigny insisted on the binding force of legal customs and people as 'the source of the law' in works such as *Of the Vocation of Our Age for Legislation and Jurisprudence* (Savigny ed. 1831). In the *System,* the German scholar formalises such theses with the "indispensability" of legislation and the systematisations of legal science that gradually but inexorably replace the 'spirit of the people' (Berkowitz 2011, at 623). To appreciate how this 'scientific approach' works in practice, the attention should be drawn to the notion of legal personhood as the status related to the rights and obligations of human beings: this was the crucial problem with the *monstrum vel prodigium* from ancient times to Savigny's years, as noted in Chapter 3. Savigny's claim in the *System* is that only human fellows properly have rights and duties of their own, and yet, the law has the power to grant such rights of personhood to anything, such as corporations, governments, ships in maritime law, and one day, why not, intelligent robots (Savigny 1884, §§ 60 and 85). However, considering the *monstrum vel prodigium* of positive law, the "Darwin of German legal theory" (Zimmermann 2013) finds no difference between ancient and modern Roman law, since the old standards of discrimination between human beings and monsters remain "the only ones which can be asserted according to our Positive Law" (Savigny 1884, § 61, at 8).

[30] The English editions of the two volumes of Savigny's *System* are (Savigny 1979) and (Savigny 1884), respectively.

Regarding the silences of legal theory, on the other hand, there are countless examples.[31] John Austin's *Lectures on Jurisprudence* make the case (Austin 1873). Lecture XII on the "analysis of pervading notions" is devoted to the terms "right" and "person" with their interplay (*op. cit.*, at 343). Austin distinguishes between physical or natural persons and legal or fictitious persons. Following "the Roman Lawyers (from whose writings it has been borrowed by modern jurists)", a natural person is conceived of as *homo*, or man, invested with a condition, or *status*, to which correspond rights, or lack thereof. Therefore, "according to this definition, human beings who have no rights are not persons, but things… such, in the Roman Law, down to the age of the Antonines, was the position of the slave" (at 348). Austin disagrees, however, with the usual interpretation of "modern civilians" for also slaves were "persons" and hence, humans. Furthermore, as noted in Chapter 3, "numerous places in the Institutes of Gaius, in the Institutes of Justinian, and also in his Digest or Pandects" attest that slaves had their legal *status* (at 349). This excursus on ancient sources helps Austin emphasise what is important to him, namely, that the meaning of person is related to a human being considered either as invested with rights, or as subject to duties. Monarchs must not be understood as such a person, since sovereigns, properly speaking, have neither legal obligations nor legal rights (at 350). Consequently, the status of *monstrum vel prodigium* handed down by the tradition, and still valid law in the mid-1800s, simply falls outside the radar of legal theory. The silence on positive law is striking, and interesting.

This eclipse of the monster, in particular, regarding the tradition of legal positivism from the 1800s and down into the 900s, suggests that, through such silences, the shadow of Hobbes' Leviathan became larger as time went by. The thread which links the 'ultimate monster' of Hobbes' political philosophy to the silences of legal positivism does not intend to make Hobbes a simple frontrunner and advocate of this tradition because we noted that Hobbes would freely admit the weight of moral arguments and natural law in determining, for example, even the legal personhood of AI robots (as much as Kant would concede after Hobbes).[32] Still, some silences differ from others, and Hobbes' philosophy plays a decisive role in discerning some

[31] Together with such silences, there are proverbial exceptions. A first group has to do with persisting ideas of natural law theory on monstrous institutions and normative acts, notwithstanding the crisis of this tradition throughout the 1800s. See Krieger (1965): we return to this crisis and the return of natural law in the mid-1900s below in Chapter 8. A second group concerns Marxist theories and their critique to the monstrosity of capitalism: this tradition persists today. See Shaviro (2002) and McNally (2011). A variable of this group concerns how Marxist theories against the monsters of capitalism can generate monsters: see, for example, Critchlow (2021), on the "monster as dictator" (Lenin), the "revolutionary destroyer" (Mao), and the "megalomania empowered" (Fidel Castro). Finally, a third group concerns the birth of criminology and studies of anatomical pathology in the late 1800s with the monsters of Cesare Lombroso (1896, at 272), and moreover, the encyclopaedic Cesare Taruffi (1886). See also Rafter and Ystehede (2010): we dwelt on this kind of monster in Chapter 5, dealing with Foucault's abnormal. On legal arguments that support the constitutional personhood of AI robots, see below the third section of Chapter 11.

[32] In addition to Kant's monsters (see above Chapter 4), it is worth mentioning that scholars have indeed inspected also the moral, legal and logical challenges of Kant's aliens: see Conant (1991) and Clark (2001).

of them. We should be attentive to the multiple reasons for this lack of interest. Legal positivism is an intricate family as much as classical and modern natural law traditions used to be and still are. Correspondingly, to appreciate a 150 years 'silent chapter' in the history of legal monsters – from the early 1800s to the mid-1900s – it is necessary to augment the granularity of the analysis and grasp in which specific domain of legal positivism some silences of lawyers and philosophers are thought-provoking. Such silences may either concern the tyrants of classical natural law theory, the design of institutions according to modern natural law schools, or the assessment of normative acts and practices on a case-by-case basis.

Next, in Chapter 8, the aim is to focus on the silences that revolve around the legal monsters of the ancient natural law tradition, i.e. the political meaning of the formula since Plato's times. The attention is drawn to different types of legal positivism and, hence, different reasons why there has been no room for monsters in legal analysis for more than a century, such as tyrants and dictators, despots, and evil institutions. Drawing on this basis, Chapter 9 will focus on a further kind of silence: the legal monsters of the modern natural law tradition, i.e. the institutional meaning of the formula since Pufendorf's times. In both cases, the silence on legal monsters can be grasped as an eclipsis, a sort of temporary reduction or loss of reputation and relevance of the formula. Scholars would increasingly discuss monsters once again after WW II, namely when, paradoxically, not only the legal status of the *monstrum vel prodigium* of the tradition was abolished, but also the advocate of legal monism and author of the Leviathan – as the 'ultimate monster' of politics and the law – that is, Thomas Hobbes, was progressively presented as a father of modern political thought.

From a theoretical perspective, the end of the eclipse of monsters in the mid-1900s is particularly relevant. The crisis of legal positivism would have brought the return of old debates on law and morals, politics and ethics, facts and values, which the monster of Malmesbury attempted to overcome: the Cape Horn of Western legal science.

References

Alfieri, V. 2023. *Del principe e delle lettere [1778–1789]*. Sophia, France: Culturea.

Alighieri, D. 2021. *Monarchia* [1313], ed. D. Quaglioni with Latin text. Milan: Mondadori.

Arienzo, A., and A. Petrina, eds. 2013. *Literary and political influences from the reformation to the restoration*. Farnham and Burlington: Ashgate.

Armitage, D. 2006. Hobbes and the foundations of modern international thought. In *Rethinking the foundations of modern political thought*, ed. A. Brett and J. Tully, 219–235. Cambridge: Cambridge University Press.

Ashcraft, R. 1986. *Revolutionary politics and Locke's two treatises of government*. Princeton: Princeton University Press.

Aubrey, J. 1898. *Brief lives* [1669-], ed. A. Clark. Oxford: Clarendon Press.

Austin, J. 1873. *Lectures on jurisprudence*. Vol. I. London: John Murray.

Bentham, J. 1843. *Works*. vol. II, ed. J. Bowring. Edinburgh: Tait.

Berkowitz, R. 2011. From justice to justification: An alternative genealogy of positive law. *UC Irvine Law Review* 1 (3): 611–630.

Bix, B. H. 2005. Legal positivism. In *The Blackwell guide to the philosophy of law and legal theory*, ed. M. P. Golding and W. A. Edmundson, 29–49. Oxford: Blackwell.

Bobbio, N. 1993. *Thomas Hobbes and the natural law tradition*. Chicago: University of Chicago Press.

Bowle, J. 1969. *Hobbes and his critics. A study in the seventeenth century constitutionalism*. London and Plymouth: Cass.

Bramhall, J. 1844. The Catching of the Leviathann or the Great Whale [1658]. In *The works of the Most Reverend Father in God, John Bramhall, D.D., Sometime Lord Archbishop of Armagh, Primate and Metropolitan of All Ireland*, vol. 4. Oxford: J. H. Parker.

Bredekamp, H. 2020. *Leviathan: Body politic as visual strategy in the work of Thomas Hobbes*. Berlin/Boston: de Gruyter.

Cairns, H. 1946. Leibniz's theory of law. *Harvard Law Review* 60 (2): 200–232.

Casanovas, P. 2017. *Sub lege pugnamus: De la gran guerra a les grans dades*. Barcelona: Edicions Universitat Barcelona.

Chabod, F. 1964. *Scritti su Machiavelli*. Torino: Einaudi.

Clark, D. L. 2001. Kant's aliens: The anthropology and its others. *CR The New Centennial Review* 1 (2): 201–289.

Comte, A. 1858. *Positive philosophy*, trans. H. Martineau. New York: Blanchard.

Conant, J. 1991. The search for logically alien thought: Descartes, Kant, Frege, and the tractatus. *Philosophical Topics* 20 (1): 115–180.

Coyle, S. 2003. Thomas Hobbes and the intellectual origins of legal positivism. *Canadian Journal of Law & Jurisprudence* 16 (2): 243–270.

Critchlow, D. T. 2021. *Revolutionary monsters: Five men who turned liberation into tyranny*. Washington, DC: Simon and Schuster.

Croce, B. 1907. *Riduzione della filosofia del diritto alla filosofia dell'economia*. Bari: Laterza.

De Vitoria, F. 1967. *Relectio de Indis o Libertad de los Indios* [1538], ed. L. Perena and J.M. Pérez Prendes. Madrid: Consejo Superior de Investigaciones Cientificas.

Drinker Bowen, C. 1985. *The lion and the throne: The life and times of sir Edward Coke (1552–1634) [1958]*. Boston: Little, Brown & Co.

Dunn, J. 1982. *The political thought of John Locke: An historical account of the argument of the 'two treatises of government'*. Cambridge: Cambridge University Press.

Figgis, J. N. 1922. *The divine right of kings [1896]*. Cambridge: Cambridge University Press.

Filmer, R. 1680. *Patriarcha, or the natural power of kings*. London: Chiswell.

Fischer, K. 1904. *Francis Bacon und seine Schule, Entwicklungsgeschichte der Erfahrungsphilosophie*. Heidelberg: Carl Winter Universitätsbuchhandlung.

Frederick the Great. 2024. Philosophical writings, ed. A. Lifschitz, Princeton. New Jersey: Princeton University Press.

Friedrich, C. J. 1966. Philosophical reflections of Leibniz on law. Politics, and the state, *Natural Law Forum* 11:79–91.

Gauthier, D. 2022. Hobbes's social contract. In *Hobbes and political contractarianism: Selected writings*, ed. S. Dimock, C. Finkelstein, and Ch. W. Morris (pp. 3–23). Oxford: Oxford University Press.

Hampton, J. 1986. *Hobbes and the social contract tradition*. Cambridge: Cambridge University Press.

Haydn, H. 1950. *The counter-renaissance*. New York: Scribner.

Heyd, D. 1991. Hobbes on capital punishment. *History of Philosophy Quarterly* 8 (2): 119–134.

Hobbes, Th. 1889 *Behemoth, or the Long Parliament* [1681], ed. F. Tönnies. London: Simpkin, Marshall & Co.

Hobbes, Th. 2003. *On the citizen* [1642], trans. R. Tuck and M. Silverthorne. Cambridge: Cambridge University Press.

Hobbes, Th. 2004. *Leviathan [1651]*. New York: Barnes & Noble.

Kelly, M. 2007. *A Short history of western legal theory*. Oxford: Oxford University Press.
Kelsen, H. 1911. *Hauptprobleme der Staatsrechtslehre*. Heidelberg: Mohr.
Kelsen, H. 1950. Causality and imputation. *Ethics* 61 (1): 1–11.
Kenyon, J. P. 1966. *The Stuart constitution. 1603-1688. Documents and commentary*. Cambridge: Cambridge University Press.
Krieger, L. 1965. Kant and the crisis of natural law. *Journal of the History of Ideas* 26 (2): 191–210.
Landucci, S. 1972. *I filosofi e i selvaggi. 1580–1780*. Bari: Laterza.
Laslett, P. 1949. Introduction. In R. Filmer, *Patriarcha and other political works*, 1–43. Oxford: Blackwell.
Lombroso, C. 1896. *L'uomo delinquente*. Vol. 1. 5th ed. Torino: Bocca.
Macaulay, T. B. 1967. *Prose and poetry*, selected by G. M. Young. Cambridge, MA: Harvard University Press.
Machiavelli, N. 2014. *Il principe [1532]*. Turin: Einaudi.
Maitland, F. W. 1963. *The constitutional history of England [1908]*. Cambridge: Cambridge University Press.
McIlwain, Ch. H. 2008. *Constitutionalism: Ancient and modern [1940]*. Indianapolis: Liberty Fund.
McNally, D. 2011. *Monsters of the market: Zombies vampires and global capitalism*. Leiden: Brill.
Montaigne, de M. 1965. *Les Essais [1580]*. Paris: PUF.
Murphy, M. C. 1995. Was Hobbes a legal positivist? *Ethics* 105 (4): 846–873.
Pagallo, U. 1995. *Homo homini deus*. Padua: Cedam.
Pagallo, U. 1998. Bacon, Hobbes and the homo homini deus formula. *Hobbes Studies* 11 (1): 61–69.
Parkin, J. 2007. *Taming the Leviathan: The reception of the political and religious ideas of Thomas Hobbes in England 1640–1700*. Cambridge and New York: Cambridge University Press.
Paulson, S. L. 2000. On the puzzle surrounding Hans Kelsen's basic norm. *Ratio Juris* 13 (3): 279–293.
Paulson, S. L. 2008. Formalism, 'Free Law', and the 'Cognition' quandary: Hans Kelsen's approaches to legal interpretation. *The University of Queensland Law Journal* 27 (2): 7–39.
Rafter, N., and P. Ystehede. 2010. Here be dragons: Lombroso, the gothic, and social control. In *Popular culture, crime and social control*, ed. M. Deflem, 263–284. Leeds: Emerald.
Savigny, F. 1831. *Of the vocation of our age for legislation and jurisprudence* [1814], trans A. Hayward. London: Littlewood.
Savigny, F. A. 1884. Jural relations; or, the Roman law of persons as subjects of jural relations, trans W. H. Rattigan. London: Wildy.
Savigny, F. A. 1979. *System of the modern Roman law* [1867], trans. W. Holloway. Westport: Hyperion.
Scarpelli, U. 1981. *Thomas Hobbes*. Milan: Giuffrè.
Schrock, T. S. 1991. The rights to punish and resist punishment in Hobbes's leviathan. *The Western Political Quarterly* 44 (4): 853–890.
Scott, M. 1984. Machiavelli and the machiavel. *Renaissance Drama* 15:147–174.
Shaviro, S. 2002. Capitalist monsters. *Historical Materialism* 10 (4): 281–290.
Skinner, Q. 1974. Conquest and consent: Thomas Hobbes and the engagement controversy. In *The interregnum: The quest for settlement 1646–1660*, ed. G. E. Aylmer, 79–93. London: Macmillan.
Skinner, Q. 1981. Machiavelli: A very short introduction. Oxford: Oxford University Press.
Skinner, Q. 1988. Warrender and Skinner on Hobbes: A reply. *Political Studies* 36 (4): 692–695.
Stephen, L. 1876. *History of English thought in the eighteen century*. London: Smith Elder.
Taruffi, C. 1886. *Storia della teratologia*. Vol. 4. Bologna: Regia Topografica.
Tönnies, F. (1989) *Thomas Hobbes: Life and doctrine* [1896], translated by O. Hoffe, Chicago: University of Chicago Press.
Tuck, R. 1986. A new date for Filmer's patriarcha. *The Historical Journal* 29:183–186.
Villari, P. (1891), *The life and times of Niccolò Machiavelli*, translated by L. Villari, New York: Scribner's sons.
Warrender, H. 1979. Political theory and historiography: A reply to professor Skinner on Hobbes. *The Historical Journal* 22 (4): 931–940.

Weissberger, L. A. 1927. Machiavelli and Tudor England. *Political Science Quarterly* 42 (4): 589–607.
Williams, H. 2003. *Kant's critique of Hobbes: Sovereignty and cosmopolitanism.* Cardiff: University of Wales Press.
Willms, B. 1992. Philosophia prima, science and politics in Hobbes. In *Hobbes e Spinoza. scienza e politica*, ed. D. Bostrenghi, 297–311. Naples, Italy: Bibliopolis.
Zimmermann, A. 2013. The 'darwin' of German legal theory – Carl von Savigny and the German school of historical Law. *Journal of Creation* 27 (2): 105–111.

Chapter 8
Positive Thinking

This chapter examines the eclipse and return of discussions on legal monsters, drawing attention to tenets of legal positivism and the 1958 debate between Hart and Fuller on whether the acts of monstrous institutions, such as the Nazi regime, should be considered valid law (Hart), or should not deserve the name of law (Fuller). Because principles of the natural law tradition have been incorporated into most Western legal systems and their post-WW II constitutions, it may seem that traditional contrasts between natural and positive law have lost relevance. The chapter shows, however, that convergences among different and even opposite schools of legal thought can trigger what is usually dubbed as 'false friends' in linguistics. The meaning of words or formulas that sound similar to words or formulas of a different language may significantly differ, as occurs with the meaning of monster in legal arguments today.

8.1 Harsh Laws, but Laws

The silences of legal positivism on old and new 'legal monsters' concern as many reasons as the many schools of this tradition: English, French, or German, among others. Considering the meaning of resistance and opposition in the use of the formula – i.e. monsters as a source of legal criticism – a tenet of legal positivism, such as the notion of validity, clarifies the eclipse of the formula on legal monsters over more than a century, namely, from the early 1800s to the mid-1900s. According to a tenet of legal positivism,[1] value assessments are not necessary to determine what a valid law is. Instead, the attention should be drawn to how a certain act has

[1] See, among others, Gardner (2001) and Coleman & Leiter (2010). In most post-WW II legal systems, the formal validity of the law shall of course be complemented with the assessment of its constitutional legitimacy through processes of judicial review. We return to this assessment below in the third section of this chapter and in the first section of Chapter 9.

U. Pagallo, *A Theory of Legal Monsters: Repression, Resistance, Rebellion*,
Philosophical Studies Series 161, https://doi.org/10.1007/978-3-032-10771-8_8

been created. In fact, a normative act is legally valid not because of its content, i.e. whether the provisions of the law can be deemed just or right, but rather because of the established law's procedures according to which it was adopted.[2] Therefore, the more scholars draw apart what the law is from what the law ought to be, the less relevant any reference to the monsters of ancient and modern schools of natural law is. The same conclusion holds for further tenets of legal positivism, such as the theory of legislative normativism, the dogma of positive law as the unique or main source of the legal order, or the theory of non-creative interpretation, particularly popular in France with the triumph of the 'exegetical school' after the Napoleonic codification in 1804 (Halpérin 2023).

The dogma of the omnipotence of the legislator does not only entail that the activity of jurists must be understood as a declarative or mechanical interpretation of the acts set up by the lawmaker, but also, that every legal custom is relegated to a subordinate role in the theory of legal sources. We noted this eclipse of the cosmos side of the law in Chapter 6, dwelling on Hayek's ideas on spontaneous orders, evolution, and design. Yet, the dogma of the supremacy of positive law has another crucial corollary in this context, namely, the presumption that the legal system created by the legislator is free from gaps, errors, or contradictions. Every reference to the monsters of the natural law tradition becomes not simply irrelevant, but illegal. Under Art. 4 of the Preliminary Title of Napoleon's Code on "publication, effect, and application of the laws in general", the golden rule was that "the judge who shall refuse to determine under pretext of the silence, obscurity, or insufficiency of the law, shall be liable to be proceeded against as guilty of a refusal of justice".

Moreover, the silence of legal positivism on the monsters of the tradition depended on the theory of unconditional obedience, namely, the strict or even absolute duty of obedience that all legal subjects have towards the provisions of positive law. The theory (and practice) of this unconditional obedience followed as a corollary of the principle of absolute sovereignty because, as John Austin claims in *The Province of Jurisprudence Determined*, the sovereign has an unlimited legal power to enforce his commands based on a threat of sanctions, which is the subjects' equivalent to having a duty (Austin ed. 1954, at 14–18). Every attempt to resist or oppose the commands of the law on the basis of moral arguments is, according to Austin, "stark nonsense" because "the most pernicious laws, and therefore those which are most opposed to the will of God, have been and are continually enforced as laws by judicial tribunals... An exception, demurrer, or plea, founded on the law of God was never heard in a Court of Justice, from the creation of the world down to the present moment" (*op. cit.*, 185).[3]

[2] This corollary of Hobbes' principle of sovereignty was under scrutiny in the third section of Chapter 7. The approach is similarly at work in Kelsen (1981).

[3] Austin's separation between law and morality does not prevent him from using the monster formula for rhetorical purposes. In *Lectures on Jurisprudence* (Austin ed. 1873), for example, Austin refers to "the monstrous and palpable mischiefs of ex post facto legislation" (*op. cit.*, at 317); or, criticises a conclusion which is "absurd and monstrous" (at 126). We noted a similar use of the formula in Bentham: see above note 25 of Chapter 7. Still, it is worth mentioning that Austin also uses the formula to condemn the opinion of some common law courts. In his lecture XXV on the rights

Against this framework, traditionally summed up with the Canon law maxim *dura lex sed lex* – the law is harsh, but it is the law – we can appreciate the ideas of Gustav Radbruch on a theory of legal monsters. Radbruch has often been presented as an advocate of legal positivism who radically changed his ideas by converting into a staunch defender of the natural law tradition as a reaction to the horrors of the Nazi regime. Radbruch would thus appear to have followed the opposite path to that of another German legal philosopher previously considered in Chapter 7, that is, Savigny. In the *Philosophy of Right* from 1932, Radbruch insists on the endless discussions about what may be deemed as legally right or just, with the corresponding "strife of legal views", to support a traditional claim of legal positivism:

> The validity of demonstrably wrong law cannot conceivably be justified. However, any answer to the question of the purpose of law other than by enumerating the manifold partisan views about it has proved impossible – and it is precisely on that impossibility of any natural law, and on that alone, that the validity of positive law may be founded. At this point relativism, so far only the method of our approach, enters our system as a structural element... Since, however, in the relativistic view of reason and science are unable to fulfill that task, will and power must undertake it. If no one is able to determine what is just, somebody must lay down what is to be legal. (Radbruch ed. 1950, at 116–117)

On the other hand, in *Five Minutes of Legal Philosophy*, Radbruch's first post-WW II work, he not only supports the traditional claim of all natural law schools, namely, the superiority of natural law over positive law, but he also advocates the more radical opinion according to which the acts of legislators that infringe principles of natural law should not be considered valid law.[4] In the phrasing of Radbruch:

> There are, therefore, principles of law that are stronger than any statute, so that a law conflicting with these principles is devoid of validity. One calls these principles the natural law or the law of reason. To be sure, their details remain somewhat doubtful, but the work of centuries has established a solid core of them and they have come to enjoy such a far-reaching consensus in the declarations of human and civil rights that only the deliberate skeptic can still entertain doubts about some of them. (Radbruch ed. 1991, at 103)

Scholars have discussed to what extent Radbruch may have actually changed his mind during the Nazi era or whether there is a continuity from the *Philosophy of Right* to *Five Minutes of Legal Philosophy* (Leawoods 2000). In this context, we can leave this debate aside and focus on Radbruch's radical claim that positive law, which is 'Schande', i.e. an ignominy or shame, should be considered void – and overruled by courts – vis-à-vis the principle of justice (Avitabile 2022, at 21). The assumption

---

of action that should be founded on injury, Austin dwells on a case of injury without intention to stress the absurdity of the Courts' opinion: "This monstrous rule of the Common Law Courts is justified by a reason which is not less monstrous" (Austin 1873, at 486). It seems fair to admit, however, that this harsh assessment does not undermine any pillar of Austin's legal positivism, from the separation between law and morals to the theory of sovereignty and law as command.

[4] Radbruch's claim has a notable precursor in Thomas Aquinas who, in the *Summa Theologica* (quest. 96, art. 4), affirms that unjust laws are not only unenforceable, but also, powerless to bind the conscience because they should be considered as legal perversions and acts of violence. All in all, unjust laws are not laws at all (Aquinas ed. 1992, at 98). We return to the multiple and even opposite readings of this text below in Chapter 10.

is obviously at odds with all tenets, dogmas, and principles of legal positivism. The practical consequences of these natural law claims became apparent in the aftermath of WW II, with the Nuremberg trial and several cases discussed before West German courts in which war criminals, spies, and informers claimed that what they did was legal under the laws of the Nazi regime which were in force at the time their actions were performed. In 1949, for example, a Court of Appeals had to decide the case of a woman who, five years earlier, wishing to get rid of her husband, denounced him to the authorities for offensive remarks against Hitler and his regime. There was no legal duty to report those acts, and yet the husband was arrested and sentenced to death, which only resulted in him being sent to the front. In the post-war trial, the wife claimed that she committed no crime because her husband's fate depended on some Nazi statutes. However, the German court held that the woman was guilty of depriving her husband of his freedom under the German criminal code. The 1934 Nazi statute, under which the husband was found guilty, had to be considered void because, in the opinion of the Bamberg Court of Appeals, that law "was contrary to the sound conscience and sense of justice of all decent human beings" (in Hart 1958, at 619).

This ruling is particularly relevant, dealing with a theory of legal monsters, because, a decade later, the case was at the core of the debate between two champions: one of the natural law tradition (Lon Fuller) and one of legal positivism (Herbert Hart). In 1958, the Harvard Law Review published Hart's *Positivism and the Separation of Law and Morals* (Hart 1958), together with Fuller's *Positivism and Fidelity to Law: a Reply to Professor Hart* (Fuller 1958). The target of Hart's criticism was twofold, i.e. on the one hand, the separation of law and morals – between law as it is and as it ought to be – in accordance with the theses of Jeremy Bentham and John Austin; and, on the other hand, Radbruch's opposite claim regarding the supremacy of natural law over positive law.

In his reply to Hart, Fuller endorsed Radbruch's views and consequently condemned Hart's distinction of law and morals. After a century of triumphant legal positivism with its silences on legal monsters, the debate revolved once again around the (political meaning in the) use of the formula as a form of resistance and opposition against tyrants and monsters with their unjust laws. It remains to be seen to what extent, even in those cases of monstrosity, such as the Nazi regime, an unjust law should no longer be deemed valid law.[5]

---

[5] A considerable amount of work has been devoted to the Hart-Fuller debate over the past decades: see, among many, Cane (2010). In the words of Martin Krygier, "much of the enduring energy and tension in the Hart-Fuller debate stems from the two protagonists' reflections on 'the testimony of those who have descended into Hell, and, like Ulysses and Dante, brought back a message for human beings'" (Krygier 2010, at 107, quoting Hart (1958), at 615). Most of the time, however, scholars overlook the monsters of this debate, including those of Homer and Dante in the *Inferno*: see above note 11 of Chapter 7. The first section of this chapter illustrates some reasons for this silence in the case of legal positivism and the so-called analytical jurisprudence. The silence is yet striking in the case of natural law theorists and the "Liber Amicorum Honouring Professor Lon L. Fuller" (Bechtler 1978). Admittedly, these discussions on the Hart-Fuller debate cover some of the problems under scrutiny in this chapter, for example, regarding international criminal law and the rule of law, law as a means and as an end, human rights and the morality of law. However, the

8.2 Return of Legal Monsters

In his 1958 essay, three years before the publication of the masterpiece *The Concept of Law*, Hart had a twofold target. The aim was to condemn both the strict separation of law and morals – which Bentham and Austin turned into a 'second nature' in the English legal and political tradition of the 1800s – and the opposite claims of natural law scholars, for example, of Radbruch's claims on justice and valid law introduced in the previous section. Hart presents Radbruch as a champion of "positive doctrines" until the Nazi tyranny converted him into an adherent of natural law theories. Hart even concedes that "it is impossible to read without sympathy Radbruch's passionate demand that the German legal conscience should be open to the demands of morality and his complaint that this has been too little the case in the German tradition" (Hart 1958, at 617). However, Hart stresses the "extraordinary naivete" of this view, as if the problem were the belief of "people like the Germans" buying into those assumptions of legal positivism, such as Austin's theory of unconditional obedience: "law is law" (*op. cit.*, 618).

Hart affirms that even Nazi laws should be considered valid, i.e. they have the force of law. Hart's example regards the Nazi 1934 statute of the previous section on the evil wife and the poor husband sent to die on the front. In Hart's opinion, the wisdom of the Court of Appeal, which held that the statute "was contrary to the sound conscience and sense of justice of all decent human beings", must be doubted. Sure enough, the 1949 ruling of the post-Nazi West German Court, as much as similar cases and decisions of other courts, "have been hailed as a triumph of the doctrines of natural law and as signalling the overthrow of positivism. The unqualified satisfaction with this result seems to me to be hysteria" (Hart 1958, at 619). The limits of every opposition of law and morals, positive and natural law, cannot be solved by simply subordinating the former to the latter.

In his response to Hart, Fuller endorses Radbruch's view with a familiar claim: the Nazi 1934 statute was a "legislative monstrosity" (Fuller 1958, at 654). Likewise, the secret Nazi act enacting the wholesale killings in concentration camps should be deemed as the greatest "legal monstrosity" (*op. cit.*, 651); whereas the improvement of planning authorities lowering the marked value of the land on which a house is built, "an unmortgageable monstrosity" (at 665). What all these monsters make clear is that unjust laws do not deserve to be called law. To think otherwise, as Hart claims, does not suggest mere theoretical nuances, but rather arrogance and conceit: "Throughout his discussion, Professor Hart seems to assume that the only difference between Nazi law and, say, English law is that the Nazis used their laws to achieve ends that are odious to an Englishman" (*op. cit.*, 650). On the contrary, according to Fuller:

> When a system calling itself law ... habitually cures its legal irregularities, even the grossest, by retroactive statutes, when it has only to resort to forays of terror in the streets, which no one dares challenge, in order to escape even those scant restraints imposed by the pretense of legality – when all these things have become true of a dictatorship, it is not hard for me, at least, to deny to it the name of law. (Fuller 1958, at 660)

---

historical and conceptual richness of the monster debate, from Greco-Roman antiquity to modern schools of natural law, is simply absent. The next sections of this chapter intend to fill this gap.

However, it is not a necessary corollary of ancient and modern natural law theories to declare unjust laws 'invalid' or to deny them even the name of law. It is noteworthy that the ancient Greek culture forged the parallelism of tyrants and monsters in the context of their tragedies, in which whatever outcome was fated to be painful and excruciating, in the wording of Aristotle, full of "fear and pity".[6] The tragedy of the legal monster – dealing, for example, with Plato's tyrants and their evil institutions – depends on the fact that they are both, i.e. monsters are evil but also legal because they execute the force of positive law.[7] Fuller's claim that the Nazi regime, through its laws, constituted a new "monstrosity" is subject to radical criticism for denying Hitler's regime the force of law, as it seems to suggest that crucial issues of justice and legal validity can be resolved on the basis of such natural law precepts, when in fact these problems are not solved at all. In the phrasing of Hart:

> The vice of this use of the principle that, at certain limiting points, what is utterly immoral cannot be law or lawful is that it will serve to cloak the true nature of the problems with which we are faced and will encourage the romantic optimism that all the values we cherish ultimately will fit into a single system, that no one of them has to be sacrificed or compromised to accommodate another. (Hart 1958, at 620)

To be fair, Fuller admitted an alternative feasible way to tackle the evil acts of monstrous institutions, i.e. enacting retroactive law. However, the decisions of the German courts in declaring the monstrous acts of the Nazi regime void were justified because such courts could not wait for the enactment of a retroactive law merely to rule over cases that had to be decided "in a situation of drastic emergency" (Fuller 1958, at 655). Fuller concedes that such an option of a retroactive law can be, under certain circumstances, desirable to make the break with the past evident (*op. cit.*, 661). Yet, Fuller does not think he contradicts himself because, in his view, there is not such an alternative as in Hart's choice "between two evils" – that is, between either leaving people unpunished or punishing them on the basis of a "retrospective legislation". Instead, a retroactive law should be deemed complementary to declaring monstrous statutes not to have the force of the law. In Fuller's phrasing:

> I, like Professors Hart and Radbruch, would have preferred a retroactive statute. My reason for this preference is not that this is the most nearly lawful way of making unlawful what was once law. Rather I would see such a statute as a way of symbolizing a sharp break with the past, as a means of isolating a kind of cleanup operation from the normal functioning of the judicial process. (Fuller 1958, at 661)

The conclusion we can draw from this part of the debate between Hart and Fuller is twofold. On the one hand, even advocates of legal positivism, in addition to supporters

[6] See Chapter XIV of Aristotle's *Poetics* (Aristotle ed. 1970), at 1452 a.

[7] See book III of Aristotle's *Politics* (Aristotle ed. 2013), at 1282 a, on the validity of unjust laws. It is worth mentioning that Hannah Arendt, when covering the Eichmann trial in Jerusalem in 1961, does not refer to Eichmann as a monster, but rather, as a prankster: "everybody could see that this man was not a 'monster,' but it was difficult indeed not to suspect that he was a clown" (Arendt 1963, at 54). An expert in Greek culture, Arendt was fully aware of the close relationship between monsters and the tragedy of a people, the "tragedy of Jewry" in this case. In denying that Eichmann is a monster, Arendt denies him any tragic relevance: Eichmann rather represents the "banality of evil".

of the natural law tradition, can deem institutions and their legislation as utterly immoral and, therefore, "monstrous". Hart is ready to concede this point (Hart 1958, at 629). Yet, on the other hand, the clash between advocates of certain natural law theories and legal positivism regards "a very precious principle of morality endorsed by most legal systems" against every retroactive criminal legislation and punishment (Hart 1958, at 619). Whereas, in the natural law approach endorsed by Radbruch and Fuller, also a legal monster may entail a plain case – meaning that such unjust law does not simply deserve the name of law – Hart, on the contrary, suggests that all (this class of) legal monsters entail a legal hard case, which is not just solved by overruling positive law in the name of justice but rather by making the choice between leaving evil people unpunished, or endorsing retroactive laws and criminal reform through the lawmaking of courts. As a result, the drawbacks of every tight separation between law and morals are not fixed by simply subordinating the former to the latter and, hence, overruling the former with the latter. Instead, we must be attentive to the balance that the law must strike among multiple regulatory systems in society, which includes the ideal and highly unlikely scenario of unanimous moral opinions and ethical doctrines (Pagallo 2016). In Hart's phrasing, "the most important single lesson to be learned from this form of the denial of the Utilitarian distinction [between law and morals] is the one that the Utilitarians were most concerned to teach: when we have the ample resources of plain speech we must not present the moral criticism of institutions as propositions of a disputable philosophy" (Hart 1958, at 620–621).

We noted that the increasing popularity of the formula 'legal monster' over the past decades can be understood as a corollary of the crisis of tenets of legal positivism triggered by the horrors of the Nazi regime and of totalitarianisms from the 1900s. And in fact, those tenets of legal positivism – such as theories of legislative normativism, unconditional obedience, or pure declarative interpretation of the acts of lawmakers – have all been questioned by international and regional declarations on human rights as well as by the transplant of natural law principles into several national constitutions, for example, in Japan (in 1947), Italy (1948), and West Germany (1949). This new legal framework, however, does not entail any subordination of positive law to a principle of justice and natural law. Although some scholars presented it "as a triumph of the doctrines of natural law", according to Hart's sarcastic remarks, even advocates of the natural law tradition, such as the French philosopher Jacques Maritain, admitted that the most pressing issue of the new legal framework revolved around the enforcement of principles and provisions of international conventions in the aftermath of WW II.[8] This enforcement problem was under scrutiny in Chapter 4, dealing with the other side to the coin on legal monsters, i.e. the abolishment of the status of the *monstrum vel prodigium* handed down by the tradition.

From a theoretical viewpoint, old disputes between legal positivism and natural law did not vanish, in fact, as a result of the new post-WW II legal framework. The return of the formula on 'legal monsters' in the philosophical debate since the 1950s suggests these disputes realigned in the new context as a source of legal criticism and

---

[8] Maritain went so far as to famously declare that "yes, we agree about the rights but on conditions no one asks us why" (Maritain 1949, at 10).

resistance. Academic papers and even judicial obiter dicta have increasingly begun using the formula on 'monsters' to condemn violations of constitutional principles and human rights enshrined in positive law.[9] Yet, the ideal takeover between the two sides to the coin on legal monsters in the mid-1900s – with, on the one hand, the abolishment of inhuman treatment for people with birth defects and, on the other, the new popularity of the political meaning of the formula on monstrous tyrants – triggered some problems of its own. The threat is clear in retrospect: the more scholars use the formula on monsters to criticise unjust laws and evil institutions, the less the meaning of the formula appears precise and coherent because the success of the formula exposes its users to the same criticism that Hart made of Fuller's arguments, i.e. it seems we can address and even fix critical issues of justice and legal validity drawing on the natural law precepts enshrined in national charts and international conventions, although these problems of justice and legal validity are not solved at all.

To corroborate the assumption, the following section further inspects two of the issues under scrutiny in the debate between Fuller and Hart, namely, Fuller's claim on the monstrosity of retroactive legislation and Hart's distinction between plain and hard legal cases. The aim is to clarify traditional problems of justice and legal validity, taking into account the novelties of today's law vis-à-vis the return of the image of legal monsters. These problems require 'right answers' for a new legal framework.

8.3 Right Answers

Scholars refer today to the formula 'legal monster' as a metaphor that may cover ideas as different as the theses of supporters of legal positivism (Hart's evil laws) and the natural law tradition (Fuller's monsters). The metaphor can sometimes be employed so that distinguishing between legal positivism and natural law approaches is irrelevant, for example, to determine whether a normative act is 'monstrous' because it is laid down on pure individual basis or implemented with retroactive effects. Both the sources of today's positive law and tenets of legal theory would justify this conclusion.[10] And yet, this convergence of opinions in using the formula can be superficial.

---

[9] The popularity of the formula on legal monsters was illustrated so far with Singapore's 2021 foreign interference bill; the 2022 reform of an international trade agreement; and Italy's 2024 right to image of cultural property. See above Chapters 5 and 6. Further examples of the popularity of the formula are provided below in the final section of this chapter as well as in Chapters 9, 10, and 11.

[10] As regards the illegitimacy of normative acts laid down on individual basis, see the third section of Chapter 6 with the rulings of the Italian Constitutional Court. The illegitimacy of retroactive normative acts is inspected below in this section with the provisions of the ECHR framework. In legal theory, the monstrosity of retroactive legislation in criminal law does not only depend on claims of natural law supporters, such as Fuller. Also, some advocates of legal positivism would freely concede this point. For example, according to Joseph Raz and the essential principles that allow a legal system to uphold the rule of law, the claim is that all laws should be prospective and the courts should have review powers over the implementation of such principle (Raz 1979). As

Consider one of the most controversial points of the debate between Fuller and Hart, such as the retroactivity of the law and a basic tenet of the rule of law, according to which "everything which is not prohibited is allowed".[11] In criminal law, this principle is connected to the clause of immunity summed up, in continental Europe, with the formula of the principle of legality, i.e. "no crime, nor punishment without a criminal law" (*nullum crimen nulla poena sine lege*). Even though certain behaviours might be deemed monstrous, for example, the evil wife getting rid of her husband thanks to the 1934 Nazi act, it is a tenet of the rule of law that individuals can be held criminally liable for such behaviour only on the basis of an explicit criminal norm. This was the problem at stake with the Nuremberg trial in the aftermath of WW II. In 1950, the European Convention on Human Rights, the 'ECHR', endorsed the principle of legal certainty and the rule of law, but with a savings provision. The first paragraph of Art. 7 ECHR establishes that "[n]o one shall be held guilty of any criminal offence on account of any act or omission which did not constitute a criminal offence under national or international law at the time when it was committed". The savings provision of Art. 7(2), which aims to cover such exceptional cases as the Nuremberg trial against the Nazis, states:

> This article shall not prejudice the trial and punishment of any person for any act or omission which, at the time when it was committed, was criminal according to the general principles of law recognized by civilized nations.

It may seem that some claims of the natural law tradition, such as Fuller's legal monsters in the debate with Hart, have thus been endorsed by the principles of today's positive law. Monstrous acts and institutions – such as those under scrutiny in the dispute between Hart and Fuller – would justify (European) courts to declare such acts void in accordance with "general principles" that may accommodate both the assumptions of natural law and legal positivistic theories.[12] We noted this kind of conceptual ambiguity and potential source of misapprehension with the International Bill of Rights and the constitutional framework set up in the aftermath of WW II. Although scholars may agree in defining a retroactive criminal act as 'monstrous', there is a key difference between doing so on the grounds of the infringement of (the principles of) positive law, or because the monstrosity depends on the infringement of principles of natural law enshrined in positive law. Such a critical difference in how to grasp the principles of the legal system can also be overlooked by those scholars

---

stressed in the next section of this chapter, this convergence may however entail 'false friends'. We return to Raz's principles below in Chapter 9.

[11] We noted in the previous section of this chapter that, according to Hart, retroactive acts entail choosing between two evils (Hart 1958, at 619). On the other hand, according to Fuller, a retroactive act would contradict the third of the minimal conditions of the law (Fuller 1964): see above the third section of Chapter 6.

[12] In accordance with tenets of legal positivism, every reference to the general principles must not only draw on the provisions of positive law in a certain legal order, but also, this is a well-known technique to comply with the presumption that the legal system created by the legislator has no gaps. In criminal law, the technique entails however the further problem to distinguish 'extensive interpretations' of the law from the use of analogy. See Fletcher (1998, at 79 and 208).

who follow the tenets of another popular approach today, such as Ronald Dworkin's legal hermeneutics and his theory on the 'unique right answer' (Dworkin 1985).[13]

Dworkin claims that, even in complex cases, such as the case of the evil woman getting rid of her husband thanks to a Nazi statute, jurists can find the 'right answer' for every argument at hand. Dworkin admits the idea of natural law scholars, according to whom 'legal monsters' may entail plain cases: jurists can find a uniquely correct answer for all the hard cases of the law by conceiving the principles of the legal system as normative statements with deontological, rather than teleological meaning. By following the logic of yes or no, or what is good for all, scholars could, in fact, identify the principles of the system that fit with the established law so as to apply such principles in a way that interprets the case in the best possible light. This approach fits like a glove with certain rulings, such as the 2009 ruling of the Court of Cassation in Italy, where a legal monster is defined as every act that sets "uncomprehensible legal solutions that defy the logic of the system".[14] As Dworkin states in *A Matter of Principle*, we "must read through what other judges in the past have written not only to discover what these judges have said, or their state of mind when they said it, but to reach an opinion about what these judges have collectively done, in the way that each of our novelists formed an opinion about the collective novel so far written"(Dworkin 1985, at 159).

In the following section of this chapter, we return to Dworkin's ideas on the hard cases of the law. What is relevant here to stress concerns four different meanings that the formula 'legal monsters' assumes today, i.e. after the crisis of legal positivism with the strict separation of law and morals. Following more than a century of eclipse in the use of the metaphor, scholars' use of the monster formula can be appreciated in accordance with four different perspectives. They concern:

(i) Today's subordination of national legislation to constitutional principles and conventions of international law, so that legal monsters are triggered by acts and institutions that infringe such principles and conventions;
(ii) Fuller's subordination of positive law to natural law, so that legal monsters shall not be considered as valid proper law;
(iii) Hart's distinction (but no separation) of law and morals, so that legal monsters entail a choice between two evils;

[13] We met his ideas above in the fourth section of Chapter 3. Dworkin's critique of legal positivism has been dissected over the past four decades: see Nino (1980), Himma (2002), Coleman and Leiter (2010). Among the counter-criticisms, see Habermas (1996) on the effects of Dworkin's "right answer thesis" as regards risks of judicial paternalism, lack of focus on democratic legitimisation and public discourse, down to the idealisation of the courts' role vis-à-vis the principle of equality. Moreover, some scholars have accused Dworkin to be a naïve abstract thinker, whose autonomous individual is fruit of the faith on pure reason, overlooking the role of communities, family, and traditions on human conduct and social order – in a nutshell, "a monster" (Gaylin and Jennings 1996). This picture has been considered "unworthy of two authors connected with the Hastings Center" (Nagel 1996). As promised in the introduction of this book, I leave this kind of debate on monstrous colleagues aside to focus on Dworkin's theoretical contribution to a theory of legal monsters with his ideas on 'unique right answers'.

[14] See above note 19 of Chapter 6.

(iv) Dworkin's theory of the unique right answer, so that jurists can determine in all the hard cases of the law whether we are dealing with a legal monster, or not.

A theory of legal monsters should be attentive to these different and even opposite meanings that the popularity of the formula brings forth today. The threat of misunderstanding is real and can be grasped through Maxime Koessler and Jules Derocquigny's work on "the false friends" of linguistics (Koessler and Derocquigny 1928). When dealing with words or formulas that may look similar to words or formulas of a different language, their meaning may differ significantly. Those who use the metaphor on legal monsters should take sides between the first and second meaning of the formula (i.e. positive law vs natural law), between the second and third use of the image (i.e. Fuller vs Hart's views), or endorsing or rejecting the fourth option (i.e. the viability of Dworkin's unique right answer).[15]

Accordingly, the next section focuses on the price to be paid for the popularity of the formula 'legal monsters' after its long eclipse under the tenets of legal positivism in the 1800s and until the mid-900s. Potential misunderstandings may depend on the context in which the image is employed, or on ambiguities of positive law, or on simple theoretical negligence. All in all, there are several false friends out there.

8.4 False Friends

Scholars often refer to monsters regardless of strict theoretical assumptions, which may lead to confusion and misapprehensions. In Chapter 6, drawing on Fuller's *The Morality of Law*, we dwelt on eight cases in which jurists can reasonably deem a normative act monstrous.[16] However, how to grasp this legal monstrosity, i.e. either concerning the ends of the law or rather the means through which the law intends to attain such ends, remains controversial. For example, in Hart's review of Fuller's

---

[15] Against Dworkin's 'unique right answer' thesis, for example, Hart claims that "there is no possibility of treating the question raised by the various cases as if there were one uniquely correct answer to be found, as distinct from an answer which is a reasonable compromise between many conflicting interests" (Hart 1961, at 128). Hart formalises on this basis the thesis put forward three years earlier in the debate with Fuller, i.e. the tragedy of monstrous institutions entails the choice between two evils. Some scholars claim that Dworkin's thesis should be understood as a direct response to Hart's views on judicial discretion and the 'open texture' of the law, so that, in later work, Dworkin would provide "a more helpful scrutiny on ambiguous, open-textures, or unclear applications, and argument of relevant legal language" (Bix 1995, at 77). Other scholars, on the contrary, claim that "Dworkin's 'one-right-answer' thesis is crucial for understanding Dworkin's entire political and legal theory because of that theory's reliance on the status of value, particular moral value" (Guest 2016). While admitting softer theses in Dworkin's later work, also scholars such as Bix admit that "Dworkin's interpretative (holistic) approach did not fit the practice" (Bix 1995).

[16] We noted in Chapter 6 that the monstrosity may depend on the fact that the normative act is *ad personam*, secret, retroactive, unintelligible, inconsistent, subject to over-frequent revision, beyond human nature, or finally, randomly dispensed.

book (Fuller 1964), we noted Hart's ironical question as to what sense Fuller's legal conditions can ever be thought of as a "morality", because they seem to be more like means for effective legislation and, moreover, they appear only as moral as the enterprise they make possible (Hart 1965). On the other hand, Fuller could respond that the role of these legal conditions is not simply instrumental since they represent a morality of respect for the freedom and dignity of the agents addressed by the law (Fuller 1964).

Opposite ideas on the means and ends of the law represent only a part of a more general problem. The false friends of this section draw attention to the fact that the apparent convergence of scholars in defining normative acts and institutions as 'monstrous' should not lead us to overlook crucial differences between the tenets of natural law, legal positivism, or legal hermeneutics. The crisis of old tenets of legal positivism – under scrutiny in the previous sections of this chapter – may have favoured this convergence and still, this convergence entails a paradox and a warning. The paradox concerns the abundance of different meanings in the current use of the formula on 'monsters' after decades of silence brought forth by axioms and dogmas of legal positivism in the same years in which the strict legal meaning of the *monstrum vel prodigium* progressively dissolved. The warning concerns the fact that scholars rarely pay attention to this connection. Natural law advocates were the first to use the image of monsters as a symbol of unjust laws to assert that such laws would not even deserve to be called law. Yet, no natural law scholar has ever asked to declare void more than two millennia of natural and positive law repression of people with birth defects as a result of unjust laws and brutal treatment of human fellows.

A theory of legal monsters should thus be attentive to all 'false friends' of the field. Contrary to the masters of suspicion of Chapter 5, the aim is not to dissect what such false friends may conceal, but rather, to grasp the different meanings in which the formula 'legal monster' is used and which of these uses makes sense, i.e. whether the legal meaning is proper, coherent, and legitimate. To attain this end, both descriptive and prescriptive, the four observables of the analysis – introduced in the previous section of this chapter and regarding today's constitutionalism, natural law theory, legal positivism, and legal hermeneutics – must be refined. We can take sides between the different meanings of the formula on monsters today, i.e. between positive law and natural law, between means and ends of legislation, or whether a unique right answer may exist, drawing on the teachings of the natural law schools from the 1700s. In particular, attention must be drawn to how such schools used to distinguish between requirements of legal monstrosity for normative acts or for whole institutions (see Chapter 6).

The reason for this differentiation hinges on a fundamental asymmetry. Whilst all evil institutions trigger monstrous laws, it does not follow that every monstrous normative act entails the presence of a despicable institution. Until the late 1700s, it was commonplace among natural law schools, both classical and modern, to claim that also decent institutions can embrace monster laws. Although censorship constraints shall never be underestimated, there is even our sense of humour in the 1736 Royal Order for the appointment of Deans to the University of Valencia, where the Order refers to previous 'monsters' that make apparent the abhorrence of the regulation (see Chapter 5). Monstrous are the acts, not the colleagues.

Further examples of this old natural law argument were stressed in previous sections of this book. For instance, the 2009 ruling of the Court of Cassation in Italy, which defined a ruling of the Santa Maria Capua Vetere Tribunal and "the complex history that had generated" as a "legal monster", does not suggest that such Court – and the Italian republican institutions for that matter – are monstrous. There is a clear separation between the assessment of legal acts and the corresponding state or institution. However, today's popularity of an old natural law argument may entail a 'false friend'. Consider the 2012 debate at the European University Institute on the Fiscal Compact Treaty signed in March of that year (Kocharov 2012). That international treaty raised a host of tricky issues concerning its compatibility with EU law, national sovereignty, institutional balance and democratic accountability. These problems were summarised, albeit in an interrogative form, with the well-known formula: *Another legal monster?* We may wonder whether such a question should be understood as the side effect of the monstrosity of the whole EU institutions, according to the opinion of certain scholars (Allott 2003), or whether the attention is drawn to a bad or unjust law that, for one reason or another, should be more radically deemed as monstrous.

This critical distinction of natural law between monster acts and evil institutions has often been overlooked in today's legal theory. The reasons may simply depend on the context of the discussion. For example, in the debate between Hart and Fuller, their focus was on the monstrosity of the Nazi regime and hence, the monstrosity of the acts that followed as a result: the evil wife's 1934 statute is only an instance of how monstrous acts necessarily follow monstrous institutions. However, the critical distinction between decent institutions and monster acts has also been ignored as a result of legal positivistic views on legislative normativism, unconditional obedience, or declarative reading of norms.[17] One point of honour for most schools of legal positivism was, after all, the dogma of positive law as a complete and coherent system, free from contradictions and gaps pursuant to a 'systematic interpretation' of the law. Today, normative acts of legislators shall be assessed against principles and provisions that provide thresholds to determine whether such acts are legitimate or, conversely, illegitimate and even monstrous. This assessment is the bread and butter of specialists in constitutional law at both the national and regional levels, as well as of specialists in human rights protection at the international level. The metaphor of the monster aims to emphasise a critical disruption in the legal order. Most of the time, the monstrosity depends on either the means of the legislation or the material practice that infringes the principles of the system.[18]

[17] It is worth mentioning that Fuller, considering in particular Austin's command theory and Kelsen's pure doctrine of the law, calls them monstrous. See *The Law in Quest of Itself*, in which Fuller refers to "the methodological impurity of the school of analytical jurists, which pretended to straddle the gap between the world of fact and the world of law with a gaseous sort of monster which purported to be of both worlds" (Fuller 1999, at 76).

[18] The initiatives of UN institutions against the monsters of human rights violations are countless. See the UN Human Rights' campaign "Learn, Speak Up and Act!", which aimed to raise awareness

Yet, blatant violations of constitutional law or systematic infringements of the international Bill of Rights do not prevent further quarrels of legal theory. From a methodological viewpoint, by drawing attention to provisions of positive law and their enforcement, legal theory disputes can be clarified with three potential classes of false friends and their variables.[19] They regard:

(i) The confusion between monstrous institutions and monstrous normative acts, or legal practices, whereas their distinction sheds light on how the former depends on the latter. It would be difficult to prove any institutional monstrosity or the evilness of any monstrous tyrant without proof of the monstrosity of specific acts or practices[20];
(ii) The further confusion between the requirements of institutional monstrosity and normative monstrosity. Whereas, in international law, cases of monstrosity mostly regard the flagrant violation of human rights, constitutional monsters may also concern further issues of institutional balance, national sovereignty, or crass bureaucracy[21];
(iii) The peculiarity of controversies regarding constitutional law vis-à-vis particular provisions or institutions. Against every simplification, cases of monstrosity can be specific to a certain legal tradition or culture.[22]

The new observables of the analysis provide the method for testing claims of legal monstrosity. The attention is drawn, first of all, to the normative acts that shall be eventually considered monstrous vis-à-vis the corresponding legal framework that is

---

about racism, xenophobia, racial discrimination and other forms of intolerance. The overall intent is "how to dismantle the monster". See the document at https://www.ohchr.org/en/get-involved/stories/we-have-figure-out-how-dismantle-monster. The same holds for some initiatives of the Human Rights Watch organization, for example, on "a monster and a test case". The document is available at https://www.hrw.org/news/2005/10/06/monster-and-test-case. Scholars have been attentive to this monstrous state of the art: among many, see Guzman (2013).

[19] The three classes of false friends do not include today's supporters of strict positivistic views, such as followers of Hans Kelsen's pure legal doctrine. Those scholars should be understood in fact as straight opponents of every use of metaphors on monsters. We return to these ideas with their drawbacks below in Chapter 10.

[20] The assumption does not entail any kind of strict normativism, according to which every analysis on institutions should ultimately be reduced to an analysis of norms. This book has stressed time and again the role of social practices, legal cultures and traditions, as well as the ethos on which legal systems rest. We return to this differentiation between norms and institutions below in Chapter 10.

[21] Consider the 2024 press release of the EPP, the largest political group in the European Parliament, opposing a proposal of the European Commission on the so-called "Deforestation Law", dubbed as "an administrative monster". See the document at https://www.eppgroup.eu/newsroom/deforestation-law-a-bureaucratic-monster-must-be-delayed. In addition to administrative monsters, constitutional issues and cases of monstrosity may also regard the violation of fundamental rights. On the "mission of modern constitutionalism" as a bulwark for the protection of such rights and against the emergence of powers out of any control, see Waldron (2012) and Sajó & Uitz (2017).

[22] The dynamics of legal transplants and rejections, i.e. how legal norms and principles of a certain legal order may be adopted, or imposed into another jurisdiction, often emphasises the specific features of each legal system with the rejection crisis that can follow as a result of such legal transplants. See Watson (1993), Graziadei (2019), and Pagallo (2020).

necessary for such an assessment. Depending on the claim, i.e. either regarding the monstrosity of a certain normative act or a whole institution, the requirements for such a monstrosity vary, though they may also overlap in accordance with observables (ii) and (iii) of the analysis on the false friends of this section.

Concerning cases of institutional monstrosity, the requirements regard either the international framework of the Bill of Rights, the constitutional safeguards of the legal system under scrutiny, or both. The constitutional safeguards may refer to specificities of that legal system, or common principles of the law, for example, safeguards against retroactive legislation or bans on torture and inhuman treatments. As a result, the requirements of monstrosity regarding normative acts may be related to infringements of constitutional and international law, as much as the means of legislation that contradict the ends to be attained. Certain requirements, such as the congruency and consistency, coherence and intelligibility of the normative act, often necessitate the expertise of national jurists to determine the legal monstrosity in accordance with the third observable of the analysis on cases that are specific to a certain legal order, tradition, or culture. Drawing on such criteria of normative monstrosity, we can thus assess the monstrosity of a whole legal order by determining whether the infringement of constitutional safeguards is blatant and disruptive, or the violation of human and fundamental rights odious and systematic.

It is against these differentiations that we can go back to the opinions of legal scholars on monsters, introduced in the previous section of this chapter, to determine whether the monstrosities of the law shall be grasped as a question of means-end efficiency, or whether a unique right answer exists for all the cases at hand, or whether such a monstrosity entails a more radical issue of legitimacy and legal validity in connection with traditional oppositions between natural law scholars and supporters of positivistic views. To address these questions, the framework and methodology provided in this section shall be tested through a case study of positive law. This is the level of abstraction necessary to avoid theoretical disputes that may be interesting, but have no connection with reality. This is why the next chapter focuses on a particular legal system: the law of the EU institutions.[23] EU law is indeed an intriguing and fruitful case study because it has been a generous source of legal monsters for scholarly debates over the past 25 years. EU law tests our ideas of positive law and legal theory, considering the requirements of monstrosity for both institutions and normative acts, as much as quarrels of legal theory on procedures and validity, means and ends of the law, plain or hard legal cases.

[23] Drawing on the methodology of this chapter, I leave the inspection of further cases of institutional and normative monstrosity at the national or regional level to my fellow legal scholars. This assessment seems particularly necessary in US law under the current President. On the one hand, a panoply of books and articles dwells on Trump's monsters and monstrosities: I checked 50 of them simply relying on the database of Google scholar services. On the other hand, few of such studies examine the strict legal side of the metaphor and, even so, they mostly focus on particular cases of monstrosity: see for example Sohoni (2018), Muller (2019), and Fine (2020). Such a research should of course be complemented with the analysis of Trump's second term.

From a methodological viewpoint, the state of the art in positive law is crucial because claims of legal monstrosity should be appreciated against a particular constitutional order to determine whether some of its acts and practices can be conceived of as monstrous and, therefore, whether an institution shall be deemed monstrous or, vice versa, whether the focus is on decent institutions that may endorse monstrous acts. By drawing attention to a particular legal order, such as EU law, it does not follow that principles and provisions of international law are irrelevant, or that general principles of legal theory are inappropriate. Instead, claims on international law constraints or principles of legal theory are necessarily finetuned through the national or regional specificities of positive law.

In light of today's popularity of legal and political uses of the formula on monsters, the overall aim of the next chapter is thus to make such uses sound and precise, especially considering the valued function of criticism and resistance that the image has transmitted since ancient times. To prevent the monster metaphor from being used improperly today, we came up with a methodology that also gets rid of false friends.

References

Allott, P. 2003. Epilogue: Europe and the dream of reason. In *European constitutionalism beyond the state*, ed. J. H. H. Weiler and M. Wind, 202–225. Cambridge: Cambridge University Press.

Aquinas, Th. 1992. *Treatise on Law (Summa Theologica Questions 90–97)*, ed. S. Parry. Chicago: Gateway.

Arendt, H. 1963. *Eichmann in Jerusalem: A report on the banality of evil.* New York: Viking Press.

Aristotle. 1970. Poetics, trans. G.F. Else. Ann Arbor: The University of Michigan Press.

Aristotle. 2013. *Politics*, trans. C. Lord, Chicago and London: Chicago University Press.

Austin, J. 1873. *Lectures on jurisprudence.* Vol. I. London: John Murray.

Austin, J. 1954. *The province of jurisprudence determined [1832].* London: Weidenfeld & Nicolson.

Avitabile, L. 2022. *Legalità e giustizia.* Turin: Giappichelli.

Bechtler, T. W., ed. 1978. *Law in a social context: Liber amicorum honouring professor Lon L. Fuller*. Deventer: Kluwer.

Bix, B. H. 1995. Ronald Dworkin's right answer thesis. In B. H. Bix, *Law, language, and legal determinacy*, 77–132. Oxford: Clarendon.

Cane, P., ed. 2010. *The Hart-Fuller debate in the twenty-first century.* Oxford and Portland: Hart.

Coleman, J. L., and B. Leiter. 2010. Legal Positivism. In *A companion to philosophy of law and legal theory*, ed. D. Patterson, 228–248. Oxford: Blackwell.

Dworkin, R. 1985. *A Matter of Principle.* Oxford: Oxford University Press.

Fine, S. 2020. Monsters, Inc.: The Fightback. In *The shifting border*, ed. A. Shachar, 99–117. Manchester: Manchester University Press.

Fletcher, G. P. 1998. *Basic Concepts of Criminal Law.* Oxford: Oxford University Press.

Fuller, L. L. 1958. Positivism and fidelity to law: A reply to professor Hart. *Harvard Law Review* 71 (4): 630–672.

Fuller, L. L. 1964. *The morality of law.* rev. ed. New Haven, CT: Yale University Press.

Fuller, L. L. 1999. *The law in quest of itself*. Union, NJ: The Lawbook Exchange.

Gardner, J. 2001. Legal positivism: 5 1/2 myths. *American Journal of Jurisprudence* 46:199–228.

Gaylin, W., and B. Jennings. 1996. *The perversion of autonomy.* New York: The Free Press.

Graziadei, M. 2019. Comparative Law, Legal Transplants, and Receptions. In *The Oxford Handbook of Comparative Law*, ed. M. Reimann and R. Zimmermann, 441–473. Oxford: Oxford University Press.

Guest, S. 2016. Dworkin's 'one-right-answer' thesis. *Problema Anuario de Filosofía y Teoría del Derecho* 10:3–21.

Guzman, A. 2013. International organizations and the Frankenstein problem. *European Journal of International Law* 24 (4): 999–1025.

Habermas, J. 1996. *Between facts and norms: contributions to a discourse theory of law and democracy*, trans. W. Rehg, Cambridge: Polity Press.

Halpérin, J. L. 2023. École de l'Exégèse. In *Encyclopaedia of the philosophy of law and social philosophy*, ed. M. Sellers and S. Kirste, 837–840. Dordrecht: Springer.

Hart, H. L. A. 1958. Positivism and the separation of law and morals. *Harvard Law Review* 71 (4): 593–629.

Hart, H. L. A. 1961. *The concept of law*. Oxford: Clarendon Press.

Hart, H. L. A. 1965. Book review: Lon Fuller, The morality of law. *Harvard Law Review* 78:1281–1296.

Himma, K. E. 2002. Situating Dworkin: The logical space between legal positivism and natural law theory. *Oklahoma City University Law of School* 27:41–150.

Kelsen, H. 1981. On the basis of legal validity. *American Journal of Jurisprudence* 26:178–189.

Kocharov, A. (ed.) 2012. Another legal monster? An EUI debate on the fiscal compact treaty, EUI LAW, Fiesole, Italy, available at https://hdl.handle.net/1814/21496, accessed on September 8, 2025.

Koessler, M., and J. Derocquigny. 1928. *Les faux amis: ou, Les trahisons du vocabulaire anglais (conseils aux traducteurs)*. Paris: Vuibert.

Krygier, M. 2010. The Hart-Fuller debate, transitional societies, and the rule of law. In *The Hart-Fuller debate in the twenty-first century*, ed. P. Cane, 107–134. Oxford and Portland: Hart.

Leawoods, H. 2000. Gustav Radbruch: An extraordinary legal philosopher. *Washington University Journal of Law and Policy* 2:489–515.

Maritain, J. 1949. *Introduction, in human rights: Comments and interpretations*, 9–17. New York: Columbia University Press.

Muller, E. L. 2019. Korematsu, Hirabayashi, and the second monster. *Texas Law Review* 98:735–756.

Nagel, Th. 1996. The cult of the individual, *The New York Times*, September 8, available at https://archive.nytimes.com/query.nytimes.com/gst/fullpage-9C06E2DF1E38F93BA3575AC0A960958260.html, accessed on 8 September 2025.

Nino, C. S. 1980. Dworkin and legal positivism. *Mind* 89 (356): 519–543.

Pagallo, U. 2016. Even angels need the rules: AI, roboethics, and the law. In *ECAI 2016: Frontiers in artificial intelligence and applications*, vol. 285, 209–215. Amsterdam: IOS Press.

Pagallo, U. 2020. The collective dimensions of privacy in the information era: A comparative law approach.*Annuario di diritto comparato e studi legislativi*. Vol. XI, 115–138.

Radbruch, G. 1950. Legal Philosophy, in *The Legal Philosophies of Lask, Radbruch, and Dabin*, trans. K. Wilk, 47-226. Cambridge, MA: Harvard University Press.

Radbruch, G. 1991. Five minutes of legal philosophy. In *Philosophy of Law*, ed. J. Fienberg and H. Gross, 103–104. Belmont: Wadsworth.

Raz, J. 1979. *The authority of law*. Oxford: Oxford University Press.

Sajó, A., and R. Uitz. 2017. *The constitution of freedom: An introduction to legal constitutionalism*. Oxford: Oxford University Press.

Sohoni, M. 2018. The Trump administration and the law of the Lochner era. *Georgetown Law Journal* 107:1323–1391.

Waldron, J. 2012. Constitutionalism: A skeptical view (May 1, 2012), *New York university school of law,* public law research paper no. 10-87, available at SSRN: https://ssrn.com/abstract=1722771, accessed on 8 September 2025.

Watson, A. 1993. *Legal transplants: An approach to comparative law*. Athens: University of Georgia Press.

Chapter 9
Decent Institutions, Monster Laws

The European Union provides a fruitful case study for a theory of legal monsters because scholars have sometimes presented either the EU as a monster, or some EU normative acts as monstrous. This chapter aims to show that claims on the monstrosity of the EU institutions are usually unhinged, although it is fair to concede that certain EU acts can be deemed monstrous. To support this twofold assumption, the analysis defines the requisites of legal monstrosity, i.e. what a legal monster is supposed to be, by distinguishing between conditions of validity for normative acts and sound institutions. At the end of the day, the EU case study shows that also decent institutions can embrace monster laws.

9.1 A New Legal Order

From time to time, scholars have presented the EU institutions as a sort of political monstrosity. To appreciate the claim, we should put it in context. Despite the general international legal framework, every legal order has its own specificities: they depend on different legal cultures and traditions, the constitution of the system, and the moral grounds on which every legal order lies. Certain features of the EU institutions make them unique. According to the rulings of the EU Court of Justice in Luxembourg since the early 1960s, the 1957 Treaty of Rome, which established the European Economic Community (EEC), set up "a new legal order of international law".[1] Five reasons would support the doctrine of the Court of Justice about the uniqueness of EU law. These reasons help clarify some constitutional tenets of EU law that are relevant to a theory of legal monsters:

---

[1] See the third point of the summary of the 1963 ruling *Van Gend & Loos* in case 26 from 1962, i. e., according to the standard quotation, ECLI:EU: C:1963:1. The text refers also to the Court's ruling in *Costa v. Enel* (i.e. ECLI:EU:C:1964:66), and *Simmenthal* (ECLI:EU:C:1978:49).

U. Pagallo, *A Theory of Legal Monsters: Repression, Resistance, Rebellion*,
Philosophical Studies Series 161, https://doi.org/10.1007/978-3-032-10771-8_9

i. The Member States (MS) have limited their sovereign rights, although within certain fields, to create the new European institution: subjects of the new legal system are not only the MS, but also their "nationals" (Court of Justice, *Van Gend & Loos* ruling, no. 3 of the summary);
ii. The law, in accordance with "the spirit, the general scheme and the wording" of the Treaty of Rome, has "direct effects" on its subjects, whether MS or individuals, thus bypassing the MS legislation (*Van Gend & Loos*, no. 5 of the summary);
iii. EEC law directly confers rights upon — and obligations on — both MS and individuals, including other individuals as third parties to a lawsuit (*Van Gend & Loos*, no. 3 of the second part of the summary);
iv. Within the limited fields of EEC law, it follows the "supremacy" of the new law over the MS' own national law (Court of Justice, *Costa v. Enel* ruling, no. 6 of the summary from July 1964);
v. In all cases in which European and national law, either precedent or subsequent, enter into conflict, all national courts must not apply their own law but give immediate effect to directly applicable European law (Court of Justice, *Simmenthal* ruling from March 1978, no. 4 of the summary).

Another peculiarity of EU law concerns the protection of both the MS' constitutional rights and the human rights of the 1950 European Convention (ECHR). Since the aim was primarily to establish a common market, the Treaty of Rome did not mention any protection of human rights. The Court of Luxembourg aimed to fill this gap through the hermeneutical criterion of the "general principles of law" in the pioneering rulings of *Internationale Handelsgesellschaft* (from 1970), *Nold* (1974), and *Hauer* (1979). The European Court of Justice established the protection of human rights as an "integral part" of EEC law, referring to the common constitutional traditions of the MS and, in part, the ECHR framework. Some MS' High Courts, for example, the German Federal Constitutional Tribunal in Karlsruhe or the Italian Constitutional Court in Rome, openly confronted the Justices in Luxembourg through the 1960s and 70s, claiming to be entitled to the 'last word', or *Kompetenz-Kompetenz*, in case of conflict between national and EU law. However, this human rights confrontation progressively changed over the decades, up to the point that certain MS, like Germany for example, had to change their own constitution for infringement of fundamental rights on the basis of the new European legal system. For example, Art. 12a(4) of the German constitution was amended in December 2000, following the ruling of the Court of Justice of 11 January 2000, according to which EU law "precludes the application of national rules, such as those of German law, which exclude women in general from military employment involving the use of weapons".[2]

The uniqueness of EU law presents a further peculiarity related to its institutional design. The Treaty of Rome set up and shaped the EU institutions in the hottest years of the Cold War. The political constraints of the era recommended the "functionalism" of one of its Founding Fathers, Jean Monnet. Since it was impossible to build the new legal common house in a top-down way — i.e. through a constitution and

[2] See the *Tanja Kreil v Bundesrepublik Deutschland* ruling (ECLI:EU:C:2000:2).

the original powers of federal institutions — the only way to tackle litigation among old sovereigns in Europe was to start building the new common house according to a bottom-up approach, i.e. through the creation of a common market with its "four liberties": the free movement of goods, persons, capital, and services. Therefore, considering this pragmatic approach, it comes as no surprise that the design of the European institutions is often the bane of law students who have to tell, for example, the difference between the Council of Europe, i.e. a 'classic' international organisation related to the ECHR legal framework, and the European Council, which is the EU institution that defines the general political direction and priorities of the 'new legal system in international law'. A result of this pragmatic approach is that, in this new legal order, the protection of human rights concerns not only the constitution of 27 MS with their High Courts, but also two European authorities: the European Court of Human Rights in Strasbourg and the Court of Justice in Luxembourg with the distinct work of both a Council of Europe and a European Council.

To make things even more intricate, the European Union, formally established with the Maastricht Treaty in 1993, did not substitute the previous organisations with a single personhood of international law: the institutions of EU law, even after the creation of the EU in 1993, were still the European Coal and Steel Community, the European Atomic Energy Community, and the European Economic Community. These 'communities' impersonated for more than a decade the new 'union' before the corresponding organisations at the international level, for example, the European Council as regards certain international relations, the European Commission and the Council vis-à-vis negotiations of the European Economic Area, and the Commission as 'observer' before the UN. This institutional labyrinth was a source of embarrassment even for the EU institutions.

By the late 1990s, after the Maastricht Treaty and the creation of a common currency, the euro, the next grand project was the Constitution for Europe (2003). From the late 1990s to 2005, i.e. the year of the Dutch and French referendum on whether to embrace the European Constitution, a hot debate ignited the whole continent. A fragment of this debate is captured by a series of articles posted on the first online Italian law journal (filosofiadeldiritto.it), which my professor, Francesco Gentile, and I created in 1999. Vanity aside, it is against this framework of scholarly debates — which, for the first time, saw people interact via the new services of the web 1.0 — that we can appreciate the monstrous side of this story. In the early 2000s, two experts of EU law, Joseph Weiler and Marlene Wind, edited a volume on *European Constitutionalism beyond the State*, i.e. one of the thornier issues at that time (another hot topic being whether a European citizen and public opinion existed or could ever exist). Weiler and Wind chose Philip Allott for the last chapter or 'epilogue' of their volume (Allott 2003). The chapter is relevant for a theory of legal monsters, offering an opportunity to begin testing the requirements of every institutional monstrosity at the EU level.

Allott, nowadays emeritus of public international law at Cambridge, was never tender with the European project. In 1999, defining *The Concept of European Union* (Allott 1999), the intent was to stress the struggle 'between reason and imagination' in the legal and political design of the European institutions. His phrasing is rather sharp:

> The European Union is a waking dream of the bulimic political imagination, offering ... only the dream of all politico-bulimic dreams, a dream which is no longer merely a dream. (Allott 1999, at 36)

A few years later, Allott rephrased the claim, taking inspiration from the famous aquatint *The Sleep of Reason Produces Monsters* by Francisco Goya in 1799. In Allott's opinion, because of the lack of a well-ordered and coherent structure of the EU institutions, what we should expect from the European integration process is a monster. Moreover, attention should be drawn to a well-known sore point: the democratic deficit of such institutions. Discussing the new constitutional tenets of the continent, the European society must have had a foundational role, for example, conceiving the European constitution as a 'self-constituting' act of such European society (Allott 2003). However, Goya's satirical spirit was gone not only in Allott's analysis, but also, in the debate that followed with the reviews of the new legal monster. In the words of Nico Krisch:

> Philip Allott may be today's Pufendorf, except that is yet unclear whether the idea of reason he believes in is, like that of his predecessor, on the rise; in these late-modern or even post-modern times, he may well fight a losing battle. (Krisch 2005, at 321)

A new legal order of international law, such as the EU law since the early 1960s, ended forty years later with the old question of whether a legal system can trigger a legal monster. We can understand some of the reasons for both views, namely, Allott's thesis that, in the 1990s and early 2000s, the political design of the EU institutions looked bizarre even to its supporters; and Kirsch's criticism, which reminds us of Hart's remarks to Radbruch and many natural law supporters: the road to hell remains paved with good intentions.[3] Supporters of monster views and grandchildren of Pufendorf, however, have the burden to argue what kind of monster the EU institutions could be without contradicting themselves, either dealing with a Platonic "monstrous tyrant", a Fuller's "institutional monster", or a Hartian choice "between two evils". For a theory of legal monsters, it is crucial to inspect and take sides in this kind of debate on whether the EU can properly be deemed a legal monster and, in such a case, what type of monster the EU institutions could ever be.

---

[3] Against every Goya-like dream of reason, it is worth mentioning that the use of right reason, or principles of natural law in the phrasing of Hart, can well "serve to cloak the true nature of the problems with which we are faced and will encourage the romantic optimism that all the values we cherish ultimately will fit into a single system" (Hart 1958, at 620). We dwelt on Hart's warning above in Chapter 8.

9.2 The EU as a Monster

Rumours on the monstrosity of the EU have been greatly exaggerated. In Chapter 8, we noted the threshold for this assessment related to constitutional principles and the protection of human rights. All in all, we can say that among the several problems of the EU institutions — from the democratic deficit to a Brussels comitology — scholars and European citizens do not have to confront themselves with a systematic infringement of rights, or blatant violations of Treaties, as their existential priority. The same holds for a Pufendorf-like monster as a source of inspiration for Allott's claims on the monstrosity of the EU institutions. Pufendorf's remarks on the German Holy Roman Empire did not refer to the arbitrariness and irregularity of the institution as a problem of aesthetics and design for the German state in the mid-1600s: Such design problems were strictly related to the balance of power among state institutions.[4] Although the EU institutions, admittedly, still have to tackle a long list of problems, those problems do not entail any blatant violation of treaties, balance of power, international law, and even the natural law rights cherished by Pufendorf, such as the rights on contracts, family law, or property. The constitutionalist shift of the EU institutions over the past decades supports this conjecture.[5]

On the other hand, Allott's suggestion that only a 'self-constituting act' of the European society could establish a well-ordered and coherent structure of the EU institutions (Allott 2003), contradicts his own idea of the monstrosity of the EU 2003 constitutional project. We may even concede that the lack of a self-constituting act of the European society — the fulcrum of every nomos and ethos of the EU institutions — was a terrible mistake. Yet, it was just the European society, particularly French and Dutch voters, who struck down the whole constitutional project with their referendum in 2005. The same holds for the 2016 referendum in the UK. It speaks volumes that discussions over alleged monstrosities mostly revolved around the mutual accusations between supporters and opponents of Brexit.[6]

---

[4] According to Pufendorf (2007), the German empire did not fit any classic form of state, such as monarchy, aristocracy, or democracy. The monstrosity depended on moving away from the dictates of sound political science, or geometry, rather than accommodating any traditional wisdom. See above the second section of Chapter 6, and Osiander (2010).

[5] It is worth mentioning that, since the early 2000s, most scholars claim exactly the opposite of what Allott's monster may suggest. In technological regulation and the challenges of Artificial Intelligence, for example, some reckon that "in the last twenty years, the policy of the European Union in the field of digital technologies has shifted from a liberal economic perspective to a constitution-oriented approach" (De Gregorio 2021). According to this view, which draws on work of Waldron (2012) and Sajó & Uitz (2017), the intent is to protect people's rights by controlling every de facto power outside legal control (Pagallo 2022a). Other scholars similarly think that in "the global battle to regulate technology" three competing regulatory approaches are at stake, not only the market-driven approach of US law and the State-driven approach of China, but also, the rights-driven approach of EU law (Bradford 2023). Although we may disagree with Bradford's tripartition on models of legal regulation, or claims of "a constitution-oriented approach", there is no reasonable standard out there which supports Allott's idea that the EU is a monster.

[6] See above the second section of Chapter 3.

Four years after Allott's paper on Pufendorf-like EU monsters, in December 2007, the MS approved another agreement, the Lisbon Treaty, which entered into force in December 2009. The agreement cured the anomaly of the European institutions by conferring international personhood to the Union, thus unifying the old three European communities. Also, the new Treaty formally adopted the EU Charter of Fundamental Rights (CFR) enshrined in the 2000 Treaty of Nice. In the opinion of certain scholars, however, even these new steps of the EU project did not fix the original sin of the EU institutions. This time, the accusation of monstrosity came from Germany and can be summed up with the title of a pamphlet that Hans Magnus Enzensberger published in 2011, i.e. *Brussels, the Gentle Monster* (Enzensberger 2011).

The author was a poet and costume critic. His book does not expect to provide a strict legal analysis, though it sheds light on some criticalities of EU law (the real monsters). The mocking, ironic, and even melancholic tone of this European denunciation has nothing to do with the monstrous institutions under scrutiny in the previous chapters of this book, either dealing with the monsters of the *Vindiciae contra tyrannos*, the monsters of Coke or Pufendorf, or the monsters of the debate between Hart and Fuller. Also, Enzensberger's monster differs from Allott's monstrosity, although dwelling on the same institutions. After all, Enzensberger's monster was gentle. This view reminds us of the conditions that, with a healthy dose of sarcasm, make legislation look monstrous. Against requirements of monstrosity, which were under scrutiny in Chapters 6 and 8 of this book — from Fuller's eight 'ingredients' for sound legislation to the case law of the Italian Court of Cassation — *The Gentle Monster* has the merit to stress how often the bizarre rules of EU law, together with the opaque and even labyrinthine bureaucracy of the European Commission, put these conditions for sound legislation under stress. In the wording of Enzensberger:

> Even the Treaty of Lisbon, a substitute constitution which serves as the legal basis of the Union, is distinguished by the fact that merely reading it presents even the most willing European citizen with insuperable difficulties ... It cannot be by chance that even constitutional lawyers have difficulty understanding this prose. Unfortunately, we can assume that this was indeed the intention of the authors. (Enzensberger 2011, at 7–8)

The exaggerations in *Brussels, the Gentle Monster* — an oxymoron, in the end — highlight three critical points for a theory of legal monsters. First, legally speaking, Enzensberger as much as Allott was mistaken for the EU is not an institutional monster. Below, in Chapter 10, the focus of the analysis will be on those hard cases that regard whether and to what extent a legal system, state, or institution can be properly deemed as legally monstrous. The threshold is determined by blatant systematic violations of international law, such as human rights infringements, or constitutional safeguards at the national or regional level. The open problems of EU law do not arguably entail any institutional monstrosity according to this threshold.[7] The test for the monstrosity of the EU institutions is satisfied neither through any natural law

[7] The claim in this section can be verified with the comprehensive analysis provided in Craig & De Búrca (2021) and Barnard & Peers (2023). Regarding the CFR in particular, see Peers et al. (2021).

argument, nor based on today's constitutional (and human rights) standards, nor by relating them to some persisting pillar of legal positivism. In fact, scholars should be attentive to how the political meaning of the formula 'legal monsters' always entails a tragedy, such as Hart's dilemma of choosing "between two evils".[8]

Second, Enzensberger nonetheless has a point: decent institutions can trigger monsters, and the EU is no exception. We noted that this natural law argument, also popular in the common law tradition with William Blackstone in the mid-1700s, has become popular after the crisis of positivism in legal theory today (see Chapter 8). The assumption was illustrated with the case law of the Italian Court of Cassation, according to which a normative act, an administrative regulation, or a court ruling, can be a 'legal monster'. However, the ruling does not mean that the Parliament in Rome or another public authority should be considered monstrous. Such dogmas of legal positivism, from the theory of legislative normativism and the mechanical interpretation of the norms to the theory of unconditional obedience, faded away to prevent jurists from denouncing the monstrosity of certain acts. The constitutional and international tenets of today's legal framework have set the standard for distinguishing decent institutions from monster laws.

Third, it remains the open question of which aspects of Enzensberger's gentle monster can properly be understood as legal monsters. At times, the assessment of the conditions that make legal acts or statutes look monstrous — for example, retroactive or secret laws — may not require any particular expertise of positive law. However, requirements of congruency and consistency, coherence and intelligibility, often necessitate such expertise to determine the monstrosity of a normative act and the "logic of the system", according to the jargon of the Italian Court of Cassation. Therefore, the next section aims to discuss the conditions of monstrosity that affect certain normative acts through the case study of EU law because requirements of monstrosity should be tested against the sources of positive law with the specificities of every legal system. The issue does not revolve around whether an institution is monstrous, but rather whether a specific legislation, act, or provision is. EU law provides a rich source of examples of what may occur in other jurisdictions: even decent institutions can establish monstrous normative acts.

9.3 EU's Monster Laws: Three Case Studies

Over the centuries, scholars and philosophers have dissected the requirements that turn normative acts into genuine laws. Positive law has been assessed against principles of natural law, or customs and traditions of legal systems, to determine the legitimacy of acts and institutions. In certain cases, the contrast of positive law with principles of 'right reason' has been deemed so monstrous that, from ancient to modern constitutionalism, rules of positive law were considered illegitimate or void. To illustrate this contrast, previous parts of the book have dwelt on Fuller's eight

[8] The dilemma was illustrated in the second section of Chapter 8.

conditions on the 'morality of law'. Such hypotheticals drew attention to cases in which positive law challenges the very idea of what the law is supposed to be, hence appearing as a monster. Such assessment entails that acts of positive law should not have the force of the law because they either protect mere personal interests; or they are secret; retroactive; unintelligible; contradictory; ever changing; incoherently administered; or unfeasible to obey (Fuller 1964). According to an old Roman saying, nobody is held to that which is impossible, *ad impossibilia nemo tenetur*.

We noted in Chapter 8 that principles of natural law have been enshrined in current positive law through the constitutions of some Western countries after WW II and with regional conventions and international agreements, in particular, the international Bill of Rights. This incorporation of natural law into positive law suggests, however, that claims of normative monstrosity today — for example, the infringement of human dignity pursuant to the 1948 Preamble of the UDHR — must be substantiated with the interpretation of the norms and procedures, duties and obligations, of positive law that aim to protect against this or that kind of monstrosity. The procedural constraints, norms, and principles that are at work, for example, with the CFR legal framework at the EU level clarify this point.[9] To determine the monstrosity of a certain act, advocates of natural law schools, legal positivism, legal hermeneutics, or constitutionalism, must assess the design and material scope of a certain EU legislation, drawing on the common ground of the means through which the ends of such legislation can be attained. Considering the sources of EU law, we can repeat what Radbruch claimed in *Five Minutes of Legal Philosophy*, i.e. that the "work of centuries" has provided a "solid core" of principles which "have come to enjoy such a far-reaching consensus in the declarations of human and civil rights that only the deliberate skeptic can still entertain doubts about some of them" (Radbruch 1991). A methodological common ground and overlapping of natural law principles with principles of today's EU law have provided that "solid core" and "far-reaching consensus" among scholars regarding the meaning of the terms framing the legal question, the ways such terms are related to each other in legal reasoning, and the role of the principles that are at stake in the case.[10]

---

[9] The role that moral arguments play in these cases, according to certain scholars, concerns more 'soft ethics', than 'hard ethics', because of the incorporation of ethical arguments and moral principles into the fabric of positive law. In hard ethics, the focus is on what should or should not be done against current legislation, or in spite of it; in soft ethics, the aim is to amend and ameliorate the legislation (Floridi 2018). This soft approach characterised, for example, the report on *Trustworthy AI* released by the High-Level Expert Group that the European Commission set up in 2018 on the ethical principles for the normative challenges of AI (HLEG 2019). These recommendations were transplanted into the hard law of the Artificial Intelligence (AI) Act in July 2024 under Art. 1 and 95 of the Regulation. See Pagallo (2025a).

[10] This agreement of the legal community does not entail that no hard case may exist in EU law, nor that a sort of Dworkin's unique right answer may fix each of them. On the contrary, it is this agreement that supports the very distinction between plain and hard cases, also but not only, in EU law (Pagallo and Durante 2016).

The aim of the following paragraphs, however, is not to illustrate on this basis the long list of cases of normative monstrosity in EU law.[11] Instead, the focus will be on whether a specific normative act, such as the AI Act, Reg. (EU) 2024/1689 of EU law, can reasonably be grasped as a legal monster. The case study of EU law is helpful for a theory of legal monsters because it sheds light on four facets of monstrosity related to the ambitious aim of the EU legislators to adopt the first all-encompassing legislation on Artificial Intelligence (AI) across the board. The Regulation represents a tenet of the EU data strategy and digital policy over the past decade, and so, a demanding test for how to set the threshold of monstrosity under scrutiny in this book. Therefore, the attention is drawn to the standards of legal assessment — relating to the meaning of the terms framing the legal question, and how the interplay of such terms is grasped in accordance with the principles of EU law — against 'four ingredients' of Fuller's list.[12] Despite disputes of legal theory,[13] these "minimum conditions" make it apparent why certain legal provisions look monstrous:

i) Fuller's ingredient no. 4 on normative acts that are unintelligible;
ii) Fuller's ingredient no. 5 on normative acts that are incongruous, or inconsistent, rather than non-contradictory;
iii) Fuller's ingredient no. 6 on the future-proofing of the law vis-à-vis acts that are subject to over-frequent revision; and,
iv) Fuller's ingredient no. 7 on normative acts that defy human nature.

In all these cases, what is legally at stake is neither institutional monstrosity nor abstract human dignity, but rather the question of how to set the bar of evaluation and

[11] In addition to the cases mentioned in the fourth section of Chapter 8 (we return to further cases of monstrosity in EU law, concerning the e-privacy directive (Debusser 2005), and the regulation of internet cookies (Leenes and Kosta 2015; Mellet and Beauvisage 2019), in Chapter 11.

[12] The whole list was illustrated in the third section of Chapter 6.

[13] As one might expect, the eight ingredients of Fuller's "internal morality of law" have been the subject of much criticism. For example, according to Ronald Dworkin, Fuller's *The Morality of Law* can be deemed "an unsuccessful attempt to establish a novel claim about law and morality" (Dworkin 1965, at 668). An overall view of such criticisms in Nicholson (1974). Some other scholars have nonetheless defended Fuller's claims, for example, Colleen Murphy: "I defend Lon Fuller's view that the rule of law has conditional non-instrumental as well as instrumental moral value" (Murphy 2005, at 239). Regardless, Fuller's eight principles have been either integrated by natural law advocates, or amended by legal positivists (Rundle 2021). For example, as far as the latter are concerned, Joseph Raz suggests that a legal system can uphold the rule of law only on the basis of eight essential principles: (i) all laws should be prospective, open, and clear; (ii) laws should be relatively stable; (iii) the making of particular laws or orders should be guided by open, stable, clear, and general rules; (iv) the independence of the judiciary must be guaranteed; (v) the principles of natural justice, such as open and fair hearing, or absence of bias, must be observed; (vi) the courts should have review powers over the implementation of the other principles; (vii) the courts should be easily accessible; and, (viii) the discretion of the crime-preventing agencies should not be allowed to pervert the law (Raz 1979, at 214–218). Despite theoretical quarrels, it is noteworthy that Fuller's ingredients no. 4, 5, 6 and 7, under scrutiny in the following paragraphs of the analysis, overlap with Raz's principles (i), (ii), and (iii). This similarity may trigger new false friends. We return to this risk in the last section of this chapter and, moreover, as the subject matter of Chapter 10.

determine whether a legal text is decently clear, consistent, resilient, or impossible to obey, in accordance with the EU constitutional framework of fundamental rights safeguards (CFR).

The next three sub-paragraphs of this section intend to address the issue with a twofold aim: On the one hand, to show that even complex legal texts that are hardly readable or even contradictory do not necessarily entail cases of monstrosity (Sect. 9.3.1); on the other hand, to emphasise that even interpreting such a complex text as the AI Act in its best possible light does not prevent the creation of a normative monster (Sections 9.3.2 and 9.3.3).

9.3.1 On Clarity and Legal Certainty

The AI Act includes 180 recitals, 68+ definitions, 113 articles, and 13 annexes. At times, the complexity of the legal text is such that the examples of Enzensberger's *Brussels, the Gentle Monster* seem like child's play. Such an intricacy does not mean that it is impossible to extract any clear or coherent meaning from the text any more than it would be to square circles through stochastic methods in the legal domain. What is certain, however, is that the addressees of the regulation cannot be ordinary citizens but rather super experts in EU law (Greenstein and Zamboni 2025). The overall design of the regulation leaves one perplexed. From the first draft released by the European Commission in April 2021 to the final text adopted by the Council and the Parliament in July 2024, different approaches to the regulation of the technology — AI as the material scope of the legislation — have piled up as pie flats in the official document of the EU Regulation.

The AI Act was born as, in the jargon of EU lawyers, a 'horizontal regulation', i.e. an all-encompassing legislation that political reasons of compromise between the Commission, the Parliament, and the Council have complemented with a myriad 'vertical provisions'. The mix regards the regulation of specific AI models and systems, such as the "general purpose" AI models of the Regulation, and further 'vertical provisions' in fields such as civil aviation (Art. 102 and 108 of the AI Act); agriculture and forestry vehicles (Art. 103); marine equipment (Art. 105); and rail systems interoperability (Art. 106). The AI Act thus entails coordination problems with further fields of EU regulation. Recital 10 of the AI Act intends to make clear that the regulation does not "affect" the provisions of the general data protection regulation, the 2016 GDPR. Likewise, Recital 11 affirms that the Act should be understood without "prejudice" to Reg. 2022/2065 on a single market for digital services. Further, Recital 141 clarifies that the safeguards of the Act have to be intended "in accordance with" Reg. 2022/868 on data governance and Reg. 2023/2854 on fair access to and use of data. Further problems of coordination concern how the provisions of the AI Act are related to another field of legal governance and regulation: EU environmental law (Pagallo 2025a).

A further issue of the Act, in addition to problems of clarity and legal certainty, i.e. Fuller's ingredient no. 4, has to do with the overall approach of the regulation. Since the proposal of the European Commission in April 2021, the AI Act was presented as a risk-based regulation. The final version of the Act has kept the original distinction of four different types of risk:

i) Unacceptable risks;
ii) High-risk uses of AI systems;
iii) Other than high-risk uses of AI systems; and,
iv) AI systems in between such high-risk and low-risk deployments of technology.

Having discovered further models of AI in 2023, namely, the general-purpose AI models — which include large language models (LLMs), such as Chat GPT, generative AI, and foundation AI — the Brussels lawmakers added a further kind of risk to the original quadripartition of the regulation:

v) "Systemic risk" under Art. 3 no. 65 of the definitions provided in the AI Act.

Notwithstanding these five different types of risk, one can reasonably doubt that the AI Act really is a risk-based regulation (Ebers 2025). Rather than relying upon an empirical analysis of the probabilities of events, their consequences, and costs to determine the level of risk on which forms of accountability and responsibility may rely, what is considered risky under the AI Act rests on the apodictic assertion of the legislator under Art. 5 (unacceptable risk) and 6 (high risk) of the Act.

In particular, Art. 6 refers to the lists of Annex I and Annex III of the Regulation. Annex I covers a set of twenty "harmonised" directives and regulations, whilst Annex III details the areas of high risk under Art. 6(2) of the Act. The problem with this risk-based approach is that the distinction between high-risk and other risk uses of AI, once detached from empirical evidence, exposes itself to the threat that certain uses of technology may fall within the loopholes of such a political distinction. Lawmakers may attempt to tackle this threat through legal presumptions.[14] Even in this case, it remains to be seen how the Act should tackle those risks, such as the environmental impact of the technology, which is politically considered low risk and, hence, mostly devolved to the goodwill of the private sector through the voluntary codes of conduct set up in Art. 95 of the Act.

Such problems of legal design in the AI Act, regarding the intricacy of the wording and the certainty of the overall regulation with further different pieces of EU law, do not entail that the legislation cannot attain its ends. The anomalies in the legislative design of the AI Act do not make the regulation as such ineffective. In the previous section, we noted that the bar this book sets for the monstrosity of normative acts is stricter than Allott's EU monster or Enzensberger's EU monster. Several provisions of the Act are indeed hardly intelligible (Fuller's ingredient no. 4); or incongruous and inconsistent (Fuller's no. 5). Art. 10(3) of the 2021 Proposal even requested what

---

[14] This is the case of the "high-impact capabilities" of AI models, for example, GPT-4 measured in floating point operations (FLOPs) with "significant impact on the internal market due to its reach" (Recital 111 of the Act). The EU law makers have in fact established the legal presumption that all LLMs, such as GPT-4, have 'high impact capabilities' pursuant to Art. 51(1) of the legislation since the pre-training for GPT-4 just required about 10^25 FLOPS in 2024. Most computer scientists, however, consider this threshold either arbitrary or meaningless (Hooker 2024).

is impossible to obey by defying human nature, namely, the Commission's idea that AI data training should have been "free of errors" (Fuller's no. 7). It is a well-known truth of computer science that there is no such thing as a software without bugs.[15]

However, EU interpreters may still adopt the "principle of charity" of Donald Davidson (Davidson 1984), according to whom, when interpreting someone or something like the AI Act, there is no choice but to ascribe to it overall logicality and rationality as well as beliefs and utterances which are mostly true, to find consistency in the complex legal framework. Therefore, for the sake of argument, we may concede that there is still a remedy for all shortcomings of the regulation under scrutiny in this paragraph with aims of harmonisation and risk governance. Is there another way in which (certain provisions of) the AI Act must be considered monstrous?

9.3.2 On Equality

The protection of fundamental rights is a mantra of the AI Act. Such protection regards Fuller's ingredient no. 5 of what makes legal acts sound or vice versa monstrous, i.e. lack of congruence and consistency against Art. 20 of the EU Charter of Fundamental Rights (CFR) on the principle of equality before the law. We noted that a problem with the design of the Act is not only what the legislation defines as high-risk uses of AI, but also, what may entail a high-risk impact on society and the protection of fundamental rights. This is what occurs with the carbon footprint and energy requirements of the technology as well as the use of minerals and fossil fuels, water consumption, or global warming potential of AI vis-à-vis the right to a high level of environmental protection enshrined in EU law with Art. 37 CFR.

Scholars have repeatedly stressed that the development of AI systems and models can imperil crucial environmental resources for current and future generations (Wilson and van der Velden 2022). The pressure on rare-earth elements generated by the computing industry, together with the increasing volume of e-waste, can have important socio-political implications for developing countries and vulnerable populations (Heacock et al. 2016), especially considering threats of dependency from private actors who own and operate AI systems and infrastructures (Bolton et al. 2021; Zuiderwijk et al. 2021). Some scholars think that digital technologies, as much as AI systems, should be properly conceived of as a technology of extraction. In the wording of Kathy Crawford, "from the minerals drawn from the earth, to the labour pulled from low-wage information workers", AI fuels "a shift toward undemocratic governance and increased inequity" (Crawford 2021). It is thus against this framework that we can appreciate why the AI Act only covers a part of the environmental issues brought forth by uses of AI under the high-risk management procedures of Art. 9 and the fundamental rights impact assessment of Art. 27 of the Regulation. The political choice to leave the environmental sustainability of the technology mostly to

[15] Art. 10(3) and Recital 67 of the AI Act still pretend that "training, validation and testing data sets" shall be "free of errors" but only "to the best extent possible".

voluntary initiatives put in place by providers of AI systems through the formation of codes of conduct remains a source of significant concern (Gailhofer et al. 2021; Silva et al. 2025; Ylönen 2025).

In addition, the AI Act's framework should be confronted with that which the European Commission expects from scholars when they present their Horizon Europe projects for funding. In these cases, under Art. 19 of Reg. (EU) 2021/695, there is a compulsory self-assessment of the environmental implications of every scientific project, which includes:

i) The description of uses of AI with power consumption and carbon footprint, among others;
ii) The list of legal sources, including regulations and the ethical guidelines for trustworthy AI that AI systems of the project shall abide by;
iii) The ways in which the project intends to minimise or prevent negative impacts on the environment;
iv) Risk mitigation plans.

The AI Act could have imposed a similar compulsory environmental self-assessment for both high-risk and other than high-risk uses of AI.[16] By endorsing the voluntary clauses of Art. 95, the threat of the Act is that scholars will have to face more legal burdens and environmental responsibilities for their EU projects than those of heavyweight companies for their AI systems in the EU market.

Admittedly, the AI Act will be at full speed only on 2 August 2026, thus remaining open to multiple readings and implementations. Following Davidson's principle of charity, we can hope that the environmental level of protection will be determinant in the risk management obligations set up in Art. 9 of the Act; that the fundamental rights impact assessment of Art. 27 will be good enough together with the safeguard clauses of Art. 95 on codes of conduct; and that the governance mechanisms of the Regulation will detect and tackle all environmental impacts of AI that may fall within the loopholes of the Act. However, even in the best possible light, the premises are not promising for four reasons:

i) The set of uses of AI under Art. 9 (risk management) is limited;
ii) The impact assessment under Art. 27 (fundamental rights) is even more limited;
iii) The safeguards of Art. 95 (codes of conduct) are voluntary; and,
iv) The criteria for the environmental assessment under Art. 37 CFR are open to divergent interpretations, that is, between environmental sustainability and the sustainable development of AI uses.[17]

[16] As a matter of fact, the Commission vetoed every compulsory environmental self-assessment because a class of AI systems and uses had to remain free from all regulatory constraints and administrative burdens. This was the plan since the very beginning with the Commission's pyramid illustrating the risk-based approach of the Regulation in spring 2021. At the base of the pyramid were indicated the low risk uses of AI for which no obligations should have to be established: see Pagallo (2025a).

[17] The fundamental right to the high quality of the environment pursuant to Art. 37 CFR has in fact to be interpreted in accordance with the 'integration principle' of Art. 7–10 and 12–13 of the Lisbon

Consequently, the contrast between the compulsory environmental self-assessment of scholars under the Horizon Europe programs and the overall approach of the Regulation reflects an uncertain state of legal affairs, which is even strident considering the duties of scholars under Reg. (EU) 2021/695 against the principle of equality before the law enshrined in Art. 20 CFR. It is only up to a complex legal combination of potentially convergent hermeneutical solutions to make it feasible to avert a monstrous outcome. This bet of the legislator on a sort of four-variable astral conjunction is what assumes the form of a legal monster. The bet seems more similar to an astrological guess than an astronomical calculation.

9.3.3 On Future-proofing

One critical threat of technological regulation is the over-frequent revision of the law to cope with the pace of technological innovation, according to Fuller's ingredient no. 6. The effect can be either hindering technological innovation or continuously amending the law, threatening the principle of legal certainty. The field of civil aviation provides a cautionary tale with the regulation of drones. The EU lawmakers first endorsed with Reg. (EU) 2008/216 a highly decentralised network for the governance and regulation of "unmanned aerial" vehicles (UAV) and systems (UAS): Most powers were up to the MS and their national civil aviation authorities. However, the design of the overall regulation soon led to the fragmentation of the EU legal system with a wave of extremely detailed regulations and prohibitions on the use of drones by authorities such as the Italian Civil Aviation Authority, or 'ENAC' (Pagallo 2017). The EU lawmakers had to intervene with Reg. (EU) 2018/1139 on common rules for drones in the field of civil aviation (Bassi 2019). The centralisation of this new legal framework, also dubbed the General Regulation, did not prevent further threats of fragmentation and over-frequent revision of legal texts. The overall picture is indeed discouraging. A full array of delegated and implementing regulations of the European Commission (EC) have followed the General Regulation through five different waves of legislative activism so far:

i) Reg. 2019/945 and the so-called Drones Regulation (Reg. 2019/947);
ii) The U-space regulatory package (Reg. 2021/664, Reg. 2021/665 and Reg. 2021/666);
iii) The EC Implementing Regulation 2023/203;
iv) New five EC regulations, i.e., from Delegated Reg. (EU) 2024/1107 to the Implementing Regulation (EU) 2024/1111;
v) The consolidated version of Regulation (EU) 2018/1139 incorporating Reg. (EU) 2024/2803, also dubbed SES2+ recast.

Treaty on what is (socially, economically and financially) sustainable. This means that the range and number of interests to be accommodated in the impact assessment process may decrease the relevance that the green safeguards should have in such assessment of environmental sustainability (McIntyre 2013; Peers et al. 2021; Pagallo et al. 2022).

On top of this, the set of opinions, guidance materials, and technical standards released by the European Aviation Security Agency, or 'EASA', complement the legal framework. At the time of writing, we are still waiting for the first use of air-taxis for commuters, or for package delivery in urban centres, or for drugs and medications, supplies and tests for patients being treated at home. The AI Act threatens a similar fate. It is a sort of paradox that Recital 4 of the Act shall remind us of how "AI is a fast evolving family of technologies that contributes to a wide array of economic, environmental and societal benefits across the entire spectrum of industries and social activities". The principle of 'technological neutrality' — and for that matter, every legal technique that may help the law to prevent the obsolescence of regulations aiming to govern advancements of technology[18] — was first enshrined in the 2021 draft of the Commission and then discarded in the institutional trialogue with Parliament and Council (Pagallo 2025b). How the AI Act intends to tackle the known-unknowns and even the unknown-unknowns of its own provisions can generate monsters.

To corroborate the conjecture, attention should be drawn to the legal techniques of the AI Act against its own obsolescence. On the one hand, as much as occurs in the field of drone regulation, powers are devolved back to the Commission with the delegated acts of Art. 58, 60, 68, 72, 92, and 101 of the AI Act. On the other hand, a significant role is played by the manifold fronts of Art. 112 on the evaluation and review of the whole Act. For example, every year the Commission will have to assess whether the list of Annex III and that related to Art. 5 on high-risk uses of AI should be amended (Art. 112(1)). Every four years, by the end of this decade, lawmakers shall discuss, among other things, whether "extending existing area headings or adding new area headings in Annex III" (no. 2). Reports should include the assessment of how national competent authorities implement the regulation, state of penalties, harmonised standards, and "the number of undertakings that enter the market after the entry into application of this Regulation" (no. 4). 2 August 2028 will be particularly relevant because, in addition to the previous provisions of Art. 112, this is the first deadline for the Commission's reports on the functioning of the AI Office, progress on the development of standards, and the impact and effectiveness of the Codes of conduct (respectively no. 5, 6 and 7 of Art. 112).

Therefore, by August 2028, it is likely that lawmakers in Brussels will be spoiled for choice as to where the AI Act has to be amended, especially considering the exponential growth of innovation, from computing power to data availability for further AI models, systems, and approaches that shall be reasonably expected in the next future. However, how the AI Act intends to tackle its own obsolescence threatens a new legal monster: The problem is not solved by devolving powers back to the Commission, complementing the definitions of the Act, integrating the lists of Annexes, or checking the effectiveness of myriad provisions. Instead, it regards the

[18] On legal techniques that can help the law prevent failings in technological regulation, see Reed (2012). The principle of technological neutrality, in particular, establishes that legal regulations apply in identical ways whatever the technology. Both Recital 15 of the EU general data protection regulation (GDPR), and the right to authorise communication of a work to the public in the field of EU copyright law illustrate this legal technique against risks of inefficacy and normative obsolescence.

original aim of the legislation, its risk-based approach. Whether or not the AI Act must be considered a risk-based regulation, a straight risk assessment of the uses of AI remains problematic given the uncertainties associated with the notion of risk and the corresponding protection of rights; the difficulty in assessing all risks raised by specific uses of AI; the costs related to such assessment; and the future-proofing of the law. It is an awful mistake to address the threats of legal obsolescence through a continuous revision of the law. Such means exacerbate the troubles with the ends of the entire legislation and put the principle of legal certainty at risk. Previous shortcomings of EU legislators with the regulation and governance of drones have taught nothing.[19] To err is human, to persist in making the same mistake is legally monstrous.

9.4 Institutional Design

Institutional design plays a crucial role in forging monstrous laws. Contrary to those monsters of EU law, such as Allott's monster (i.e. the hubris of EU law) or Enzensberger's monster (i.e. the pedantic kindness of the EU technocrat), the focus of this chapter has been on what the law is called to do by stressing that rules of lawmakers, even endorsing a principle of hermeneutical charity, can trigger conflicts between ends, for instance, ensuring safety and security against risky uses of AI vis-à-vis the protection of fundamental rights, such as the right to a high level of environmental protection and the principle of equality in EU law. The monstrosity can depend on how lawmakers design the regulation because of incompetency or political constraints.[20] For example, we noted that since the first draft of the AI Act, the Commission vetoed any compulsory environmental self-assessment for commercial uses of the technology because, as a matter of principle, a class of AI systems and uses of technology had to remain free from every regulatory constraint and administrative burden. The compromise of the final text in July 2024, notwithstanding the efforts of the European Parliament (Gailhofer et al. 2021), set the regulatory burden well below the bar of constraints and safeguards that have been established with Art. 19 of Reg. (EU) 2021/695 on EU scientific funding for Horizon Europe projects.

[19] Similar shortcomings affect the governance of autonomous vehicles or, in the phrasing of the European regulations 2022/1426 and 2022/2236, "automated driving systems". Unlike what is happening in many US cities with Waymo's robotaxis services, for example, we are waiting for the implementation of these technologies on European roads. Although many implementation problems concern the member states, it speaks volumes that, at the time of writing, the European Commission is still working on simplifying its own labyrinthine rules. See Pagallo (2022b).

[20] Consider the EU e-money directive 46 from 2000 which reminds of how the regulatory claims of the law may fail vis-à-vis digital innovation because of lack of technological expertise. After the implementation of the directive, which aimed at expanding traditional forms of centralisation to online interaction, new forms of payment, such as PayPal, made the legal regulation obsolete. The EU legislators in Brussels had to amend themselves with a new directive, n. 110 from 2009.

Although we may understand the political constraints of the compromise, an act does not stop being a monster for that comprehension.

By distinguishing monstrous acts from decent institutions — for example, most MS of the EU have a long list of cases discussed before the European Court of Human Rights which have not turned them into legal monsters[21] — the intent has been to provide a method to ascertain cases of normative monstrosity on the basis of a legal threshold. Drawing on Fuller's 'minimum conditions' of the law (Fuller 1964), the attention was drawn to four classes of monstrous acts, although it should be admitted that the threshold, *pace* Fuller, has been determined through the analysis of whether such normative acts represent reasonable means for effective legislation. Such reasonability was understood either according to the specificity and uniqueness of a legal order, such as the law of the EU institutions, or acknowledging that certain classes of monstrous acts are common to all legal systems, for example, ever changing legislation. This common property of all legal systems was further elucidated in connection with that which makes institutions decent, i.e. the protection of constitutional safeguards vis-à-vis the international Bill of Rights.

However, the distinction between normative and institutional monstrosity does not intend to overlook how certain normative acts can go together with monstrous institutions. The monstrous design of certain acts, or parts of them, may affect the soundness of every legal order. Therefore, the meaning of institutional design can be intended either as the technical or instrumental way to attain or safeguard certain rights and principles, or in accordance with the soundness of the ends that regard the material scope of the legislation. The exercise of legal hermeneutics on the monsters of this chapter must hence be supplemented with all those cases in which a normative act turns a decent institution into a monster, or is the output of a monstrous institution. This is the further political meaning of the formula that can be traced back to the equalisation of tyrants with monsters since ancient times, and that nowadays refers to all those legal systems that are well below the threshold with which we tested the EU pedigree on human rights and further constitutional safeguards against potential monsters.

Consider current monstrous institutions, if any, such as Kim Jong-un's North Korea or Maduro's Venezuela, that is, countries in which international and regional standards on human rights protection and constitutional safeguards are systematically

---

[21] Some data are instructive. In 2023, for example, 52 judgements concerning Italy were issued. 48 of these found at least one violation of ECHR rights. The majority (23 cases) had to do with the violation of Art. 6; in particular, 8 cases on the right to fair trial, 8 on excessive length of proceedings, and 5 on the execution of a judgement. Further sets of violations regarded Art. 1, Protocol 1 on the right to property (16 cases); Art. 5 on personal freedom and security (14 cases); Art. 8 on privacy (10 cases); and Art. 3 on inhuman or degrading treatments (9 cases). Despite this series of violations, no academic or advocacy group has seriously denounced the Italian Republic as a monstrous institution. The statistical report of the ECHR rulings is available at the ECHR website: see, accessed on September 8, 2025 from https://www.echr.coe.int/d/stats-violation-2023-eng?p_l_back_url=%2Fsearch%3Fq%3Dstate%2Bstatistics%2B2023&p_l_back_url_title=Search%20+%20https://www.echr.coe.int/statistical-reports.

infringed.[22] This scenario is critical for a theory of legal monsters because it brings us back to the 'false friends' of Chapter 8 concerning the distinction between monstrous institutions and normative monsters after the crisis of legal positivism. The plan of tyrannical institutions with human rights violations and constitutional infringements poses a critical problem of legal theory. The tyrant does not only draw attention to standards of legal evaluation at work in this chapter with the international Bill of Rights, regional Declarations and Charters, and most Western constitutions. Also, focus must be on what should be done against evil institutions until they have power.

This latter problem introduces a new function of the metaphor on legal monsters, i.e. monsters as the symbol for an open, organised, and even armed resistance to the government or ruler (Turchetti 2001). Previous parts of this book have only partially touched upon this further function of the image. We noted in Chapter 2 that Aristotle, in *Politics* (1267 a), mentions the honour that may be bestowed to those who kill a tyrant, not those who murder thieves. Cicero followed suit by grounding tyrannicide on the precepts of natural law (*On Duties*, III, 4). In Chapter 6, the problem was at stake with the claims of the *Vindiciae contra tyrannos* against the monstrous tyrants of the late 1500s, and Locke's right to resist in the late 1600s. In Chapter 8, the debate between Hart and Fuller dwelt on whether the acts of those monstrous institutions, such as the Nazi regime, or Kim Jong-un's North Korea and Maduro's Venezuela for that matter, have to be considered valid law. The formula 'legal monster' is not simply understood in these cases as a source of legal criticism, as occurred throughout this chapter with the case study of EU law. Instead, the formula 'legal monster' must be grasped as a symbol of rebellion, thus entailing the further issue of whether and to what extent subjects have legal rights under such monstrous circumstances.

The next chapter aims to clarify how criticism and resistance against legal monsters can turn into open revolt under the use of the metaphor as a symbol for such a resistance. In Pufendorf's terms, the focus is again on 'institutional monsters', rather than 'monstrous normative acts', although considering what Pufendorf — following Hobbes — explicitly rejected, i.e. a right to resist such evil sovereigns or rulers. After using the formula on monsters as the target of legal repression, or as a source of legal criticism, it is thus necessary to inspect this third use of the metaphor that opposes repression and brings any criticism to the limit of open rebellion. A new set of issues on legal rights, interpretation of normative texts, and validity of the law follows as a result of this third function of the formula. Although decent institutions can nurture monstrous laws, it is only monstrous institutions with their normative acts that mostly raise tragic choices.

[22] As regards Kim Jong-un's North Korea see, among many, Tan (2010), Goedde (2018), and Khaerunnisa (2022). We return to Maduro's Venezuela below in the second section of Chapter 10.

References

Allott, P. 1999. The concept of European union. *Cambridge Yearbook of European Legal Studies* 2:31–59.

Allott, P. 2003. Epilogue: Europe and the dream of reason. In *European constitutionalism beyond the state*, ed. J. H. H. Weiler and M. Wind, 202–225. Cambridge: Cambridge University Press.

Barnard, C., and S. Peers, eds. 2023. *European union law*. Oxford: Oxford University Press.

Bassi, E. (2019). European drones regulation: Today's legal challenges. In *International Conference on Unmanned Aircraft Systems (ICUAS)*, Atlanta, GA, USA, 443–450.

Bolton, M., R. Raven, and M. Mintrom. 2021. Can AI transform public decision-making for sustainable development? An exploration of critical earth system governance questions. *Earth System Governance* 9:100116.

Bradford, A. 2023. *Digital empires: The global battle to regulate technology*. Oxford: Oxford University Press.

Craig, P., and D. De Búrca, eds. 2021. *The evolution of EU law*. Oxford: Oxford University Press.

Crawford, K. 2021. *Atlas of AI: Power, politics, and the planetary costs of artificial intelligence: The real worlds of artificial intelligence*. New Haven, CT: Yale University Press.

Davidson, D. 1984. *Inquiries into truth and interpretation*. Oxford: Clarendon Press.

De Gregorio, G. 2021. The rise of digital constitutionalism in the European union. *International Journal of Constitutional Law* 19 (1): 41–70.

Debusser, F. 2005. The EU e-privacy directive: A monstrous attempt to starve the cookie monster? *International Journal of Law and Information Technologies* 13:70–97.

Dworkin, R. 1965. Philosophy, morality, and law. *University of Pennsylvania Law Review* 113:668–690.

Ebers, M. 2025. Truly risk-based regulation of artificial intelligence-how to implement the EU's AI act. *European Journal of Risk Regulation* 16:684–703.

Enzensberger, H. M. 2011. *Brussels, the gentle monster: Or the disenfranchisement of Europe*. London: Seagull.

Floridi, L. 2018. Soft ethics and the governance of the digital. *Philosophy and Technology* 31 (1): 1–8.

Fuller, L. L. 1964. *The morality of law*. revised ed. New Haven, CT: Yale University Press.

Gailhofer, P. et al. (2021). *The role of artificial intelligence in the European green deal, study for the special committee on artificial intelligence in a digital age (AIDA)*. Policy Department for Economic, Scientific and Quality of Life Policies. Luxembourg: European Parliament.

Goedde, P. 2018. Human rights diffusion in North Korea: The impact of transnational legal mobilization. *Asian Journal of Law and Society* 5 (1): 175–203.

Greenstein, S., and M. Zamboni. 2025. Navigating the legislative dilemma: Evaluating the EU AI act's approach to regulating emerging technologies. *The Theory and Practice of Legislation* 13(3): 312–352.

Hart, H. L. A. 1958. Positivism and the separation of law and morals. *Harvard Law Review* 71 (4): 593–629.

Heacock, M., et al. 2016. E-waste and harm to vulnerable populations: A growing global problem. *Environmental Health Perspectives* 124 (5): 550–555.

HLEG. (2019). High-level expert group on artificial intelligence's ethics guidelines for trustworthy AI, Brussels, European commission. Accessed on September 8, 2025 from https://digital-strategy.ec.europa.eu/en/library/ethics-guidelines-trustworthy-ai.

Hooker, S. (2024). *On the limitations of compute thresholds as a governance strategy. arXiv preprint*, arXiv:2407.05694.

Khaerunnisa, A. 2022. The roles of the United Nations human right council (UNHRC) in handling the human rights cases in political prison camp North Korea. *Mediasi Journal of International Relations* 5 (2): 46–63.
Krisch, N. 2005. Europe's constitutional monstrosity. *Oxford Journal of Legal Studies* 25 (2): 321–334.
Leenes, R., and E. Kosta. 2015. Taming the cookie monster with Dutch law—A tale of regulatory failure. *Computer Law & Security Review* 31 (3): 317–335.
McIntyre, O. 2013. The principles of integration and interrelationships in international law related to sustainable development: sobering lessons from EU law. In *Confronting ecological and economic collapse: Ecological integrity for law*, ed. L. Westra, P. Taylor, and A. Michelot, 104–119. London: Routledge.
Mellet, K., and T. Beauvisage. 2019. Cookie monsters. Anatomy of a Digital Market Infrastructure. *Consumption Markets & Culture* 23 (2): 110–129.
Murphy, C. 2005. Lon Fuller and the moral value of the rule of law. *Law and Philosophy* 24:239–262.
Nicholson, P. P. 1974. The internal morality of law: Fuller and his critics. *Ethics* 84 (4): 307–326.
Osiander, A. (2010). Irregulare aliquod corpus et monstro simile: Can historical comparisons help understand the European union?, SSRN 1648807. Accessed on September 8, 2025 from https://papers.ssrn.com/sol3/papers.cfm?abstract_id=1648807.
Pagallo, U. (2017). From automation to autonomous systems: A legal phenomenology with problems of accountability. In *International Joint Conferences on Artificial Intelligence Organization (IJCAI-17)*. Melbourne, 17–23.
Pagallo, U. 2022a. The politics of data in EU law: Will it succeed? *Digital Society* 1:20.
Pagallo, U. 2022b. The politics of self-driving cars. In *Autonomous vehicle ethics: The trolley problem and beyond*, ed. R. Jenkins, D. Černy, and T. Hríbek, 159–175. Oxford: Oxford University Press.
Pagallo, U. 2025a. On twelve shades of green: Assessing the levels of environmental protection in the artificial intelligence act. *Minds & Machines* 35:10.
Pagallo, U. 2025b. LLMs meet the AI act: Who's the sorcerer's apprentice? *Cambridge Forum on AI: Law and Governance* 1:1e.
Pagallo, U., J. Ciani Sciolla, and M. Durante. 2022. The environmental challenges of AI in EU law: Lessons learned from the artificial intelligence act (AIA) with its drawbacks. *Transforming Government: People, Process and Policy* 16 (3): 359–376.
Pagallo, U., and M. Durante. 2016. The pros and cons of legal automation and its governance. *European Journal of Risk Regulation* 7 (2): 323–334.
Peers, S., T. Hervey, J. Kenner, and A. Ward, eds. 2021. *The EU charter of fundamental rights: A commentary*. Oxford: Hart.
Pufendorf, S. (2007). *The present state of Germany*, trans. E. Bohun. Indianapolis: Liberty Fund.
Radbruch, G. 1991. Five minutes of legal philosophy. In *Philosophy of law*, ed. J. Fienberg and H. Gross, 103–104. Belmont: Wadsworth.
Raz, J. 1979. *The authority of law*. Oxford: Oxford University Press.
Reed, Ch. 2012. *Making laws for cyberspace*. Oxford: Oxford University Press.
Rundle, K. 2021. The morality of the rule of law: Lon L. Fuller. In *The Cambridge companion to the rule of law*, ed. J. Meierhenrich and N. Loughlin, 186–201. Cambridge: Cambridge University Press.
Sajó, A., and R. Uitz. 2017. *The constitution of freedom: An introduction to legal constitutionalism*. Oxford: Oxford University Press.
Silva, S. R., D. C. Vadillo, and A. P. Andrés. 2025. Green AI and AI act: Pioneering legislation or merely an environmental statement? *Revista Catalana de Dret Ambiental* 16 (1): 1–38.
Tan, M. H. 2010. A state of rightlessness: The egregious case of North Korea. *Mississippi Law Journal* 80:681–709.
Turchetti, M. 2001. *Tyrannie et tyrannicide de l'Antiquité à nos jours*. Paris: PUF.

Waldron, J. (2012). *Constitutionalism: A skeptical view*, NYU School of Law, Public Law Research Paper No. 10-87. Available at SSRN: https://ssrn.com/abstract=1722771, accessed on 8 September 2025.

Wilson, C., and M. van der Velden. 2022. Sustainable AI: An integrated model to guide public sector decision-making. *Technology in Society* 68:101926.

Ylönen, M. 2025. Reconceptualising the Brussels effect. *JCMS: Journal of Common Market Studies*. https://doi.org/10.1111/jcms.13731.

Zuiderwijk, A., Y.-C. Chen, and F. Salem. 2021. Implications of the use of artificial intelligence in public governance: A systematic literature review and a research agenda. *Government Information Quarterly* 38:101577.

Chapter 10
Paths to Rebellion

This chapter examines the use of the formula 'legal monsters' as a symbol of open, organised, and armed resistance against rulers and governments. The analysis inspects what a rebel is supposed to be by stressing differences with revolutionary men and what rights, if any, rebels may have vis-à-vis discrepancies of opinions among scholars (and institutions). Discussions on rebel's rights are understood in connection with either the internal perspective of the social group, which accepts and uses the rules of a legal system as their guide to appraisal and conduct, or the external stance of observers who do not necessarily accept such rules. The overall aim is to illustrate multiple paths to rebellion and to take sides on whether the unjust rules of monstrous governments should be considered valid law in the interplay between formal and material sources of the legal phenomenon.

10.1 Rebels and Revolutions

Rebels have claimed moral rights against monstrous tyrants since ancient times. This book has traced this use of the formula back to Plato's philosophy and the idea that tyrants are the opposite of the Philosopher-King and his wisdom. In Roman times, from Cicero's *On Duties* to Seneca's *Hercules Furens* and his fight against monsters, the rebel's rights included the killing of the tyrant.[1] In Chapter 6, we noted that this use of the formula on monstrous tyrants was still alive in the late 1500s, for example, with the *Vindiciae contra Tyrannos*, in which the 'third question' of the essay is on "whether it is lawful to resist a ruler who is oppressing or ruining the country, and how far such resistance may be extended; by whom, how, and by what right or law it is permitted" (Brutus ed. 1924). In the second of the *Two Treatises of Government*, Locke even pokes fun at those scholars, such as the Scottish royalist and Catholic

[1] See Cicero (ed. 1887, at III, 4), and Seneca (ed. 1917, at 895), respectively.

U. Pagallo, *A Theory of Legal Monsters: Repression, Resistance, Rebellion*, Philosophical Studies Series 161, https://doi.org/10.1007/978-3-032-10771-8_10

writer William Barclay – who coined the term 'Monarchomachs' in *De Regno et Regali Potestate* from 1600 – because of the limits Barclay sought to establish for all theories of tyrannicide that were popular in his times (Locke ed. 1823, at § 230).

Locke's irony rests on two main reasons, i.e. the nature of rebellions and their legal meaning. On the one hand, those constraints, such as Barclay's ideas on people's right to defend themselves but not to attack their prince, nor to avenge any past violence, or exceed "the bounds of due reverence and respect", would only be a sort of imaginary resistance (Locke 1823, § 234). Indeed, in Locke's view, there is no such thing as particular restraints for forms of rebellion because rebels and institutions find themselves confronted in a state of war (*op. cit.*, § 226). This state of war does not mean that legal complaints should be just silenced on the battlefield: Chapter XVI of the second *Treatise* makes it clear that just wars can be differentiated from unjust wars. Force and power, as a result, are not the criteria for establishing what the law is but rather the means to protect the individuals' rights. We return to this interplay between force and the law with the corresponding rebel's legal rights in the following section.

On the other hand, regarding the political foundation of the rebel's claims, they concern the natural roots of the rights and how they refer to a certain legal tradition. The rebellion against the monster and even the killing of a king have been considered in both ancient and modern times as a restoration of the constitution and the laws of the land. The foundational act of the community does not aim to reset the political order but rather to re-establish it, as occurs with Locke's claim on the people's right to provide for "their safety anew" (Locke 1823, § 226). This legal anchorage is still at work with the American Revolution in which, drawing on Locke's ideas on individual rights and property – but also on Montesquieu's assumptions on separation of political powers and Rousseau's civic liberty and the constitution of freedom – the aim of a 'new beginning' is at the core of many revolutionary claims in the former British colonies. Hannah Arendt's account of the American Revolution provides an idealised version of this view, according to which the goal of the Founding Fathers could be understood as the antithesis of what occurred a decade later with the 'year zero' of the French Revolution in 1789, and later, with the Soviet Revolution in 1917.[2] In Arendt's phrasing:

> Historically speaking, the men of the American Revolution, like their colleagues on the other side of the Atlantic, had been wrong when they thought they were merely revolving back to an 'early period' in order to retrieve ancient rights and liberties. But, politically speaking, they had been right in deriving the stability and authority of any given body politic from its beginning, and their difficulty had been that they could not conceive of a beginning except as something which must have occurred in a distant past. (Arendt ed. 2006, at 190)

Arendt's interpretation of the American Revolution must be taken cautiously because the understanding of those events should consider the novelty not only every Founding Father, but also the most traditional of rebels, must deal with. Concerning,

[2] The year zero of the French Revolution has to be intended literally: in 1792, the Legislative Assembly established 1 January 1789 as Year I. See Zerubavel (1977) and Shaw (2011). Regarding the vicissitudes of time in the Soviet Revolution, see Williams (1995) and Petrone (2000).

for example, the American Revolution, it was soon apparent that the 1776 agreement between the former thirteen colonies – the so-called Articles of the confederation – would not have prevented risks of fragmentation. Even the war of resistance against the United Kingdom under the orders of George Washington illustrated the threat. The lack of food, shoes, clothing, or ammunition of the Continental Army is vastly documented in American history (Wright 1983). Moreover, the further expansion of American colonies westward, towards the border of the Mississippi River, worsened such a threat of fragmentation because one of the main drivers of the ethos of the American Revolution concerned the 'distance' between *we the people* and a King with his parliament in London. The quest for new territories could have accrued such a distance between the former colonies and the last-generation explorers, and, in fact, Spain, France, and the United Kingdom were all ready to benefit from this American expansion with their own settlements around the borders of the newborn fragile United States. It is not by chance that the troubling years that followed the Declaration of Independence until the framing of the federal Constitution in 1787 are often dubbed as the 'second' American revolution (Ellis 2002).

Arendt's distinction between 'new beginnings' and 'years one', although controversial, is nonetheless fruitful for a theory of legal monsters because it draws attention to a crucial difference between the rebels' traditional claims on their right to resist and the aim of revolutionary men to establish a new political order, for example, according to the tenets of the Marxist tradition (Buchanan 1982). Both rebels and revolutionary men may symbolise their political target as a monster: in addition to the *Vindiciae*, for example, in Chapter 5, we noted that this was a popular way to refer to King Louis during the French revolution. However, only rebels would justify their opposition to the monster in accordance with the ancient customs of the land, i.e. a legal claim that has no role in revolutionary thinking because what revolutionary men claim is a political right – to sovereignty, independence, or self-determination – that can be even redundant or, in Karl Marx's jargon, *petite bourgeois*. Following this view (Ypi 2014), the fight against monsters has to do with the materialisation of 'scientific demonstrations' regarding the transition from capitalism to communism (Fraser 2000; McNally 2011). Therefore, among the many problems of all revolutionary men, the least relevant issue would consist in Arendt's difficulty of the Founding Fathers to conceive of a beginning which did not occur in a distant past. The revolutionary problem of how to envisage the institutional beginning of a new order works the other way around for those who incite or legitimate revolts against monsters by hinging on customs and traditions: it is only in this latter case that the more the legal anchorage of resistance can be traced back to the past, the better for the claims of the rebel's legal rights.

Further aims of rebellions and revolutions have suggested, however, more nuanced approaches (Weede and Muller 1998; Selbin 2010). A rebel's intent can be to set up a new government and advocate secessions or irredentist goals, whilst today revolutions can be justified with the defence of human rights. The potential overlapping of rebel and revolutionary claims – together with different types of rebellions and revolutions – can be grasped as the observables and variables of an analysis that falls within the two ends of a spectrum. At one end, there is the rebel's claim on a right to resist grounded on the traditional laws of the land; at the other end of the spectrum, we find a Marxist revolutionary man whose intent is to establish a new political order from scratch. Multiple kinds of institutional monsters follow as a result of this differentiation. For example, according to Karl Marx's phrasing in the *Capital*:

> By turning his money into commodities that serve as the material elements of a new product, and as factors in the labour-process, by incorporating living labour with their dead substance, the capitalist at the same time converts value, i.e., past, materialised, and dead labour into capital, into value big with value, a live monster that is fruitful and multiplies. (Marx ed. 1887, I, 1, 7)

From a legal viewpoint, the manifold differences among monstrous institutions pose a host of common issues that are particularly relevant for a theory of legal monsters. Such issues regard:

(i) The interplay between force, power, and the law;
(ii) The interplay between the formal sources of the law and all facts and acts that create, change, or extinguish the rules of a legal order notwithstanding such formal sources, i.e. what civil lawyers dub as the 'material sources' of the law;
(iii) The validity of the law and its rules.

It is against this framework that the next section brings attention back to the question of what kind of rights, if any, people have in the act of resistance against a monstrous institution. As previous uses of the formula 'monster' suggest, i.e. monsters either as a target of legal regulation or a source of opposition and criticism, this third use of 'monster' as a symbol of rebellion must be understood in legal terms. Whereas, in previous parts of this book, the focus was on requirements that make institutions look monstrous, thereby inciting the revolt (see Chapters 6 and 7), here the aim is to examine the interplay between material and formal sources of the legal phenomenon, i.e. between force, power and the law, to put issues of legal validity in the proper light.

10.2 Rebels' Rights

Generations of scholars have debated what rights rebels may have. In the previous section, we dwelt on Locke's ideas as a supporter of those rights as legal rights. The argument can be summed up with § 155 of the second *Treatise*, according to which "the people have a right to remove [the executive power] by force" because the "true remedy of force without authority is to oppose force to it" (Locke 1823). So goes the argument that all monsters of tyranny put themselves into a state of war against their own people who are thus right in deeming their rulers the aggressor. Any target of resistance and rebellion is legitimate because such a monstrous authority is liable to be treated accordingly. *À la guerre comme à la guerre*. This conclusion is true in all states and under every condition. In Locke's phrasing:

> For when men, by entering into society and civil government, have excluded force, and introduced laws for the preservation of property, peace, and unity amongst themselves, those who set up force again in opposition to the laws, do rebellare—that is, bring back again the state of war, and are properly rebels, which they who are in power, by the pretence they have to authority, the temptation. (Locke 1823, at § 226)

There are, of course, manifold variables of legal theories about rebels' rights. In addition to Locke's views in *Two Treatises of Government*, the previous section mentioned theories of tyrannicide which can be traced back to ancient times, from Cicero to Seneca. Today, many legal systems have endorsed and enshrined a right to resist. For example, as a response to the horrors of the Nazi regime, Art. 20(4) of the 1949 West Germany Constitution establishes that "all Germans shall have the right to resist any person seeking to abolish this constitutional order if no other remedy is available". Likewise, France followed suit with the Preamble of the 1958 Constitution that indirectly refers to the right to resist enshrined in Art. 2 of the 1789 Declaration. Similarly, more than 40 countries have set the fundamental law to recognise this right to resist in their post-fascist, post-colonial, or post-Soviet era (Ginsburg et al. 2012).

However, a rebel's legal right to resist remains highly controversial. The reasons can be either theoretical or practical. Concerning the theoretical side of the right to resist, it seems fair to admit that there have been as many critics of this right as supporters. Chapter 8 stressed tenets of legal positivism that directly contradict or oppose the endorsement of this right. It is worth mentioning that, although from a natural law perspective, Kant also embraced this view. Contrary to some oscillations of his philosophical ideas on monsters – as seen in Chapter 4 – there is no room in Kant's legal theory for either monstrous tyrants or a right to resist.[3] Corollaries of the sovereignty principle that Kant adopts, for example, in 'Theory and Practice' from 1793 make this point clear (Kant ed. 1996). Although the essay's subtitle sounds 'against Hobbes', Kant follows a Hobbesian approach because, in his view, if the sovereign could be coerced, he would not be head of state, and all "the ascending series of subordination would go on to infinity". Likewise, if there were two such persons, "neither would be subject to coercive laws and one could not do any unjust act to the other, which is impossible". Whilst Kant concedes what Locke and all theories of tyrannicide claim, i.e. that institutions from time to time can turn out to be so evil that people will "judge in all probability" that a certain legislation of positive law is "detrimental to their happiness", Kant's conclusion is just the opposite of Locke's: "What should they do? Rebel? There can be only one answer: that people have no choice but to obey" (Kant 1996, at 298).

On the other hand, concerning the practical side of every rebellion, attention must be drawn to issues of force and power. Consider Locke's right to remove the monster by force: the scenario entails a state of war in which power, rather than the law, practically determines who is the ruler. There are two possibilities: either there is a

---

[3] Kant did not think he contradicts himself because of his enthusiasm for the 1789 French Revolution as a transfer of sovereignty to the people. Rather, it was the execution of the monster, i.e. King Louis XVI in January 1793, that which should be conceived of as a perversion of the principle of popular sovereignty. See Maliks (2022).

'supreme judge' who assesses a rebel's act of resistance – but then, according to the objections raised by Hobbes or Kant, that supreme judge would be the sovereign – or no such ultimate judge exists on Earth, but only God in Heaven. Locke opts for this latter hypothetical:

> But, farther, this question, Who shall be judge? cannot mean that there is no judge at all. For where there is no judicature on earth to decide controversies amongst men, God in heaven is judge. He alone, it is true, is judge of the right. But every man is judge for himself, as in all other cases so in this, whether another hath put himself into a state of war with him, and whether he should appeal to the supreme judge, as Jephthah did. (Locke 1823, at § 241)

Further practical problems with the rebel's right to resist concern the enforcement of this right even when the international community agrees that a certain institution is monstrous. Maduro's Venezuela clarifies the point.[4] The monster has materialised through starvation and disease, massive waves of crime and dramatic mortality rates, hyperinflation and huge emigration, which have whipped the country for more than a decade (Yilmaz 2024). At the apex of an escalating starvation in 2017, more than half of the population's income was not enough to meet basic nutritional needs: three-quarters of Venezuelans lost over 8 kg each on average. By the late 2010s, the UN reported thousands of extrajudicial killings per year. In 2021, one Venezuelan out of five had left the country; in July 2024, seeking a third consecutive term, Maduro's administration likely falsified the results of the presidential election, repressing the political opposition and forcing its leader to flee the country and seek for asylum in Spain (Corrales and Kronick 2025). Over the past 15 years, the European Union, the United States and other countries have applied sanctions against government officials and members of the military and security forces. Since 2017, representatives of twelve Central and South American countries have established the Lima Group to find a peaceful exit to the Venezuelan crisis. However, at the time of writing, Maduro is still in power and planning to accomplish his third six-year term, which began on 10 January 2025.

The practical problems with every right to rebellion – against such monstrous regimes as Maduro's Venezuela, if any – can be understood in accordance with the drawbacks of today's international legal system and, moreover, with the popular distinction in legal theory between the 'internal' and 'external' point of view (Hart 1994). Such a distinction does not mean that we should imagine ourselves as Venezuelan citizens living under Maduro's rule, nor as scholars dwelling on this case simply examining it from abroad. Instead, a theory of legal monsters should

[4] See an overall view of Venezuela's most tragic decades in Polga-Hecimovich and Sanchez Urribarri (2025), in which the control of information and criminal governance, autocratic international cooperation and authoritarian capitalism, the instrumentalisation of emigration and the Venezuelan diaspora are elucidated. In the phrasing of the editors of the volume, "scholars, journalists, and other public voices have written a lot about Hugo Chávez… However, fewer people seem interested in or paid serious attention to his salsa-dancing, moustachioed successor, who has been in power for over a decade and ushered Venezuela into dictatorship, despite often being underestimated by his critics… We hope that scholars, politicians, and citizens in other places around the globe can draw some lessons from Venezuela's descent into authoritarianism in order to avoid the same fate" (*op. cit.*, at xvii).

be attentive to how claims on the rebel's legal right to resist or on people's self-determination concern practical aspects of norm-acceptance as well as theoretical interests in describing, for example, how Venezuelans may regard and respond to Maduro's rules. As Aristotle warns us, even the eviler of tyrannies finds support in (this or that part of) the community.[5]

So far, the analysis of this chapter has dwelt on the internal point of view regarding the rebel's legal rights against acts of monstrous institutions. The attention was drawn to whether a certain legal system endorses a right to resist, whether a legal community agrees on the monstrosity of a certain institution and, in case of agreement, to what extent forms of support for rebels and their opposition to the monster are deemed necessary. However, several problems have piled up as a result of this perspective. First, we noted the contrast between different opinions, such as Locke's and Kant's conflicting views on the legal right to resist. Second, variants concerning each of such views, for example, requirements and conditions for the right to resist suggest multiple and even opposite ways to conceive such a legal right.[6] Third, each of such views entails contradictions. On the one hand, consider Locke's opinion that a legal right to resist should be admitted: Locke freely concedes that this view ends up with a state of war in which force, rather than the law – that is, God rather than any human justice – is called to define who is the ruler (Locke 1823, at § 241). Leaving aside Locke's problems of theodicy with variables of secularisation,[7] it follows that it is not the formal sources of the law that qualify the facts of life, but the other way around: it is the result of the war confrontation that defines what the law ultimately would be. On the other hand, regarding Kant's opposing opinion that a legal right to resist would be worse than the issue it aims to address, the thesis is subjected to Locke's objection that some legal rules will not prevent the people from resisting the oppressor, "for when the people are made miserable, and find themselves exposed to the ill usage of arbitrary power… give them out for whom or what you please, the same will happen" (Locke 1823, at § 224). Therefore, in addition to the formal sources of the law, i.e. what a legal system determines as the acts or facts that legitimately create the law within that given legal order, the attention should be drawn to what civil lawyers call the 'material sources' of the law or sources *extra* or *contra ordinem.*[8]

[5] See above the second section of Chapter 2. The community, of course, includes international sovereigns, such as China and Russia, which for one reason or another have supported the monster in Caracas.

[6] The plurality of opinions concerning the right to resist does not only regard old debates among supporters of this right, for example, among the 'Monarchomachs'. Also, this debate is well alive today at national and international levels. See Rajagopal (2002); Caney (2015); Finlay (2015); and Delmas (2018).

[7] See for example Kelsen (1973). In this context, however, it suffices to repeat what Spinoza affirms in his *Ethics*, namely, "they will pursue you from cause to cause until you are glad to take refuge in the will of God, that is, the asylum of ignorance" (Spinoza ed. 1941, at 33). The next section of this chapter intends to address such an *ignorantiae asylum* through the material, rather than formal sources of the law.

[8] See Rotolo (2005) and Bell (2018). Most work is not translated however into English and regards this or that jurisdiction of civil law, such as Italy (Paladin 1996); Spanish-speaking countries (Guibourg 2000); or France (Goltzberg 2018); among others.

The focus should be on acts or facts that create binding rules in a specific legal order, regardless of whether such a legal order includes those acts and facts among its sources, especially if those acts and facts, as occurs with every rebellion, oppose the public authority and even the formal sources of the legal system.[9]

To address this interplay between formal and material sources of the law, the following section aims to complement the analysis of whether, and to what extent, a legal right to resist exists from an internal point of view with the external point of view of legal theory. The intent is to shed light on problems of legal validity that regard the existence of evil institutions and, moreover, what to do with such monstrous institutions until the tyrant has power.

10.3 Inside Out

Herbert Hart introduced the distinction between the internal and external point of view in *The Concept of Law* from 1961 (Hart ed. 1994).[10] However, since Hart did not provide any general treatment of such two kinds of legal statements in his book, scholars have vividly discussed the meaning of the distinction over the past decades. For example, some reckon that the 'internal' point of view represents the 'insider's perspective', that is, according to Stephen Perry, the level of abstraction through which we can grasp "how the practice looks to at least some of the practice's participants, from the inside" (Perry 1995, at 97). Likewise, according to Gerry Postema, the internal point of view concerns "beliefs, attitudes, judgments, and understandings of participants. The practice has an 'inside,' the 'internal point of view' of participants" (Postema 1998, at 32). By contrast, other scholars assert that Hart's internal point of view does not simply represent the insider's perspective; instead, the stance plays four different roles in Hart's legal theory (Shapiro 2006). First, the internal point of view draws attention to someone's particular kind of motivation towards the rules of the law, that is, in Hart's phrasing, "a member of the group which accepts and uses them as guides to conduct" (Hart 1994, at 89). Second, the internal point of view clarifies a crucial condition of existence for social and legal rules in opposition to such theories, as Kelsen's, in which the law hinges on the threat of sanctions (Kelsen 1941). Third, the internal point of view makes both the legal practice and theory

[9] The 'material sources' are often grasped as the content of legal precepts in the common law tradition: see for example Pound (1946). An understanding of the material sources of the law closer to the views of civil lawyers is popular among international law experts: see Thirlway (2019) and Degan (2024).

[10] Remarkably, Hart does not refer to this distinction of internal and external viewpoints in his 1958 essay on the separation of law and morals, which was under scrutiny in Chapter 8. Yet, Hart admits a right to resist in both his debate with Fuller and *The Concept of Law*, although considering it as a moral, rather than legal right. On the one hand, "a concept of law which allows the invalidity of law to be distinguished from its immorality, enables us to see the complexity and variety of these separate issues" (Hart 1994, at 211). On the other hand, going back to the debate with Fuller, "Hart was convinced that resistance to tyranny would be encouraged, rather than discouraged, by a positivist disposition to maintain a clear separation between law and morality" (Lacey 2007).

intelligible by drawing attention to the role that norm-acceptance has in every legal system. And fourth, this perspective provides "a naturalistically acceptable semantics for legal statements" (Shapiro 2006, at 1158).

On the other hand, the external point of view with the corresponding legal statements refers to three hypotheticals. First, the external point of view refers to every "observer" who is concerned with the rules but "does not himself accept them" (Hart 1994, at 89). Second, the external point of view can be understood in connection with those members of the group who do not accept the rules of their legal system. For example, supporters of the right to resist under a jurisdiction which formally forbids every resistance would assume such an external point of view. Third, one might adopt this view to describe the law in accordance with the beliefs, attitudes, judgments, and understandings of the members of the group who accept and use the rules of a certain legal system as guides to conduct. According to certain scholars, this is the external point of view which Hart adopts as a legal theorist (Shapiro 2006, at 1160).

Legal statements related to the external point of view are relevant for a theory of legal monsters because they can be further comprehended in connection with the case study of such a monstrous institution, as introduced in the previous section with Maduro's Venezuela. The humanitarian crisis of the South American country casts light on all nuances of Hart's external point of view. Three observables of the analysis follow as a result:

(i) The practical problem of those who do not accept the rules under a specific legal order. Dealing with opposition and resistance, it is more than likely that even in those legal systems where the people's right to resist is formally recognised, disagreement and confrontation characterise every discussion among members of the group, e.g., between supporters of Maduro's administration and its opposition;
(ii) The theoretical problem of legal theorists dissecting this legal confrontation, for example, ascertaining the disagreement that may regard the principles of the system;
(iii) The theoretical problem of every observer, be it an advocate of philosophical behaviourism or Kelsen's pure doctrine of law, according to whom the problem does not revolve around taking sides between parties to the conflict. Instead, the aim is to determine the degree of compliance in the population or the effectiveness of the whole legal institution.[11]

The first observable represents a necessary but insufficient ingredient of the analysis. Arguably, there would not be any use of the metaphor for monsters as a source of criticism, resistance and rebellion without this external point of view in a certain legal

[11] In Kelsen's wording, "a legal norm [is] valid only when it belongs to a legal order which is in the main effective" (Kelsen 1941, at 70). We return to this assumption below in the next section of this chapter.

order.[12] The disagreement that follows as a result, however, does not raise any particular hard cases as regards, for example, Maduro's Venezuela because, concerning the second observable of the analysis, a robust consensus exists in the international community about the systematic violation of human rights that has turned such institution into a legal monster. To admit this agreement, we do not have to buy into any argument about 'unique right answers' – as mentioned in Chapter 8 when dealing with Dworkin's legal hermeneutics. Instead, it is Maduro who has taken to referring himself to other institutions or opponents as monsters. For instance, in October 2024, the Venezuelan President described Israeli Prime Minister Benjamin Netanyahu as a "monster created by the European Union and the US Empire", comparing Netanyahu to Hitler, and adding that even Hitler did not dare to do what Netanyahu was doing. In February 2024, during a television program, Maduro similarly affirmed that Hitler was "a monster created by Western elites", regretting that "today, the criminal military apparatus of Israel has the same encouragement, funding and support".[13]

Lest we fall into Maduro's rhetorical trap, however, his accuses of monstrosity should not make us overlook what is legally at stake, i.e. what to do with this legal monster as long as it has power and, moreover, how to grasp the normative acts of this monster according to the third observable of the analysis in this section. The problem does not only concern the enforcement of international principles or the degree of success in regional initiatives. Also, the focus should be on the normative acts set up by such a monstrous institution with the corresponding issues of legal validity. Those were the issues under scrutiny in Chapter 8, inspecting the debate between Hart and Fuller on the monstrous acts of the Nazi regime. In that context, attention was drawn to the disagreement among jurists who, as observers, may endorse three different external points of view:

(i) Those who do not admit that any normative act or institution can be deemed monstrous according to traditional claims of legal positivism;
(ii) Those who admit that some institutions can be evil and still, their normative acts are valid laws in accordance with, for example, Hart's view;
(iii) Those who deny such monstrous acts the name of law as occurs, for example, with Fuller's claims and some radical theses of natural law advocates.

In Chapter 8, this theoretical disagreement concerned the statutes of a defunct regime. What is under scrutiny in this context is different because the assessment of moral

[12] The careful reader will note that this was the assumption of the analysis on whether the EU institutions should be considered monstrous according to the opinion of certain scholars: see the first two sections of Chapter 9.

[13] The warrants of arrest for Netanyahu and Yoav Gallant for crimes against humanity (and war crimes) pose a hard case. The warrants were issued by the International Criminal Court in the ICC Pre-Trial first Chamber's proceedings in the Hague. On 24 April 2025, the ICC Appeals Chamber admitted Israel's appeal against such a decision under Art. 82(1)(a) of the Rome Statute, remanding "the matter to the Pre-Trial Chamber for it to decide anew on the substance of the jurisdictional challenge" (§ 66 of the ruling CC-01/18 OA2). At the time of writing, the Pre-Trial Chamber has yet to deliver its new ruling. In any event, the (pre-)trial arguably raises a case of disagreement under the second observable of the analysis in this section. Contrary so far to Maduro's evil actions, however, Netanyahu and Gallant's decisions are at least being challenged in court.

principles and issues of legal validity are related to a monstrous institution that is still effective in repressing every form of criticism, opposition, and rebellion. This is precisely the case of Maduro's Venezuela.

The next section assumes that such scenarios, such as the ongoing legal vicissitudes of the South American country, shed critical light on the claims of those who do not accept the rules under a certain legal order vis-à-vis Hart's more extreme 'external' point of view, i.e. the theoretical stance of every legal observer regarding cases of disagreement on how the validity of the law and its efficacy interplay. The focus should be on discussions of moral theories about notions of what is right or wrong to determine how such claims are further related to the legal analysis of what is valid or not. Would the effectiveness of the law be the last word about questions of legal validity, or pace Kelsen, should we take sides also in these cases?

10.4 Ethos and Valid Law

We noted the opposite views on a legal right to resist, such as Locke's and Kant's, although both concede the state of war that follows such an institutional confrontation. This state of war has often been used as evidence by some scholars, such as Kelsen, to claim the opposite result of what advocates of a certain legal positivism and some natural law schools affirm. Against the contention that coercion is a necessary but insufficient condition of every legal order, according to, for example, Hart's 'secondary rules' of the law, Kelsen notes that it is still the power of coercion that is crucial in every conflict and state of war. And, against the theses of the natural law tradition with the supremacy of natural law over positive law, Kelsen warns that such an assessment of moral principles and opinions would be the cause, rather than the solution, for such a state of conflict. The only sound way out is a formal or 'pure' approach to validity problems. In the wording of the *General Theory of Law and State*, "a norm is considered to be legally valid on the condition that it belongs to a system of norms, to an order which, on the whole, is efficacious" (Kelsen 1945, at 42).

Whilst the validity of a norm is a formal issue that depends on two conditions – i.e. a norm is valid if it is based on another valid norm and on the corresponding authorisation of who creates such a legal norm – the overall validity of the system ultimately hinges on its own efficacy. Therefore, Kelsen adopts the radical stance of the observer who tackles on this basis all problems of the internal point of view in coping with the legal right to resist, or the problem of whether institutions can be deemed legal monsters (*op. cit.*, 122). Although Kelsen concedes certain differences between the efficacy of national and international law, the threshold for the validity of the law ultimately concerns information about the states of reality. In Kelsen's words:

> According to this principle of international law, an actually established authority is the legitimate government, the coercive order enacted by this government is the legal order, and

> the community constituted by this order is a State in the sense of international law, in so far as this order is, on the whole, efficacious. (Kelsen 1945, at 121)

Both Kelsen's theoretical stance of the observer and certain approaches of natural law converge in the opinion that unjust norms are legally valid. According to Kelsen, such a statement would be a truism; following, for example, Aristotle's *Politics* (1282 a), it is this assessment on regulations that "are good or bad, just or unjust" – but still valid law – what lets us appreciate the existence of multiple political organisations that depend on the prevalence of certain social classes as well as how multiple kinds of constitution relate to different forms of justice (Aristotle 1944, at 231).[14] Correspondingly, Aristotle's political realism emphasises the shortcomings of all radical claims of certain natural law advocates, according to whom unjust norms are not proper law. Such was Fuller's opinion mentioned in Chapter 8 And in fact, we may even concede that Fuller's intent was noble, i.e. to prevent a sort of Hegelian night where all institutions, whether monstrous or not, look efficaciously grey. The price for such a noble intention, however, is a series of drawbacks as a sort of *schöne Seele*, or beautiful soul, to go on with Hegel's jargon.[15]

The problems with those claims, such as Fuller's assumptions on the invalidity of unjust laws, are both theoretical and practical. The theoretical problems regard what the law is supposed to do, i.e. its functions. Aristotle would remind us that the law is a regulatory system that often competes with other regulatory systems in society, such as social customs or economics. Therefore, the ideal and highly unlikely scenario of unanimous moral opinions must be understood in connection with the balance that the institutional forum of the law is called to strike among such multiple regulatory systems.[16] This institutional process is at work either regarding old contrasts between natural law and positive law, or the functioning of legal systems after WW II in which principles of the natural law tradition would have been incorporated into the foundation of positive law. Even in this latter case, the implementation of the law must go through the mediation of the legal community regarding the meaning of

[14] Scholars often present an idealised image of Aristotle's political teachings, which should definitely be abandoned. We noted in Chapter 2 that Aristotle considered tyrannies in connection with the political relationship between master and slave, mentioning in *Politics* the honour that may be bestowed to those who kill a tyrant. Therefore, according to Aristotle, it is true that lawmakers should take care of virtue and make the citizens good by forming habits in them (*The Nichomachean Ethics*, at 1102 a, and 1103 b, respectively); however, Aristotle would freely admit that this care is the open problem of politics. See *op. cit.*, at 1150 a, in addition to the excerpt from *Politics* cited in the text.

[15] See Hegel (1988, at 383), on conscience, evil, and its forgiveness.

[16] It is worth noting that also the most relevant precursor of natural law theories on the legal invalidity of unjust laws, i.e. Thomas Aquinas, has been understood in multiple and even opposite ways. The text in Aquinas (1992, at 38), on which see note 4 of Chapter 8, has been interpreted literally by Damich (1985) and Soper (2007), among others. By contrast, other scholars have stressed that Aquinas' maxim either should be further qualified to prevent blatant self-contradictions or a "dramatization" of his thought (Finnis 1990); or grasped as a "weak natural law theorist" (George 1999).

the terms framing the legal question and how such terms may relate to each other vis-à-vis the principles of the system and their substantiation in the legal order.[17]

On the other hand, claims on the invalidity of unjust law trigger the illusion that problems could be solved this way when they are not. The practical drawback of Fuller's ideas and similar natural law assertions can be appreciated either after or before the demise of the monstrous tyrant. The first scenario was under scrutiny in Chapter 8. By arguing that the normative acts of monstrous institutions, such as the Nazi regime, do not even deserve to be called law (Fuller 1958, at 660), scholars overlook the tragic choices that the end of such a regime necessarily entails. Once the political community breaks free from the legal monster, we noted that the choice is either leaving evil people unpunished or punishing them on the basis of retroactive legislation, i.e. the choice between two evils (Hart 1958, at 620). When the focus is on the second scenario of monstrous institutions that still exercise power, as occurs at the time of writing with Maduro's Venezuela, the drawback of Fuller's ideas is even more evident. Declaring, today, the invalidity of the July 2024 political election may have symbolic relevance as a way to express solidarity with the victims of such a monstrous institution. And yet, strictly speaking, such posture is toothless, especially considering that in the best possible scenario – i.e. once the tyrant is gone – lawmakers will have to confront themselves once again with the choice between two evils. Unjust laws are still law.

However, this strict distinction of legal validity from moral arguments does not mean that ethos and moral arguments play no relevant role in the legal domain. By stressing the function of the metaphor on legal monsters as a source of criticism, resistance, and rebellion throughout the centuries, the previous parts of this book have insisted upon coercion as a necessary but insufficient condition of the legal phenomenon. In the previous section of this chapter, in particular, we noted not only the role that moral arguments and principles play in the formation and implementation of the law through its own institutions and procedures, statuses and customs, but also how beliefs, attitudes, judgments, and understandings of old legal subjects and today's citizens are crucial in the functioning and resilience of the law. Drawing on Aristotle's warnings, this interplay of morals and the law, opinions and legal sources, statutory and customary law, works both ways. The analysis of the *monster vel prodigium* of the tradition showed that strong claims of natural law on the invalidity of unjust laws have never questioned this tradition of positive law and that the moral grounds of the community and even the lack of pathos for our human fellows with

[17] How the institutional process of the law works in practice was illustrated in Chapter 9. In the third section, for example, we noted that the moral principle of human dignity is protected with duties upon public authorities and private parties through the implementation of normative acts that must be clear and prospective, non-contradictory and coherently administered, or feasible to obey. The attention was also drawn to the adoption of the Ethics guidelines for trustworthy AI of the High-Level Expert Group on Artificial Intelligence in 2019, and their implementation in the provisions of the AI Act pursuant to Recitals 7, 27 and 165 of the EU regulation.

birth defects paved the way for some of the ugliest chapters of the Western legal tradition and its resilience over the centuries.[18]

Going back to the opposite views on a legal right to resist, the state of war which follows such an institutional confrontation, and certain claims of value-free observers – such as Kelsen's theoretical stance on the efficacy of the law – we may thus wonder how to address monstrous institutions when they still have power. Leaving aside Kelsen's troubles with his own strict separation of law and morals,[19] might he not have a point in asserting that the only choice is to follow the duel of strength and force, ultimately assigning the legal right to whoever emerges victorious from the battlefield?

The specificity of the case on monstrous institutions – the subject matter of this chapter – emphasises critical drawbacks of Kelsen and his followers. Regarding today's positive law, the qualifying adjective of some rulers, governments and institutions as monstrous is not a rhetorical trick. Monstrosity refers to the blatant systematic violation of human rights and, at times, of the constitutional safeguards that go together with hyperinflation and starvation, appalling mortality rates and disease, or people casting their vote through massive emigration rates. In the best possible light, self-styled value-free observers may only repeat Lucretius' words in *De rerum natura.* So goes the poem:

> It is sweet, when on the great sea the winds trouble its waters, to behold from land another's deep distress; not that it is a pleasure and delight that any should be afflicted, but because it is sweet from what evils you are yourself exempt. It is sweet also to look upon the mighty struggles of war arrayed along the plains without sharing yourself in the danger. (Lucretius ed. 1866, at 28)[20]

Regarding a theory of legal monsters, "the lofty and serene positions well fortified by the learning of the wise" should not lead us to overlook that every rebellion against monstrous institutions entails tragic cases and hard choices. Such tragic

[18] Legal customs can indeed be monstrous as much as acts of parliaments and court's rulings can occasionally be. In addition to the case study of this book on the *monstrum vel prodigium*, the analysis has dwelt on further cases of customary law regarding slavery, torture and even cannibalism. The list, alas, could be expanded with further examples of ritualistic violence, child violence, and female genital mutilation. The threshold for assessing the monstrosity of such social practices and customs brings us back to the requirements of monstrosity examined in this book, namely the "minimum conditions" of Fuller's The *Morality of Law* integrated with the analysis of violations of the International Bill of Rights or constitutional guarantees. The tragedy of monstrosity is sometimes compounded by the fact that social practices lead to the self-destruction of the community that has adopted such practices. See Diamond (2011).

[19] Kelsen's main problem revolves around the content, rather than the function of his 'basic norm' which "is responsible for the unity of the legal order" (Kelsen 1941, at 63). The basic norm of international law, which is the source of the validity of every national legal order, states *pact sunt servanda*, freely translated by Kelsen as "the States ought to behave as they have customarily behaved" (Kelsen 1945, at 369). This obligation, however, is either categorical, or hypothetical in Kantian terms. In the first case, it presupposes a moral duty; in the second case, there is no real unity, but only a presupposed fiction: *ex injuria jus oritur* (Kelsen 1945, at 214). The same Kantian impasse applies to Kelsen's basic norm at the national level.

[20] A brilliant reading of Lucretius' image and its manifold interpretations in Blumenberg (1996).

cases and hard choices have been ignored over the past decades either pursuant to variables of legal positivism (such as Kelsen's), strong natural law claims (such as Fuller's), or certain approaches to legal hermeneutics (such as Dworkin's). Three scenarios make the assumption clear. They bring us back to all nuances of the 'external point of view' of the law (see the previous section). The first scenario concerns resistance against rulers with no uniquely right answer. The lack of such answers may depend on controversies about principles, loopholes of the law, or even natural law interpretations that entail the need for a reasonable compromise.[21] Although the lack of unique right answers does not entail any sheer relativism, history is full of wars and tragedies between parties that had all their good reasons.[22] In addition to every unique right answer posture, also strong natural law theories simply fall short, or are dangerously misleading, in tackling such tragedies of human life as a sort of plain case.

The second scenario regards a right rebellion against a proper monster who yet, at least momentarily, prevails. Despite terminological uncertainties in today's political lexicon, such as between autocracies, ochlocracies, despotic regimes, dictatorships, or one-party rulers (Turchetti 2008), attention must be drawn to all those institutions that enslave their subjects, i.e. tyrannies. This is, so far, the tragic situation of today's Venezuela. In this case, the calamity of institutional violence adds to the tragedy of monstrous laws that are still valid laws. Also, under such circumstances, every strong natural law theory appears self-complacent or deadly wrong. It is not by chance that ancient Greeks coined the political image of the monster in the context of their tragedies. We noted that opposite claims on the radical nullity of unjust laws, as well as theories on uniquely right answers, are deceptive and deceiving. Tyrannies are tragic because they are evil and still have the force of the law.

The third scenario concerns the right rebellion against the monster that finally gets rid of the monstrous institution. Even in this case of triumph, there is room for tragedy. In Hart's jargon, triumphant rebels must choose "between two evils". The issue is not solved either substantially nor formally. In addition to the substantial flaws of strong natural law postures or one-size-fits-all hermeneutics, consider Kelsen's 'pure' doctrine of law, according to which either leaving evil people unpunished or adopting retroactive legislation is not an insurmountable problem (Kelsen 1945, at 44). What matters would regard the procedures according to which norms are adopted, thus

[21] See note 16 of this chapter on how even Thomas Aquinas' theory on the legal invalidity of unjust laws has led to multiple and even opposite ways; and note 15 in Chapter 8, referring to Hart's objections to Dworkin. Hard legal cases brought forth by technological innovation with its unique challenges provide further instances of the shortcomings that follow Dworkin's approach: see Pagallo (2013 and 2024). Dworkin, however, seems ready to soften his own claims: "For every route that Hercules took from that general conception to a particular verdict, another lawyer or judge who began in the same conception would find a different route and end in a different place, as several of the judges in our sample cases did. He would end differently because he would take leave of Hercules, following his own lights, at some branching point sooner or later in the argument" (Dworkin 1986, at 412). We return to these hermeneutical issues below in Chapter 11.

[22] Dworkin's problems with the justification of state's use and withholding of force is explored by Ehrenberg (2016, at 55). Among too many wars and tragedies, see Brands and Edel (2019), O'Driscoll (2019), and for an Aristotelian view, Ullman (1942).

being open to (almost) every possible content.[23] However, the price for this purity is too high because Kelsen's level of abstraction simply overlooks a critical condition for the existence of social and legal rules, such as the kind of motivation that members of a group must have towards the rules of the law as "guides to conduct" (Hart 1994, at 89). Throughout the previous chapters of this book, attention was drawn to how the content of the law is a critical ingredient of the analysis, since it is just the content of the law that may spark criticism, opposition, resistance or open rebellion to the public authority. Kelsen's formalisms are unsatisfactory because they ignore the physiological conditions of the functioning of every legal system and, moreover, the reasons why legal orders shall occasionally address tragic choices.

Rebellion is a last resort option that must always be considered. By reversing Hobbes' ideas, we may say that only a monster law can address the challenges that arise with the extinction of a monstrous institution. The institutional forum of the law shall have to take charge of these hard choices through the mediation of the legal community in the determination and implementation of the principles of the system with its constitutional safeguards. We noted this institutional process at work with the implementation of the principle of dignity into post-WW II legal systems (Chapters 4 and 8), as much as with the determination of the new principles and provisions that shall address the challenges of emerging technologies in today's law (Chapter 9). This institutional process clarifies the shortcomings of unique right answers-theories and the opposite drawbacks of formalist views and strong natural law claims. The current information revolution poses an increasing set of challenges that will test this institutional process. The law should be ready to tackle a new generation of legal monsters with their corresponding hard cases.

References

Aquinas, Th. 1992. *Treatise on Law* (Summa Theologica Questions 90–97), ed. S. Parry, Chicago: Gateway.

Arendt, H. 2006. *On revolution [1963]*. New York: Penguin.

Aristotle. 1944. *Politics*, trans. H. Rackham. Cambridge, MA: Harvard University Press; London: Heinemann.

Bell, J. 2018. Sources of law. *The Cambridge Law Journal* 77 (1): 40–71.

Blumenberg, H. 1996. *Shipwreck with spectator*, trans S. Rendall. Cambridge, MA: MIT Press.

Brands, H., and C. N. Edel. 2019. *The lessons of tragedy: Statecraft and world order*. New Haven and London: Yale University Press.

Brutus, S.J. 1924. *Vindiciae Contra Tyrannos. A defense of liberty against tyrants* [1579], trans Ch. H. McIlwain. London: Bell & Sons.

Buchanan, A. 1982. *Marx and justice: The radical critique of liberalism*. London: Methuen.

Caney, S. 2015. Responding to global injustice: On the right to resistance. *Social Philosophy and Policy* 32 (1): 51–73.

Cicero, M.T. 1887. De Officiis, trans A.P.Peabody. Boston: Little, Brown & Co.

[23] Such normative constraints, however, are logical, for example, contradictory rules and legal antinomies, rather than substantial restrictions: see Kelsen (1945, at 408).

Corrales, J., and D. Kronick. 2025. How Maduro Stole Venezuela's Vote. *Journal of Democracy* 36 (1): 36–49.

Damich, E. J. 1985. The essence of law according to Thomas Aquinas. *The American Journal of Jurisprudence* 30 (1): 76–96.

Degan, V. D. 2024. *Sources of international law.* Leiden: Brill.

Delmas, C. 2018. *A duty to resist: When disobedience should be uncivil.* Oxford: Oxford University Press.

Diamond, J. 2011. *Collapse: How societies choose to fail or succeed.* rev. ed. New York: Penguin.

Dworkin, R. 1986. *Law's empire.* Cambridge, MA: Harvard University Press.

Ehrenberg, K. M. 2016. *The functions of law.* Oxford: Oxford University Press.

Ellis, J. J. 2002. *Founding brothers.* New York: Vintage.

Finlay, C. J. 2015. *Terrorism and the right to resist: A theory of just revolutionary war.* Cambridge: Cambridge University Press.

Finnis, J. 1990. Natural law and legal reasoning. *Cleveland State Law Review* 38 (1): 1–13.

Fraser, I. 2000. Hegel and Marx on needs: The making of a monster. In *The Hegel-Marx connection*, ed. T. Burns and I. Fraser, 146–166. London: Palgrave Macmillan.

Fuller, L. L. 1958. Positivism and Fidelity to Law: A Reply to Professor Hart, *Harvard Law Review, 71*(4): 630–672.

George, R. P. 1999. Kelsen and Aquinas on the natural-law doctrine. *Notre Dame Law Review* 75 (5): 1625–1646.

Ginsburg, T., D. Lansberg-Rodriguez, and M. Versteeg. 2012. When to overthrow your government: The right to resist in the world's constitutions. *UCLA Law Review* 60:1184–1260.

Goltzberg, S. 2018. *Les sources du droit. Que sais-je.* Paris: PUF.

Guibourg, R. 2000. Fuentes del derecho, *Enciclopedia Ibero-Americana de Filosofia* 2:177–197.

Hart, H. L. A. 1958. Positivism and the Separation of Law and Morals, *Harvard Law Review, 71*(4): 593–629.

Hart, H. L. A. 1994. *The concept of law [1961].* Oxford: Oxford University Press.

Hegel, G.W.F. 1988. *Phenomenology of spirit* [1807], trans A.V. Miller. Delhi: Motilal Banarsidass.

Kant, I. 1996. On the common saying: that may be correct in theory, but it is of no use in practice [1793], In *Immanuel Kant, Practical Philosophy*, trans. and ed. M.J. Gregor, vol. 8, 273–309. Cambridge: Cambridge University Press.

Kelsen, H. 1941. The pure theory of law and analytical jurisprudence. *Harvard Law Review* 55 (1): 44–70.

Kelsen, H. 1945. *General theory of law and state*, trans A. Wedberg. New York: Russell & Russell.

Kelsen, H. 1973. God and the state. In *Essays in legal and moral philosophy*, ed. H. Kelsen, 61–82. Dordrecht: Springer.

Lacey, N. 2007. H.L.A. Hart's rule of law: The limits of philosophy in historical perspective. *Quaderni Fiorentini* 36:1203–1224.

Locke, J. 1823. *Two treatises of government [1689].* London: Tegg & Co.

Lucretius, T. 1866. *De rerum natura*, trans A. Boyle. Cambridge: Deighton Bell.

Maliks, R. 2022. *Kant and the French revolution.* Cambridge: Cambridge University Press.

Marx, K. 1887. Capital: A critique of political economy, vol. I, book 1: The process of production of capital, trans. S. Moore and E. Aveling, Moscow: Progress Publishers, available at https://www.marxists.org/archive/marx/works/download/pdf/Capital-Volume-I.pdf, accessed on 8 September 2025.

McNally, D. 2011. *Monsters of the market.* Leiden, The Netherlands: Brill.

O'Driscoll, C. 2019. *Victory: The triumph and tragedy of just war.* Oxford: Oxford University Press.

Pagallo, U. 2013. *The laws of robots: Crimes, contracts, and torts.* Dordrecht: Springer.

Pagallo, U. 2024. *The new laws of outer space: Ethics, legislation, and governance in the age of artificial intelligence.* Oxford: Hart.

Paladin, L. 1996. *Le fonti del diritto italiano.* Bologna: Il Mulino.

Perry, S. R. 1995. Interpretation and methodology in legal theory. In *Law and interpretation*, ed. A. Marmor, 97–135. Oxford: Oxford University Press.

Petrone, K. 2000. *Life has become more joyous, comrades: Celebrations in the time of Stalin.* Bloomington and Indianapolis: Indiana University Press.
Polga-Hecimovich, J., and R. Sanchez Urribarri, eds. 2025. *Authoritarian consolidation in times of crisis: Venezuela under Nicolás Maduro.* New York: Routledge.
Postema, G. J. 1998. Jurisprudence as practical philosophy. *Legal Theory* 4:329–357.
Pound, R. 1946. Sources and forms of law. *Notre Dame Law Review* 21 (4): 247–314.
Rajagopal, B. 2002. International law and social movements: Challenges of theorizing resistance. *Columbia Journal of Transnational Law* 41 (2): 397–433.
Rotolo, A. 2005. Sources of law in the civil law. In *A treatise of legal philosophy and general jurisprudence*, ed. C. Roversi, 728–779. Dordrecht: Springer.
Selbin, E. 2010. *Revolution, rebellion, resistance: The power of story.* London: Bloomsbury Publishing.
Seneca. 1917. Tragedies, trans. F.J. Miller, Cambridge, MA: Harvard University Press.
Shapiro, S. 2006. What is the internal point of view? *Fordham Law Review* 75 (3): 1157–1170.
Shaw, M. 2011. *Time and the French revolution: The republican calendar, 1789-year xiv.* Rochester, NY: Boydell & Brewer.
Soper, P. 2007. In defense of classical natural law in legal theory: Why unjust law is no law at all. *Canadian Journal of Law & Jurisprudence* 20 (1): 201–223.
Spinoza, B.. 1941. *Ethics*, trans. A. Boyle, London: Dent.
Thirlway, H. 2019. *The sources of international law.* Oxford: Oxford University Press.
Turchetti, M. 2008. 'Despotism' and 'Tyranny'. Unmasking a tenacious confusion. *European Journal of Political Philosophy* 7 (2): 159–182.
Ullman, B. L. 1942. History and tragedy. *Transactions and Proceedings of the American Philological Association* 73:25–53.
Weede, E., and E. N. Muller. 1998. Rebellion, violence and revolution: A rational choice perspective. *Journal of Peace Research* 35 (1): 43–59.
Williams, R. C. 1995. The Russian revolution and the end of time: 1900-1940. *Jahrbücher für Geschichte Osteuropas* 3:364–401.
Wright, R. K. 1983. *The continental army.* Washington, DC: Center of Military History, United States Army.
Yılmaz, O. 2024. A political, economic and humanitarian crisis: Venezuela crisis. In *Black swan: Economic crises*, ed. B. Açıkgöz, vol. III, 175–214. Singapore: Springer.
Ypi, L. 2014. On revolution in Kant and Marx. *Political Theory* 42 (3): 262–287.
Zerubavel, E. 1977. The French republican calendar: A case study in the sociology of time. *American Sociological Review* 42 (6): 868–877.

Chapter 11
A Look into the Future

This chapter examines a new generation of digital monsters with the interplay between institutional, normative, and technological meanings of monstrosity. Attention is drawn to the challenges posed by AI systems and the robots equipped with them, interpreted through Imre Lakatos' epistemological suggestions on 'monster barring', 'monster adjustment', and 'lemma incorporation'. The aim is twofold. On the one hand, the focus is on the unique challenges brought forth by a new generation of artificial agents to stress that a novel normative monstrosity complements the old meanings of the metaphor at the institutional and legislative levels. On the other hand, against techno-deterministic stances on the apocalyptic future of monstrous AI systems out of human control, the chapter claims that scholars should be attentive to the mid- and even short-term provisions of legislators. While advocates of techno-deterministic positions rightly emphasise certain peculiarities of the technology under exam, they fall short in neglecting the ways in which, for better or worse, the decisions of today's lawmakers are going to shape the future.

11.1 Digital Monsters

Since the mid-1990s, the novelties of our time have been summarised in terms of "being digital" (Negroponte ed. 2015); the "information age" (Castells ed. 1998); and later, in the 2000s, the "data-driven society" (Pentland 2013); or, the "fourth revolution" (Floridi 2014). The overall idea is that the impact of technology — from personal computers to current autonomous artificial agents, such as AI systems and robots — deeply affects who we are, as well as what we know and what we do, both offline and in cyberspace. Since the very beginning of their history, human societies have been bound by the use of information and communication technologies (ICTs), and moreover, by their most basic form: writing. However, over the centuries, human societies have depended on energy and essential resource-related technologies. What

U. Pagallo, *A Theory of Legal Monsters: Repression, Resistance, Rebellion*, Philosophical Studies Series 161, https://doi.org/10.1007/978-3-032-10771-8_11

is new in today's societies is that, for the first time ever, human societies depend on ICTs and, further, on data and information as their vital resources (Pagallo 2015).[1] It will come as no surprise that scholars have increasingly begun to speak of digital monsters in this new era.

There are three kinds of digital monsters. According to the differentiations of this book on normative acts and institutions, a first kind of monster has to do with the digitalisation of human societies and hence, of states and public institutions. For example, in 2003, two scholars and advocates of the American Civil Liberties Union, Jan Stanley and Barry Steinhardt, claimed that "a combination of lightning-fast technological innovation and the erosion of privacy protections threaten to transform the United States into a Surveillance Society" — in short, a "bigger monster [with] weaker chains" (Stanley and Steinhardt ed. 2014). The same trend holds for popular narratives on current threats of surveillance capitalism with the massive collection and commodification of personal data by corporations (Zuboff 2019). The monster functions as the synecdoche of rhetorics, in which either the whole is used for a part, or a part is employed for the whole. Therefore, attention is drawn, on the one hand, to a part used for the whole, as occurs, for example, with the "monster carbon footprint of surveillance capitalism" (Davey 2020). On the other hand, the whole may be used for a part, as illustrated by the voracious logic of capitalism and the "darkening of the digital dream" (Zuboff 2019, at 7). According to this view, "the image of technology as an autonomous force with unavoidable actions and consequences" makes technology look like a monster: "The monster did it, not Victor Frankenstein" (Zuboff 2019, at 136). In the phrasing of Richard Weiskopf:

> Zuboff's new book appears as a disruptive event of truth-telling, challenging many of the taken-for-granted views on organizing the digital ... It goes beyond the bounded organization to explore the organizing principles and the 'laws of motion' that drive social action and shape our experience. The monster that we only see vaguely and cannot describe accurately is given a name: 'surveillance capitalism'. (Weiskopf 2020)

The second kind of digital monster concerns specific technology uses and corresponding legislation. This is the case, for example, of cookies that track people's movements on a website, or among different websites, to collect and store information, such as names, addresses, or credit card numbers (Trevisan et al. 2019). Some scholars refer to cookie technologies as monsters to emphasise the drawbacks of the normative attempts to govern their uses, especially in EU law (Leenes and Kosta 2015). Others reckon that the monsters are not only the cookies, because the same normative attempt to govern them, such as the EU e-privacy directive, may itself appear monstrous (Debusser 2005). Further scholars surrender to this monstrous evidence and declare that such cookie monsters "have become the backbone and the

---

[1] As stressed below in this section, today's dependence of human societies on data and information can be also understood in political-economical terms. The traditional three factors of production, i. e. land, labour and money have been complemented by the commodification of data (Cohen 2019). Accordingly, the material goods of the value chain have been joined — and more often replaced — by the intangible goods on which the wealth of today's knowledge and information societies is increasingly based.

main vehicle of a vast market infrastructure, based on its ability to transform online behavioral information into data assets, and to attach these assets to advertising products" (Mellet and Beauvisage 2019). Further digital monsters concern more troubling cases, such as the mitigation of cybercrimes against minors in India.[2]

The third kind of monster regards digital technologies as such. Considering Martin Heidegger's ideas on technology as a grotesque comprehension of the world — that which makes beings measurable and manipulable, ultimately reducing them to the status of not-beings — several advocates of this third kind of digital monstrosity have followed suit. The image of the hydroelectric plant that converts the Rhine river into a mere supplier of waterpower as a "monstrousness" (Heidegger ed. 1993, at 321), has become more sophisticated. Certain scholars discuss monsters referring to the complexities of machine learning techniques and the challenges for user experience designs (Dove and Fayard 2020). Others draw on work by Langdon Winner, Bruno Latour, and Donna Haraway, to elaborate a monster-theory "for the fascination with and aversion towards new technology" (Smits 2006).[3] In further cases, labelling digital technologies as monsters helps grasp what Heidegger's often murky and impenetrable texts would intend to convey: "a story about technology mastering humans rather than serving them" (Doctorow 2018).

Arguably, among the three dimensions of digital monstrosity with their interplay – – i.e. between the institutional, normative, and technological meanings of monstrosity — the surge of artificial intelligence (AI) and, according to the "sense-think-act" paradigm (Bekey 2005), of robots equipped with AI, has mostly attracted the attention of scholars and the public at large. What makes this technology unique has to do with the fact that humans are no longer the creators of machines, but rather, of artificial agents.[4] To prevent misapprehensions, such an agency of AI systems and smart robots does not entail any human-like property. Instead, the notion should be grasped in engineering terms. Drawing on the IEEE definition of autonomous and

---

[2] See these monsters at accessed on September 8, 2025 from https://timesofindia.indiatimes.com/blogs/voices/the-lurking-digital-monster-how-to-mitigate-cyber-crimes-against-minors/.

[3] Among the examples of monstrous technology, in addition to nuclear energy, plastics, steam engines, xenotransplantation and nanotechnology, Smits refers to the case of genetically modified (GM) food, which has triggered a popular debate on "Frankenstein food", according to Prince Charles' attack on GM food in March 1999 (Smits 2006). What all these technological monsters have in common, including the debate on "monstrous organisms" (Clancy and Clancy 2016), concerns the interplay between the law's aim to govern technology and the "Frankenstein's problem" (Winner 1978, at 306). As this section claims, this Frankenstein's legal problem is exacerbated by the agency of AI systems and smart robots. See also Latour on "hybrids" (2011), and Haraway on "cyborgs" (2013).

[4] The difference between 'machines' and 'artificial agents' can also be grasped in accordance with three orders of technology. Whereas first order technologies are those between humans and Mother Nature, for example, the axe, and second order technologies are in-between humans and other technologies, for instance, the engine, what makes third order technologies unique — from ICTs to AI models — is that such technologies work in-between other technologies that set up the environment of the system. Humans are no longer needed in the loop as a result. See Floridi (2013), Durante (2021), and Pagallo (2024).

intelligent systems (IEEE 2020, at 18), the focus should be on three properties that are particularly relevant in dealing with a new generation of monsters:

i) Interactivity: AI systems and smart robots can perceive their environment and respond to stimuli by changing the values of their own properties or inner states;
ii) Adaptability: AI systems and smart robots can improve the rules through which their properties or inner states change;
iii) Autonomy: AI systems and smart robots can modify their inner states or properties without external stimuli, thereby exerting control over their actions without any direct human intervention.

The agency of AI systems and smart robots makes them strong candidates for the title of new monsters because of either exogenous reasons, endogenous causes, or both. A 'godfather of AI', i.e. Yoshua Bengio, stressed these scenarios in an interview with *Yahoo!finance* in October 2024 (in Khorram 2024). Regarding the exogenous reasons, AI systems may turn into monsters because they can fall "in the wrong hands", for example, helping terrorists and state actors to attack and even destroy Western democracies. The causes are endogenous when considering the agency of such autonomous and intelligent systems. In Bengio's phrasing:

> And then there is the issue that many scientists have been pointing out, which is the way that we're training them now — we don't see clearly how we could avoid these systems becoming autonomous and having their own preservation goals, and we could lose control of these systems. So we're on a path to maybe creating monsters that could be more powerful than us. (in Khorram 2024)

Bengio's warning that AI systems can be out of control has become mainstream over the years (Moravec 1999). Although narratives on 'general AI', 'singularities' or 'super intelligences' may seem quite exaggerated, the risk of a Pandora's box, especially in the military sector, is real (Bringsjord et al. 2025). The threat reminds us of the cautionary tale of Karel Ĉapek's 1920 play, *Rossum's Universal Robots*, in which the word "robot" was used for the first time. The book's plot revolves around a factory producing artificial persons — that is, robots — whose rebellion ultimately leads to the extinction of the human race (Pagallo 2013, at 3–4). Some decades later, it was the father of cybernetics, Norbert Wiener, to present the automaton and the machine as "the modern counterpart of the Golem of the Rabbi of Prague", so that "I do not consider that I have taken more than an author's normal liberty in calling this book GOD and GOLEM, Inc." (Wiener 1964, at 95). Should we conclude that nothing is new under the sun?

11.2 Human Control

Over the past years, Bengio's powerful AI monsters have been the subject of institutional debates and scholarly research on the risks and threats associated with potential control losses over AI and smart robots (Pagallo 2017). The aim is to develop theoretical frameworks supporting AI systems that avoid undesirable behaviours and enable humans to keep them in check. A 'meaningful human control' (MHC) over the entire technological cycle and functioning of such autonomous systems entails two preliminary conditions that shall be satisfied: 'tracking' and 'tracing' (Mecacci et al. 2024). Tracking regards the relation between human controllers and controlled intelligent systems, i.e. the degree to which a system can respond to the intentions or reasons of the designated controllers. Tracing concerns the conditions that make such control meaningful, that is, only inasmuch as humans "are cognitively, physically and morally capable to perform their assigned tasks and fulfil their obligations" (Santoni et al. 2023).

This kind of research complements and partially overlaps with work on the mitigation of societal risks that software can pose: "taming the AI monster" through effective human oversight (Baum et al. 2025). However, as stressed in the previous section, problems of human control can also be understood the other way around, that is, not only through the meaningful control that humans must have over potentially monstrous technologies, but also the control that institutions may attempt to exert over humans through the use of technology. The example of surveillance technologies makes it clear that technology is not a simple means to attain such old ends of human control, but rather, technology affects and reshapes the ways in which either public institutions or private companies aim to attain those ends.[5]

In addition to Western monstrous surveillance capitalism, or mass surveillance states, China provides further examples. Whilst scholars have discussed whether surveillance capitalism and mass surveillance states represent the two sides of the same coin in Western democracies, they arguably are so in China. In an interview to the Bulletin of Atomic Scientists in 2022, an activist of Human Rights Watch, Maya Wang, deplored "the rise of the authoritarian surveillance technology state in China since 2017", drawing on documents of both the marketing departments of the surveillance companies that sell these systems to the government, and the police:

> The reason why I said I'm probably the first person to document these monster surveillance systems was that there was zero literature on this wherever I looked at that time.[6]

Another instance of AI monstrosity regards the Chinese efforts to set up robotic courts through the use of AI-assisted adjudication systems. The implementation

---

[5] The use of 'lethal autonomous weapon systems' corroborates the assumption of this section. By the early 2010s, experts, such as the UN special rapporteur Philip Alston, still claimed that "a missile fired from a drone is no different from any other commonly used weapon … The critical legal question is the same for each weapon: whether its specific use complies with IHL", i. e. international humanitarian law (in Pagallo 2013, at 59). By the end of the 2010s, the UN Secretary-General, António Guterres, emphasised that the use of "autonomous machines with the power and discretion to select targets and take lives without human involvement" would be "politically unacceptable, morally repugnant and should be prohibited by international law" (in Pagallo 2024, at 79). However, the devil is in the legal detail. A ban of this technology is not an easy task due to political convenience and dual uses of technology, among others. A group of governmental experts in Geneva, under the auspices of the UN institutions, is at work since 2017, although a reasonable compromise or international agreement is still out of reach.

[6] The interview is available at accessed on September 8, 2025 from https://thebulletin.org/premium/2022-09/the-high-tech-surveillance-state-is-not-restricted-to-china-interview-with-maya-wang-of-human-rights-watch/

process comprises three different stages: "1) 'intelligent perception,' 2) 'intelligent cognition,' and 3) 'intelligent decision making,' with an emphasis on the development of 'smart courts' and court automation" (Wang and Tian 2022). However, due to the limits of technology, such attempts to replace functions and requisites of the courts with the adjudicatory powers of AI systems look like a "syntax monster" (Ebrahimi Afrouzi 2024). In the best possible light, efforts of engineers and computer scientists to set up AI systems for decision-making in the legal domain aim to predict what human judges could rule in such cases, either through neural networks or machine learning techniques. It has been noted that "rather than being part of an ongoing social process in the development of the law, such determinations are more akin to forecasting the weather" (Chesterman 2022, at 13). As a result, the use of AI-assisted adjudication systems can be interpreted either as an intrepid form of legal experimentation, or more likely, as a straight way to suppress dissenting opinions and conflicting values.[7]

The twofold threat of AI — regarding either its monstrous uses or the potential uncontrollable nature of the technology — does not mean, however, that we should overlook its benefits and opportunities. At the risk of being lambasted for technocratic optimism, I must stress that there would not be such a fuss on existential threats of technology if robots and AI systems did not bring advantages and help. The author of this book confesses to having repeatedly warned against risks of technological underuse that entail a further kind of monstrosity, although invisible.[8] The whole set of benefits and promises of AI can be missed or exploited far below its full potential, and for the wrong reasons (Floridi et al. 2018). Such reasons include business disincentives and greed among data keepers, bureaucracy and professional reluctance, or public distrust in the era of conspiracy theories. I have suggested the possibility of establishing forms of accountability and liability for the activities of AI robots in contracts and business law, for example, through new forms of legal agenthood for AI systems and robots in cases of complex distributed responsibility and failures in legal causation.[9] This ambivalence of AI as both a source of opportunities and threats

---

[7] Leibniz's extraordinary reflection provides a warning sign. We met Leibniz's ideas above in Chapter 4, dealing with the reasons why monsters do not exist, and moreover, in Chapter 6, emphasising his efforts in legal computing through probability calculus, combinatorial analysis, and binary arithmetic, summed up with the motto: *Calculemus!* Scholars often present these efforts (and motto) as if Leibniz's belief were that legal reasoning could be resolved as a computation on the basis of an appropriate logical language. However, it is worth stressing that in *Disputatio de conditionibus* from 1665, amended in 1669 with the *Doctrina conditionum*, Leibniz admits that certain cases, such as inheritance disputes, must be resolved through reasons of equity, rather than legal rules. Also, Leibniz develops non-deductive forms of reasoning that have only recently been incorporated into philosophical reflection and formalised through studies of logic and artificial intelligence, including the logical analysis of legal arguments. See Pagallo (2016), and Artosi & Sartor (2018).

[8] The monster materialises with the opportunities costs of technology that, for example, are up to 2% of the Italian GDP in the health sector (Pagallo 2021). See also Pagallo and Durante (2022), and Pagallo et al. (2024).

[9] See Pagallo 2013, 2018. In particular, the notion of distributed responsibility refers to actions that result from the interplay of multiple agents, in which each action is in itself neither illegal nor necessarily immoral, but whose final result can be catastrophic. Environmental protection offers a typical

does not only concern, in any event, my personal opinion. More interestingly, this ambivalence concerns the opinions expressed by the European Parliament (EP) in some resolutions and declarations.

For example, in the meeting between Facebook's Mark Zuckerberg and the EP's political leadership in May 2018, some members of the parliament (MEPs) questioned the CEO for his company's track record with personal data protection. In particular, the focus was on the misuse of such data by Cambridge Analytica through Facebook's services for targeted political advertising (ESO 2018). Guy Verhofstadt, the EP's chief Brexit negotiator, suggested that the social media's services should have been split apart. Moreover, Verhofstadt posed Zuckerberg the alternative that either he could be remembered as a pioneer who created technology for good, "like Steve Jobs", or as "a genius who created a digital monster".[10]

A year earlier, in the Resolution from February 2017 — with recommendations to the European Commission (EC) on Civil Law Rules on Robotics — the EP invited the EC "to explore, analyse and consider the implications of all possible legal solutions" to tackle the legal challenges of technology, including a new legal status of "electronic personhood" for, at least, some of such robots (EP 2017, at § 59 f). Dealing with a theory of legal monsters and, in particular, of digital monsters, an excerpt of the Resolution deserves our attention:

> Whereas from Mary Shelley's Frankenstein's Monster to the classical myth of Pygmalion, through the story of Prague's Golem to the robot of Karel Čapek, who coined the word, people have fantasised about the possibility of building intelligent machines, more often than not androids with human features … the EP calls on the Commission to propose common Union definitions of cyber physical systems, autonomous systems, smart autonomous robots and their subcategories by taking into consideration … creating a specific legal status for robots in the long run, so that at least the most sophisticated autonomous robots could be established as having the status of electronic persons responsible for making good any damage they may cause, and possibly applying electronic personality to cases where robots make autonomous decisions or otherwise interact with third parties independently. (EP 2017, at lett. A, and § 1 & § 59 f)

In retrospect, the EP resolution was a flop as much as the dressing down of Zuckerberg a year later. Drawing on the opinion of a High-Level Expert Group in 2019 (EC 2019), the Commission discarded every legal personhood of AI systems and smart robots in the first draft of the AI Act in April 2021, and both the European Council and the EP followed suit throughout the institutional debate that ended up with the final version

---

example of this twofold scenario. On the one hand, scholars often dub the anthropogenic impact on the environment as "monstrous" (May 2021; Godin 2022). On the other hand, the behaviour of AI systems and the complexity of digital technologies may break down the classic legal cause and effect analysis. In the phrasing of Curtis Karnow, "no judge can isolate the 'legal' causes of injury from the pervasive electronic hum in which they operate, nor separate causes from the digital universe which gives them their mutable shape and shifting sense. The result is a snarled tangle of cause and effect as impossible to sequester as the winds of the air, or the currents of the ocean" (Karnow 1996).

[10] See, accessed on September 8, 2025 from https://www.independent.co.uk/news/world/europe/mark-zuckerberg-hearing-latest-facebook-data-scandal-european-parliament-cambridge-analytica-a8364191.html

of the Regulation in July 2024.[11] All in all, why should the law grant legal personhood or create any form of accountability for synthetic entities that may become powerful monsters out of control? Would not any such normative attempt be a monster itself by shielding humans from the consequences of their conduct?

Supporters of new forms of personhood for AI systems and robots — which I dub as the Robotic Liberation Front (Pagallo 2013 and 2024) — often pass accusations of monstrosity onto their opponents. For example, according to certain scholars, a new kind of legal personhood for AI systems and smart robots would prevent "the debates over slavery" that "remind us of uncomfortable parallels with the past" and "reflect ongoing tension over humanity's role in an increasingly technologized world" (Chopra and White 2011, at 186). Although AI systems can act and decide beyond human control, therefore triggering problems of alienation and human reification, the claim is that we cannot, on conceptual grounds, rule out in advance the possibility that AI systems should be given the status of legal personhood (Solum 1992). This theoretical possibility has been enthusiastically endorsed by all those scholars who embrace the scenarios of general AI and even sentient AI systems; other scholars inspect this possibility more pragmatically.[12]

Against this hard case of the law,[13] we may wonder how to take sides between accusations of monstrosity for those who recognise that robots can be legal persons and similar claims for those who deny this possibility. After all, in October 2017, a humanoid robot, called Sophia, became the first AI application to receive some form of citizenship by a country, i.e. Saudi Arabia, and other countries may follow suit at least in certain fields of the law. It should not be underestimated that granting someone, or something, legal personhood is — as has always been — a highly sensitive political issue that does not only hinge on rational choices and empirical evidence, for discretion, arbitrariness, and even bizarre or cruel decisions play a role in this context. Over the centuries, humans with birth defects have not been considered legal persons, whilst legal systems have been granting personhood to monasteries, corporations, trusts, ships in maritime law, environmental entities, and so forth. Since today's legal systems grant constitutional personhood to, for example, rivers in New Zealand and India, or the entire ecosystem in Ecuador, why not AI robots?

[11] We dwelt on the Artificial Intelligence Act of EU law in the third section of Chapter 9.

[12] Günther Teubner, for example, affirms that the law may "confer a carefully delimited legal status" to some electronic agents without making them "actors in the economy, in science, medicine, religion or somewhere else in society" (Teubner 2007, at 20). This very possibility has been discussed and supported in fields such as corporate law (Bayern et al. 2017); tax law (Oberson 2019); copyright law (Ajani 2020); and criminal law (Lagioia and Sartor 2020); among others.

[13] See above Chapters 8 and 10, in which the hard cases of the law have been discussed through cases of disagreement among scholars concerning the principles of the legal system (for example, a new status of legal person for robots); the meaning of the terms framing the legal question (for example, what is artificial intelligence); and, how such terms refer to each other (for example, what types of liability follow the potential malfunctioning of an AI system). Arguably, current discussions on AI and smart robots affect all such levels of abstraction. See Barfield and Pagallo (2020).

The uniqueness of AI technologies has updated traditional discussions on monstrous normative acts and institutions, by supplementing such debates with the presence of non-humans, that is, after the *monstrum vel prodigium* of the tradition, a new generation of autonomous artificial agents and anthropomorphic robots. Current debates on personhood for AI systems can be appreciated with mutual accusations of monstrosity against the new scenarios of either AI systems out of control, or governments exploiting the means of such technologies for surveillance purposes.

To tackle both old and new monsters, the next section claims that another kind of monster is necessary. The assumption is that Imre Lakatos' epistemology and his own theory of monsters can help us deal with new cases of disagreement among legal scholars that regard either how digital technologies reshape old forms of institutional and normative monstrosity, or how such technologies raise a set of brand new legal challenges in a terra incognita. A new monster should allow us, if not to solve, at least to clarify a new generation of hard legal cases.

11.3 Lakatos' Monsters

Logic and mathematics have their monsters (Poincaré ed. 1918, at 125). In *Proofs and Refutations*, Lakatos provides his own version of monsters with the example of a polyhedron (Lakatos 1976, at 14). Leaving aside geometrical details, attention must be drawn to what of Lakatos' formalisation of monsters and polyhedrons is relevant in the legal domain. Three basic notions follow with a methodology:

i) Monster barring: What appears to be an exception to the rule, model, or theory, is rejected as invalid, so that the theory, model or rule is accordingly refined to exclude the monstrous exception;
ii) Monster adjustment: The exception or counterexample is not rejected, but rather, reframed to fit the rule, model, or theory, for example, by refining the definitions that are at stake with the monster;
iii) Lemma incorporation: rules, models, or theories are finally reformulated to integrate the exception.

Regarding the legal diatribe of the previous section, the first step — monster barring — has to do with how the law has traditionally tackled the novelty of AI technologies. Although this is the first time legal systems have held humans accountable for what these systems 'decide' to do, the law can determine that such technological novelty does not affect principles, concepts, or rules of the law. This sort of Lakatos' rejection works either through legal mechanisms, such as forms of strict liability for designers and manufacturers of the technology, or by denying that AI systems really 'decide' after all. We noted that this is the opinion of those scholars who either reject every personhood for AI systems or aim to demystify the functioning of autonomous technologies: "The monster did it, not Victor Frankenstein" (Zuboff 2019, at 136).

The second step — monster adjustment — entails the admission that the behaviour and decision-making of AI and smart robots can affect concepts and principles of the law. This impact, however, would not trigger any adoption of new principles and concepts. Lakatos' adjustment should be legally grasped in two ways. In criminal (as opposed to civil) law, as noted in Chapter 8, individuals' responsibility is subordinated to the existence of a specific norm in accordance with the principle of legality and its Anglo-Saxon counterpart, the rule of law. Therefore, from time to time, legislators are forced to amend themselves due to technological advancements: the new generation of computer crimes in the early 1990s illustrates this kind of adjustment (Pagallo 2024, at 14). Vice versa, in civil (as opposed to criminal) law, legislators may deem it appropriate to amend certain provisions of the law to tackle the challenges of technology. This adjustment was examined in Chapter 9 with the provisions of the EU's Artificial Intelligence Act. Although new legal principles and concepts are deemed unnecessary, issues of individual responsibility and accountability may suggest amending certain rules of the law.

Finally, Lakatos' lemma incorporation sums up the core of today's hard cases on digital monsters. Whether the uniqueness of AI technologies entails the adoption of new legal principles and concepts is controversial in the legal community because either adjustments are fated to become monstrous in accordance with the assumptions of the advocates of the Robotic Liberation Front, or critics of this view reckon that it is every lemma incorporation that should be instead understood as the real monster. However, the lemma incorporation dilemma suggests a more critical problem. It can be illustrated with two different but converging claims. On the one hand, scholars may consider some adjustments of legislators as monstrous without buying into the arguments of the Robotic Liberation Front — for example, concerning the monstrosity of EU legislation aiming to govern the use of cookies. On the other hand, scholars may agree on the normative monstrosity of every normative lemma incorporation, regardless of the potentially uncontrollable nature of technology or its monstrous uses. A popular thesis among advocates of the legal personhood of AI systems, such as the parallelism between the legal status of AI systems and that of corporations as legal persons (Karnow 1996; Weitzenboeck 2001), clears this latter point. According to certain scholars, the problem with this lemma incorporation would not concern the new legal status of AI systems as corporations, but rather, the monstrosity of corporations as such (Crofts 2022).

To add a further layer of complexity to the intricacy of current legal debates, scholars' arguments can be further divided into two groups, irrespective of whether they intend to support or oppose a new legal status for AI systems and smart robots. The first group can be presented as deterministic. According to this view, the pace of technology would be so determined and powerful that it cannot be deterred by legal means (Moravec 1999; Kurzweil 2005; Kelly 2010). This belief represents the common ground for opinions such as those of scholars who warn against the monstrous nature of AI technologies or, vice versa, those who consider every legal barring of superintelligences as the real monster. It is not necessary to accept these views to admit some of their merits. All techno-deterministic stances draw attention to the particularity of the challenges posed by digital monsters vis-à-vis traditional debates on despicable institutions or monstrous normative acts. The pace of technological innovation emphasises this point because traditional issues of economic growth, average human life expectancy, or ageing of the population suggest that lawmakers have traditionally addressed problems that are linear, not exponential. Therefore, the gap between the disruptive speed of AI advancements and the slow response of law and regulators often leads to an 'AI pacing problem', which entails an increasing set of legal monster adjustments, i.e. alternative solutions to the law, policy, and regulations for AI systems and smart robots that must properly tackle the new challenges in the field (Barfield et al. 2024).

Against every techno-deterministic thesis, a second group of scholars adopts a pragmatic approach to the monster adjustments of the law (Teubner 2007). The overall assumption is that the long-run views on issues of artificial legal personality – – as in the case of the EP's 2017 resolution — crucially depend on how the law tackles its short- and mid-term issues. This group of scholars' arguments is anchored in the legal tradition of whether institutions and normative acts can be deemed monstrous. The approach was illustrated in the first section of this chapter, which discussed current debates on monstrous surveillance societies and the drawbacks of legislative attempts to tame monster cookies. What we should expect in the future regarding the use of AI systems and how to assess their impact on human societies, thus overlaps with discussions about the monstrosity of acts and legal systems that do not necessarily depend on the use of digital technologies. Thresholds of monstrosity are defined by the same requirements that were under scrutiny in the previous chapters of this book, with standards and principles of international and constitutional law for the protection of human and fundamental rights (institutional monsters), or with acts that are unintelligible, inconsistent, or subject to over-frequent revision (normative monsters).

The pragmatic approach to the monster adjustments of the law, in addition, draws attention to a critical facet of all deterministic stances on AI technologies with their digital monsters. The focus is on the disruptive moment in which AI systems not only affect concepts and principles of the law, but force the law to endorse new concepts and principles. According to the pragmatic approach, the transition from monster adjustments to lemma incorporations entails assessing whether new concepts and principles may help tackle drawbacks and loopholes of the law. Consider failures of legal causation or liability gaps that hinge on cases of distributed responsibility in which multiple accumulated actions of humans and computers may lead to cases of impunity (Karnow 1996). Such assessment revolves around conditions and steps of the transition from simple adjustments to lemma incorporations in the legal domain. It explains why adopting forms of legal experimentation, such as sandboxes and legally deregulated special zones set up in several jurisdictions, has increasingly gained traction over the past decade to grasp the steps and conditions of every potential transition.[14]

[14] Forms of technological experimentation through the creation of legally deregulated special zones were first created in Japan in the early 2010s: see Weng et al. (2015). Further forms of experimentation were — and still are — at work in the field of autonomous vehicles (Pagallo 2017). The AI Act has endorsed the idea of sandboxes under Art. 57 of the EU regulation. In general terms, such forms of legal experimentation should represent the basis on which to collect empirical data and sufficient knowledge to make rational decisions for a number of critical issues, such as improving

By contrast, most deterministic stances lack this kind of granularity. Whether advocates of robotic rights or supporters of the monstrous nature of AI technology, scholars often jump into the challenges of the future without dispensing any detail about how we may wake up one day dealing with superintelligences, sentient robots, or powerful AI systems out of control. Since the assumption of these stances is the irrelevance or incapacity of the law to deter the pace of technology, this lack of attention to how we should legally grasp the transition from every monster adjustment to any final lemma incorporation is unsurprising. However, the fact that such scholars often overlook the problems of this legal transition is critical because their reference to future monsters necessarily appears as a simple rhetorical exercise or an unhinged Sci-Fi scenario.

As a result, the next section aims to shed light on the short- and mid-term issues of the field to comprehend some further ways in which the unique challenges of AI technology may interplay with the traditional monsters of the legal tradition. Surprising monstrous reasons shall be additionally dissected to complement the requirements of monstrosity for both the institutional and normative levels.

11.4 Breaking Points

Rumours about a monstrous future in which superintelligences and robots take control over humans are widely popular among scholars and business people (Coeckelbergh 2020). In 2015, for example, the Future of Life Institute released an open letter in which Bill Gates, Elon Musk, Stephen Hawking, and others warned against the apocalyptic threat of AI and robots out of control (Pagallo 2017). A decade later, in 2023, another group of business leaders and experts, including the boss of ChatGPT, Sam Altman, claimed on the website of the Centre for AI Safety, a U.S.-based non-profit organisation, that combating AI-related risks should be "a global priority on par with other society-wide risks, such as pandemics and nuclear war" (Pagallo 2025). Scholars have imagined how such existential threats of superintelligence and monstrous AI could ever materialise (Bostrom 2014). Among such thought experiments, Robert Nozick's metaphor of the "utility monster" is particularly fruitful in this context (Nozick 1974). Although the target of his ethical criticism was the core of utilitarianism, the argument has become trendy among certain prophets of doom. So goes Nozick's thesis:

> Utilitarian theory is embarrassed by the possibility of utility monsters who get enormously greater sums of utility from any sacrifice of others than these others lose … the theory seems to require that we all be sacrificed in the monster's maw, in order to increase total utility. (Nozick 1974, at 41)

---

our understanding of how AI systems may react in various contexts and satisfy human needs, and how to better appreciate risks and threats posed by possible losses of control of AI systems, so as to keep them in check. In accordance with the spirit of our times, certain scholars interpret the aim of such regulatory sandboxes as a way "to tame innovation monsters" (Laurent 2024).

A utility monster paving the way to a monstrous AI robot, admittedly, does not require any superintelligence. Consider the Zero Intelligence ("ZI") agents developed since the robot tournaments at the Santa Fe Institute in the early 1990s. Such ZI agents were programmed to replicate the behaviour of human double-oral auction markets by generating "bids and offers selected randomly from a uniform distribution subject only to the constraint that it cannot 'deliberately' lose money" (Miller 2008). Such robots are rudimentary because oblivious to their environment and incapable of controlling the timing of their actions, or taking action to compensate for their inability to respond to the environment. Still, ZI agents can achieve sophisticated goals, such as outperforming untrained human traders in double auction experiments, thus showing that markets populated only by such robots can have the tendency of human markets to generate average prices and quantities of what economists call a "competitive equilibrium" (Pagallo 2013, at 97). This ability of ZI agents to attain a high level of allocative efficiency when determining average prices and quantities of goods exchanged in a market has been linked to Hayek's idea that in certain fields of social interaction, "intelligence" emerges from the rules of the game rather than individual choices (Sunder 2004). However, the subtleties of markets containing intelligent agents such as humans may lead to rudimentary bubbles and crash scenarios, where traders act without regard to the effects of future supply. The correspondence between the greediness of human speculators and the eagerness of ZI robots to trade not only suggested the end of projects such as the Automated Trading project sponsored by the University of Pennsylvania and Lehman Brothers in 2005, i.e. 3 years before Lehman Brothers' own collapse. Also, according to some scholars, "some of the financial troubles of late 2009 may have been caused by the involvement of such agents operating without human supervision and at speeds not amenable to human understanding or intervention" (Chopra and White 2011, at 7).

Over the past decade, also but not only in the financial sector, lawmakers have been attentive to prevent these scenarios of out-of-control artificial agents.[15] In the civilian sector, for example, in EU law, the bulk of the AI Act concerns both the high and systemic risks posed by certain technology uses that are regulated through a full array of provisions on human oversight under Art. 14 of the Regulation. Similar safeguards were set up with the Executive Order on AI of the Biden administration (White House 2023).[16] Such a race to AI regulation, according to a popular formula among scholars (Smuha 2021), does not mean that problems of meaningful control over the behaviour of AI systems and smart robots are fixed. However, current activism of lawmakers at the international and national level draws the attention to how every long-term picture of monstrous AI systems taking decisions by themselves crucially depends on the short- and mid-term regulations of the law. Whilst advocates of

[15] This "theme in political thought" is not new (Winner 1978), although advancements of AI technologies have exacerbated it. We already noted in the previous section of this chapter that the international community is currently discussing the regulation and even ban of lethal autonomous weapon systems in the military sector: see Pagallo (2024, at 81).

[16] Under Section 8 (b)(i)(A) of the Executive Order, the Act concerned, among others, the protection of consumers and patients, passengers and students. The Trump's administration got rid of this EO in the first week of the new presidency in January 2025 (White House 2025).

techno-deterministic stances properly stress some peculiarities of the technology under exam — for example, the exponential pace of AI innovation and the autonomy of the artificial agents' decision-making — such stances are flawed insofar as they overlook how today's decisions may shape the future.

Drawing on the methodology of this book on requirements of monstrosity for normative acts (Chapter 9), and institutions (Chapter 10), three observables of the analysis with their variables stress the ways in which the uniqueness of AI technologies updates those requirements. The observables regard:

i) Monstrous institutions that employ digital technologies and AI systems for further monstrous purposes, such as the systematic infringement of human rights and of constitutional safeguards through mass surveillance means of social control or autonomous lethal weapons;
ii) Decent institutions that may become monstrous for the new wrong ways in which they may use the technology, for example, the reckless automation of adjudicatory procedures;
iii) Normative acts that appear monstrous for how they attempt to govern and regulate the technology. In addition to the monstrous acts that hinge on the two previous observables of the analysis, this is the case of decent institutions that may adopt a monstrous normative act in good faith.

The first observable draws attention to the many ways in which the systematic violation of human rights and infringement of constitutional safeguards become more systematic and sophisticated. For example, in Maduro's Venezuela, state control technology is employed for surveillance, censorship, and repression through website blocking and filtering; threats to social media platforms; use of digital identification systems, such as the "Carnet de la Patria" and "Sistema Patria", which are linked to social welfare programs that potentially restrict access to essential services (Singer 2021); and apps, such as "VenApp", which is used for citizen reporting on suspicious activities (Puyosa 2021). The same holds for Kim Jong-un's North Korea, in which the use of state control technologies includes tools for surveillance of communication, such as phone calls monitoring; internet access and censorship; facial recognition and biometric databases; road traffic surveillance and overall suppression of dissent (Byman and Lind 2010; Silberstein 2020). Against this technological expertise, scholars wonder how the increasing spread of AI will shape North Korea's cyber capabilities in the coming years, which includes the use of autonomous weapons systems (Harold et al. 2022; Raska 2023). To some, North Korea may be less concerned about malfunctions of such autonomous weapons systems resulting in civilian deaths than most states, since the regime is already one of the world's worst human rights violators (Horowitz 2021).

The second observable on decent institutions that may become monstrous through the use of technology reminds us of some scandals, such as the UK postal scandal (Bath 2021; Wallis 2021; Marshall 2022); and the Dutch childcare benefits scandal (Bouwmeester 2023; Fenger and Simonse 2024). Reckless automation encompasses many different factors, such as over-reliance on technology with a rapid, poorly planned, or harmful implementation; flawed human-machine interaction; inadequate system design; and lack of human oversight; all of which can lead to the devaluation of human expertise, removal of human responsibility, reduction of human control, and erosion of human self-determination (Floridi et al. 2018, at 691). So far, it is fair to admit that most Western democratic systems have been able to address these risks: after all, we noted in previous chapters of this book that only decent institutions may concede they have adopted monstrous regulations or practices. However, whether and to what extent the oversight of these institutions through independent control, accountability to the law, and respect for fundamental rights will effectively address the challenges of technology remains an open issue, especially considering less resilient rule of law traditions. In the phrasing of the EC's 2023 *Rule of Law Report*, "the Russian war of aggression against Ukraine serves as a tragic reminder that these values can never be taken for granted" (EC 2023).

The third observable of the analysis, in particular, the variable of monstrous normative acts in good faith is particularly challenging for a theory of legal monsters. Previous parts of this book insisted on the thresholds of normative monstrosity related to the means-end efficacy of every legislation. In Chapter 9, the focus was on why certain provisions of the EU's AI Act — from the protection of fundamental rights, such as equality and a high level of environmental protection, to the threat of over-frequent revision of the Regulation — look monstrous. Likewise, in the first section of this chapter, we noted that normative efforts to tackle some technological monsters, such as the EU regulation of internet cookies, may also generate monsters. Such cases of monstrosity do not entail that defects of legislation are a sufficient condition to trigger the monstrous scenarios of out of control AI systems.[17] However, every normative act that fails to prevent such a threat is necessarily monstrous.[18] Considering cases of normative monstrosity triggered by legislative incompetence, as those stressed in the last two sections of Chapter 9, scholars have the responsibility to denounce this normative danger through the monster metaphor on the means-end efficacy of lawmaking. The interdependence of data-driven societies and the exponential growth of technological innovation make this responsibility even graver. Legislative good faith without technological know-how can sometimes be as harmful as the evil intentions of a tyrant.

---

[17] This is the case of monstrous regulations and despicable uses of AI by other legal systems also, but not only, in the military domain: see Bringsjord et al. (2025). The interdependence of data-driven societies with challenging issues regarding jurisdiction, law enforcement, and the extra-territorial effects of legislation aggravates traditional problems of monstrous organisations (Thanem 2011), and governance (Dean 2008). On the unique governance challenges of the digital age and how to tackle them, see Pagallo (2015); Poblet et al. (2019); and Paseri (2025). The aim of these new governance models should include the prevention of monstrous normative acts and practices that depend on the unique features of AI.

[18] The assessment also covers cases of legislative inertia. Drawing on Hobbes' warning, the responsibility shall be traced back to the "will of the sovereign … signified by his silence". See above the third section of Chapter 7.

References

Ajani, G. 2020. Contemporary artificial art and the law: Searching for an author. *Brill Research Perspectives in Art and Law* 3 (4): 1–84.
Artosi, A., and G. Sartor. 2018. Leibniz as jurist. In *The Oxford handbook of Leibniz*, ed. M. R. Antognazza, 641–663. Oxford: Oxford University Press.
Barfield, W., and U. Pagallo. 2020. *Advanced introduction to the law and artificial intelligence.* Cheltenham: Elgar.
Barfield, W., Y.-H. Weng, and U. Pagallo, eds. 2024. *The Cambridge handbook of the law, policy, and regulation for human–robot interaction.* Cambridge: Cambridge University Press.
Baum, K., et al. 2025. Taming the AI monster: Monitoring of individual fairness for effective human oversight. In *Model checking software*, ed. T. Neele and A. Wijs, 3–25. Cham: Springer.
Bayern, S., T. Burri, T. D. Grant, D. M. Häusermann, F. Möslein, and R. Williams. 2017. Company law and autonomous systems: A blueprint for lawyers. *Entrepreneurs, and Regulators, Hastings Science, Technology and Law Journal* 9 (2): 135–161.
Bekey, G. A. 2005. *Autonomous robots: From biological inspiration to implementation and control.* Cambridge, MA/London: MIT Press.
Bostrom, N. 2014. *Superintelligence: Paths, dangers, strategies.* Oxford: Oxford University Press.
Bouwmeester, M. 2023. System failure in the digital welfare state: Exploring parliamentary and judicial control in the Dutch childcare benefits scandal. *Recht der Werkelijkheid* 44 (2): 13–37.
Bringsjord, S., N. Sundar Govindarajulu, J. Licato, and A. Bringsjord. 2025. *Only logic can save us.* Cham: Springer.
Byman, D., and J. Lind. 2010. Pyongyang's survival strategy: Tools of authoritarian control in North Korea. *International Security* 35 (1): 44–74.
Castells, M. 1998. *The information age: Economy, society and culture.* 3 vol. Oxford: Blackwell.
Chesterman, S. 2022. All rise for the honourable robot judge? Using artificial intelligence to regulate AI. *NUS Law Working Paper* No. 2022/019, at https://doi.org/10.2139/ssrn.4252778.
Chopra, S., and L. F. White. 2011. *A legal theory for autonomous artificial agents.* Ann Arbor, MI: The University of Michigan Press.
Clancy, K. A., and B. Clancy. 2016. Growing monstrous organisms: The construction of anti-GMO visual rhetoric through digital media. *Critical Studies in Media Communication* 33 (3): 279–292.
Coeckelbergh, M. 2020 Superintelligence, monsters, and the AI apocalypse. In M. Coeckelbergh, *AI Ethics*, 11–29. Cambridge, MA:MIT Press.
Cohen, J. E. 2019. *Between truth and power: The legal constructions of informational capitalism.* Oxford: Oxford University Press.
Crofts, P. 2022. The corporate monster metaphor. *Law Text Culture* 26:73–96.
Davey, B. 2020. Surveillance capitalism at the limits to economic growth: Part 2, *Resilience*, February. Accessed on September 8, 2025 from https://www.resilience.org/stories/2020-02-07/surveillance-capitalism-at-the-limits-to-economic-growth-part-2/.
Dean, M. 2008. Governing society. The story of two monsters. *Journal of Cultural Economy* 1 (1): 25–38.
Debusser, F. 2005. The EU e-privacy directive: A monstrous attempt to starve the cookie monster? *International Journal of Law and Information Technologies* 13:70–97.
Doctorow, C. 2018. I've created a monster! (and so can you). In *Franken book.* Cambridge, MA: The MIT Press. Accessed on September 8, 2025 from https://www.frankenbook.org/pub/ive-create-a-monster/release/1.
Dove, G. and A.-L. Fayard 2020. Monsters, metaphors, and machine learning, In *Proceedings of the 2020 CHI Conference on Human Factors in Computing Systems*, 1–17. ACM: New York.
Durante, M. 2021. *Computational power: The impact of ICT on law, Society and Knowledge.* London: Routledge.
Ebrahimi, Afrouzi A. 2024. John Robots, Thurgood Martian, and the Syntax Monster: A New Argument Against AI Judges. *Canadian Journal of Law & Jurisprudence*1–28.

European Commission (EC). 2019. *Liability for Artificial Intelligence and Other Emerging Digital Technologies,* Directorate-General for Justice and Consumers Publications Office. Accessed on September 8, 2025 from https://data.europa.eu/doi/10.2838/573689.

European Commission (EC). 2023. *2023 rule of law report*. Communication COM(2023) 800 final, Brussels.

European Parliament (EP). 2017. Report with recommendations to the commission on civil law rules on robotics, Report A8–0005/2017. Accessed on September 8, 2025 from https://www.europarl.europa.eu/doceo/document/A-8-2017-0005_EN.html.

European Sources Online (ESO). 2018. Meeting between Facebook's Mark Zuckerberg and European parliament's political leadership, *Cardiff EDC.* Accessed on September 8, 2025 from https://www.europeansources.info/record/meeting-between-facebooks-mark-zuckerberg-and-european-parliaments-political-leadership/.

Fenger, M., and R. Simonse. 2024. The implosion of the Dutch surveillance welfare state. *Social Policy & Administration* 58 (2): 264–276.

Floridi, L. 2013. Technology's in-betweenness. *Philosophy and Technology* 26:111–115.

Floridi, L. 2014. *The fourth revolution: How the infosphere is reshaping human reality*. Oxford: Oxford University Press.

Floridi, L., J. Cowls, M. Beltrametti, R. Chatila, P. Chazerand, V. Dignum, Ch. Luetge, R. Madelin, U. Pagallo, F. Rossi, B. Schafer, P. Valcke, and E. Vayena. 2018. AI4People—An ethical framework for a good AI society: opportunities. Risks, Principles, and Recommendations, *Minds and Machines* 28 (4): 689–707.

Godin, G. 2022. Monstrous things: Horror, othering, and the Anthropocene. *Post-Medieval Archaeology* 56 (2): 116–126.

Haraway, D. 2013. The promises of monsters: A regenerative politics for inappropriate/d others. In *Cultural studies*, ed. L. Grossberg, C. Nelson, and P. Treichler, 295–337. Abingdon: Routledge.

Harold, S.W., Beauchamp-Mustafaga, N., Jun, J., Myers, D., and D. Grossman 2022. Will artificial intelligence hone North Korea's cyber 'all-purpose sword'?, *Korea Economic Institute of America*, March, report no. 7. Accessed on September 8, 2025 from https://keia.org/wp-content/uploads/2022/03/KEI_SMA_Harold-Mustafaga-Jun-Myers-Grossman.pdf.

Heidegger, M. 1993. The question concerning technology [1953]. Trans. William Lovitt, with rev. David Farrell Krell. In *Martin Heidegger: Basic Writings*, ed. David Farrell Krell, rev. expanded edition, 311–41. London: Routledge.

Horowitz, M. C. 2021. When speed kills: Lethal autonomous weapon systems, deterrence and stability. In *Emerging technologies and international stability*, ed. T. S. Sechser, N. Narang, and C. Talmadge, 144–168. London: Routledge.

IEEE Standard Association. 2020. IEEE Recommended Practice for Assessing the Impact of Autonomous and Intelligent Systems on Human Well-being, IEEE 7010–2020, 16, 1–96. Accessed on September 8, 2025 from https://doi.org/10.1109/IEEESTD.2020.9084219.

Karnow, C. E. A. 1996. Liability for distributed artificial intelligence. *Berkeley Technology Law Journal* 11:147–183.

Kelly, K. 2010. *What technology wants*. New York: Viking.

Khorram, J. 2024. AI 'Godfather' Yoshua Bengio: We're 'creating monsters more powerful than us'. *Yahoo! finance*, 12 October. Available at https://finance.yahoo.com/news/ai-godfather-yoshua-bengio-were-creating-monsters-more-powerful-than-us-120042014.html?guccounter=1&guce_referrer=aHR0cHM6Ly93d3cuZ29vZ2xlLmNvbS8&guce_referrer_sig=AQAAAEWknLC0HSZg95rQL0kZ2oPDCNBEXFJF75yNnhDOB_TC7FLeocIHzEEqvK2qLlOA10HxPgc-EkCWVw21XoELOS2e8mNpPhJ23MPhs9W5ANbLi2BCroWrF8eel2iw-5uLzja0RktQxnotLN501r7EBAghVZ1QLFsVh-DO7BnkdpI0.

Kurzweil, R. 2005. *The singularity is near*. New York: Viking.

Lagioia, F., and G. Sartor. 2020. AI systems under criminal law: A legal analysis and a regulatory perspective. *Philosophy and Technology* 33:433–465.

Lakatos, I. 1976. *Proofs and refutations: The logic of mathematical discovery*, ed. J. Worrall and E. Zahar. Cambridge: Cambridge University Press.

Latour, B. 2011. Love your monsters. *Breakthrough Journal* 2 (11): 21–28.
Laurent, B. 2024. Innovation monsters in the sandbox. *Practicing Anthropology* 46 (1): 71–78.
Leenes, R., and E. Kosta. 2015. Taming the cookie monster with Dutch law—A tale of regulatory failure. *Computer Law & Security Review* 31 (3): 31–335.
Marshall, P. 2022. Scandal at the post office: The intersection of law, ethics and politics. *Digital Evidence and Electronic Signature Law Review* 19:12–28.
May, L. 2021. Confronting ecological monstrosity: Contemporary video game monsters and the climate crisis. *M/C Journal* 24 (5): 2804.
Mecacci, G., D. Amoroso, L. Cavalcante Siebert, D. Abbink, J. van den Hoven, and F. Santoni de Sio, eds. 2024. *Research handbook on meaningful human control of artificial intelligence systems*. Cheltenham: Elgar.
Mellet, K., and T. Beauvisage. 2019. Cookie monsters. Anatomy of a Digital Market Infrastructure, *Consumption Markets & Culture* 23 (2): 110–129.
Miller, R. M. 2008. Don't let your robots grow up to be traders: Artificial intelligence, human intelligence, and asset-market bubbles. *Journal of Economic Behavior and Organization* 68 (1): 153–166.
Moravec, H. 1999. *Robot: Mere machine to transcendent mind*. London: Oxford University Press.
Negroponte, N. 2015. *Being digital*. New York: Vintage.
Nozick, R. 1974. *Anarchy, state, and utopia*. Malden, MA: Basic Books.
Oberson, X. 2019. *Taxing robots*. Cheltenham: Elgar.
Pagallo, U. 2013. *The laws of robots: crimes, contracts, and torts*. Dordrecht: Springer.
Pagallo, U. 2015. Good onlife governance: On law, spontaneous orders, and design. In *The onlife manifesto: Being human in a hyperconnected era*, ed. L. Floridi, 161–177. Cham: Springer.
Pagallo, U. 2016. *Leibniz*. Milan: Kluwer.
Pagallo, U. 2017. From automation to autonomous systems: A legal phenomenology with problems of accountability. In *Proceedings of the Twenty-Sixth International Joint Conference on Artificial Intelligence (IJCAI-17)*, Melbourne, Australia, August 19–25, 2017, 17–23. Palo Alto, CA: International Joint Conferences on Artificial Intelligence Organization.
Pagallo, U. 2018. Vital, sophia, and Co-The quest for the legal personhood of robots. *Information* 9 (9): 230.
Pagallo, U. 2021. *Il dovere alla salute. Sul rischio di sottoutilizzo dell'intelligenza artificiale in ambito sanitario*. Milano: Mimesis.
Pagallo, U. 2024. *The New Laws of Outer Space: Ethics, Legislation, and Governance in the Age of Artificial Intelligence*. Oxford: Hart.
Pagallo, U. 2025. LLMs meet the AI act: Who's the sorcerer's apprentice. *Cambridge Forum on AI: Law and Governance* 1:e1.
Pagallo, U., and M. Durante. 2022. The Good, the bad, and the invisible with its opportunity costs: Introduction to the 'J' special issue on "the impact of artificial intelligence on law". *J—Multidisciplinary Scientific Journal* 5 (1): 139–149.
Pagallo, U., S. O'Sullivan, N. Nevejans, et al. 2024. The underuse of AI in the health sector: opportunity costs, success stories, risks and recommendations. *Health and Technology* 14 (1): 1–14.
Paseri, L. 2025. *Il governo dei dati. Interesse pubblico, altruismo e partecipazione*. Turin: Giappichelli.
Pentland, A. S. 2013. The data-driven society. *Scientific American* 309 (4): 78–83.
Poblet, M., P. Casanovas, and V. Rodríguez-Doncel. 2019. *Linked democracy: Foundations, tools, and applications*. Cham: Springer.
Poincaré, H. 1918. *Science and Method [1908]*, trans. F. Maitland, London: Nelson.
Puyosa, I. 2021. Venezuela: 21st-century authoritarianism in the digital sphere. In *Social media impacts on conflict and democracy*, ed. L. Schirch, 194–204. London: Routledge.
Raska, M. 2023. North Korea's evolving cyber strategies and operations: Toward weapons of mass effectiveness. In *North Korea's foreign policy: The Kim Jong-un regime in a hostile world*, ed. S. A. Snyder and K.-A. Park, 173–200. London: Rowman and Littlefield.

Santoni de Sio, F., G. Mecacci, S. Calvert, et al. 2023. Realising meaningful human control over automated driving systems: A multidisciplinary approach. *Minds & Machines* 33:587–611.

Silberstein, B. K. 2020. How high-tech can boost regime stability in North Korea. *Orbis* 64 (4): 589–598.

Singer, F. 2021. 'Sistema patria': A new digital tool for social control in Venezuela, *El País English*, 24 April.

Smits, M. 2006. Taming monsters: The cultural domestication of new technology. *Technology in Society* 28 (4): 489–504.

Smuha, N. A. 2021. From a 'Race to AI' to a 'Race to AI regulation': Regulatory competition for artificial intelligence. *Law, Innovation and Technology* 13 (1): 57–84.

Solum, L. B. 1992. Legal personhood for artificial intelligence. *North Carolina Law Review* 70:1231–1287.

Stanley, J., and B. Steinhardt. 2014. Bigger monster, weaker chains: The growth of an American surveillance society. In *Ethics and emerging technologies*, ed. R. L. Sandler, 269–284. London: Palgrave Macmillan.

Sunder, S. 2004. Markets as artifacts: Aggregate efficiency from zero-intelligence traders. In *Models of a man: Essays in memory of Herbert A. Simon*, ed. M. Augier and J. Marsch, 501–519. Cambridge, MA: MIT Press.

Teubner, G. 2007. Rights of non-humans? Electronic agents and animals as new actors in politics and law. Max Weber lecture at the European University Institute of Fiesole. Available at https://cadmus.eui.eu/bitstream/handle/1814/6960/MWP_LS_2007_04.pdf.

Thanem, T. 2011. *The monstrous organization*. Cheltenham, UK: Elgar.

Trevisan, M., S. Traverso, E. Bassi, and M. Mellia. 2019. 4 years of EU cookie law: Results and lessons learned. *Proceedings on Privacy Enhancing Technologies* 2:126–145.

Wallis, N. 2021. *The great post office scandal*. Bath: Bath Publishing.

Wang, N., and M. Y. Tian. 2022. 'Intelligent justice': AI implementations in China's legal systems. In *Artificial intelligence and Its discontents: Social and Cultural Studies of Robots and AI*, ed. A. Hanemaayer. Cham: Palgrave Macmillan.

Weiskopf, R. 2020. Book review: The age of surveillance capitalism. The fight for a human future at the new frontier of power. *Organization* 27 (6): 975–978.

Weitzenboeck, E. M. 2001. Electronic agents and the formation of contracts. *International Journal of Law and Information Technology* 9:204–234.

Weng, Y.-H., Y. Sugahara, K. Hashimoto, and A. Takanishi. 2015. Intersection of "Tokku" special zone, robots, and the law: A case study on legal impacts to humanoid robots. *International Journal of Social Robotics* 7 (5): 841–857.

White House. 2023. *Executive order on the safe, secure, and trustworthy development and use of artificial intelligence, October 30*. USA: Washington D.C.

White House. 2025. *Executive order on removing barriers to American leadership in artificial intelligence, January 23*. USA: Washington D.C.

Wiener, N. 1964. *God and Golem, Inc. A comment on certain points where cybernetics impinges on religion*. Cambridge, MA: MIT Press.

Winner, L. 1978. *Autonomous technology: Technics-out-of-control as a theme in political thought*. Cambridge, MA: MIT Press.

Zuboff, S. 2019. *The age of surveillance capitalism: The fight for a human future at the new frontier of power*. New York: PublicAffairs.

Conclusion

Formulas on monsters have played a critical role over more than 2500 years of Western legal and political thought. This volume has insisted on the difference between what is dead and what is alive in the use of such metaphors. What is dead concerns the image of human monsters as targets of legal repression, i.e. the 'legally dead' people of the tradition. Human beings—whether people with congenital disabilities, pirates, criminals, terrorists, illegal immigrants, or lesbians and homosexuals—have all inalienable and absolute rights, for example, a right against any inhuman treatment. The claim rests on moral arguments and pillars of today's law that were under scrutiny in the fourth chapter of this volume on the chronicle of a 'legal death'. The assumption does not mean that normative acts and practices of states and public authorities cannot openly contradict principles of human rights or fundamental rights protection. However, should this be the case, the only monster would be the lawmaker who treats human fellows as monsters of the tradition. The claim also applies to the hypothesis that current law should be abolished, thus reinstating the formal treatment of people with birth defects, slaves, or enemies of the institutions. The only function of the metaphor of the 'legally dead' people of ancient and modern times would be that of criticism, resistance, and rebellion.

What is legally alive with the metaphor on monsters concerns the other facet of the functions of the formula related to the body politic, rather than the individuals' body, that is, the subjects rather than the objects of the law. The analysis of the body politic has distinguished requirements of monstrosity for either normative acts or political institutions. This differentiation hinges on a fundamental asymmetry: whilst monstrous normative acts must be expected as a result of monstrous institutions, decent institutions can also adopt monstrous normative acts. The asymmetry has practical and theoretical relevance. As regards the practical side of the asymmetry, the fact that certain institutions should be deemed monstrous casts light on how rulers exercise their legal and political power. Despite their dissenting opinions, Plato and Aristotle warn us against why and how democratic regimes can turn into tyrannies. The threshold of monstrosity does not regard any numerical distinction of

U. Pagallo, *A Theory of Legal Monsters: Repression, Resistance, Rebellion*, Philosophical Studies Series 161, https://doi.org/10.1007/978-3-032-10771-8

monarchies, aristocracies, and democracies, in addition to the plethora of one-person or one-party rule systems, despotic regimes, ochlocracies, oligarchies, or autocracies. Instead, today as much as back then, the focus should be on whether rulers and legislators violate the law, seek their own profit rather than the benefit of their subjects, and govern against their people. History has always been a generous source of tyrannical monsters that enslave their people and, alas, our era in no exception.

On the other hand, the distinction between monstrous institutions and monstrous normative acts also has a theoretical relevance because the threshold of monstrosity set up in this book aims to address a thorny issue of legal theory. Over the past century, scholars have analysed—and have been deeply divided on—whether the functioning of political organisations can be reduced to a set of norms, for example, according to the tenets of Kelsen's doctrine (Kelsen 1945). Alternatively, such a set of norms would be a necessary but insufficient condition for understanding how legal orders function in a specific culture and tradition. This latter view was emphasised by a French legal philosopher, Maurice Hauriou, who claimed that every legal system involves "an idea of a work or enterprise that is realised and endures juridically in a social milieu" (Hauriou ed. 1970, at 99). The panoply of legal cultures, traditions, customs, and the dynamics of legal transplants and rejections in multiple jurisdictions confirm this conjecture: norms and rules pass, but institutions endure. Still, it seems fair to admit that any claim of institutional monstrosities shall be substantiated with the monstrous properties of this or that normative act or practice. This condition applies especially—but not exclusively—to every democratic institution that turns itself into a tyranny.

The volume fleshed out different requirements of normative monstrosity. Adapting Lon Fuller's suggestions (Fuller 1964), an act is not simply wrong but monstrous when the act is laid down on an individual basis, or when it is secret, retroactive, unintelligible, incongruous or inconsistent, subject to over-frequent revision, unfeasible to obey, or randomly dispensed. Such requirements of monstrosity were complemented with the analysis of violations of the international Bill of Rights or of constitutional safeguards. *Pace* Fuller and his claims on the "internal morality of law", the reasons for such a monstrosity do not necessarily depend on the evil ends a certain act or practice intends to attain. We can reverse the Kantian idea that a nation of devils can establish a state of good citizens, if they "have understanding" (Kant ed. 1999, at 366), by saying that even a nation of angels would need the law for their coordination. It is often unnecessary to address the philosophical quarrel of the ends that justify a certain legislation in considering it monstrous. In most cases, by following Occam's razor, paying attention to the consistency of the means through which a legislation intends to attain its ends is sufficient.

This means-end approach was illustrated with samples of EU lawmaking, in particular, some provisions of the AI Act, which either contradict the principle of equality—as regards the environmental responsibilities of the subjects in the legal order—or entail the over-frequent revision of legal texts to tackle technological advancements. Further cases of normative monstrosity included legislation crafted for individual purposes. In addition to William Blackstone's remarks in the mid-1700s, attention was drawn to certain laws passed by the Italian Parliament during

Silvio Berlusconi's governments which aimed at protecting the interests of the political leader. In all these cases, it is not the institution, whether Blackstone's England, the Italian Republic, or the EU legislators, that appears monstrous, but rather the specific normative act they adopt. This book argued that the monstrosity of normative acts or practices is a necessary but insufficient condition of institutional monstrosity. As a result, how should we grasp the end(s) of the law?

This book has identified the requirements of institutional monstrosity by taking up the ancient idea of tyrants who break the law, and specifying that such infringement of national and international principles and legislation should be blatant, or systematic. The threshold does not entail any quantitative affair, although followers of Friedrich Engels—or of Plato's numerology, for that matter—may still claim that this is one of those cases where quantity transforms into quality (Engels ed. 1954, at 213). The systematic violation of human rights or constitutional safeguards breaks the bond of political obligation as well as the social trust in legal norms as guides to conduct. When the source of criticism or resistance is not a specific normative act or practice but rather the institution itself, citizens cannot rely on those who created the monster to get rid of it. Despite Engels' examples from physics, or Plato's distance of 729 between tyrants and philosopher-kings, no one-size-fits-all answer exists. We noted that even a single normative act can be sufficient to turn an institution into a monster, and yet, it can be tricky to determine whether, for example, Mussolini's Italy had to wait for the Racial Law in November 1938 with the Royal Decree no. 1728 to become a monstrosity. Scholars might claim that such a monstrosity should be traced back to the 'Rocco law' on the one party rule system of Act no. 1019 from May 1928; or even earlier and much likelier, back to the 'Acerbo law' no. 2444 from 1923. This latter law rigged elections in April 1924 and led to Giacomo Matteotti's denunciation of the regime before the Chamber of Deputies in May of that same year. Matteotti was vilely assassinated on 10 June 1924.

Although clear-cut cases of institutional and normative monstrosity do exist, the book stressed that thresholds for the assessment of every institutional or normative monster are exposed to cases of reasonable disagreement. Scholars may discuss whether the violation of constitutional safeguards should be deemed blatant, the infringement of human rights systematic, or the ends of legislation wrong. Throughout the chapters of this book the attention was drawn to the shortcomings of Dworkin's thesis on 'unique right answers'. Disagreements of the legal community may depend on different traditions, customs, and cultures on how to interpret the concepts of the system and their interplay vis-à-vis the principles of national or international law. Also, divergent opinions can regard the principles of the law that may fall short in coping with the unique challenges of our times. For example, risks and threats posed by AI systems and models have required complementing the set of core principles commonly used in bioethics—namely, beneficence, non-maleficence, autonomy and justice—with a new principle of "explicability" to understand and hold to account the decision-making of AI (Floridi et al. 2018). It would be hard to buy into the idea that such a new principle of explicability, later endorsed by the European legislator, could have been inferred as the unique right answer from the previous tenets of the law on justice and autonomy, among others.

Disagreements of the legal community are also relevant for a theory of legal monsters by warning against crying wolf exaggerations. Presenting an institution or a normative act as a monster involves a grave responsibility because the function of the metaphor is to identify and denounce what is legally deplorable and unacceptable. Against any easy multiplication of monsters, the book accordingly set the bar of assessment high. It is not enough to claim that a certain regime, current surveillance societies, or potentially out-of-control AI systems are monstrous. It is necessary to substantiate such claims on the basis of case law, provisions of positive law, or the practice of states and institutions. Such a burden of proof does not entail that requirements are too strict or open to opposing readings. The drawbacks of the unique right answer-thesis do not entail any sheer relativism. Plain cases of normative and institutional monstrosity exist, such as Mussolini's Italy or Maduro's Venezuela. By following the same standard, some claims of EU institutional monstrosity were rejected as unhinged, although it should be admitted that certain provisions of EU law can be considered monstrous. After all, only decent institutions may concede they embraced a monstrous act.

The book dwelt on several examples of this institutional acknowledgement, such as the Italian Court of Cassation's doctrine on normative monsters. This circumstance suggests that such normative acts are not only more numerous than monstrous institutions, but also that they are potentially less controversial. To substantiate the claim, the analysis drew attention to another asymmetry that follows as a result of the distinction between conditions of monstrosity for normative acts and institutions. On the one hand, we noted that every analysis of cases of normative monstrosity is restricted to this or that legislation or practice, mostly regarding the soundness of such act or behaviour through a means-end investigation that can set aside the assessment of the whole jurisdiction, i.e. Hauriou's institutional "idea of a work or enterprise". On the other hand, cases of institutional monstrosity presuppose this hermeneutical effort of assessment over specific normative acts or practices, and yet, they also entail critical problems of legal theory as regards the overall validity of the order set up by monstrous institutions. In addition to the role of criticism towards every despicable custom or statute, cases of institutional monstrosity emphasise the further function of the monster metaphor as a symbol of resistance and rebellion.

Conflicts and the potential state of war that follow every institutional monstrosity shall be assessed—and even legitimised—vis-à-vis the constitutional safeguards and the international Bill of Rights infringed by the monstrous tyrant. Although Locke poked fun at those who intended to set limits to the right to resist in § 230 of his second treatise of government, even Locke admitted certain limits that shall ground the legitimacy of this legal right (Locke ed. 1823, at § 226). I stressed that such infringements should be blatant or systematic. However, by referring to the international Bill of Rights or the safeguards of national constitutions, it could be questioned that this book's criteria for the assessment of institutional monsters rests on the contingent convergence of today's positive law with some tenets of the natural law tradition. All in all, positive law can be changed, and even Maduro's Venezuela or similar monstrous institutions do not lack international support on how to interpret or defend the status quo. By following a Kelsenian approach to these kinds of monstrosity, the only option would be that of an aseptic observer. Still, it is not by chance that the ancient Greek culture coined the image of the monster in the context of their tragedies. This legacy suggests that our own era's tragedies will not be fixed through legal formalisms nor through opposite natural law claims with variables of unique right answers. Against every strong claim of certain natural law theorists, this book argued that all institutional monsters entail a tragedy because the rules of such a monster are valid law. Likewise, against every assertion of unique right answers, this volume stressed that every population that finally breaks free from a tyranny will be confronted with hard choices. And, against every formalism of the aseptic observer, the attention was drawn to how the price for those views, such as Kelsen's pure doctrine of law, is to simply ignore the functioning of legal systems.

Coercion is a necessary but insufficient component of the legal phenomenon. No theory of legal monsters would be meaningful without the conditions that make such a use of force legitimate and selective. This book described how, despite such conditions of legitimacy may have changed over the centuries, monsters are still the rulers who violate the law, seek their own profit over everything else, and govern against their people. Even in this case, the claim should not be grasped as an endorsement of natural law claims. The fact that norms and rules of both statutory and customary law function as guides to conduct and are related to beliefs, attitudes, judgments or opinions in the political community represents a double-edged sword. For better or worse, the resilience of every legal order rests on people's ethos, and yet, the monster metaphor illustrated the reasons why this interplay between law and ethos works both ways. The image has represented one of the darkest pages of Western history with the lack of pathos for our human fellows with congenital disabilities as much as a noble intent to oppose the horrors of humanity. Discriminating this noble sense of criticism and resistance is critical today because of the widespread, although undifferentiated, use of the metaphor—which includes institutional monsters denouncing enemies or dubbing their targets as the only monsters. This sense of criticism and resistance is fundamental because we live in an age where a new generation of digital monsters complements the old monsters of the tradition.

The uniqueness of our age depends on this mix of humans, normativity, and technology. The novelty of autonomous artificial agents' decision-making suggests that lawmakers' efforts to govern the uses of technology may generate normative monsters, or that public institutions may attempt to update the means of social control through the configuration of a monstrous surveillance society, the reckless automation of adjudicatory procedures, and the syntax monsters of robotic courts, among others. The threat is not only to perpetuate old forms of human control through new means, but also to create novel monsters through the incapacity to keep the technology under human control. This is the threat that John von Neumann reportedly referred to his wife Klári in spring 1945, by dubbing the hydrogen bomb that he and his colleagues were creating at Los Alamos as "a monster whose influence is going to change history, provided there is any history left" (Hargittai and Hargittai 2015, at 30). If possible, this scenario is worsened by the use of autonomous weapons systems, such as monstrous AI systems making use of monstrous hydrogen bombs (Johnson 2023). The monstrous rulers' temptation to play a sorcerer's apprentice game can be strengthened by the failure of decent institutions in tackling such third-party's out-of-control AI systems.

This book recommended a mid- and even short-term approach to these monstrous scenarios: also rudimental forms of AI systems and robots can trigger dire outcomes. Moreover, any long-run view of such threats relates to how the law will tackle the short- and mid-term issues posed by autonomous systems. The responsibility of scholars increases as a result, and should be confronted with the opportunism of some AI businessmen who, especially in the United States—after playing crying wolf and denouncing the perils of their own technology in the early 2020s (see above Chapter 11)—changed their mind with the advent of a new administration a few years, or even a few months, later. The responsibility of scholars is greater because the examination of whether monstrous normative acts and institutions may materialise shall be supplemented with the analysis of a terra incognita. Although the mid- and short-term approach of this volume aimed to prevent further crying wolf games on singularity disruptions or superintelligences, it can be tricky to determine the breaking point where the use of technologies otherwise beneficial can become monstrous, and hence, the public at large must be alerted.

The overall intent of this reflection, however, was not to be either exhaustive or self-complacent in the critique of monsters. There is no room for claims of completeness, on the one hand, because we noted that the assessment of the requirements of monstrosity may entail the expertise of positive law with the peculiarities of multiple jurisdictions: a theory of legal monsters must limit itself to providing the conceptual framework, a method, and how to test this method through a series of case studies. On the other hand, there cannot be any intellectual pleasure in coping with the monsters of certain legal systems, especially in countries where one grew up, lived, is accustomed to, or is a citizen. The eventuality of decent institutions adopting monstrous normative acts is a motive of concern and embarrassment as much as any institutional monstrosity, a source of sorrow and distress. The bottom line is the tragic condition of some human societies and the hard choices they will face, even in the best possible scenario of their liberation from the monstrous tyrant.

What is up to scholars is thus a powerful tool of criticism. The function of the metaphor is to draw the attention of the legal community and the public opinion to normative acts and institutions that are not only wrong or unjust, but monstrous. This double appeal to the legal community and the public at large is fundamental because every criticism in the name of monsters would be meaningless once deprived of ears to hear and eyes to see. It comes as no surprise that political monsters have been the target of comedians and satirists since ancient times, aiming to raise the audience's alertness, sensibility, or consciousness (Sommerstein 2009). The recipient of legal criticism is thus the expert, but also, and above all, those whose beliefs, attitudes, judgments or opinions are critical in the functioning of the legal system. This role of all fellow citizens explains why technical considerations on normative or institutional monstrosity have always been supplemented with the irony, parody, or derision of satiric poets and comedians. They all help lay the king bare.

Since the introduction of this book, attention was drawn to this role of irony. The second chapter mentioned Seneca's *Pumpkinification* of the Roman emperor

Claudius, as well as Marcus Terentius Varro's mockery of Crassus and Pompey, who managed Caesar's election as consul, all portrayed as the "three-headed monster". Juvenal, likely the greatest among Roman satiric poets, similarly depicted deplorable authorities, human follies, or reasons of ignorance and baseless fear as monstrous (e.g., Juvenal ed. 1958, at 66). According to Aristotle's remarks in *Poetics* (1452 a), irony can be grasped at the heart of tragedy as "a reversal", i.e. "a shift of what is being undertaken into the opposite" (Aristotle ed. 1970, at 35). This "peripety" suggests why the analysis of the legal interplay between coercion and criticism, between objects and subjects of the law, between the individuals' body and the body politic, may leverage the weapon of irony against the tragedies of the legal phenomenon. After all, we saw this irony at work throughout the chapters of this book with the reflection of Socrates, Cicero, Seneca, Pufendorf, Locke, Hart, and Enzensberger, among many others.

Tyrants famously have little sense of humour. Their susceptibility, however, must not provoke any discouragement for the persistent need to resort to the monster metaphor. Cicero and Seneca's troubles with the politics of their times, Montaigne's disdain for his own corrupt society, or Pufendorf's annoyance with the German Empire's design, remind us of how we are still always in great company. A theory of legal monsters shall be reflective until the end.

References

Aristotle. 1970. *Poetics*, trans. G.F. Else. Ann Arbor: The University of Michigan Press.

Engels, F. 1954. *Dialectics of nature* [1883], trans. C. Dutt. Moscow: Progress Publishers.

Floridi, L., J. Cowls, M. Beltrametti, R. Chatila, P. Chazerand, V. Dignum, Ch. Luetge, R. Madelin, U. Pagallo, F. Rossi, B. Schafer, P. Valcke, and E. Vayena. 2018. AI4People—An ethical framework for a good AI society: Opportunities, risks, principles, and recommendations. *Minds and Machines* 28 (4): 689–707.

Fuller, L. L. 1964. *The morality of law*. revised ed. New Haven, CT: Yale University Press.

Hargittai, I., and B. Hargittai. 2015. *Wisdom of the Martians of science: In their own words with commentaries*. Singapore: World Scientific.

Hauriou, M. 1970. The theory of the institution and the foundation: A study in social vitalism [1925]. In *The French institutionalists: Maurice Hauriou, Georges Renard, Joseph T. Delos*, ed. A. Broderick, 93–124. Cambridge, MA and London, England: Harvard University Press.

Johnson, J. 2023. *AI and the bomb: Nuclear strategy and risk in the digital age*. Oxford: Oxford University Press.

Juvenal. 1958. *The Satires*, trans. R. Humphries. Bloomington: Indiana University Press.

Kant, I. 1999. Perpetual peace [1795]. In *The Cambridge edition of the works of Immanuel Kant: Practical philosophy*, trans. M. Gregor, vol. 8. Cambridge: Cambridge University Press.

Kelsen, H. 1945. *General theory of the law and the state*, trans. A. Wedberg. Cambridge, MA: Harvard University Press.

Locke, J. 1823. *Two treatises of government* [1689]. London: Tegg & Co.

Skinner, Q. 1981. Machiavelli: A very short introduction. Oxford: Oxford University Press.

Sommerstein, A. H. 2009. Monsters, ogres, and demons in old comedy. In *Talking about laughter: And other studies in Greek comedy*, 155–175. Oxford: Oxford University Press.

Thym, D. 2020. The end of human rights dynamism? Judgments of the ECtHR on 'hot returns' and humanitarian visas as a focal point of contemporary European asylum law and policy. *International Journal of Refugee Law, 32*(4) 569–596.

Appendix I
Table of Case Law

(Numerical references are to the chapter and section of citation)

EU Court of Justice

Costa v Enel (1964)	§ 9.1
Hauer (1979)	§ 9.1
Internationale Handelsgesellschaft (1970)	§ 9.1
Nold (1974)	§ 9.1
Simmenthal (1976)	§ 9.1
Tanja Kreil v Bundesrepublik Deutschland (2000)	§ 9.1
Van Gend & Loos (1963)	§ 9.1

European Court of Human Rights

N. v. The United Kingdom (2008)	§ 5.3
Paposhvili v. Belgium (2016)	§ 5.3
VM and others v. Belgium (2015)	§ 5.3

Germany

Bamburg Court of Appeals, The Grudge Informer Case (1949)	§ 8.1; 8.2

International Criminal Court

Situation in the State of Palestine (ongoing)	§ 10.3

U. Pagallo, *A Theory of Legal Monsters: Repression, Resistance, Rebellion*, Philosophical Studies Series 161, https://doi.org/10.1007/978-3-032-10771-8

Italy

Constitutional Court's ruling no. 13 from 2004	§ 6.3
Constitutional Court's ruling no. 26 from 2007	§ 6.3
Constitutional Court's ruling no. 262 from 2009	§ 6.3
Court of Cassation (criminal section I)'s ruling 17854 (2009)	§ 6.3; 8.3; 8.4
Court of Cassation (united sections)' ruling 14890 (2010)	§ 6.3
Court of Cassation (criminal section II)'s ruling 853 (2012)	§ 6.3
Court of Cassation (civil section III)'s ruling 9324 (2019)	§ 6.3
Court of Cassation (civil section IV)'s ruling 8658 (2020)	§ 6.3
Court of Cassation (criminal section VI)'s ruling 20677 (2024)	§ 6.3
T.A.R. Friuli-Venezia Giulia section I's ruling 530 (2013)	§ 6.3
Tribunale Como section III (March 2018)	§ 6.3

United Kingdom

England's Court of Common Pleas, Thomas Bonham v College of Physicians (1610)	§ 6.4
England's Court of Common Pleas, The Mary Portington's Case (1614)	§ 3.2
England's Court of High Commission, Peacham's Case (1614)	§ 6.4
England's Court of King's Bench, The Case of Commendams (1616)	§ 6.4; 7.2
Great Britain's Court of Appeal, Civil Division, Re A (Children) Conjoined Twins: Surgical Separation (2000)	§ 3.2; 4.3

Appendix II
Table of Conventions and Declarations

(Numerical references are to the chapter and section of citation)

European Law

Convention for the Protection of Human Rights and Dignity of the Human Being with regard to the Application of Biology and Medicine (1997)	§ 4.3
Convention on Human Rights (1950)	§ 4.1; 4.4; 9.1
–ECHR's Art. 1, Protocol 1	§ 9.4
–ECHR's Art. 3	§ 4.4; 5.4; 9.4
–ECHR's Art. 5	§ 9.4
–ECHR's Art. 6	§ 9.4
–ECHR's Art. 7	§ 8.3
–ECHR's Art. 8	§ 9.4

France

Declaration of the Rights of Man and of the Citizen (1789)	§ 4.3
–Art. 1	§ 4.3
–Art. 2	§ 10.2
–Art. 6	§ 4.3
Reference to the Declaration in the 1958 Constitution	§ 10.2

U. Pagallo, *A Theory of Legal Monsters: Repression, Resistance, Rebellion*, Philosophical Studies Series 161, https://doi.org/10.1007/978-3-032-10771-8

United Nations

Convention against Torture and Other Cruel, Inhuman or Degrading Treatment or Punishment (1984)	§ 5.4
Covenant on Civil and Political Rights (1966)	§ 4.1
Covenant on Economic, Social, and Cultural Rights (1966)	§ 4.1
Declaration on the Rights of Mentally Retarded Persons (1971)	§ 4.1
Declaration on the Rights of Disabled Persons (1975)	§ 4.1
Rome Statute (1998)	§ 10.3
Universal Declaration of Human Rights (1948)	§ 4.1; 4.3; 4.4; 9.3
–UDHR's Art. 5	§ 4.4; 5.4

United States

Declaration of Independence (1776)	§ 10.1

Appendix III
Table of Legislation and Other Normative Acts

(Numerical references are to the chapter and section of citation)

EU Law (primary legislation)

Charter of Fundamental Rights (2000/2009)	§ 9.2; 9.3
–Art. 20	§ 9.3.2
–Art. 37	§ 9.3.2
Fiscal Compact Treaty, or Treaty of Stability (2012)	§ 8.4
Lisbon Treaty (2007)	§ 9.1; 9.2, 9.3.3
Maastricht Treaty (1993)	§ 9.1
Treaty of Nice (2000)	§ 9.1
Treaty of Rome (1957)	§ 9.1

EU Law (secondary legislation)

Delegated Reg. (EU) 2024/1107 to 2024/1111 (drones)	§ 9.3.3
Directive 2000/46/EC (e-money)	§ 9.4
Directive 2002/58/EC (e-privacy)	§ 11.1
Directive 2009/110/EC (new e-money provisions)	§ 9.4
Implementing Reg. 2023/203 (drones)	§ 9.3.3
Reg. 2008/216 (civil aviation)	§ 9.3.3
Reg. 2016/679 (the GDPR)	§ 9.3; 9.3.1; 9.3.3
Reg. 2018/1139 (common rules for drones)	§ 9.3.3
Reg. 2019/947 (drones regulation)	§ 9.3.3
Reg. 2021/664-665-666 (U-space for drones)	§ 9.3.3
Reg. 2021/695 (Horizon projects)	§ 9.3.2; 9.4

(continued)

U. Pagallo, *A Theory of Legal Monsters: Repression, Resistance, Rebellion*, Philosophical Studies Series 161, https://doi.org/10.1007/978-3-032-10771-8

(continued)

Reg. 2022/868 (data governance)	§ 9.3.1
Reg. 2022/1426 and 2022/2236 (autonomous vehicles)	§ 9.3.3
Reg. 2022/2065 (digital services)	§ 9.3.1
Reg. 2023/2854 (fair access to and use of data)	§ 9.3.1
Reg. 2024/1689 (the AI Act)	§ 9.3; 10.2; 10.4
–Appendix I	§ 9.3.1
–Appendix III	§ 9.3.1; 9.3.3
–Art. 1	§ 9.3
–Art. 3	§ 9.3.1
–Art. 5	§ 9.3.1; 9.3.3
–Art. 6	§ 9.3.1
–Art. 9	§ 9.3.2
–Art. 10	§ 9.3.1
–Art. 14	§ 11.4
–Art. 27	§ 9.3.2
–Art. 51	§ 9.3.1
–Art. 57	§ 11.3
–Art. 95	§ 9.3.1; 9.3.2
–Art. 102	§ 9.3.1
–Art. 103	§ 9.3.1
–Art. 105	§ 9.3.1
–Art. 106	§ 9.3.1
–Art. 108	§ 9.3.1
–Art. 112	§ 9.3.3
–Delegated Acts of the EU Commission	§ 9.3.3
–Recital 4	§ 9.3.3
–Recital 7	§ 10.4
–Recital 10	§ 9.3.1
–Recital 11	§ 9.3.1
–Recital 27	§ 10.4
–Recital 67	§ 9.3.1
–Recital 111	§ 9.3.1
–Recital 141	§ 9.3.1
–Recital 165	§ 10.4

France

Napoleon's Code: Art. 4 of the Preliminary Title	§ 8.1

Germany

Art. 12a(4) of the Grundgesetz (amendment)	§ 9.1
Art. 20(4) of the Grundgesetz (right to resist)	§ 10.2
Law Concerning the Head of State of the German Reich (1934)	§ 6.2; 7.1; 7.3

Italy

Act 2444 from 1923 (legge Acerbo)	Conclusions
Act. 1019 from 1928 (legge Rocco)	Conclusions
Act. 140 from 2003 (legge Boato)	§ 6.3
Act. 46 from 2006 (legge Pecorella)	§ 6.3
Act. 124 from 2008 (lodo Alfano)	§ 6.3
Art. 49(2) criminal code	§ 4.1
Art. 96 civil procedural code	§ 4.1
Royal Decree 1728 from 1938 (Racial Law)	Conclusions

Roman Law

Ius Liberorum	§ 3.1; 3.2
Lex Papia et Poppaea	§ 3.1
Romulus' regulation of monsters	§ 2.3; 3.1
Twelve Tables	§ 2.3; 3.1

Spain

Royal Order for the Appointment of Deans in Valencia (1736)	§ 5.2; 6.2

Uganda

The Anti-homosexuality Act (2023)	§ 5.3

United States

Biden's Executive Order on AI (2023)	§ 11.4
Trump's Executive Order on AI (2025)	§ 11.4

Bibliography

Addo, M. K., and N. Grief. 1998. Does article 3 of the European convention on human rights enshrine absolute rights? *European Journal of International Law* 9 (3): 510–524.
Aeschylus. 2017. *Eumenides*, trans. E. D. A. Morshead, Melbourne: Scribble. Accessed on September 8, 2025 from http://classics.mit.edu/Aeschylus/eumendides.html.
Ajani, G. 2020. Contemporary artificial art and the law: Searching for an author. *Brill Research Perspectives in Art and Law* 3 (4): 1–84.
Alfieri, V. 2023. *Del principe e delle lettere [1778–1789]*. Sophia (France): Culturea.
Alighieri, D. 2021. In *Monarchia [1313]*, ed. D. Quaglioni. Milan: Mondadori.with Latin text
Allély, A. 2003. Les enfants malformés et considérés comme prodigia à Rome et en Italie sous la République. *Revue des études anciennes* 105 (1): 127–156.
Allott, P. 1999. The concept of European union, *Cambridge yearbook of European. Legal Studies* 2:31–59.
Allott, P. 2003. Epilogue: Europe and the dream of reason. In *European constitutionalism beyond the state*, ed. J. H. H. Weiler and M. Wind, 202–225. Cambridge: Cambridge University Press.
Andocides. 1998. *Antiphon & Andocides*, trans. M. Gagarin and D.M. MacDowell. Austin: University of Texas Press.
Angelucci, D. 2022. From the sublime to the monstrous. *Two Interpretations of Kant, Con-textos Kantianos: International Journal of Philosophy* 15:287–296.
Aquinas, Th. *1992*. In *Treatise on law (summa Theologica questions 90–97)*, ed. S. Parry. *Chicago: Gateway.*
Arendt, H. 1963. *Eichmann in Jerusalem: A report on the banality of evil*. New York: Viking Press.
Arendt, H. 2006. *On revolution [1963]*. New York: Penguin.
Arienzo, A., and A. Petrina, eds. 2013. *Literary and political influences from the reformation to the restoration*. Farnham and Burlington: Ashgate.
Aristotle. 1943. *Generation of animals*, trans. A.L. Peck. Cambridge, MA: Harvard University Press.
Aristotle. 1944. *Politics*, trans. H. Rackham. Cambridge, MA: Harvard University Press.
Aristotle. 1970. *Poetics*, trans. G.F. Els. Ann Arbor: The University of Michigan Press.
Aristotle. 2000. *The nichomachean ethics*, trans. R. Crisp. Cambridge: Cambridge University Press.
Aristotle 2013. *Politics*, trans. C. Lord. Chicago and London: Chicago University Press.

U. Pagallo, *A Theory of Legal Monsters: Repression, Resistance, Rebellion*, Philosophical Studies Series 161, https://doi.org/10.1007/978-3-032-10771-8

Armitage, D. 2006. Hobbes and the foundations of modern international thought. In *Rethinking the foundations of modern political thought*, ed. A. Brett and J. Tully, 219–235. Cambridge: Cambridge University Press.
Artosi, A., and G. Sartor. 2018. Leibniz as Jurist. In *The Oxford handbook of Leibniz*, ed. M. R. Antognazza, 641–663. Oxford: Oxford University Press.
Ashcraft, R. 1986. *Revolutionary politics and Locke's two treatises of government*. Princeton: Princeton University Press.
Asma, S. T. 2009. *On monsters: An unnatural history of our worst fears*. Oxford: Oxford University Press.
Aubrey, J. 1898. In *Brief lives [1669]*, ed. A. Clark. Oxford: Clarendon Press.
Austin, J. 1873. *Lectures on Jurisprudence*. Vol. I. London: John Murray.
Austin, J. 1954. *The province of jurisprudence determined [1832]*. London: Weidenfeld & Nicolson.
Avitabile, L. 2022. *Legalità e giustizia*. Turin: Giappichelli.
Bakewell, G. W. 2017. The voice of Aeschylus in Plato's republic. In *Voice and voices in antiquity: Orality and literacy in the ancient world*, ed. N. Slater, vol. 2, 260–276. Leiden: Brill.
Barfield, W., and U. Pagallo. 2020. *Advanced introduction to the law and artificial intelligence*. Cheltenham: Elgar.
Barfield, W., Y.-H. Weng, and U. Pagallo, eds. 2024. *The Cambridge handbook of the law, policy, and regulation for human–robot interaction*. Cambridge: Cambridge University Press.
Barnard, C., and S. Peers, eds. 2023. *European union law*. Oxford: Oxford University Press.
Bassi, E. 2019. European drones regulation: Today's legal challenges, In *International Conference on Unmanned Aircraft Systems (ICUAS)*, Atlanta, GA, USA, IEEE 443–450.
Baum, K., et al. 2025. Taming the AI monster: Monitoring of individual fairness for effective human oversight. In *Model checking software*, ed. T. Neele and A. Wijs, 3–25. Cham: Springer.
Bayern, S., T. Burri, T. D. Grant, D. M. Häusermann, F. Möslein, and R. Williams. 2017. Company law and autonomous systems: A blueprint for lawyers. *Entrepreneurs, and Regulators, Hastings Science, Technology and Law Journal* 9 (2): 135–161.
Beagon, P. 1992. *Roman nature: The thought of Pliny the elder*. Oxford: Clarendon Press.
Bechtler, T. W., ed. 1978. *Law in a social context: Liber Amicorum honouring professor Lon L. Fuller*. Deventer: Kluwer.
Behme, T. 2002. Pufendorf's doctrine of sovereignty and its natural law foundations. In *Natural law and civil sovereignty*, ed. I. Hunter and D. Saunders, 43–58. London: Palgrave Macmillan.
Bekey, G. A. 2005. *Autonomous robots: From biological inspiration to implementation and control*. Cambridge, MA/London: MIT Press.
Bell, J. 2018. Sources of law. *The Cambridge Law Journal* 77 (1): 40–71.
Bentham, J. 1843. In *Works*, ed. J. Bowring, vol. II. Edinburgh: Tait.
Berkowitz, R. 2011. From justice to justification: An alternative genealogy of positive law. *UC Irvine Law Review* 1 (3): 611–630.
Berry, A., and J. Browne. 2022. Mendel and Darwin. *Proceedings of the National Academy of Sciences* 119 (30): e2122144119.
Bix, B. H. 1995. Ronald Dworkin's right answer thesis. In *Law, language, and legal determinacy*, 77–132. Oxford: Clarendon.
Bix, B. H. 2005. Legal positivism. In *The Blackwell guide to the philosophy of law and legal theory*, ed. M. P. Golding and W. A. Edmundson, 29–49. Oxford: Blackwell.
Blackstone, W. 1871. *Commentaries on the laws of England*. Callaghan and Cockcroft: In Four Books, Chicago.
Blackstone, W. 1979. Commentaries on the laws of England. In *Of the rights of things*, vol. 2. Chicago: University of Chicago Press.
Blank, A. 2021. Pufendorf and Leibniz on duties of esteem in diplomatic relations. *Journal of International Political Theory* 18 (2): 186–204.
Bloch, R. 1963. *Les prodiges dans l'antiquité classique: Grèce, Étrurie et Rome*. Paris: PUF.
Blumenberg, H. 1996. *Shipwreck with Spectator*, trans. S. Rendall. Cambridge, MA: MIT Press.

Bobbio, N. 1993. *Thomas Hobbes and the natural law tradition.* Chicago: University of Chicago Press.

Bök, C. 1992. The monstrosity of representation: Frankenstein and rousseau. *ESC: English Studies in Canada* 18 (4): 415–432.

Bolton, M., R. Raven, and M. Mintrom. 2021. Can AI transform public decision-making for sustainable development? An exploration of critical earth system governance questions. *Earth System Governance* 9:100116.

Bostrom, N. 2014. *Superintelligence: Paths, Dangers, Strategies.* Oxford: Oxford University Press.

Bouwmeester, M. 2023. System failure in the digital welfare state: Exploring parliamentary and judicial control in the Dutch childcare benefits scandal. *Recht der Werkelijkheid* 44 (2): 13–37.

Bouwsma, W. J. 1975. The two faces of humanism: Stoicism and Augustinianism in renaissance thought. In *Itinerarium Italicum: The profile of the Italian renaissance in the mirror of its European transformations*, ed. H. A. Oberman, 3–60. Leiden: Brill.

Bowle, J. 1969. *Hobbes and his critics. A study in the seventeenth century constitutionalism.* London and Plymouth: Cass.

Boyer, A. D. 1997. Understanding, authority, and will: Sir Edward Coke and the Elizabethan origins of judicial review. *Boston College Law Review* 39 (1): 43–94.

Bracton, H. 1968. *On the laws and customs of England 1240-1260*, trans. S.E. Thorne. vols 1-4, Cambridge, MA: Harvard University Press.

Bradford, A. 2023. *Digital empires. The global battle to regulate technology.* Oxford: Oxford University Press.

Bramhall, J. 1844. The catching of the Leviathann or the Great Whale [1658]. In *The works of the most reverend father in God, John Bramhall, D.D., sometime Lord Archbishop of Armagh, primate and metropolitan of all Ireland, vol. 4*, ed. J. Vesey, Oxford: J. H. Parker.

Brands, H., and C. N. Edel. 2019. *The lessons of tragedy: Statecraft and world order*. New Haven and London: Yale University Press.

Bredekamp, H. 2020. *Leviathan: Body politic as visual strategy in the work of Thomas Hobbes.* Berlin/Boston: de Gruyter.

Brent, R. L. 1967. Medicolegal aspects of teratology. *The Journal of Paediatrics* 71 (2): 288–298.

Bringsjord, S., N. S. Govindarajulu, and J. Oswald. 2023. Universal cognitive intelligence, from cognitive consciousness, and Lambda (Λ). In *Computational approaches to conscious artificial intelligence, vol. 5 of Machine Consciousness*, ed. A. Chella, 127–168. Singapore: World Scientific Publishing.

Bringsjord, S., N. Sundar Govindarajulu, J. Licato, and A. Bringsjord. 2025. *Only logic can save us*. Cham: Springer.

Brooks, T. 2012. *Hegel's political philosophy*. Edinburgh: Edinburgh University Press.

Brutus, S.J. 1924. *Vindiciae Contra Tyrannos. A defense of liberty against tyrants* [1579], trans. Ch. H. McIlwain. London: Bell & Sons.

Buchanan, A. 1982. *Marx and justice: The radical critique of liberalism*. London: Methuen.

Byman, D., and J. Lind. 2010. Pyongyang's survival strategy: Tools of authoritarian control in North Korea. *International Security* 35 (1): 44–74.

Cadava, E. 2006. The monstrosity of human rights. *PMLA* 121 (5): 1558–1565.

Cairns, H. 1946. Leibniz's theory of law. *Harvard Law Review* 60 (2): 200–232.

Calasso, F. 1957. *I glossatori e la teoria della sovranità. Studio di diritto comune pubblico.* Milan: Giuffrè.

Cane, P., ed. 2010. *The hart-fuller debate in the twenty-first century.* Oxford and Portland: Hart.

Caney, S. 2015. Responding to global injustice: On the right to resistance. *Social Philosophy and Policy* 32 (1): 51–73.

Canguilhem, G. 1991. *The normal and the pathological [1966].* New York: Zone Books.

Casanovas, P. 2017. *Sub lege pugnamus. De la gran guerra a les grans dades.* Barcelona: Edicions Universitat Barcelona.

Castells, M. 1998. *The information age: Economy, society and culture.* Vol. 3. Oxford: Blackwell.

Chabod, F. 1964. *Scritti su Machiavelli.* Torino: Einaudi.

Chaitin, G. 2006. *Meta-math! The Quest for Omega.* New York: Knopf Doubleday.
Chesterman, S. 2022. *All rise for the honourable robot judge? Using artificial intelligence to regulate AI*, NUS Law Working Paper No. 2022/019. Available at https://doi.org/10.2139/ssrn.4252778.
Chetail, V. 2016. Sovereignty and migration in the doctrine of the law of nations: An intellectual history of hospitality from Vitoria to Vattel. *European Journal of International Law* 27 (4): 901–922.
Chopra, S., and L. F. White. 2011. *A legal theory for autonomous artificial agents.* Ann Arbor, MI: The University of Michigan Press.
Christianson, A. L. 2013. Attaining human dignity for people with birth defects: A historical perspective. *South African Medical Journal* 103 (12:1): 1014–1019.
Chroust, A. H. 1979. Some critical remarks about Samuel Pufendorf and his contributions to jurisprudence. *American Journal of Jurisprudence* 24 (1): 72–85.
Cicero, M. T. 1829. *The Republic.*, trans. G. W. Featherstonhaugh,. New York: Carvill.
Cicero, M. T. 1887. *De Officiis*, trans. A.P. Peabody. Boston: Little, Brown & Co.
Cicero, M. T. 1923. *De Senectute, De Amicitia, De Divinatione.*, trans. W.A. Falconer,. Cambridge, MA: Harvard University Press.
Cicero, M. T. 1928. *The Verrine orations.*, trans. L. H. G. Greenwood. Cambridge, MA: Harvard University Press.
Cicero, M. T. 1928. *On the laws.*, trans. C.W. Keynes. Cambridge, Ma: Harvard University Press.
Clancy, K. A., and B. Clancy. 2016. Growing monstrous organisms: The construction of anti-GMO visual rhetoric through digital media. *Critical Studies in Media Communication* 33 (3): 279–292.
Clark, D. L. 2001. Kant's aliens: The anthropology and its others, *CR. The New Centennial Review* 1 (2): 201–289.
Clewis, R. R. 2009. *The kantian sublime and the revelation of freedom.* Cambridge: Cambridge University Press.
Coeckelbergh, M. 2020. *Superintelligence, monsters, and the AI apocalypse, AI ethics*, 11–29. MIT Press.
Cohen, J. E. 2019. *Between truth and power: The legal constructions of informational capitalism.* Oxford: Oxford University Press.
Cohen, J. J. 1996. *Monster theory: Reading culture.* Minneapolis: University of Minnesota Press.
Coke, E. 1826. In *The reports of Sir Edward Coke*, ed. J. H. Thomas and J. H. Fraser. London: J. Butterworth and Son.13 parts in 6 vols
Coke, E. 1817. *The institutes of the law of England 1628–1644, 4 vols.* London: W. Clarke.
Coleman, J. L., and B. Leiter. 2010. Legal positivism. In *A companion to philosophy of law and legal theory*, ed. D. Patterson, 228–248. Oxford: Blackwell.
Colletti, L. 1972. *From rousseau to lenin.* New York: NYU Press.
Comte, A. 1858. *Positive philosophy, trans. H. Martineau.* New York: Blanchard.
Conant, J. 1991. The search for logically alien thought: Descartes, kant, frege, and the tractatus. *Philosophical Topics* 20 (1): 115–180.
Constant, B. 2016. The liberty of the ancients compared with that of the moderns. In *Democracy: A reader*, ed. R. Blaug and J. Schwarzmantel, 108–110. New York Chichester, West Sussex: Columbia University Press.
Corrales, J., and D. Kronick. 2025. How maduro stole Venezuela's vote. *Journal of Democracy* 36 (1): 36–49.
Coyle, S. 2003. Thomas hobbes and the intellectual origins of legal positivism. *Canadian Journal of Law & Jurisprudence* 16 (2): 243–270.
Craig, P., and D. De Búrca, eds. 2021. *The evolution of EU law.* Oxford: Oxford University Press.
Crawford, K. 2021. *Atlas of AI: Power, politics, and the planetary costs of artificial intelligence. The real worlds of artificial intelligence.* New Haven, CT: Yale University Press.
Crifò, G. 1999. *Prodigium e diritto: il caso dell'ermafrodita.* Naples: Jovene.
Critchlow, D. T. 2021. *Revolutionary monsters: Five men who turned liberation into tyranny.* Washington, DC: Simon and Schuster.
Croce, B. 1907. *Riduzione della filosofia del diritto alla filosofia dell'economia.* Bari: Laterza.

Crofts, P. 2022. The corporate monster metaphor. *Law Text Culture* 26:73–96.
Crowther, P. 1989. *The Kantian sublime: From morality to art*. Oxford: Clarendon Press.
d'Holbach, P.-H. T. 1990. In *Système de la nature [1781]*, ed. J. Boulad-Ayoub. Paris: Fayard.
Dahl, R. A. 1957. The concept of power. *Behavioral Science* 2 (3): 201–215.
Damich, E. J. 1985. The essence of law according to Thomas Aquinas. *The American Journal of Jurisprudence* 30 (1): 76–96.
Darwall, S. L. 2012. Pufendorf on morality, sociability, and moral powers. *Journal of the History of Philosophy* 50 (2): 213–238.
Darwin, Ch. 1901. *The descent of man.* new ed. London: John Murray.
Darwin, Ch. 1964. *On the origin of species, facsimile of the first edition [1859].* Cambridge: Harvard University Press.
Davey, B. 2020. Surveillance capitalism at the limits to economic growth: Part 2, Resilience, February. Accessed on September 8, 2025 fromhttps://www.resilience.org/stories/2020-02-07/surveillance-capitalism-at-the-limits-to-economic-growth-part-2/.
Davidson, D. 1984. *Inquiries into truth and interpretation.* Oxford: Clarendon Press.
de E., Vattel. 2008. In *The law of nations, or, principles of the law of nature [1758]*, ed. B. Kapossy and R. Whatmore. Liberty Fund: Indianapolis.
De Gregorio, G. 2021. The rise of digital constitutionalism in the European Union. *International Journal of Constitutional Law* 19 (1): 41–70.
de Montaigne, M. 1965. *Les Essais [1580].* Paris: PUF.
de Montaigne, M. 2003. *The complete essays.*, trans. M.A. Screech. London: Penguin.
De Vitoria, F. 1967. In *Relectio de Indis o Libertad de los Indios [1538]*, ed. L. Perena and J. M. Pérez Prendes. Madrid: Consejo Superior de Investigaciones Cientificas.
De Wilde, M. 2018. Enemy of all humanity: The dehumanizing effects of a dangerous concept. *Netherlands Journal of Legal Philosophy* 47 (2): 158–175.
Dean, M. 2008. Governing society. The story of two monsters. *Journal of Cultural Economy* 1 (1): 25–38.
Debusser, F. 2005. The EU e-privacy directive: A monstrous attempt to starve the cookie monster? *International Journal of Law and Information Technologies* 13:70–97.
Degan, V. D. 2024. *Sources of international law.* Leiden: Brill.
Del Lucchese, F. 2019. *Monstrosity and philosophy: Radical otherness in Greek and Latin culture.* Edinburgh: Edinburgh University Press.
Delmas, C. 2018. *A duty to resist: When disobedience should be uncivil.* Oxford: Oxford University Press.
Dembour, M.-B. 2015. *When humans become migrants.* Oxford: Oxford University Press.
Diamond, J. 2011. *Collapse: How societies choose to fail or succeed.* Revised ed. New York: Penguin.
Diderot, D. 2001. *Rameau's nephew, and other works*, trans. J. Barzun and R.H. Bowen. Indianapolis/Cambridge: Hackett.
Dionysius of Halicarnassus. 1937. *Roman antiquities, Volume I: Books 1–2, trans. E. Cary.* Cambridge, MA: Harvard University Press.
Dobelmann, J. 2020. The right to resist in the approach of Samuel Pufendorf's De Iure naturae et gentium and De officio hominis et civis. *Archiv für Rechts und Sozialphilosophie* 106 (4): 487–508.
Doctorow, C. 2018. I've created a monster! (And so can you), In *Frankenbook*. The MIT Press. Accessed on September 8, 2025 from https://www.frankenbook.org/pub/ive-create-a-monster/release/1.
Dove, G., and A.-L. Fayard. 2020. Monsters, metaphors, and machine learning. In *Proceedings of the 2020 CHI conference on human factors in computing systems*, 1–17. New York: ACM.
Drinker Bowen, C. 1985. *The lion and the throne. The life and times of Sir Edward Coke [1956].* Boston: Little, Brown & Company.
Dunn, J. 1982. *The political thought of John Locke: An historical account of the argument of the 'two treatises of government'.* Cambridge: Cambridge University Press.

Durante, M. 2021. *Computational power: The impact of ICT on law, society and knowledge.* London: Routledge.
Dworkin, R. 1965. Philosophy, morality, and law. *University of Pennsylvania Law Review* 113:668–690.
Dworkin, R. 1985. *A matter of principle.* Oxford: Oxford University Press.
Dworkin, R. 1986. *Law's empire.* Cambridge, MA: Harvard University Press.
Ebers, M. 2025. Truly risk-based regulation of artificial intelligence-how to implement the EU's AI act. *European Journal of Risk Regulation* 16:684–703.
Ebrahimi, Afrouzi A. 2024. John robots, thurgood martian, and the syntax monster: A new argument against AI judges. *Canadian Journal of Law & Jurisprudence* 37:1–28.
Edwards, A. J. 2025. *Report of the special rapporteur on torture and other cruel, inhuman or degrading treatment or punishment*, U.N. Doc. A/HRC/58/55. Available at https://docs.un.org/en/A/HRC/58/55. 6 February 2025.
Ehirim, U. G. 2025. Public morality and constitutionalism in restricting LGBTQ+ Rights: A legal analysis of Nigeria, Ghana, and Uganda. *International Journal of Constitutional and Administrative Law* 1 (1): 42–68.
Ehrenberg, K. M. 2016. *The functions of law.* Oxford: Oxford University Press.
Einolf, C. J. 2007. The fall and rise of torture: A comparative and historical analysis. *Sociological Theory* 25 (2): 101–121.
Eljaiek-Rodríguez, E. 2024. Blood: The monstrification of immigrants in U.S. politics, *Free Voice*, issue 40 (Blood), August. Accessed on September 8, 2025 from https://shuddhashar.com/monsters-that-poison-the-blood-the-monstrification-of-immigrants-in-u-s-politics/.
Ellis, J. J. 2002. *Founding brothers.* New York: Vintage.
Engels, F. 1954. *Dialectics of nature [1883], trans. C. Dutt.* Moscow: Progress Publishers.
Enzensberger, H. M. 2011. *Brussels, the gentle monster: Or the disenfranchisement of Europe.* London: Seagull.
Erasmus. 2003. *The education of a Christian prince [1516], trans. L. Jardine.* Cambridge: Cambridge University Press.
Euchner, W. 2017. *John locke zur einführung.* Hamburg: Junius Verlag.
European Commission (EC). 2019. *Liability for artificial intelligence and other emerging digital technologies*, Directorate-general for justice and consumers publications office. Accessed on September 8, 2025 from https://data.europa.eu/doi/10.2838/573689.
European Commission (EC). 2023. *2023 rule of law report, communication COM (2023) 800 final.* Brussels: European Commission (EC).
European Parliament (EP). 2017. *Report with recommendations to the commission on civil law rules on robotics*, Report A8–0005/2017. Accessed on September 8, 2025 from https://www.europarl.europa.eu/doceo/document/A-8-2017-0005_EN.html.
European Sources Online (ESO). 2018. *meeting between Facebook's mark Zuckerberg and European parliament's political leadership*, Cardiff EDC. Accessed on September 8, 2025 from https://www.europeansources.info/record/meeting-between-facebooks-mark-zuckerberg-and-european-parliaments-political-leadership/.
Evêque, R. 2020. The legal treatment of hermaphroditism in ancient rome. from persecution to integration, *Gender based approaches to the law and Juris Dictio in Europe*, hal open science. Accessed on September 8, 2025 from https://hal.science/hal-03891789/document.
Eyerman, R. 1981. False consciousness and ideology in Marxist theory. *Acta Sociologica* 24 (1–2): 43–56.
Fairbanks, D. J. 2020. Mendel and Darwin: Untangling a persistent enigma. *Heredity* 124:263–273.
Fenger, M., and R. Simonse. 2024. The implosion of the Dutch surveillance welfare state. *Social Policy & Administration* 58 (2): 264–276.
Figgis, J. N. 1922. *The divine right of kings [1896].* Cambridge: Cambridge University Press.
Filmer, R. 1680. *Patriarcha, or the natural power of kings.* London: Chiswell.
Fine, S. 2020. Monsters, Inc.: the fightback. In *The shifting border*, ed. A. Shachar, 99–117. Manchester: Manchester University Press.

Finlay, C. J. 2015. *Terrorism and the right to resist: A theory of just revolutionary war*. Cambridge: Cambridge University Press.
Finnell, R. H. 1999. Teratology: General considerations and principles. *Journal of Allergy and Clinical Immunology* 103 (2): S337–S342.
Finnis, J. 1990. Natural law and legal reasoning. *Cleveland State Law Review* 38 (1): 1–13.
Finnis, J. 2004. Natural law: The classical tradition. In *The Oxford handbook of jurisprudence and philosophy of law*, ed. J. L. Coleman and S. J. Shapiro, 1–61. Oxford: Oxford University Press.
Fischer, K. 1904. *Francis bacon und seine Schule: Entwicklungsgeschichte der Erfahrungsphilosophie*. Heidelberg: Carl Winter Universitätsbuchhandlung.
Fishbayn, L. 2007. Not quite one gender or the other: Marriage law and the containment of gender trouble in the United Kingdom. *American University Journal of Gender Social Policy and the Law* 15 (3): 413–441.
Fletcher, G. P. 1998. *Basic concepts of criminal law*. Oxford: Oxford University Press.
Floridi, L. 2013. *Ethics of information*. Oxford: Oxford University Press.
Floridi, L. 2013. Technology's in-betweenness. *Philosophy and Technology* 26:111–115.
Floridi, L. 2014. *The fourth revolution: How the infosphere is reshaping human reality*. Oxford: Oxford University Press.
Floridi, L. 2018. Soft ethics and the governance of the digital. *Philosophy and Technology* 31 (1): 1–8.
Floridi, L., J. Cowls, M. Beltrametti, R. Chatila, P. Chazerand, V. Dignum, Ch. Luetge, R. Madelin, U. Pagallo, F. Rossi, B. Schafer, P. Valcke, and E. Vayena. 2018. AI4People—An ethical framework for a good AI society: Opportunities, risks, principles, and recommendations. *Minds and Machines* 28 (4): 689–707.
Foucault, M. 2003. *Abnormal: Lectures at the college de france 1974–1975*. London: Verso.
Franchini, L. 2016. Lo status dell'ermafrodita ed il problema della determinazione del sesso prevalente, *Teoria e storia del diritto privato. Rivista Internazionale on line* 9:1–35.
Fraser, I. 2000. Hegel and Marx on needs: The making of a monster. In *The Hegel-Marx connection*, ed. T. Burns and I. Fraser. London: Palgrave Macmillan.
Frederick the Great. 2024. In *Philosophical writings*, ed. A. Lifschitz. Princeton, NJ: Princeton University Press.
Freedman, L. 2024. The revival of classical monsters in the Italian renaissance. In *The Oxford handbook of monsters in classical myth*, ed. D. Felton, 470–492. Oxford: Oxford University Press.
Freeman, B. 1987. Frankenstein with Kant: A theory of monstrosity, or the monstrosity of theory. *SubStance* 16 (1): 21–31.
Friedman, J. B. 1981. *The monstrous races in medieval art and thought*. Cambridge, MA: Harvard University Press.
Friedrich, C. J. 1966. Philosophical reflections of Leibniz on law, politics, and the state. *Natural Law Forum* 11:79–91.
Fuller, L. L. 1958. Positivism and fidelity to law: A reply to professor Hart. *Harvard Law Review* 71 (4): 630–672.
Fuller, L. L. 1964. *The morality of law*. revised ed. New Haven, CT: Yale University Press.
Fuller, L. L. 1999. *The law in quest of itself, Union*. NJ: The Lawbook Exchange.
Gadamer, H. G. 1983. *Dialogue and dialectic: Eight hermeneutical studies on Plato*. New Haven, CT: Yale University Press.
Gadamer, H. G. 1984. The hermeneutics of suspicion. *Man and World* 17:313–323.
Gailhofer, P., et al. 2021. *The role of artificial intelligence in the European green deal, Study for the special committee on Artificial Intelligence in a Digital Age (AIDA), Policy Department for Economic, Scientific and Quality of Life Policies*. Luxembourg: European Parliament.
Galton, F. 1904. Eugenics: Its definition, scope and aims. *American Journal of Sociology* 10 (1): 1–25.
Gardner, J. 2001. Legal positivism: 5 1/2 myths. *American Journal of Jurisprudence* 46:199–228.

Gauthier, D. 2022. Hobbes's social contract. In *Hobbes and political contractarianism: Selected writings*, ed. S. Dimock, C. Finkelstein, and Ch. W. Morris. Oxford: Oxford University Press.
Gaylin, W., and B. Jennings. 1996. *The perversion of autonomy*. New York: The Free Press.
Gellius. 1927. *Attic Nights. Volume I: Books 1–5*, trans. J.C. Rolfe. Cambridge, MA: Harvard University Press.
Gentile, M. 1930. Platone autore di drammi filosofici. *Rivista di Filosofia Neo-Scolastica* 22:427–435.
George, R. P. 1999. Kelsen and aquinas on the natural-law doctrine. *Notre Dame Law Review* 75 (5): 1625–1646.
Gest, J. M. 1909. The writings of Sir Edward Coke. *The Yale Law Journal* 18 (7): 504–532.
Ghadessi, T. 2018. *Portraits of human monsters in the renaissance: Dwarves, Hirsutes, and Castrati as idealized anatomical anomalies*. Kalamazoo, MI: Medieval Institute Publications.
Ginsburg, T., D. Lansberg-Rodriguez, and M. Versteeg. 2012. When to overthrow your government: The right to resist in the world's constitutions. *UCLA Law Review* 60:1184–1260.
Godin, G. 2022. Monstrous things: Horror, othering, and the Anthropocene. *Post-Medieval Archaeology* 56 (2): 116–126.
Goedde, P. 2018. Human rights diffusion in North Korea: The impact of transnational legal mobilization. *Asian Journal of Law and Society* 5 (1): 175–203.
Goltzberg, S. 2018. *Les sources du droit. Que sais-je*. Paris: PUF.
Graff, G.M. 2014. The green monster, politico, November/December. Accessed on September 8, 2025 from https://www.politico.com/magazine/story/2014/10/border-patrol-the-green-monster-112220/.
Gramsci, A. 1977. In *Quaderni del carcere*, ed. A. Gerratana, vol. I. Turin: Einaudi.
Graziadei, M. 2019. Comparative law, legal transplants, and receptions. In *The Oxford handbook of comparative law*, ed. M. Reimann and R. Zimmermann, 441–473. Oxford: Oxford University Press.
Green, L. 1988. *The authority of the state*. Oxford: Oxford University Press.
Greenstein, S., and M. Zamboni. 2025. Navigating the legislative dilemma: Evaluating the EU AI act's approach to regulating emerging technologies. *The Theory and Practice of Legislation* 2025:1–41.
Gregory, D. 2006. The black flag: Guantánamo Bay and the space of exception. *Geografiska Annaler: Series B, Human Geography* 88 (4): 405–427.
Guest, S. 2016. Dworkin's 'one-right-answer' thesis. *Problema Anuario de Filosofía y Teoría del Derecho* 10:3–21.
Guibourg, R. 2000. Fuentes del derecho. *Enciclopedia Ibero-Americana de Filosofia* 2:177–197.
Guzman, A. 2013. International organizations and the Frankenstein problem. *European Journal of International Law* 24 (4): 999–1025.
Gwyn, W. B. 1991. Cruel Nero: The concept of the tyrant and the image of Nero in western political thought. *History of Political Thought* 12 (3): 421–455.
Haara, H., and K. Saastamoinen. 2022. Esteem and sociality in Pufendorf's natural law theory. *British Journal for the History of Philosophy* 32 (2): 265–283.
Habermas, J. 1996. *Between facts and norms: Contributions to a discourse theory of law and democracy, trans. W. Rehg*. Cambridge: Polity Press.
Hadgopoulos, D. J. 1973. Thrasymachus and legalism. *Phronesis* 18 (3): 204–208.
Halberstam, J. 1995. *Skin shows: Gothic horror and the technology of monsters*. Durham and London: Duke University Press.
Hall, J. 2009. Serving the times: Cicero and Caesar the dictator. In *Writing politics in imperial Rome*, ed. W. J. Dominik, J. Garthwaite, and P. A. Roche, 89–110. Leiden, The Netherlands: Brill.
Halliwell, S. 1984. Plato and Aristotle on the denial of tragedy. *Proceedings of the Cambridge Philological Society* 30:49–71.
Halpérin, J. L. 2023. École de l'Exégèse. In *Encyclopedia of the philosophy of law and social philosophy*, ed. M. Sellers and S. Kirste, 837–840. Dordrecht: Springer.

Hampton, J. 1986. *Hobbes and the social contract tradition.* Cambridge: Cambridge University Press.

Haraway, D. 2013. The promises of monsters: A regenerative politics for inappropriate/d others. In *Cultural studies*, ed. L. Grossberg, C. Nelson, and P. Treichler, 295–337. Abingdon: Routledge.

Hargittai, I., and B. Hargittai. 2015. *Wisdom of the Martians of science: In their own words with commentaries.* Singapore: World Scientific.

Harold, S. W., Beauchamp-Mustafaga, N., Jun, J., Myers, D., and D. Grossman 2022. Will artificial intelligence Hone North Korea's cyber 'all-purpose sword'?, *Korea Economic Institute of America*, March, report no. 7. Accessed on September 8, 2025 from https://keia.org/wp-content/uploads/2022/03/KEI_SMA_Harold-Mustafaga-Jun-Myers-Grossman.pdf.

Hart, H. L. A. 1958. Positivism and the separation of law and morals. *Harvard Law Review* 71 (4): 593–629.

Hart, H. L. A. 1965. Book review: Lon fuller, the morality of law. *Harvard Law Review* 78:1281–1296.

Hart, H. L. A. 1994. *The concept of law [1961].* Oxford: Oxford University Press.

Hauriou, M. 1970. The theory of the institution and the foundation: A study in social vitalism [1925]. In *The French institutionalists: Maurice Hauriou, Georges Renard, Joseph T. Delos*, ed. A. Broderick, 93–124. Cambridge, MA and London, England: Harvard University Press.

Haydn, H. 1950. *The counter-renaissance.* New York: Scribner.

Hayek, F. A. 2021. In *Law, legislation and liberty: A new statement of the liberal principles of justice and political economy [1982]*, ed. J. Shearmur. Chicago: Chicago University Press.

Hazleton, R. 1995. The tort monster that ate Dow corning, *The Wall Street Journal.* May 17, at A21.

Heacock, M., et al. 2016. E-waste and harm to vulnerable populations: A growing global problem. *Environmental Health Perspectives* 124 (5): 550–555.

Hegel, G. W. F. 1988. *Phenomenology of spirit [1807].*, trans. A.V. Miller,. Delhi: Motilal Banarsidass.

Hegel, G. W. F. 1999. On the scientific ways of treating natural law, on its place in practical philosophy, and its relation to the positive sciences of right. In *Political writings*, ed. L. Dickey and H. B. Nisbet, 102–180. Cambridge: Cambridge University Press.trans. H. B. Nisbet

Hegel, G. W. F. 2001. *The philosophy of history, trans. J. Sibree.* Kitchener: Batoche Books.

Heidegger, M. 1993. The question concerning technology [1953], trans. W. Lovitt with revisions by D. F. Krell, in D. F. Krell (ed.). *Martin Heidegger: Basic writings*, revised and expanded edition, pp. 311–41, London: Routledge.

Herries, A. I., et al. 2020. Contemporaneity of Australopithecus, Paranthropus, and early homo erectus in South Africa. *Science* 368 (6486): eaaw7293.

Heyd, D. 1991. Hobbes on capital punishment. *History of Philosophy Quarterly* 8 (2): 119–134.

Hicks, S. R. C. 2004. *Explaining postmodernism: Skepticism and socialism from rousseau to foucault.* Tempe and New Berlin/Milwaukee: Scholargy Publishing.

Hill, Ch. 1997. The many-headed monster. In *Intellectual origins of the English revolution–revisited*, ed. Ch. Hill, 327–337. Oxford: Oxford University Press.

Himma, K. E. 2002. Situating Dworkin: The logical space between legal positivism and natural law theory. *Oklahoma City University Law of School* 27:41–150.

HLEG. 2019. *High-level expert group on artificial intelligence's ethics guidelines for trustworthy AI*, Brussels, European Commission. Accessed on September 8, 2025 from https://digital-strategy.ec.europa.eu/en/library/ethics-guidelines-trustworthy-ai.

Hobbes, Th. 1889. In *Behemoth, or the long parliament [1681]*, ed. F. Tönnies. London: Simpkin, Marshall & Co.

Hobbes, Th. 2003. *On the citizen [1642].*, trans. R. Tuck and M. Silverthorne. Cambridge: Cambridge University Press.

Hobbes, Th. 2004. *Leviathan [1651].* New York: Barnes & Noble.

Hooker, S. 2024. On the limitations of compute thresholds as a governance strategy, *arXiv preprint*, arXiv:2407.05694.

Horowitz, M. C. 2021. When speed kills: Lethal autonomous weapon systems, deterrence and stability. In *Emerging technologies and international stability*, ed. T. S. Sechser, N. Narang, and C. Talmadge, 144–168. London: Routledge.

Hourani, G. F. 1962. Thrasymachus' definition of justice in Plato's 'Republic'. *Phronesis* 7 (2): 110–120.

Hunter, I. 2023. Introduction: Life, work and historical context. In *The Cambridge companion to Pufendorf*, ed. K. Haakonssen and I. Hunter, 1–32. Cambridge: Cambridge University Press.

IEEE Standard Association 2020. *IEEE recommended practice for assessing the impact of autonomous and intelligent systems on human well-being.* IEEE 7010–2020, 16, 1–96. Accessed on September 8, 2025 from https://doi.org/10.1109/IEEESTD.2020.9084219.

Johnson, C. W. 1845. *The life of Sir Edward Coke: Lord chief justice of England in the reign of James I with memoirs of his contemporaries.* London: H. Colburn.

Johnson, J. 2023. *AI and the bomb: Nuclear strategy and risk in the digital age.* Oxford: Oxford University Press.

Johnson, K. R. 2010. It's the economy, stupid: The hijacking of the debate over immigration reform by monsters, ghosts, and goblins (or the war on drugs, war on terror, narcoterrorists, etc.). *Chapman Law Review* 13 (3): 583–614.

Joy, L. S. 1992. Epicureanism in renaissance moral and natural philosophy. *Journal of the History of Ideas* 53 (4): 573–583.

Juvenal. 1958. *The Satires, trans. R. Humphries.* Bloomington: Indiana University Press.

Kant, I. 1951. *Critique of judgement [1790].*, trans. J.H. Bernard. New York: Hafner.

Kant, I. 1974. *On the old saw: That may be right in theory but it won't work in practice [1793].*, trans. E.B. Ashton. Philadelphia: University of Pennsylvania Press.

Kant, I. 1996. On the common saying: That may be correct in theory, but it is of no use in practice [1793], In *Immanuel Kant, practical philosophy*, trans. and eds. M.J. Gregor, vol. 8, pp. 273–309, Cambridge: Cambridge University Press.

Kant, I. 1997. *Critique of practical reason, trans. M. Gregor*. Cambridge: Cambridge University Press.

Kant, I. 1999. Perpetual peace [1795]. In *The Cambridge edition of the works of Immanuel Kant: Practical philosophy, trans. M. Gregor*, vol. 8. Cambridge: Cambridge University Press.

Kant, I. 2013. *The moral law. Groundwork of the metaphysic of morals [1785].*, trans. H.J. Paton. London/New York: Routledge.

Kantorowicz, E. 2016. *The king's two bodies: A study in medieval political theology [1957].* Princeton: Princeton University Press.

Kaplan, J. 2022. Undocumented zombies: US-Mexican immigration, the walking dead, and the effort/shape of monsters. In *Monsters in performance*, ed. M. Chemers and A. Santana, 213–227. London: Routledge.

Karnow, C. E. A. 1996. Liability for distributed artificial intelligence. *Berkeley Technology Law Journal* 11:147–183.

Kelley, D. R. 1990. *The human measure: Social thought in the western legal tradition.* Cambridge, MA: Harvard University Press.

Kelly, K. 2010. *What technology wants.* New York: Viking.

Kelly, M. 2007. *A short history of western legal theory.* Oxford: Oxford University Press.

Kelsen, H. 1911. *Hauptprobleme der Staatsrechtslehre.* Heidelberg: Mohr.

Kelsen, H. 1945. *General theory of the law and the state, trans. A. Wedberg.* Cambridge, MA: Harvard University Press.

Kelsen, H. 1950. Causality and imputation. *Ethics* 61 (1): 1–11.

Kelsen, H. 1973. God and the state. In *Essays in legal and moral philosophy*, ed. H. Kelsen, 61–82. Dordrecht: Springer.

Kelsen, H. 1981. On the basis of legal validity. *American Journal of Jurisprudence* 26:178–189.

Kenyon, J. P. 1966. *The Stuart constitution. 1603-1688. Documents and commentary.* Cambridge: Cambridge University Press.

Kevles, D. J. 1999. Eugenics and human rights. *BMJ* 319 (7207): 435–438.

Khaerunnisa, A. 2022. The roles of the United Nations human right council (UNHRC) in handling the human rights cases in political prison camp North Korea. *Mediasi Journal of International Relations* 5 (2): 10019.

Khorram Y. 2024. AI 'Godfather' Yoshua Bengio: We're 'creating monsters more powerful than us', *Yahoo! Finance*, October 12. Accessed on September 8, 2025 from https://finance.yahoo.com/news/ai-godfather-yoshua-bengio-were-creating-monsters-more-powerful-than-us-120042014.html.

Klein, E. 2025. Now is the time of monsters, *The New York Times*, 12 January.

Kocharov, A., ed. 2012. *Another legal monster? An EUI debate on the fiscal compact treaty*. Fiesole, Italy: EUI LAW. Available at https://hdl.handle.net/1814/21496.

Koessler, M., and J. Derocquigny. 1928. *Les faux amis: ou, Les trahisons du vocabulaire anglais (conseils aux traducteurs)*. Paris: Vuibert.

Krieger, L. 1965. Kant and the crisis of natural law. *Journal of the History of Ideas* 26 (2): 191–210.

Krisch, N. 2005. Europe's constitutional monstrosity. *Oxford Journal of Legal Studies* 25 (2): 321–334.

Kroger, J. R. 2017. The philosophical foundations of Roman law: Aristotle, the Stoics, and Roman theories of natural law. In *Cicero and modern law*, ed. R. O. Brooks, 229–268. London: Routledge.

Krygier, M. 2010. The hart-fuller debate, transitional societies, and the rule of law. In *The hart-fuller debate in the twenty-first century*, ed. P. Cane, 107–134. Oxford and Portland: Hart.

Kurzweil, R. 2005. *The singularity is near*. New York: Viking.

Lacey, N. 2007. H.L.A. Hart's rule of law: The limits of philosophy in historical perspective. *Quaderni Fiorentini* 36:1203–1224.

Lacy, R. B., and H. van Houtum. 2020. Death as policy: The EU's criminalisation of solidarity with undocumented migrants. In *Expanding boundaries*, ed. J. P. Laine et al., 72–84. London: Routledge.

Lagioia, F., and G. Sartor. 2020. AI systems under criminal law: A legal analysis and a regulatory perspective. *Philosophy and Technology* 33:433–465.

Lakatos, I. 1976. Proofs and refutations. In *The logic of mathematical discovery*, ed. J. Worrall and E. Zahar. Cambridge: Cambridge University Press.

Land, I., ed. 2008. *Enemies of humanity: The nineteenth-century war on terrorism*. New York: Palgrave Macmillan.

Landucci, S. 1972. *I filosofi e i selvaggi. 1580–1780*. Bari: Laterza.

Lanza, D. 1977. *Il tiranno e il suo pubblico*. Turin: Einaudi.

Laslett, P. 1949. Introduction. In *Patriarcha and other political works*, ed. R. Filmer, 1–43. Oxford: Blackwell.

Laslett, P. 1964. Market society and political theory. *The Historical Journal* 7 (1): 150–154.

Latour, B. 2011. Love your monsters. *Breakthrough Journal* 2 (11): 21–28.

Laurent, B. 2024. Innovation monsters in the sandbox. *Practicing Anthropology* 46 (1): 71–78.

Leakey, R. E., and A. C. Walker. 1976. Australopithecus, homo erectus and the single species hypothesis. *Nature* 261 (5561): 572–574.

Leawoods, H. 2000. Gustav Radbruch: An extraordinary legal philosopher. *Washington University Journal of Law and Policy* 2:489–515.

Lee Malcolm, J., ed. 1999. *The struggle for sovereignty: Seventeenth-century English political tracts*. Vol. 1. Indianapolis: Liberty Fund.

Leenes, R., and E. Kosta. 2015. Taming the cookie monster with Dutch law—A tale of regulatory failure. *Computer Law & Security Review* 31 (3): 317–335.

Leibniz, G. W. 1995. *Theodicy: Essays on the goodness of god, the freedom of man and the origin of evil [1710]*., trans. E.M. Huggard. La Salle, Ill: Open Court.

Lemos, F. 2014. Kant e o monstro. *Kriterion* 129:189–203.

Lessig, L. 1999. *Code and other laws of cyberspace*. New York: Basic Books.

Levine, A. 1993. *The general will: Rousseau, Marx, communism*. Cambridge: Cambridge University Press.

Locke, J. 1823. *Two treatises of government [1689]*. London: Tegg & Co.
Locke, J. 1993. A letter concerning toleration [1690]. In *Political writings*, ed. D. Wootton, 390–436. Indianapolis: Hackett Publishing.
Locke, J. 1997. *An essay concerning human understanding [1689]*. London: Penguin.
Lombroso, C. 1896. *L'uomo delinquente*. Vol. 1. 5th ed. Torino: Bocca.
Long, K. 2016. Montaigne on monsters and monstrosity. In *The Oxford handbook of Montaigne*, ed. P. Desan, 715–731. Oxford: Oxford University Press.
Long, R. T. 2009. Thrasymachus and the relational conception of authority. In *An anthology of philosophical studies, 3*, ed. P. Hanna, 27–36. Athens: Atiner.
Lovejoy, A. 2001. *The great chain of being: A study of the history of an idea [1936]*. Cambridge, MA: Harvard University Press.
Luban, D. 2018. The enemy of all humanity. *Netherlands Journal of Legal Philosophy* 47 (2): 112–137.
Lucretius, T. 1866. *De rerum natura, trans. A. Boyle*. Cambridge: Deighton Bell.
Lukács, G. 1972. *History and class consciousness: Studies in Marxist dialectics [1927]*. Cambridge, MA: MIT Press.
Maas, M., ed. 2005. *The Cambridge companion to the age of Justinian*. Cambridge: Cambridge University Press.
Macaulay, T. B. 1967. *Prose and poetry, selected by G. M. Young*. Cambridge, MA: Harvard University Press.
Machiavelli, N. 2014. *Il Principe [1532]*. Turin: Einaudi.
Macpherson, C. B. 1962. *The political theory of possessive individualism: Hobbes to Locke*. Oxford: Clarendon Press.
Maitland, F. W. 1963. *The constitutional history of England [1908]*. Cambridge: Cambridge University Press.
Maliks, R. 2022. *Kant and the French revolution*. Cambridge: Cambridge University Press.
Mangham, A. 2023. *We are all monsters: How deviant organisms came to define Us*. Cambridge, MA: MIT Press.
Mann, J. 1998. Dignity and health: The UDHR's revolutionary first article. *Health and Human Rights* 3 (2): 30–38.
Maritain, J. 1949. Introduction. In *Human rights: Comments and interpretations*, 9–17. UNESCO, New York: Columbia University Press.
Marshall, P. 2022. Scandal at the post office: The intersection of law, ethics and politics. *Digital Evidence and Electronic Signature Law Review* 19:12–28.
Martinich, A. P. 1999. *Hobbes: A biography*. Cambridge: Cambridge University Press.
Marx, K. 1887. Capital: A critique of political economy, vol. I, *Book 1: The process of production of capital*, trans. S. Moore and E. Aveling. Moscow: Progress Publishers. Accessed on September 8, 2025 from https://www.marxists.org/archive/marx/works/download/pdf/Capital-Volume-I.pdf.
Marx, K., and F. Engels. 1956. *The holy family, or critique of critical criticism [1844], trans. R. Dixon*. Moscow: Foreign Languages Publishing House.
Marx, K., and F. Engels. 1976. *The German ideology [1846]*. Moscow: Progress Publishers.
May, J. M. 1996. Cicero and the beasts. *Syllecta Classica* 7:143–153.
May, L. 2021. Confronting ecological monstrosity: Contemporary video game monsters and the climate crisis. *M/C Journal* 24 (5): 2827.
McIlwain, Ch. H. 2008. *Constitutionalism: Ancient and modern [1940]*. Indianapolis: Liberty Fund.
McIntyre, O. 2013. The principles of integration and interrelationships in international law related to sustainable development: Sobering lessons from EU law. In *Confronting ecological and economic collapse: Ecological integrity for law*, ed. L. Westra, P. Taylor, and A. Michelot, 104–119. London: Routledge.
McNally, D. 2011. *Monsters of the market: Zombies, vampires and global capitalism*. Leiden: Brill.
Mecacci, G., D. Amoroso, L. Cavalcante Siebert, D. Abbink, J. van den Hoven, and F. Santonio de Sio, eds. 2024. *Research handbook on meaningful human control of artificial intelligence systems. Cheltenham: Elgar*.

Mellet, K., and T. Beauvisage. 2019. Cookie Monsters. Anatomy of a digital market infrastructure. *Consumption Markets & Culture* 23 (2): 110–129.

Méndez, J. E. 2015. *Report of the special rapporteur on torture and other cruel, inhuman or degrading treatment or punishment*, U.N. Doc. A/HRC/28/68. Available at https://www.refworld.org/pdfid/550824454.pdf. 5 March 2015.

Miller, R. M. 2008. Don't let your robots grow up to be traders: Artificial intelligence, human intelligence, and asset-market bubbles. *Journal of Economic Behavior and Organization* 68 (1): 153–166.

Montesquieu. 1989. *The spirit of the laws [1748].*, trans. A.M. Cohler, B.C. Miller and H.S. Stone. Cambridge: Cambridge University Press.

Moravec, H. 1999. *Robot: Mere machine to transcendent mind*. London: Oxford University Press.

Mousourakis, G. 2012. *Fundamentals of Roman private law*. Heidelberg: Springer.

Moya, D., and G. Milios, eds. 2021. *Aliens before the European court of human rights: Ensuring minimum standards of human rights protection*. Leiden: Brill.

Muller, E. L. 2019. Korematsu, hirabayashi, and the second monster. *Texas Law Review* 98:735–756.

Murphy, C. 2005. Lon fuller and the moral value of the rule of law. *Law and Philosophy* 24:239–262.

Murphy, M. C. 1995. Was Hobbes a legal positivist? *Ethics* 105 (4): 846–873.

Murphy, T. 2004. *Pliny the elder's natural history: The empire in the Encyclopaedia*. Oxford: Oxford University Press.

Naddaff, R. 2002. *Exiling the poets: The production of censorship in Plato's republic*. Chicago and London: University of Chicago Press.

Nagel, Th. 1996. The cult of the individual, *The New York Times*, September 8. Accessed on September 8, 2025 from https://archive.nytimes.com/query.nytimes.com/gst/fullpage-9C06E2DF1E38F93BA3575AC0A960958260.html.

Negroponte, N. 2015. *Being digital*. New York: Vintage.

Neufeld, R. 2022. Investment law's monstrous reform. In *The Oxford handbook of international trade law*, ed. D. Bethlehem et al., 2nd ed. Oxford: Oxford University Press.

Newman-Stille, D. 2010. Morality and monstrous disability in topographia Hibernica. In *The Treatment of disabled persons in medieval Europe*, ed. W. J. Turner and T. V. Pearman, 231–257. Lewiston, N.Y: Edwin Mellen Press.

Nicholson, P. P. 1974. Unravelling Thrasymachus' arguments in "The Republic". *Phronesis* 19 (3): 210–232.

Nicholson, P. P. 1974. The internal morality of law: Fuller and his critics. *Ethics* 84 (4): 307–326.

Nino, C. S. 1980. Dworkin and legal positivism. *Mind* 89 (356): 519–543.

Noyes, W. 1890. The insanity of jean Jacques Rousseau. *The American Journal of Psychology* 3 (3): 406–429.

Nozick, R. 1974. *Anarchy, state, and utopia*. Malden, MA: Basic Books.

Nuzzo, L. 2013. Foucault and the enigma of the monster. *International Journal for the Semiotics of Law-Revue internationale de Sémiotique juridique* 26:55–72.

Oberson, X. 2019. *Taxing robots*. Cheltenham: Elgar.

O'Driscoll, C. 2019. *Victory: The triumph and tragedy of just war*. Oxford: Oxford University Press.

O'Hara, D. T. 2003. Neither gods nor monsters: An untimely critique of the "Post/human" Imagination. *boundary* 30 (3): 107–122.

Osiander, A. 2010. Irregulare Aliquod corpus Et Monstro simile: Can Historical comparisons help understand the European Union?, *SSRN 1648807*. Accessed on September 8, 2025 from https://papers.ssrn.com/sol3/papers.cfm?abstract_id=1648807.

Pagallo, U. 1995. *Homo Homini deus*. Padua: Cedam.

Pagallo, U. 1998. Bacon, hobbes and the homo homini deus formula. *Hobbes Studies* 11 (1): 61–69.

Pagallo, U. 2005. Plato's Daoism and the Tübingen school. *Journal of Chinese Philosophy* 32 (4): 597–613.

Pagallo, U. 2011. Robots of just war: A legal perspective. *Philosophy & Technology* 24:307–323.

Pagallo, U. 2013. *The laws of robots: Crimes, contracts, and torts*. Dordrecht: Springer.

Pagallo, U. 2013. Online security and the protection of civil rights: A legal overview. *Philosophy & Technology* 26:381–395.

Pagallo, U. 2015. Good on life governance: On law, spontaneous orders, and design. In *The on life manifesto: Being human in a hyperconnected era*, ed. L. Floridi, 161–177. Cham: Springer.

Pagallo, U. 2015. *Il diritto nell'età dell'informazione*. Turin: Giappichelli.

Pagallo, U. 2016. *Leibniz*. Milan: Kluwer.

Pagallo, U. 2016. Even angels need the rules: AI, roboethics, and the law. In *ECAI 2016: Frontiers in artificial intelligence and applications*, vol. 285, 209–215. Amsterdam: IOS Press.

Pagallo, U. 2017. From automation to autonomous systems: A legal phenomenology with problems of accountability. In *International joint conferences on artificial intelligence organization (IJCAII-17), Melbourne*, 17–23.

Pagallo, U. 2018. Vital, Sophia, and Co.—The quest for the legal personhood of robots. *Information* 9 (9): 230.

Pagallo, U. 2020. The collective dimensions of privacy in the information era: A comparative law approach. *Annuario di diritto comparato e studi legislativi* XI:115–138.

Pagallo, U. 2021. *Il dovere alla salute. Sul rischio di sottoutilizzo dell'intelligenza artificiale in ambito sanitario*. Milano: Mimesis.

Pagallo, U. 2022. The politics of data in EU law: Will it succeed? *Digital Society* 1:20.

Pagallo, U. 2022. The politics of self-driving cars. In *Autonomous vehicle ethics: The trolley problem and beyond*, ed. R. Jenkins, D. Černy, and T. Hríbek, 159–175. Oxford: Oxford University Press.

Pagallo, U. 2024. *The new laws of outer space: Ethics, legislation, and governance in the age of artificial intelligence*. Oxford: Hart.

Pagallo, U. 2024. Introduction to a theory of legal monsters: From Greco Roman teratology to the EU artificial intelligence act. *i-lex* 17 (1): 53–73.

Pagallo, U. 2025. On twelve shades of green: Assessing the levels of environmental protection in the artificial intelligence act. *Minds & Machines* 35:10.

Pagallo, U. 2025. LLMs meet the AI act: Who's the sorcerer's apprentice?, Cambridge forum on AI: Law and governance, 1. In *Taming the leviathan: The reception of the political and religious ideas of Thomas Hobbes in England*, ed. J. Parkin, 1640–1700. Cambridge and New York: Cambridge University Press.

Pagallo, U., J. Ciani Sciolla, and M. Durante. 2022. The environmental challenges of AI in EU law: Lessons learned from the artificial intelligence act (AIA) with its Drawbacks. *Transforming government: People, process and policy* 16 (3): 359–376.

Pagallo, U., and M. Durante. 2016. The pros and cons of legal automation and its governance. *European Journal of Risk Regulation* 7 (2): 323–334.

Pagallo, U., and M. Durante. 2022. The good, the bad, and the invisible with its opportunity costs: Introduction to the 'J' special issue on "the impact of artificial intelligence on law". *J* 5 (1): 139–149.

Pagallo, U., S. O'Sullivan, N. Nevejans, et al. 2024. The underuse of AI in the health sector: Opportunity costs, success stories, risks and recommendations. *Health and Technology* 14 (1): 1–14.

Paladin, L. 1996. *Le fonti del diritto italiano*. Bologna: Il Mulino.

Palladini, F. 2023. Polemics and controversies: Regarding the Eris scandica. In *The Cambridge companion to Pufendorf*, ed. K. Haakonssen and I. Hunter, 263–294. Cambridge: Cambridge University Press.

Paseri, L. 2025. *Il governo dei dati. Interesse pubblico, altruismo e partecipazione*. Turin: Giappichelli.

Paulson, S. L. 2000. On the puzzle surrounding Hans Kelsen's basic norm. *Ratio Juris* 13 (3): 279–293.

Paulson, S. L. 2008. Formalism, 'Free Law', and the 'Cognition' quandary: Hans Kelsen's approaches to legal interpretation. *The University of Queensland Law Journal* 27 (2): 7–39.

Peers, S., T. Hervey, J. Kenner, and A. Ward, eds. 2021. *The EU charter of fundamental rights: A commentary*. Oxford: Hart.

Pentland, A. S. 2013. The data-driven society. *Scientific American* 309 (4): 78–83.
Perry, S. R. 1995. Interpretation and methodology in legal theory. In *Law and interpretation*, ed. A. Marmor, 97–135. Oxford: Oxford University Press.
Petrone, K. 2000. *Life has become more joyous, comrades: Celebrations in the time of Stalin.* Bloomington & Indianapolis: Indiana University Press.
Piirimäe, P. 2019. Men, monsters and the history of mankind in Vattel's law of nations. In *Early modern natural law*, ed. S. Zurbuchen, 159–185. Leiden: Brill.
Pines, C. L. 1993. *Ideology and false consciousness: Marx and his historical progenitors.* Baltimore: SUNY Press.
Pinfari, M. 2019. *Terrorists as monsters: The unmanageable other from the French revolution to the Islamic state.* online ed. New York: Oxford Academic.
Piro, F. 2011. Rationality of the irregular. Political communities and constitutional Devices in Leibniz. *Studia Leibnitiana* 43 (1): 36–53.
Plato. 1977. *Plato's cosmology. The Timeus of Plato.*, trans. F. M. Cornford. Indianapolis/Cambridge: Hackett.
Plato. 2000. *The republic, trans. T. Griffith.* Cambridge: Cambridge University Press.
Poblet, M., P. Casanovas, and V. Rodríguez-Doncel. 2019. *Linked democracy: Foundations, tools, and applications.* Cham: Springer.
Poincaré, H. 1918. *Science and method [1908], trans. F. Maitland.* London: Nelson.
Polga-Hecimovich, J., and R. Sanchez Urribarri, eds. 2025. *Authoritarian consolidation in times of crisis: Venezuela under Nicolás maduro.* New York: Routledge.
Polifka, J. E., and J. M. Friedman. 2002. Medical genetics: 1. Clinical teratology in the age of genomics. *Canadian Medical Association Journal* 167 (3): 265–273.
Popper, K. R. 1962. *The open society and its enemies.* London: Routledge and Kegan.
Postema, G. J. 1998. Jurisprudence as practical philosophy. *Legal Theory* 4:329–357.
Pound, R. 1946. Sources and forms of law. *Notre Dame Law Review* 21 (4): 247–314.
Pufendorf, S. 1729. *Of the law of nature and nations [1672].* Carew ed. London: Walthoe et al. publishers.
Pufendorf, S. 2003. De officio hominis et civis [1672/1691], trans. A Tooke [1735]. In *The whole duty of man, according to the law of nature*, ed. I. Hunter and D. Saunders. Indianapolis: Liberty Fund Press.
Pufendorf, S. 2007. *The present state of Germany [1667], trans. E. Bohun.* Indianapolis: Liberty Fund.
Puyosa, I. 2021. Venezuela: 21st-century authoritarianism in the digital sphere. In *Social media impacts on conflict and democracy*, ed. L. Schirch, 194–204. London: Routledge.
Radbruch, G. 1950. *Legal philosophy, in the legal philosophies of Lask, Radbruch, and Dabin, trans. K. Wilk.* Cambridge: Harvard University Press.
Radbruch, G. 1991. Five minutes of legal philosophy. In *Philosophy of law*, ed. J. Fienberg and H. Gross, 103–104. Belmont: Wadsworth.
Rafter, N., and P. Ystehede. 2010. Here be dragons: Lombroso, the gothic, and social control. In *Popular culture, crime and social control*, ed. M. Deflem, 263–284. Leeds: Emerald.
Rai, A. S. 2004. Of monsters: Biopower, terrorism and excess in genealogies of monstrosity. *Cultural studies* 18 (4): 538–570.
Rajagopal, B. 2002. International law and social movements: Challenges of theorizing resistance. *Columbia Journal of Transnational Law* 41 (2): 397–433.
Raska, M. 2023. North Korea's evolving cyber strategies and operations: Toward weapons of mass effectiveness. In *North Korea's foreign policy: The Kim Jong-un regime in a hostile world*, ed. S. A. Snyder and K.-A. Park, 173–200. London: Rowman and Littlefield.
Rawls, J. 2005. *Political liberalism [1993].* New York: Columbia University Press.
Raz, J. 1979. *The authority of law.* Oxford: Oxford University Press.
Reale, G. 1997. *Toward a new interpretation of Plato.* Washington, DC: Catholic University of America Press.
Reed, Ch. 2012. *Making laws for cyberspace.* Oxford: Oxford University Press.

Richards, E. 1994. A political anatomy of monsters, hopeful and otherwise: Teratogeny, transcendentalism, and evolutionary theorizing. *Isis* 85 (3): 377–411.

Richardson, A. 1991. From Emile to Frankenstein: The education of monsters. *European Romantic Review* 1 (2): 147–162.

Ricoeur, P. 1970. *Freud and philosophy: An essay on interpretation.* New Haven and London: Yale University Press.

Ricoeur, P. 2013. *Le conflit des interprétations. Essais d'herméneutique.* Paris: Média Diffusion.

Riley, P. 2009. The legal theory of Pufendorf. In *A treatise of legal philosophy and general jurisprudence*, ed. E. Pattaro et al., 421–431. Dordrecht: Springer.

Román, E., and M. A. Olivas. 2013. *Those damned immigrants: America's hysteria over undocumented immigration.* Vol. 1. New York: NYU Press.

Romano, B. 2013. *Giudizio giuridico e giudizio estetico, Da Kant verso Schiller*. Turin: Giappichelli.

Romm, J. 2025. *Plato and the tyrant.* New York: Norton.

Rotolo, A. 2005. Sources of law in the civil law. In *A treatise of legal philosophy and general jurisprudence*, ed. C. Roversi, 728–779. Dordrecht: Springer.

Rousseau, J. J. 1889. *Emile, or concerning education [1762], trans. E. Worthington.* Boston: Heath & Co.

Rousseau, J. J. 1992. *The reveries of the solitary walker [1782].*, trans. C.E. Butterworth. Indianapolis/Cambridge: Hackett.

Rousseau, J. J. 1997. *Rousseau's social contract and other later political writings, edited and trans. V. Gourevitch.* Cambridge: Cambridge University Press.

Rousseau, J. J. 2003. *On the social contract [1765].*, trans. G.D.H. Cole. New York: Dover.

Rundle, K. 2021. The morality of the rule of law: Lon L. Fuller. In *The Cambridge companion to the rule of law*, ed. J. Meierhenrich and N. Loughlin, 186–201. Cambridge: Cambridge University Press.

Ruskola, T. 2013. *Legal orientalism: China, the United States, and modern law.* Cambridge, MA: Harvard University Press.

Russell, A. 2016. *The politics of public space in republican Rome.* Cambridge: Cambridge University Press.

Rustad, M. L., and T. H. Koenig. 2002. Taming the tort monster: The American civil justice system as battleground of social theory. *Brooklyn Law Review* 68 (1): 1–122.

Saastamoinen, K. 2006. Liberty and natural rights in Pufendorf's natural law theory. In *Transformations in medieval and early-modern rights discourse*, ed. V. Mäkinen and P. Korkman, 225–265. Dordrecht: Springer.

Saether, A. 2017. *Natural law and the origin of political economy: Samuel Pufendorf and the history of economics.* London/New York: Routledge.

Saint-Hilaire, E. G. 1822. *Philosophie anatomique des monstruosité humaines.* Paris: Rignaux.

Sajó, A., and R. Uitz. 2017. *The constitution of freedom: An introduction to legal constitutionalism.* Oxford: Oxford University Press.

Santoni de Sio, F., G. Mecacci, S. Calvert, et al. 2023. Realising meaningful human control over automated driving systems: A multidisciplinary approach. *Minds & Machines* 33:587–611.

Savigny, F. A. 1831. *Of the vocation of our age for legislation and jurisprudence [1814], trans. A. Hayward.* London: Littlewood.

Savigny, F. A. 1884. *Jural relations; or, the Roman law of persons as subjects of jural relations*, trans. W. H. Rattigan. London: Wildy.

Savigny, F. A. 1979. *System of the modern roman law [1867], trans. W. Holloway.* Westport: Hyperion.

Scarpelli, U. 1981. *Thomas Hobbes.* Milan: Giuffrè.

Schneider, S. 1999. Monsters as (uncanny) metaphors: Freud, lakoff, and the representation of monstrosity in cinematic horror. *other Voices* 1 (3): 167–191.

Schrage, E. J. H. 1995. Capable of containing a reasonable soul. In *Colatio Iuris Romani*, ed. R. Feenstra, A. S. Hartkamp, J. E. Spruit, P. J. Sijpesteijn, and L. C. Winkel, vol. 2, 469–488. Amsterdam: J.C. Gieben.

Schrock, T. S. 1991. The rights to punish and resist punishment in Hobbes's leviathan. *The Western Political Quarterly* 44 (4): 853–890.
Scott, M. 1984. Machiavelli and the Machiavel. *Renaissance Drama* 15:147–174.
Seaford, R. 1998. Tragic money. *The Journal of Hellenic Studies* 118:119–139.
Seidler, M. 2007. Introduction. In *The present state of Germany*, ed. S. Pufendorf, ix–xxviii. Indianapolis: Liberty Fund.
Seidler, M. 2021. Pufendorf's moral and political philosophy, In E.N. Zalta (ed.), *The Stanford Encyclopaedia of philosophy*. Accessed on September 8, 2025 from https://plato.stanford.edu/entrieS/pufendorf-moral/.
Selbin, E. 2010. *Revolution, rebellion, resistance: The power of story*. London: Bloomsbury Publishing.
Seneca, L. A. 1917. *Tragedies.*, trans. F.J. Miller. Cambridge, MA: Harvard University Press.
Seneca, L. A. 2009. *Apocolocyntosis.*, trans. W.H.D. Rouse. Auckland: The Floating Press.
Shanks, T. 2014. Toleration and democratic membership: John Locke and Michel de Montaigne on monsters. *Political Theory* 43 (4): 451–472.
Shapiro, S. 1996. What is the internal point of view? *Fordham Law Review* 75 (3): 1157–1170.
Sharpe, A. 2007. Structured like a monster: Understanding human difference through a legal category. *Law and Critique* 18 (2): 207–228.
Sharpe, A. N. 2010. *Foucault's monsters and the challenges of law*. Abingdon: Routledge.
Shaviro, S. 2002. Capitalist monsters. *Historical Materialism* 10 (4): 281–290.
Shaw, M. 2011. *Time and the French revolution: The republican calendar, 1789-Year xiv*. Rochester, NY: Boydell & Brewer.
Shepard, T. H., M. Barr Jr., R. L. Brent, A. Hendrickx, D. Kochhar, G. Oakley, and W. J. Scott Jr. 2000. A history of the teratology society. *Teratology* 62 (5): 301–316.
Silberstein, B. K. 2020. How high-tech can boost regime stability in North Korea. *Orbis* 64 (4): 589–598.
Silva, S. R., D. C. Vadillo, and A. P. Andrés. 2025. Green AI and AI act: Pioneering legislation or merely an environmental statement? *Revista Catalana de Dret Ambiental* 16 (1): 1–38.
Simon, H. A. 1996. *The sciences of the artificial [1969]*. Cambridge, MA: MIT Press.
Singer, F. 2021. 'Sistema Patria': A new digital tool for social control in Venezuela, *El País English*, 24 April.
Skinner, Q. 1974. Conquest and consent: Thomas Hobbes and the engagement controversy. In *The interregnum: The quest for settlement 1646–1660*, ed. G. E. Aylmer, 79–93. London: Macmillan.
Skinner, Q. 1978. *The foundations of modern political thought, vol. 2: The age of reformation.* Cambridge: Cambridge University Press.
Skinner, Q. 1988. Warrender and Skinner on Hobbes: A Reply. *Political Studies* 36 (4): 692–695.
Smits, M. 2006. Taming monsters: The cultural domestication of new technology. *Technology in Society* 28 (4): 489–504.
Smuha, N. A. 2021. From a 'Race to AI' to a 'Race to AI Regulation': Regulatory competition for artificial intelligence. *Law, Innovation and Technology* 13 (1): 57–84.
Sohoni, M. 2018. The Trump administration and the law of the Lochner era. *Georgetown Law Journal* 107:1323–1391.
Solum, L. B. 1992. Legal personhood for artificial intelligence. *North Carolina Law Review* 70:1231–1287.
Sommerstein, A. H. 2009. Monsters, ogres, and demons in old comedy. In *Talking about laughter: And other studies in Greek comedy*, 155–175. Oxford: Oxford University Press.
Soper, P. 2007. In defense of classical natural law in legal theory: Why unjust law is no law at all. *Canadian Journal of Law & Jurisprudence* 20 (1): 201–223.
Sophocles. 1887. *Oedipus Tyrannus, trans. R. Jebb.* Cambridge: Cambridge University Press.
Spalding, A. 2022. *The treatment of immigrants in the European court of human rights.* Oxford: Hart.
Spinoza, B. 1941. *Ethics, trans. A. Boyle.* London: Dent.

Stanley, J., and B. Steinhardt. 2014. Bigger monster, weaker chains: The growth of an American surveillance society. In *Ethics and emerging technologies*, ed. R. L. Sandler, 269–284. London: Palgrave Macmillan.
Stephen, L. 1876. *History of English thought in the eighteen century*. London: Smith Elder.
Steyn, J. 2004. Guantanamo Bay: The legal black hole. *International & Comparative Law Quarterly* 53 (1): 1–15.
Stothard, P. 2022. *Crassus: The first tycoon*. New Haven: Yale University Press.
Strauss, L. 1953. *Natural right and history*. Chicago: University of Chicago Press.
Stromberg, R. N. 1951. History in the eighteenth century. *Journal of the History of Ideas* 12 (2): 295–304.
Sudai, N. 2022. Sex ambiguity in early modern common law (1629-1787). *Law and Social Inquiry* 47 (2): 478–513.
Sunder, S. 2004. Markets as artifacts: Aggregate efficiency from zero-intelligence traders. In *Models of a man: Essays in memory of Herbert A. Simon*, ed. M. Augier and J. Marsch, 501–519. Cambridge, MA: MIT Press.
Talmon, J. 1919. *The origins of totalitarian democracy*. London: Mercury Books.
Tan, M. H. 2010. A state of rightlessness: The egregious case of North Korea. *Mississippi Law Journal* 80:681–709.
Tanner, J. R. 1962. *English constitutional conflicts of the seventeenth century. 1603–1689 [1928]*. Cambridge: Cambridge University Press.
Tarrant, D. 1955. Plato as dramatist. *The Journal of Hellenic Studies* 75:82–89.
Taruffi, C. 1886. *Storia della teratologia*. Vol. 4. Bologna: Regia Topografica.
Tedeschini, M. 2021. Il mostro è un paradosso. *Studi di estetica* XLIX, IV (2): 240–259.
Teubner, G. 2007. Rights of non-humans? Electronic agents and animals as new actors in politics and law, max weber lecture at the European university institute of Fiesole. Accessed on September 8, 2025 from https://cadmus.eui.eu/bitstream/handle/1814/6960/MWP_LS_2007_04.pdf.
Teubner, G. 2011. Economics of gift—Positivity of justice: The mutual paranoia of Jacques Derrida and Niklas Luhmann. *Theory, Culture and Society* 18:29–47.
Teubner, G. 2019. *Critical theory and legal autopoiesis: The case for societal constitutionalism*. Manchester: Manchester University Press.
Thanem, T. 2011. *The monstrous organization. Cheltenham, UK: Elgar*.
Thirlway, H. 2019. *The sources of international law*. Oxford: Oxford University Press.
Tönnies, F. 1989. *Thomas Hobbes: Life and doctrine [1896], trans. O. Hoffe*. Chicago: University of Chicago Press.
Trevisan, M., S. Traverso, E. Bassi, and M. Mellia. 2019. 4 years of EU cookie law: Results and lessons learned. *Proceedings on Privacy Enhancing Technologies* 2:126–145.
Troshynski, E. I., and J. D. Weiner. 2016. Freak show: Modern constructions of ciceronian Monstra and Foucauldian monstrosity. *Law, Culture and the Humanities* 12 (3): 741–765.
Tuck, R. 1986. A new date for Filmer's Patriarcha. *The Historical Journal* 29:183–186.
Turchetti, M. 2001. *Tyrannie et tyrannicide de l'Antiquité à nos jours*. Paris: PUF.
Turchetti, M. 2008. Despotism' and 'Tyranny'. Unmasking a tenacious confusion. *European Journal of Political Philosophy* 7 (2): 159–182.
Tyerman, T., and T. Van Isacker. 2024. 'Here there be monsters': Confronting the (Post) coloniality of Britain's borders. *Review of International Studies* 51:1–21.
Ullman, B. L. 1942. History and tragedy. *Transactions and Proceedings of the American Philological Association* 73:25–53.
Vavouras, E. 2021. Natural right and historicism: From Thucydides to Marx. *Cogito-Multidisciplinary Research Journal* 1:7–20.
Verner, L. 2014. Medieval monsters, in theory and practice. *Medicina nei Secoli: Journal of History of Medicine and Medical Humanities* 26 (1): 43–68.
Villari, P. 1891. *The life and times of Niccolò Machiavelli, trans. L. Villari*. New York: Scribner's sons.

Voltaire. 2012. *An essay on universal history, the manners, and spirit of nations [1756], trans. Th. Nugent*. London, Nurse: Ulan Press.

von Friedeburg, R. 2003. Natural jurisprudence, argument from history and constitutional struggle in the early enlightenment: The case of Gottlieb Samuel Treuer's polemic against absolutism in 1719. In *Early modern natural law theories*, ed. T. J. Hochstrasser and P. Schröder, 141–167. Dordrecht: Springer.

von Leyden, W. 1981. *Hobbes and Locke: The politics of freedom and obligation*. New York: Palgrave.

Waldron, J. 2012. Constitutionalism: A skeptical view, *New York university school of law*, Public law research Paper No. 10-87. Available at SSRN: https://ssrn.com/abstract=1722771. Accessed on 1 May 2012.

Wallace, W. M. 2015. *Sir Walter Raleigh*. Princeton, NJ: Princeton University Press.

Wallis, N. 2021. *The great post office scandal*. Bath: Bath Publishing.

Wang, N., and M. Y. Tian. 2022. 'Intelligent justice': AI Implementations in China's Legal Systems. In *Artificial intelligence and its discontents. Social and cultural studies of robots and AI*, ed. A. Hanemaayer. Cham: Palgrave Macmillan.

Warrender, H. 1979. Political theory and historiography: A reply to professor skinner on Hobbes. *The Historical Journal* 22 (4): 931–940.

Wartofsky, M. W. 1952. Diderot and the development of materialist monism. *Diderot Studies* 2:279–329.

Watson, A. 1993. *Legal transplants: An approach to comparative law*. Athens: University of Georgia Press.

Watson, A., ed. 1997. *The digest of Justinian*. Philadelphia: University of Pennsylvania Press.

Weede, E., and E. N. Muller. 1998. Rebellion, violence and revolution: A rational choice perspective. *Journal of Peace Research* 35 (1): 43–59.

Weinreb, L. L. 1987. *Natural law and justice*. Cambridge, MA: Harvard University Press.

Weinstock, J. A., ed. 2020. *The monster theory reader*. Minneapolis: University of Minnesota Press.

Weiskopf, R. 2020. Book review: The age of surveillance capitalism. The fight for a human future at the new frontier of power. *Organization* 27 (6): 975–978.

Weissberger, L. A. 1927. Machiavelli and Tudor England. *Political Science Quarterly* 42 (4): 589–607.

Weitzenboeck, E. M. 2001. Electronic agents and the formation of contracts. *International Journal of Law and Information Technology* 9:204–234.

Weng, Y.-H., Y. Sugahara, K. Hashimoto, and A. Takanishi. 2015. Intersection of "Tokku" special zone, robots, and the law: A case study on legal impacts to humanoid robots. *International Journal of Social Robotics* 7 (5): 841–857.

Whaley, J. 2022. Politics and the constitution of the empire. In *The Cambridge companion to Pufendorf*, ed. L. Haakonssen and I. Hunter, 33–59. Cambridge: Cambridge University Press.

White House. 2023. *Executive order on the safe, secure, and trustworthy development and use of artificial intelligence*, October 30, Washington D.C., USA.

White House. 2025. *Executive order on removing barriers to American leadership in artificial intelligence*, January 23, Washington D.C., USA.

Wiener, N. 1964. *God and golem, Inc. A comment on certain points where cybernetics impinges on religion*. Cambridge, MA: MIT Press.

Williams, H. 2003. *Kant's critique of Hobbes: Sovereignty and cosmopolitanism*. Cardiff: University of Wales Press.

Williams, R. C. 1995. The Russian revolution and the end of time: 1900-1940. *Jahrbücher für Geschichte Osteuropas* 3:364–401.

Willms, B. 1992. Philosophia prima, science and politics in Hobbes. In *Hobbes e Spinoza. Scienza e politica*, ed. D. Bostrenghi, 297–311. Naples (Italy): Bibliopolis.

Wilson, C., and M. van der Velden. 2022. Sustainable AI: An integrated model to guide public sector decision-making. *Technology in Society* 68:101926.

Winner, L. 1978. *Autonomous technology: Technics-out-of-control as a theme in political thought*. Cambridge, MA: MIT Press.

Wolfe, C. T. 2005. The materialist denial of monsters. In *Monsters and philosophy*, ed. C. T. Wolfe, 187–204. London: College Publications.

Wolff, Ch. 1934. *The law of nations according to the scientific method [1749].*, trans. J. H. Drake. Oxford: Clarendon Press.

Wright, R. K. 1983. *The continental army*. Washington, DC: Center of Military History, United States Army.

Yılmaz, O. 2024. A political, economic and humanitarian crisis: Venezuela crisis. In *Black swan: Economic crises*, ed. B. Açıkgöz, vol. III, 175–214. Singapore: Springer.

Ylönen, M. 2025. Reconceptualising the Brussels effect. *JCMS: Journal of Common Market Studies* 63:13731. https://doi.org/10.1111/jcms.13731.

Ypi, L. 2014. On revolution in Kant and Marx. *Political Theory* 42 (3): 262–287.

Zerubavel, E. 1977. The French republican calendar: A case study in the sociology of time. *American Sociological Review* 42:868–877.

Zimmermann, A. 2013. The 'Darwin' of German legal theory-carl von Savigny and the German school of historical law. *Journal of Creation* 27 (2): 105–111.

Zizek, S. 2010. A permanent economic crisis, new left review, July/August, no. 64.

Zuboff, S. 2019. *The age of surveillance capitalism: The fight for a human future at the new frontier of power*. New York: Public Affairs.

Zuiderwijk, A., Y.-C. Chen, and F. Salem. 2021. Implications of the use of artificial intelligence in public governance: A systematic literature review and a research agenda. *Government Information Quarterly* 38:101577.

MIX
Papier aus verantwortungsvollen Quellen
Paper from responsible sources
FSC® C105338

If you have any concerns about our products,
you can contact us on
ProductSafety@springernature.com

In case Publisher is established outside the EU,
the EU authorized representative is:
Springer Nature Customer Service Center GmbH
Europaplatz 3, 69115 Heidelberg, Germany

Printed by Libri Plureos GmbH
in Hamburg, Germany